NEWCASTLE

Scott Bevan was born in Newcastle and is a writer, journalist, broadcaster and playwright. He is the author of eight books, including *The Harbour, Return To The Hunter, Battle Lines: Australian Artists At War, Water from the Moon: A Biography of John Fawcett* and *Bill: The Life of William Dobell*. His documentary work includes *Oll: The Life and Art of Margaret Olley, The Hunter* and *Arthur Phillip: Governor, Sailor, Spy*.

NEWCASTLE
The Lives and Times of a City

SCOTT BEVAN

NEWSOUTH

UNSW Press acknowledges the Bedegal people, the Traditional Owners of the unceded territory on which the Randwick and Kensington campuses of UNSW are situated, and recognises the continuing connection to Country and culture. We pay our respects to Bedegal Elders past and present.

A NewSouth book

Published by
NewSouth Publishing
University of New South Wales Press Ltd
University of New South Wales
Sydney NSW 2052
AUSTRALIA
https://unsw.press/

Our authorised representative in the EU for product safety is Mare Nostrum Group B.V., Mauritskade 21D, 1091 GC Amsterdam, The Netherlands (gpsr@mare-nostrum.co.uk).

© Scott Bevan 2025
First published 2025

10 9 8 7 6 5 4 3 2 1

This book is copyright. Apart from any fair dealing for the purpose of private study, research, criticism or review, as permitted under the *Copyright Act*, no part of this book may be reproduced by any process without written permission. Inquiries should be addressed to the publisher.

A catalogue record for this book is available from the National Library of Australia

ISBN   9781742238043 (paperback)
        9781761179006 (ebook)
        9781761178108 (ePDF)

Cover design Alex Ross
Cover images Auscape International Pty Ltd/Alamy Stock Photo
Internal design Josephine Pajor-Markus
Printer Griffin Press

All reasonable efforts were taken to obtain permission to use copyright material reproduced in this book, but in some cases copyright could not be traced. The author welcomes information in this regard.

CONTENTS

Introduction 1

Chapter One: HARBOUR CITY 11

Chapter Two: THE CITY'S HEART 59

Chapter Three: PUB ROCK CITY 106

Chapter Four: CITY OF COAL AND STEEL 144

Chapter Five: SURF CITY 190

Chapter Six: CITY OF VILLAGES 240

Chapter Seven: CITY OF NOW WHAT? 297

Acknowledgements 319

Select Bibliography 322

Notes 329

INTRODUCTION

Not for the first time in its history, Newcastle finds itself on shifting ground.

Only it is not an earthquake rocking the city's foundations, as it did in 1989, or subsidence due to one of the old mines worming under Newcastle. It is the perception of the city that is shifting. For Newcastle is in uncharted territory, standing at a spot many of its long-time residents are unfamiliar with.

Their hometown is being widely noticed and deeply loved by people not from here. The place that was born as a dumping ground for convicts judged too recalcitrant even for the penal settlement of Sydney, the place that has been maligned for most of its history as a dirty industrial city, the place that has been satirised in popular culture, is being lavished with compliments.

Newcastle is a place that travellers have habitually skirted around, barely touching the city's fringes as they have determinedly kept driving north or south on holidays or headed west into the nation's heart. And those fringes still don't exactly encourage a traveller to stop, as they are tasselled with warehouses and factories or the remains of heavy industries, confirming what many have imagined Newcastle to be. However, drive into Newcastle and you see a change, to both the city and people's assumptions about it. And that is what many are doing, no longer passing by Newcastle but heading into it. Some are even coming to Newcastle for holidays. Before Covid-19 played havoc with travel, the city had 5.1 million visitors in 2019.[1] After pandemic-related restrictions eased, visitors have been finding their way back to Newcastle.

The city has been widely 'discovered' and recognised by travel and lifestyle magazines internationally, and it has won accolades, including being named as the best destination with a population over 5000 in the 2023 NSW Top Tourism Towns Awards. So Newcastle is no longer a place to avoid. It is a destination.

Others are more than visiting Newcastle; they're staying. In recent years, the city's population has been steadily growing. With the changes Covid-19 imposed on daily life, people's desire to move out of major cities to regional areas also spread like a virus. According to the report *Big Movers 2023*, released by the Regional Australia Institute, Newcastle is one of the most popular local government areas people have been heading to. In the report, Newcastle is cited as an area that has 'grown at Sydney's expense'.[2]

At Sydney's expense. Now there is a statement that grabs the attention, and perhaps puts a smile on the face, of a person from Newcastle, or, as they are known, a Novocastrian. For Sydney is the city that has cast the longest shadow over Newcastle. Indeed, Newcastle is often referred to as New South Wales' second city. *Second*. Novocastrians are well aware of who is first.

Being only about 160 kilometres to the north of Sydney, Novocastrians have been close enough to feel, and to imagine, the comparisons with the Emerald City and all the glittering marvels it holds. Conversely, Novocastrians have felt, or imagined, that many of those in Sydney have viewed Newcastle as a 'hole'. Certainly, Newcastle has been pocked and riddled with holes, due to coal mining. Newcastle was, in effect, born to be a hole. The attraction of coal, along with the need for a place of secondary punishment for convicts, was a primary reason for Newcastle coming into being in the early years of the 19th century. The prisoners became miners in what was, for them, a hell hole. From all the holes dug through Newcastle's history has come the coal that helped build a penal settlement into a city, and a colony into a nation. Yet from those holes has come part of Newcastle's image as a dirty joint, and, for that, it has been punished and derided. What's more, Novocastrians have lacerated themselves with that image, leaving embedded in their souls welts and wounds even deeper than the shafts and tunnels coursing through the earth beneath their feet.

To be a Novocastrian is to simultaneously wear a badge of honour on your chest and a chip on your shoulder. Furthermore, this is something all of those moving here should know. Strictly speaking, you can't become a Novocastrian. You're born as one. A Novocastrian is someone who came into the world here. And at this point, I should declare, with pride, that I'm a Novocastrian. So from here on, if I refer to the inhabitants of Newcastle as 'we' or 'us', bear that in mind.

Yet few Novocastrians speak strictly and, like so many other things in Newcastle, the definition of 'Novocastrian' seems to be changing. I have heard relatively new arrivals referring to themselves as 'Novocastrians' and they haven't been corrected by Novocastrians. A generation earlier they would have most likely had it explained to them that while they were now a part of Newcastle, they weren't Novocastrians. You could be with us and among us, and for that we would have embraced you (or, at least, we would have shaken your hand; Novocastrians weren't the embracing kind. Another change). But you couldn't have been one of us.

The people of Newcastle have been defensively proud of their city, and yet a lot of that pride has been shaped by a civic inferiority complex. As a result, you can hear Novocastrians boast that theirs is the best city in the world. Never mind it being the second city of New South Wales.

This is a city whose people and products have flowed out to the world, and have had the world arrive here, through its harbour. This city has been shaped, for better and for worse, by the global economy. Newcastle inherited its name from a town on the other side of the globe. When the colony's governor, Philip Gidley King, decided to establish a settlement by the mouth of the Hunter River in 1804, he anointed it 'Newcastle, in the County of Northumberland'. In choosing the name for the settlement, King believed that 'none appears so applicable as that of Newcastle'.[3] Presumably the presence of so much coal and a harbour, and the commercial potential that mix held for the colony, reminded the governor of that other Newcastle on the banks of the River Tyne in England's north-east. However, the settlement's first commandant, Charles Menzies, referred to Newcastle as King's Town. That is not how King saw it. In his correspondence with the commandant, the governor wrote that the settlement was named Newcastle.[4] So a little piece of northern England was planted on the New South Wales coast. Yet this part of the coast was already defined by beautiful names, marking the places and underlining their significance to the Aboriginal people for many generations. For the Worimi and the Awabakal, this area would not have reminded them of somewhere else; this was home.

Names kept being imported. Even the name ascribed to Newcastle people, Novocastrian, has a cosmopolitan, erudite air about it. Like the first European inhabitants here, the name of Latin origin was also sent out from Britain, since it had been used to define those born in Newcastle upon Tyne. While we love using the term, 'Novocastrian' doesn't quite seem to fit how we are. The erudition of the term runs counter to the 'no airs and graces' attitude that has been a Novocastrian hallmark.

And yet, despite how much Newcastle has been, and continues to be, a part of the wider world, many here have seen and cherished this place as a world unto itself.

One of the most successful advertising campaigns ever staged in Newcastle shot straight for the heart of the community: its parochialism. The campaign was for Newcastle Permanent Building Society. As a result, never has a financial institution been so loved. The sector usually rejected as being 'one of them' was avowedly one of us after this campaign. For the catchphrase was 'Our Town'. In the beautifully filmed television commercial, gleaming landmarks and beaming faces of locals were united by a jingle that took out a mortgage on your brain and, consequently, you found yourself singing along to the advertisement, which, in the chorus, rose to its shouted declaration, 'Hey, this is our town! It's here that we're born and bred!'[5] The jingle was so popular, it was released on a record. This was a song on everyone's lips, because it spoke to how we saw ourselves. Newcastle may have been officially a city for decades by the time this campaign was released in the late 1970s, but our self-perception was that we were a town. Novocastrians found comfort in being small. Perhaps it was a coping mechanism, or a delusion. Our eyes told us we were a growing industrial city, but in our hearts we were a big country town.

That television commercial also reminded us of what we had physically: stunning beaches and surrounding countryside, meticulously tended parks and gardens, and a fine harbour, easily accessible to all.

Hey, this is our beautiful town! And let's not tell anyone. Let the rest of the world continue to think we're a dirty little industrial joint.

But then came the closure of Newcastle's biggest industry of all, the Broken Hill Proprietary Company Limited (BHP) steelworks, in 1999. The arrival of a new millennium seemed destined to mark the end of our town as we knew it. For almost a century, those steelworks had provided generations of Novocastrians with a job, and they had spawned a network of businesses and industries that also created employment. What's more, 'The BHP' (and in Newcastle, such was the company's importance that most people referred to it with the definite article) produced more than just iron and steel to be exported around the globe. The steelworks had given Newcastle so much of its identity. We weren't just a coal centre but a steel town. Actually, we were known as 'Steel City'. So in that respect, we were bigger than we saw ourselves.

As an employer, the steelworks had been shrinking for years before closing. But in terms of its place in people's minds, it remained 'The BHP' until the end. When it closed, not only did about 2500 people directly lose their jobs, a city lost a huge slab of its identity and purpose.

Many Novocastrians were left grappling with two big questions: Who are we now? And what does our future hold?

While we Novocastrians were searching for answers, the closure of the BHP steelworks opened many people's eyes to Newcastle. Or, at least, that key moment in Newcastle's history invited people to view the city with fresh eyes. Like some variation of 'The Ugly Duckling' fairy tale, people suddenly saw what was there all along, and what Novocastrians have always known: Newcastle is a beautiful place.

Early on in this transformation of perception, I was sitting in a restaurant on Sydney's North Shore and heard a woman at the next table tell her fellow diners that she had just returned from Newcastle and how surprised she was by what she had 'discovered'.

'It even has its own little Paddington!' she declared. I guess she was referring to the inner-city suburb of Cooks Hill, with its historic terraces and workers' cottages.

You don't have to look too hard to find elements of Newcastle that remind you of somewhere else. While newcomers may take comfort in that, Novocastrians are still grappling with their city being something else. What's more, they are still trying to determine what that 'something else' is.

Many of those who have 'discovered' Newcastle in recent years want the place to remain as they found it or imagine it to be: small, like a village, or, a term that is applied liberally to the city now, boutique. 'Boutique' is a word you rarely heard in Newcastle until a generation ago. We didn't have boutiques. We had dress shops. Now we have boutique restaurants, boutique hotels, boutique apartment complexes, boutique boutiques; if it can be labelled 'boutique', Newcastle has it. Indeed, Newcastle itself is 'boutique'. The Visit Newcastle website has referred to it as a 'boutique city'.[6]

Yet in the tug-of-war over Newcastle's future, others have wanted the city to grow, and quickly. More than seeing what Newcastle already had, many have viewed the city as a greenfield site for their own vision and ambitions. As a result, the face of Newcastle has been dramatically changed. Whether it is a more attractive face is a subject of conversation and debate in Newcastle.

With all the interest being shown in our city, and with property prices climbing, Novocastrians have grown obsessed with real estate. In the years before 1999, if you discussed real estate at a dinner party in Newcastle, you were quickly identified as having come from Sydney. Now you'd fit right into Newcastle dinner-party talk. So, to that extent, Novocastrians are becoming like Sydneysiders. Then again, maybe it is because so many Sydneysiders are becoming 'Novocastrians'.

The people of Newcastle are used to standing on shifting ground. They are not afraid of change. So much change has been foisted on the community through the years, by governments, by business, by Mother Nature. As a result, Novocastrians are adept at adapting.

However, if a city is a mirror of its inhabitants, then we Novocastrians don't quite recognise ourselves. We knew who we were, or, at least, we were content or resigned to being told who we were. How others saw us is what we believed we were. We were coal miners, steelworkers, waterside workers, surf lovers, great sportsmen and sportswomen, tough, gritty, working class. Even those who didn't identify with those labels knew and accepted that's what Newcastle was, or was seen as. Even when Newcastle was so much more than that, and capable of being so much more. Which is one reason why so many young Novocastrians moved away. Newcastle wasn't for them. They had to change, because Newcastle, as it saw itself, didn't seem as if it was about to. But Newcastle has changed. And now the face in the mirror is familiar, but …

I'm one of those Novocastrians who moved away. I moved as a young man because opportunities took me elsewhere. I lived in quite a few places, but Newcastle was always my home. I had never worked a day in a coal mine or at The BHP (although I did some casual work at the factories my father managed, so I did get my hands dirty during holidays), but the coalopolis and Steel City had forged me and, indirectly, fed me. So wherever I was in the world, I carted Newcastle with me.

While living in Brisbane, I attended a National Rugby League match between the home team, the Broncos, and the Newcastle Knights at the newly rebuilt Lang Park stadium. As I was walking up to my seat, a bloke in Knights gear, who must have recognised me, approached and said, 'Don't you dare change sides'.

'Never!' I replied.

My answer was not based on my being a fervent Knights supporter (I'm not), but because I'm a Novocastrian. And being a Novocastrian is indelible, even more so than a tattoo commemorating the Knights' premiership wins in 1997 and 2001 (which, unlike quite a few of my fellow Novocastrians, I don't have).

After the best part of a quarter of a century living and working elsewhere, I returned to my home region full-time in 2016. I'm following the migratory pattern of so many Novocastrians. As a real estate agent told me while I was hunting for a house, I was just one of many clients he referred to as 'the boomerang kids'.

However, the home I returned to was not as I remembered it. Newcastle had changed, and it had changed in my mind.

I had returned to a city that was richer in many respects, and to a community that felt poorer in other ways.

So this book has come about, in part, as my way of exploring, and attempting to reconcile, that paradox of how my home city has changed, and continues to change, for richer and poorer.

At one point, I considered using as the book's title the hookline lyric of the 1970s hit, 'The Newcastle Song'.

'Don't you ever let a chance go by!'[7]

Only that didn't quite encapsulate the story of Newcastle. Novocastrians are skilled and experienced at grasping chances. But our city is also the way it is because of the chances squandered, dropped, or passed by. We, or those making decisions and weighing up chances on our behalf, haven't always acted according to the hookline of that song.

Which leaves me wondering what Newcastle would be if it had never let a chance go by.

I have opted to call this book *Newcastle*. It is a simple title for a story that is anything but. And we Novocastrians are anything but a simple people. Sydneysiders may consider us that. But, as we Novocastrians know, Sydneysiders know nothing.

Newcastle is a story of how a city and its people came to be. It is a story of how Novocastrians respond to shifting ground, which is riven with cracks and pocked with very deep shafts. But from the high points, the views are unsurpassed.

In many people's minds, the idea of Newcastle bleeds into surrounding areas, such as Lake Macquarie and the Lower Hunter communities. However, I'm staying inside the city's limits and exploring the 187 square kilometres that constitute the Newcastle Local Government Area. After all, wars have started for flimsier reasons than an author trying to imply that Maitland or Cessnock is just an extension of Newcastle. We are all part of the Hunter region, but those other communities have their own character, identity and history.

I have not structured the book as a history, so it is not chronological. Nor is it a guide that takes you area by area, so it is not geographical. Rather, I've taken elements of Newcastle for which it is renowned and used them as starting points to take us on a journey into the soul of this city. And to write this book, I have listened to, and included, the voices and perspectives of other Novocastrians, to the voices of those whose connection to this land reaches back generations, and to the voices of those who have made Newcastle home and, in the process, helped make this city a more diverse and interesting place. So that is why I have given the book the subtitle, *The Lives and Times of a City*. This book is not *the* story of Newcastle, but it is the sum of many stories, many lives, sketching a portrait of this place.

For those who want to know more about Newcastle, I hope this book helps you see the city for what it is, and for what it has. After all, the one statement that Novocastrians have come to hear perhaps more than any other in recent years is, 'Wow, I didn't know Newcastle was like this!'

As you'll read, Newcastle hasn't always been 'like this'.

For those who now call Newcastle home, I hope this book gives you a better understanding of where you are, and what you've let yourself in for. I have no desire to remove your rose-coloured glasses, only to perhaps broaden your vision and give those lenses a wipe. But the way you see my hometown has helped change and broaden my view, which has no doubt played a role in shaping what I've written.

For fellow Novocastrians, I trust you will read this book as a paean to a place that is far from perfect in my eyes, but for which my love is unconditional. Just as I know your love for the place is. So I hope this book is a conversation starter, and that it is one of many love stories for, and about, Newcastle.

Whatever brings you here, welcome to *Newcastle*.

CHAPTER ONE

HARBOUR CITY

IF only everyone could arrive in Newcastle from the water. This is how Newcastle is best seen.

For Newcastle is a harbour community. It has been nurtured by the harbour, its heart beats by the harbour, its people work and play on the harbour, and it is made beautiful, in no small part, thanks to the harbour.

It is a massive working harbour, with more than 2000 ships sliding in and out each year, and handling about 158 million tonnes of cargo in 2024, when I was writing this book. Coal is by far and away the dominant product the port handles. Newcastle is the world's largest coal export port. The harbour may not be that deep physically, measuring only about 15.2 metres in the main shipping channel, but it holds fathomless wealth for the region, and for the nation. The trade handled through the port was worth about $48 billion to the Australian economy in 2024. Port of Newcastle, the corporation that manages the shipping channels, the 21 commercial berths and much of the harbourside land, describes this place as 'the region's international trade gateway'.[1]

More than just a gateway, the harbour led to the birth of Newcastle, for it was from the water that this area was first seen by European eyes. However, the European eyes recorded as the first to scan this part of the coastline didn't look for long.

As James Cook and his crew sailed north in the *Endeavour* during that historic voyage along Australia's east coast in May 1770, he noted a 'small round rock or island' close to the shore but apparently didn't come closer to explore it, or find out what lay beyond.[2] And so began the long-entrenched pattern of many travellers in regard to Newcastle. Don't stop, keep heading north.

More than a quarter of a century later, in 1797, another Royal Navy officer, Lieutenant John Shortland, commanding HMS *Reliance*, sailed out of the sea and into the mouth of a river, tracing the shoreline where a city would be born.

Shortland is credited with being the first European to enter this harbour. Etched into a plaque on a historic building in the city's east, a couple of hundred metres from the harbour, is the proclamation that this is 'The vicinity of the landing place of Lieut. John Shortland. R.N. Sept. 9th 1797'.[3] So Shortland's place in Newcastle's history is set in stone, and his name has been given to a suburb nowhere near the harbour, a beachside thoroughfare, and a park. When he came across the river mouth, Shortland was searching for a group of escaped convicts who had stolen a government boat, the *Cumberland*. So perhaps those convicts, or others who had escaped from Sydney, were the first Europeans to sail into the river. Shortland never did find the convicts, but he found a harbour.

Within a few years, convicts would officially be the first European import into the Hunter. However, along the shores of the river mouth, Shortland came across what would be the Hunter's first and, to this day, most financially lucrative export: coal. In the history books, any mention of the convicts Shortland was chasing tends to drift away in favour of the black rock. For when he landed and picked up a lump of coal, John Shortland was grasping the future of a region.

Yet it wasn't just coal that Shortland saw as an asset. He also envisioned the potential the harbour held for the British Empire.

'Vessels from 60 to 250 tons may load there with ease, and completely landlocked,' Shortland wrote in a letter to his father in 1798. 'I dare say, in a little time, this river will be a great acquisition to this settlement.'[4]

Shortland named the river in honour of the colony's governor, John Hunter. That name would be printed on maps to identify a river and a region. It was also applied to the river's mouth. The harbour is known as Port Hunter. Yet in the early years of the colony, the river was commonly called by the resource to which it has been tied ever since Shortland arrived: Coal River.

The river's mouth already had a name, handed down from one generation to the next for thousands of years. To First Nations people, it was known as Yohaaba.

What Shortland saw as a great acquisition was seen as a generous provider by the Awabakal people, as the group of clans to the south of the harbour came to be known, and by the Worimi people, along the northern shores. The harbour's waters and edge were a source of food and medicine, of culture and stories, of identity.

The stretch that would cradle the settlement of Newcastle, and later the city centre, was named after a source of nourishment and beauty for the Aboriginal people. It was called Mulubinba, or Muloobinba. The Mulubin is a sea fern, so Mulubinba is the place of the sea fern.

Yet from Yohaaba, the inhabitants derived so much more than sea ferns.

'This was a virtual paradise of plenty,' says Worimi man, author and University of Newcastle professor John Maynard. 'The amount of seafood and marsupials in the area was enormous.'

What's more, the harbour provided a means of getting around, connecting those on the northern shores with those to the south.

'There was a lot of exchange across the harbour, and ceremonies were held on the shores,' he says.

What the harbour gave to the First Nations people was evident to the Europeans when they arrived on these shores. John says the Europeans were astounded to see First Nations women dive into the water and return to the surface holding large lobsters.

One of those early European arrivals was Lieutenant William Sacheverell Coke. While stationed in Newcastle in 1827, Coke wrote to his sisters in England that the 'natives ... will never live in cottages or cultivate their land, as they can kill plenty of kangaroos and catch fish'.[5]

The evidence of what this harbour has meant in the lives of First Nations people lies much deeper than in the pages of colonial letters. John Maynard explains there was a massive midden along the harbour's shores and the banks of the river, stretching for kilometres. The sum of shells, bones and ash was, as John puts it, 'recognition of thousands of years of occupation', the legacy of generations of food being prepared and feasted on.

But when the Europeans arrived, they viewed the midden differently. It was another resource ripe for using. The earliest colonial arrivals were astounded by the scale of the midden. John Harris, who, in 1801, was a member of the first survey party up the Hunter River, reported to Governor King he had never seen such quantities of oyster shells.[6]

Within a few years, when the penal settlement began taking shape on the harbour's southern shoreline, those shells served a twofold purpose. They could be collected and burned down to produce the lime needed in constructing some of the colony's finest buildings. In turn, that created work for some of the convicts sent from Sydney to Newcastle.

Along the river's north arm, where it sweeps wide and turns south on its final run to Newcastle, about 7 kilometres downstream, there was an area named Limeburners Bay. For the convicts sent there, the production of lime was not so much work as punishment. While the authorities argued the lime burners suffered little, the landmark colonial novel, *Ralph Rashleigh*, paints a dramatically different picture. The novel about the exploits of a convict, Ralph Rashleigh, was written in the 1840s by a former convict, James Tucker, who had spent time in Newcastle and the Hunter Valley. Limeburners Bay features in his novel as a place where convicts suffer dreadfully.[7]

In the novel, the river water only adds to the suffering, with the emaciated and often-flogged convicts wading out to the boats, carrying baskets filled with lime.

Water also provides a means of escape. Ralph Rashleigh and a crew of fellow convicts steal a boat and sail down the river, out of the harbour mouth and into the sea, leaving behind their 'dreaded scene of confinement'.[8]

John Maynard says the midden was progressively destroyed for the sake of producing lime. Even so, it has left its mark, and not just in the mortar holding together some of the colonial sandstone structures sitting imperiously in the heart of Sydney.

'Wherever you tread in Newcastle', John reminds me, 'there's an Aboriginal presence'.

When you are out to sea, Newcastle all but disappears into the landscape. Out there, it is easier to look back and imagine how the coastline would have appeared when the Europeans arrived.

To the south of the city are the cliffs formed over aeons, each layer telling a different and dramatic story, from the ash of distant volcanoes erupting during the Permian Period, at least 250 million years ago, to the sediment deposited from vast rivers flowing across the land. Geological forces, Father Time and Mother Nature have squeezed and folded the layers and ceaselessly sculpted the cliffs, helping give them the compelling, characterful faces they possess. To geologists, who can read the stories pressed into the layers, this is an extraordinary stretch of coastline. Sir Tannatt William Edgeworth David, the renowned scientist who was instrumental in the development of the Hunter Valley coalfields through his exploration and mapping in the 1880s, reckoned the geology of the Newcastle coastline was 'probably the finest of its kind anywhere in the world'.[9] To the rest of us, this coastline is simply stunning, whether viewed from near or far.

To the north of Newcastle, a ribbon of sand unravels along the coast for 32 kilometres to Port Stephens. Beyond the beach are vast floodplains that the sea and the river have tussled over, each leaving their mark, for millions of years, while way off in the distance, gauzed and faded by the space between, are hills and mountains.

As you approach the coast, landmarks of the city emerge. You can make out Christ Church Cathedral crowning the hill that presides over the harbour's southern shore, and a few multi-storey buildings that have risen in recent years poke their heads into view. To the north of the harbour, the arch of the Stockton Bridge, an engineering marvel that was officially opened in 1971, rises like a concrete sun out of the flat landscape.

Yet while the city takes shape before you, it is the lump of earth at the harbour's entrance that grabs your attention. This is the 'small round rock or island' that Cook and his crew spotted in 1770. When Shortland sailed into the harbour 27 years later, he was able to confirm that it was indeed an island. Shortland drew an 'Eye Sketch of Hunter's River', mapping part of the estuary. On his map, he named the landmark at the harbour entrance as Hacking Island.[10] Shortland appeared to be paying respect to a fellow naval officer. Henry Hacking had sailed on HMS *Sirius*, the flagship of the First Fleet that arrived in Port Jackson to found New South Wales in 1788. On a later version of Shortland's eye sketch, the island is referred to as Hacking's Point.

The landmark's moniker shifted through the years. On a very early map of the harbour, drawn by Francis Barrallier, a member of the 1801 survey expedition along the Hunter River, it is marked as Coal Island, and the accompanying notes pointed out that when sailing northward the feature appeared 'like a castle'. It may have been threaded with coal, but that name wouldn't stick to the island. Instead, it would become known as Nobbys.

Where that name came from has long been a point of discussion. According to a history written in 1897, a century after Shortland had sailed into the harbour, the sight of the island's green cap glistening in the sunlight attracted the naval lieutenant to cruise closer and therefore come across the river mouth. What's more, the sight beguiled him into referring to the island as the 'Nob'.[11] There are other theories, and names of people, offered as the source of Nobbys. Despite the debate over the name, what is undisputed about Nobbys is that it helps define a city. It is Newcastle's X that marks the spot.

In selfies and on postcards, in films and advertisements, and at the top of a Novocastrian's list for showing visitors around the town, there is Nobbys. The headland is not imposing in height, at less than 30 metres. It is an incisor of earth protruding from the river mouth and is crowned with a lighthouse. From another angle, Nobbys has the appearance of a curled fist, jabbing at the sea, as if warning it to keep its distance. Which the sea duly ignores.

Yet Nobbys is iconic. It is a drawcard. People want to hike up to its cap, not just to stand on the cusp of the continent, in order to stare out to sea or to gaze back at the city spread out along the river, but to simply be there.

A lighthouse has been on top of Nobbys since the late 1850s. From the 10-metre-high tower of dressed sandstone, a light still rakes the sea at night. The lighthouse has not been staffed full-time since the 1930s, and the original residences were replaced during the Second World War with cottages to accommodate military officers. For a time after the war, the cottages were home for the staff at the signal station on Nobbys, which sent weather reports to those out to sea, and back into Newcastle. These days, the cottages serve as studios for artists and writers under an initiative called Lighthouse Arts.

Since the program's launch in 2021, hundreds of creatives have worked in the stone cottages. In 2024, 44 per cent of those who had taken up a residency were from outside the region.

As Katherine McLean, the director of Hunter Writers' Centre, which runs the Lighthouse Arts initiative, says, 'we're starting to build that name'. Which means Newcastle is also building a different perception of itself, and not just in visiting artists' eyes.

Katherine has noticed more tourists making the climb up the hill, to see the artists' works on display in the small gallery and shop, and to savour the views.

'There's a reward to the challenge of the hill', she says.

However, in the face of Nobbys' growing popularity, local artists aren't about to give up their claim to the iconic rock. After all, it is a part of how they see themselves.

'Hunter artists have a sense of ownership – "this is my Nobbys" – and it's important to have that sense of place.'

Nobbys has long been a muse. The rocky nob is present throughout Australian art history. As an island, it features in the earliest colonial images, including those painted by convicts sentenced to Newcastle. Joseph Lycett was a forger who was evidently not good at getting away with his crime but was excellent at depicting the settlement where he was doing his time. Lycett's images of early Newcastle are varnished with a patina of Englishness. So in those works, he has applied a kind of forgery, pretending to be somewhere else, perhaps in an English village by the coast. Among the few identifiers he has painted into the scene to indicate he was actually in Newcastle are First Nations figures and, in the distance, the island at the harbour's entrance. Nobbys has been sketched and charted by explorers and generations of mariners, and it has been a source of inspiration for giants of Australian art in the late 20th century, including Tim Storrier, Margaret Olley and Brett Whiteley. When Whiteley did a painting of the area around the headland, conjuring the scene by applying a series of sinuous, sensuous curves on a bed of brilliant blue, for an art project and book titled *The Nobbys Collection*, it also held a note of nostalgia for him. Whiteley recalled surfing around here when he visited Newcastle as a kid.[12]

I spend a day in a Lighthouse Arts studio. It is a rainy day, ideal for being cocooned in a historical cottage on a headland. The view I have through my mizzle-spattered studio window is of Newcastle. As I write this, I'm constantly glancing up, looking at the city embraced by the sea and the river. And I can gaze at both the sea and the river filling my window. To the left, I see the dramatic curve of Nobbys Beach. To the right, the harbour bends and washes the feet of Newcastle. A huddle of tugs is loitering just outside the navigation channel, waiting for a bulk carrier to plough its way out of the sea. The big ship arrives and is guided by the tugs, as it cruises beyond the frame and out of sight, destined for the coal-loading berths upriver. The character of the two bodies of water seems worlds apart. The sea, tossed and churned by a southerly, throws great foamy rollers onto the beach. The sand sops up the surf and light, taking on a sheen for a few seconds before it is washed over again, and again. A hundred metres or so to the right, the harbour looks barely dimpled, its surface seemingly oblivious to the wind. Slicing across my view, keeping the sea and the river at bay, is a breakwater. That thin line of rock, with an apron of sand, allows Newcastle to straddle two worlds and belong in them both. In really wild weather, those two worlds all but collide. The sea engulfs the breakwater, as massive waves explode against the rocks. As the studio view shows, Newcastle, no matter the weather, is a city of the sea and the river.

My view is but one. The beauty of a lighthouse is that it offers views in every direction. In the other studios are my fellow residents, who are visual artists and writers, taking in different views, drawing on different perspectives, creating their own impressions.

Everyone can find something inspiring, even magical, about this place. And to Katherine McLean, the lighthouse and the rock on which it stands are a metaphor for what is happening in Newcastle.

'For me, culture is a kind of building block for our society', she says.

'As a daughter of Newcastle and an arts and culture worker, the fact Nobbys is being used in this way, and the arts and artists are producing new stories about the place, is just wonderful.

'There's the beacon of stories. The light [shining out to sea] brings us home, and now the light on the hill is helping bring us home through the stories we're telling about ourselves.'

Perhaps the magic and magnetic power of Nobbys lies below the surface. The First Nations people call the island Whibayganba. The original name for the landmark has been restored; it is officially dual named as Nobbys Head–Whibayganba. Indeed, that name has gone universal. NASA named a geological feature on Mars as 'Nobbys Head–Whibayganba'.

That name reaches not just across space but back in time. According to an Awabakal story about Whibayganba, a giant kangaroo lives inside the island. The kangaroo had assaulted a female wallaby, and the other wallabies were furious and wanted revenge. The kangaroo bounded away, with the wallabies chasing him. When he reached the coast, the kangaroo swam to there and hid deep inside it. The kangaroo remains inside there, entombed, but periodically he bangs his tail and the earth shakes.[13]

As John Maynard explains, the story is about Aboriginal law and justice, but it also reflects environmental knowledge. The story indicates Newcastle is prone to earthquakes. The story of the giant kangaroo resonated with greater meaning after 28 December 1989, when Newcastle was rocked by a devastating earthquake.

'You go back to 1989', John Maynard says, 'and you know the giant kangaroo is still banging his tail'.

THE colonial authorities risked rousing the giant kangaroo when they began trimming Nobbys in the mid-19th century. The island had more of a pointed top – or, as John Maynard describes it, like the head of a kangaroo – until Colonel George Barney arrived on the scene. The member of the Royal Engineers would develop quite a reputation for reshaping Australia's east coast ports, particularly Sydney Harbour, and he would leave his mark at Nobbys. In the 1830s, Barney arranged for the top of Nobbys to be lopped, with the stone used in the breakwater being built to link the island to the mainland. Twenty years on, there were plans to go even further in reshaping the harbour entrance and demolish

Nobbys, to remove the wind block it created for sail ships. Tunnels were dug into Nobbys to insert explosives and blow up the landmark. But in what was considered one of the earliest environmental protests in not just Newcastle but the colony, sections of the community, including local mariners, opposed the move, and eventually the demolition plan foundered. However, by then, Nobbys had been diminished physically. The island had been chewed into, and it had been roughly halved in height and given a flat top. On top of the hiding kangaroo, the lighthouse was built. What the engineers had taken away, the lighthouse designers replaced with the stone tower. In 1858, burning oil created the finger of light that stretched through the darkness out to sea. Technology has changed, and the beam of light has grown more powerful through the years.

Yet so often the sea has been far more powerful, and the light has not been enough to protect some from the notoriously capricious entrance to the harbour.

The price the sea and the weather demanded of sailors to reach calmer waters – and the coal – was something everyone entering the harbour was fearfully aware of before the settlement of Newcastle even came into being. The map that Francis Barrallier drew as a result of the 1801 survey expedition indicates that fear. The map outlined what this 'Coal Harbour' could mean to shipping, with a note pointing out there was good shelter from all winds, 'and plenty of room for more than 100 sail of shipping'.[14] However, when he sent a map of the harbour and its entrance to Governor King, who had ordered the survey, Barrallier wrote in a letter, 'You can see from my map what a fearsome passage one has to traverse in order to reach this beautiful river. The roaring of the waves, crashing one upon the other and breaking with a terrible noise on the steep rocks of the island, and raging as they roll onto the sands of the opposite shore, would make the most intrepid sailor tremble'.[15]

To access Newcastle Harbour has been not just terrifying at times for sailors; it has resulted in tragedy. It has been estimated that since Europeans arrived, about 200 ships have been lost in and around Newcastle's waters.

When ships enter and leave Newcastle Harbour, they are threading the eye of a maritime needle that can easily prick any sense of safe passage. To the south is Nobbys, and on the northern side of the channel there was a treacherous trap of sand and rock known as the Oyster Bank. This became the graveyard for so many ships through the years that in places their corpses lay on top of each other.

One of those corpses belongs to the *Cawarra*, which was wrecked in a dreadful gale in July 1866. The paddle steamer had her boiler fires extinguished when she was smashed by enormous waves while trying to enter the harbour. The ship and the 61 crew members on board were at the mercy of the elements. No mercy was extended. There was just one survivor, who was saved by a crew in a small lifeboat. One of the rescuers was James Johnson, who worked at Nobbys Lighthouse. For Johnson, this was maritime history repeating; he had been the sole survivor of the *Dunbar* disaster at Sydney Heads in 1857, when 121 people died.

The *Cawarra* wasn't the only casualty of that gale. About 100 lives and at least five vessels were lost in or near Newcastle's waters. The Oyster Bank played a role in wrecking four of the five ships.[16]

The residents' reaction to the tragedy of the *Cawarra* demonstrated Newcastle was a harbour town, in good times and terrible. Many had stood in the storm, watching the death of the *Cawarra* and hoping for lives to somehow be saved. In the days after, they retrieved the bodies bobbing on the water and nudging into the shore, and then an estimated 1500 attended the mass burial on the hill overlooking the harbour at Christ Church Cathedral, with thousands more lining the streets to honour the funeral procession as it passed.

Novocastrians knew then what they know now. Novocastrians know what the sea gives them, and how easily the sea can take it all away. Even life itself. Especially life. Never mind the harbour carrying a city's and region's lifeblood. Its waters are a memento mori, a memorial for all the lives lost in the quest to reach here, or for all those who dare to venture beyond here.

The memorials take firmer shape around the harbour. Along the southern foreshore, close to the harbour entrance, is a monument honouring merchant seafarers killed in times of war. Along the east coast of Australia, 277 merchant mariners died during the Second World War, when ships were attacked by Japanese submarines. The monument features an anchor in repose on the curved monument, which features a quote from Shakespeare's *King Lear*, 'Hark, do you hear the sea?' From here, when the sea is roused, you can hear it. And you can see it, just beyond Nobbys, looking so benign and so seemingly endless. Out there, the water is no longer a memento mori. The sea can delude you into believing everything goes on forever.

Over the corpses of that fatal gale of 1866, over the wrecks of other ships that came to grief on the Oyster Bank, is another memorial to the price of being tied to the sea. A breakwater was built from the Stockton shore, covering the Oyster Bank, along with the remains of the ships it had claimed, with the purpose of making the entrance to the harbour safer and preventing yet more vessels from ending up on the mass grave. While the breakwater is intended to prevent history repeating, it also acknowledges what has gone before – and what lies beneath. The path topping the 800 or so metres of the northern breakwater is known as Shipwreck Walk. Along the walk, poking above the rock wall, is an epitaph written in rust for the ships lost. Actually, it is the corpse of one of the ships, rising from the grave. It is the wreck of the *Adolphe*, a four-masted barque that was shoved by huge seas onto the Oyster Bank, and onto another lost ship, the *Colonist*, in 1904. And there the French barque has remained for more than a century, her wreck built into the breakwater as though she has rammed it, with her bowsprit pointing towards the city she would never reach. The *Adolphe* has turned into a tourist attraction. You can stand on a viewing platform and peer into her rotting corpse, watching fish glide amid her flaking rib cage. This wreck may be a symbol of the perils of maritime life, but the *Adolphe* carries such an elegance and beauty, she is like a siren calling you onto the rocks.

From here, across the 400 metres of water at the harbour's entrance, is the southern breakwater. Most people call it 'Nobbys Breakwater'. This engineered structure, begun by convicts, shackles what was once an island to the mainland. This was one of the Europeans' earliest local projects to shape the landscape to suit their needs.

In the earliest days of the colony, smaller vessels would enter the harbour through the channel between the island and the southern headland. But it could be perilous for a mariner, and the force of waves and sand being washed in only made the harbour entrance trickier for ships to navigate.

In 1818, the colony's fifth governor, Lachlan Macquarie, was visiting the penal settlement when he decided the channel between 'Coal Island' and the southern headland should be filled in 'for the purpose of deepening the main channel or entrance into the harbour',[17] as he wrote in his journal. By the following afternoon, decision had turned into action, with the governor laying a foundation stone to mark the start of work on the breakwater. He added that the commandant of Newcastle, Captain James Wallis, had proposed that 'it should bear my name'.[18] While Macquarie Pier began with a sprint, it would take 28 years to complete the 500-metre-long breakwater to Nobbys. Later the breakwater was extended beyond Nobbys to improve the entrance for shipping.

The tussle between human ambitions and needs and the ceaseless force of Mother Nature has continued in the harbour and along its shores. The harbour is the product of not just what comes in from the sea but also what is washed down the river. The Hunter River picks up vast amounts of sediment in its 470-kilometre journey to the sea, and it dumps much of what it collects in its own mouth.

'What comes down the river is mud, which basically consists of silt and clay, and the further you get to the entrance is sand, and that's mostly brought in from the ocean side', says Ron Boyd.

Ron, an honorary professor of Earth Sciences at the University of Newcastle who lives by the mouth of the Hunter in Stockton, says the meeting of the river and the sea created a maze of hazards and a navigational nightmare for early colonial mariners.

'The channel was about six metres deep when the Europeans first arrived', Ron says, adding that much of the harbour was shallower than that.

As the colony developed and the Hunter Valley opened to settlers, what was increasingly coming down the river were products, such as timber and wool, to be loaded onto ships. But many ships went further upriver to the port town of Morpeth to load cargo. Coal was being loaded into ships in Newcastle, but even so the shallow water around the wharves meant vessels had to be moved into deeper parts of the harbour and loaded with boxes of coal transported by barges. Many ships simply couldn't attempt to enter the port because the harbour was too shallow. As the demand for Hunter coal increased in the mid-1800s, the only thing deepening was the frustration of businesspeople.

'Newcastle had a terrible reputation because so many ships came to grief trying to get in and out', explains harbour historian Rosemary Melville. 'You weren't going to buy your coal from here if it was going to end up in the drink.'

Unable to tame the wilful moods of nature, engineers and politicians figured they could at least 'train' the river mouth in a bid to deepen the harbour. The man who would reshape much of the harbour, and Newcastle as a harbour town, was a young engineer named Edward Orpen (known as EO) Moriarty. In one respect, he was following in the wake of his father, Captain Merion Moriarty, who, as Portmaster for New South Wales, had carried out a review of Newcastle Harbour and was instrumental in building a wharf and a small boat harbour in the 1840s. But the younger Moriarty would go much further. Appointed the engineer for Hunter River Improvements in 1855, EO Moriarty devised a plan to deepen the harbour and make the entrance safer for ships. So much hope, as well as money, was invested in turning that plan into reality. After all, the fortunes of businesses and the future of a port city rested on it.

According to Rosemary Melville, when Alexander Brown, a member of the prominent Hunter coal mining family, later travelled to the United States on a business trip, he took samples of his product and a copy of Moriarty's plan to reassure potential customers.

Moriarty's plan was far-reaching in scale and time. Wherever you look around the harbour, chances are you're seeing what Moriarty foresaw. It was he who proposed a northern breakwater from Stockton and the extension of the southern breakwater, beyond Nobbys. Moriarty plotted the reworking of the harbour's western and southern edges into what he called a fair, gentle curve to improve the flow of water. As a result, massive reclamation and dredging projects saw shorelines straightened, and a long point that would become known as The Dyke was sculpted from the edge of what was called Bullock Island on the north-western side of the harbour. Just like Nobbys, this island wasn't left alone; these days it is connected to the mainland and forms the suburb of Carrington. The Dyke was shaped from ships' ballast. So what was designed to entice ships from around the world to Newcastle was, in part, constructed from shards of the globe brought into the harbour by those vessels. A writer inspecting The Dyke in 1877 noted, 'Here we have geological specimens from every part of the world. The whole expanse of ground has been built up of ballast from the ships that come to our harbour. In one place we tread upon a layer of London flint, next a collection of stones from the shores of the sunny Mediterranean'.[19]

By the 1880s, with the numbers of ships growing, the city's annual nautical almanac could assert Newcastle was 'the principal shipping port of the northern district of New South Wales, and the emporium of the coal trade'.[20] However, the almanacs continued to carry pages of instructions and warnings for the masters of ships entering and leaving the port.

EO Moriarty may not have been in Newcastle for long, but his influence has been profound. More than drawing the plan for a reshaped harbour, and for a working port, those hands of his steered Newcastle towards being a fine harbour city.

Rosemary Melville says, 'I think he was crucial to the development of the port and, by extension, the city.

'The changes he made to the port made it a viable port, and it wouldn't have been without that reshaping. So he laid the foundations for what was to come afterwards.'

Long after Moriarty had left town, the transition of lines on paper to rock walls and reclamation along the shores continued. An area for ships to berth, known as The Basin, was constructed off the southern end of Bullock Island, and felled forests were laid along the harbour's edge as new wharves were built. Training walls were built, and work on the breakwaters was carried out. Stretches of rock in the bed were blasted to deepen the harbour, a practice that went on well into the 20th century.

By 1983, the main harbour channel had been deepened to 15.2 metres, with the completion of a massive project that had required the removal of millions of tonnes of rock and sediment. Yet that feat of engineering has meant nothing to the ways of water. The river and the sea never tire of trying to fill in the harbour, so the ceaseless task for Port of Newcastle is to maintain the main channel's depth by dredging.

As Calvin Grills, the dredge superintendent for Port of Newcastle, told me in 2022, maintaining the channel's depth was a bit like painting the Sydney Harbour Bridge. You never actually finish; you just start again.[21]

Dredging has been an integral part of Newcastle Harbour life since the mid-1800s. A 2020 study estimated that since 1859, about 140 million cubic metres of sediment had been dredged and removed from the port.[22]

These days, the ship seen in the port more than any other is the *David Allan*, named after an early harbour master. The ship glides past Nobbys, in and out of the harbour, day in, day out. For the *David Allan* is Port of Newcastle's dredging ship, or, to give the 71-metre vessel its full title, a trailing suction hopper dredger. Working with another vessel, the *Lydia*, which sweeps the harbour bed, the *David Allan* is like a nautical vacuum cleaner, sucking up vast volumes of sediment into its hold. Then the ship ploughs out into the open sea, to a disposal ground just off the coast, where the ship's hull cleaves apart and the sediment sinks into the depths. Basically, the *David Allan* opens its hull on large hydraulic hinges so that the hulls of other ships don't get stuck on the harbour bed.

Each year, the *David Allan* removes about 250 000 cubic metres of silt and sand from the 9-kilometre stretch of the channel from the harbour's entrance to the coal loaders furthest upriver. However, those averages are washed away whenever there is a major flood and massive amounts of sediment – along with all manner of debris on the surface – are whooshed into the river mouth.

After the 1955 Hunter Valley flood disaster, for instance, about 2.3 million cubic metres of sand and silt had to be removed, while in more recent times, the channel's depth was reduced to 14.4 metres after a series of flood events in 2021 and 2022. As a result, to return the channel to 15.2 metres, the dredging crews removed a year's worth of sediment in the first three months of 2022.[23]

Even at that depth, there may be little more than a metre's clearance for the biggest ships when their bellies are filled with coal.

So as surely as the river and the sea continue to bring in sediment, the dredging will continue. As Ron Boyd points out, this river mouth doesn't offer any option.

Ron explains that estuaries are 'time limited'.

'Over time, a big river like the Hunter will fill [the estuary] up all the way out to Nobbys.'

Not that he expects that to happen. Human ambitions will continue to prevail over Mother Nature, especially when so much money is tied up in keeping the shipping channels open.

'I think there will always be enough money to have a big enough dredge to make it navigable, no matter what', Ron says.

STANDING sentinel on a hill on the south-eastern edge of the harbour, in a landmark face-off with Nobbys, is Fort Scratchley.

In the early colonial days, this hill held not a fort but a coal-fired beacon for mariners. It was known as Signal Hill.

Yet the colonial authorities were keenly aware that not all ships were welcome into the harbour, and that this vital coal port needed to be defended for the sake of not just the colony but the British Empire. In the 1880s, the fort was built on Signal Hill, and deep into it, with a series of tunnels.

More than half a century later, at the height of the Second World War, Fort Scratchley was called on to do what it was built for: to defend Newcastle. For the first time in the fort's history, its guns were fired in anger when, at 2.17 am on 8 June 1942, a threat surfaced just off the coast in Stockton Bight.

A Japanese submarine, *I-21*, targeted the industrial city, which was integral to the Allied war effort. The night was suddenly illuminated by star shells. Then the Japanese fired high-explosive shells on the BHP steelworks and the port, and at the fort. The number of shells fired on the city has been debated, from 26 to 34 rounds. But it was enough to jolt the city awake.

The fort's two guns responded, firing four salvos at the submarine, which slipped into the depths. According to Frank Carter, a long-time president of Fort Scratchley Historical Society, this has been the only time land-based guns in Australia have been fired in a naval engagement. In less than half an hour, silence returned to Newcastle. Most of the Japanese shells didn't explode, so they caused minimal damage, no deaths and only a couple of reported injuries. A bombardier was on his way to Fort Scratchley when a shell exploded near him and he was knocked unconscious by shrapnel. When he came to, the bombardier rushed to the nearby fort to take up his post, unaware he had shrapnel embedded in his head.[24] While the physical impact of the attack on Newcastle was minimal, any notion of peace was shattered. War had reached the heart of the city.

'Most people don't realise how close the Japanese came to here', says Frank Carter. 'We know the Japanese attacked Darwin and the Top End, most people know there was an attack on Sydney Harbour, but they've forgotten about this.'

To Frank Carter, the fort is a bulwark against forgetting. He feels deeply connected to this place, having served here as a member of the Australian Army's Citizen Military Forces until the fort shut in 1972. Today it operates as a museum. Within its thick stone walls are exhibits outlining the fort's history, among them artefacts from that night in 1942.

Visitors can also explore the tunnels, imagining what it was like in the fort's early days, when light came not from electricity but flames, and there were magazines filled with gunpowder. All this time on, as you zig and zag ever deeper under the fort, you can almost feel the tension the soldiers must have dealt with, keeping naked flames and powder from ever meeting. The layers of human experience, and the levels of discomfort, lie even deeper in this hill. Convicts tunnelled the settlement's first mines somewhere under here, burrowing into the coal seams.

As you trudge further into what seems like an unsolvable puzzle, the darkness engulfs you, until natural light trickles over the walls and ceiling, and you arrive at an emplacement with a view to the outside world. The room seems to expand as your eyes adjust to the brilliant light pouring in through a slot cut into the side of the hill. A sea breeze riffles through the concrete cocoon, bringing a sense of relief.

Frank says more and more visitors are trekking deep into Newcastle's history. About 100 000 visited the fort in 2023–2024. The fort doesn't just offer a window to times past; it marks time. Each day at 1 pm, a cannon is fired, and that has coincided with a time ball dropping on the tower of the former Customs House, just down the hill. Those two actions have recreated a cornerstone of daily harbour life dating back to the 1870s, when mariners in port relied on the cannon fire and dropping time ball to check their ship's chronometers, which were vital at sea to determine longitude and help work out a ship's position. The fort has played other roles: a dramatic setting for receptions, an open-air gallery for sculpture exhibitions, and a stunning platform to scan and survey the harbour and a changing cityscape.

'As far as a military point of view is concerned, we're obsolete', says Frank. 'But we're a force to be reckoned with in Newcastle's tourist industry.'

What's more, in Frank's eyes, the fort remains a symbol of Newcastle's character.

'It just shows Newcastle will survive', he says. 'We were here in 1942, and we'll be here in another 100 years. And hopefully the fort will be a premier attraction!'

AROUND so much of the harbour's edges, where we walk now we would have once been walking on water. Or perhaps trudging through mud. In the spirit of EO Moriarty, or in the pursuit of money, so much of the foreshore has changed. And it continues to change.

At the eastern end of Newcastle's harbour shore, where people amble and jog, cycle and picnic, clipper ships once berthed. Stars of the seas, such as the *Cutty Sark* and the *Thermopylae*, rested here, being loaded with wool and preparing to race against time, the winds and the waves back to Britain.

In the early years of the harbour's development, the border between water and earth was blurry around here. The terrain was swampy, according to historian Rosemary Melville, so a boardwalk of wood was constructed, allowing those working on the waterfront to avoid sliding into the mire.

By the late 1800s, the eastern end of the southern foreshore had been reclaimed further, and it was webbed with rail lines bringing products, from coal and wool to foodstuffs, to the wharves. In the early years of the 20th century, the coal was also being directed towards a power station built here. For more than 50 years, Zaara Street Power Station produced not just electricity for the railways and the residents of Newcastle, but also the black soot that sprinkled the east end of the city. That helped provide the icing to Newcastle's reputation as a dirty place.

Once Zaara Street Power Station shut in the mid-1970s, the shell presided over increasingly derelict land. Eventually the old power station was demolished, yet still this stunning piece of earth nestled between the harbour and the sea lay dormant, stitched with rusting rail lines and knotted with weeds. It was as though Newcastle was incapable of seeing the beauty right before its eyes, instead swapping one vision of ugliness for another. Perhaps we didn't expect anything better for ourselves.

With the bicentenary of the European settlement of Australia in 1988 approaching, the land was reimagined as a foreshore park. A parcel was devoted to a residential development, which included social housing. That caused controversy. Land that had been allowed to lie forlorn for so long was suddenly deemed by some of the project's critics to be too good for social housing. The development went ahead, taking its place beside historic terraces that once housed waterside workers and mariners and their families and overlooking the new parkland. The coal soot in the air has long dissipated, replaced with the scent of salt wafting over from the sea a couple of hundred metres away. Memories of the power station and the swampy earth lie deep beneath the foreshore park's lawn.

The foreshore was once indented with small quays and boat harbours. Boats carrying passengers and supplies slid in and out of the little harbours. One of the boat harbours fed the city's markets, as produce was ferried downriver from the farms along the Hunter. As well as providing space for landing produce, the boat harbour hosted watermen, the taxi drivers of the 19th century, ferrying passengers around the port. The boat harbour lives on in name only. It was filled in long ago, providing the foundations for the demands of the new and dominant form of transport. The area is now the Boat Harbour Car Park, sited along a thoroughfare whose name reminds us of another harbour hallmark largely no longer there: Wharf Road.

Along the water's edge, however, there remain echoes of the old boat harbours. The stretch near the harbour's entrance, where the princesses of sail bobbed and mingled with the rising regents of steam, was known as Queen's Wharf, in honour of Queen Victoria. When the monarch changed, so did the name, to King's Wharf. However, Queen's Wharf still exists along the Newcastle shoreline, only now it applies to a precinct further into the port. It was named in honour of Queen Elizabeth II, who officially opened it in 1988. Queen's Wharf was yet another bicentennial project in the city. The most conspicuous feature of Queens Wharf was a 40-metre-high observation tower that had the appearance of an erect penis. Or, as many Novocastrians called it, 'The Big Cock'. If this structure was meant to be a symbol of Newcastle's potency, it flopped. Instead, it was an object of ridicule, and a tourist attraction for the wrong reasons. Even the city's former lord mayor, Nuatali Nelmes, described the tower as having an unfortunate shape and considered it a blight on the city's landscape.[25] So down the tower came in 2018. The foreshore doesn't appear castrated as a result of the tower's demolition. Indeed, in city planning, as in most things in life, sometimes less is more.

Queens Wharf is where the Stockton Ferry loads and unloads passengers, on average about 1000 people each day, as it criss-crosses the harbour from pre-dawn to late at night. A passenger ferry has linked the community of Stockton, on the northern shore, with Newcastle since 1854. The harbour has long been a binding agent for the communities around the shoreline. In the past, ferries beetled across the water from the city to stops around the port, carrying residents home, as well as transporting the occupants of the floating community docked in the harbour. As the legendary sea shanty performer, author and sailor Stan Hugill wrote of Newcastle in his book, *Sailortown*, 'All the wharves and innumerable jetties around the harbour are reached by many small ferries, and in the windbag days every ferry, nightly, was choked with sailors bound ashore seeking, in the streets of the town, booze, girls, and general pleasure'.[26]

Now there is just this solitary ferry service. But seeing the Stockton Ferry, incessantly stitching together the northern and southern shores, provides a reassuring constant, like watching a metronome. While the city changes before our very eyes, the ferry ploughs on like time itself. Indeed, when you step onto the ferry, time seems to slow down. It may take only about three minutes to complete the 700-metre voyage across the harbour on the ferry, but the gift of travelling on water is that it bestows you with the belief you have all the time in the world. Little wonder some don't want the journey to end. A ferryman for the company operating the service told me how quite a few passengers hopped on not to hop off on the other side but to simply enjoy the ride across the harbour and back again.[27]

Back at Queens Wharf, people drink and dance on the jetty that serves as a beer garden for a waterfront hotel. In the small quay framed by the wharf, you rarely see a boat moored; only on special occasions, such as when long-distance sailor Tony Mowbray (who is from nearby Lake Macquarie, so not a Novocastrian but close enough in a moment of triumph) completed his solo and unassisted round-the-world voyage in 2001. He was welcomed home by a crowd of thousands along the foreshore. However, the usual absence of boats doesn't mean the wharf framing the quay is unused and unpeopled. Fishers dangle a line from it, kids use it as a diving platform, somersaulting through space before splintering the surface, and each Australia Day, hundreds thrash and stroke their way to Stockton and back in the Newcastle Harbour Swim. So Queens Wharf is not so much a boat harbour as a people's harbour.

Further to the east, there is more than an echo of the historical boat harbours. A small quay is cocooned by stone walls wearing the marks of time and tide. This boat harbour was built in 1866, as part of the pilot station. From here boats would head towards the sea, their occupants helping guide visiting ships into the port and then out again. However, pilots had been assisting ships in and out of the harbour since 1812, with the first boats rowed by convicts.

Also heading out of the little harbours were the crews of the famed 'butcher boats', rowing furiously to be the first to reach an arriving ship and secure a food supply contract. Lifeboat crews would also leave behind the security and relative calm of a boat harbour, rowing into the wildest weather, steering towards peril to rescue those in danger on the seas. A lifeboat service had operated out of the harbour since 1838, but crews were coming to the rescue of stricken vessels before that. Many of the earliest crew members were convicts. The most renowned lifeboat in the harbour was the *Victoria*, which was based just near the pilot station, and whose crew was celebrated for saving all 32 on board the stricken *Adolphe* in 1904.

From this 19th century boat harbour, pilot boats still come and go, although they are mostly transporting marine pilots across the harbour to a heliport. The majority of marine pilot transfers to ships arriving and departing are now done by helicopter in Newcastle. The pilot is delivered to the deck of a ship rather than having to climb a ladder in all sorts of conditions, fair and foul.

That little harbour, right beside the Port Authority of NSW building, provides Newcastle's Harbour Master, Captain Vikas Bangia, with a view to the long tradition he was joining. And from his office, Vikas has a view of the harbour entrance.

Vikas first cruised through that entrance in 2009, during his 21-year career on ships, so he was aware the city was right beside the harbour. Since 2020, Vikas has been Newcastle's Harbour Master. But the job is about more than regulating the movement of ships in and out of the port. The connection between the harbour and the city, beyond mere proximity, became apparent to him very quickly. While house hunting, Vikas was surprised when he told the real estate agent what he did, and the reply was, 'It's an honour to meet you'.

In Newcastle, the harbour master personifies not only what this city has but part of what this city is.

'One thing I had to change as a mindset is that I'm Harbour Master for the port as well as for the community', says Vikas, who had three harbour master postings prior to moving to Newcastle. 'Here you're under scrutiny twenty-four hours a day, the whole port, because every person who is walking or taking their dog for a walk, we're just in front of them.

'The economic benefits [of the port], everyone knows about, but for me, it's part of being a Novocastrian. You grow up, come to Nobbys, and you look at such large ships coming in. They look like a monster entering there. It's an amazing feeling.'

There is no shortage of ships to gaze at or, for Vikas and his team of about 50, to keep an eye on. On average, based on 2023 figures, a ship arrives or leaves every three hours.

While he can see the ships passing by, Vikas spends little time gazing out of his office window. Anyway, he has had his fill of water views.

'I've done my twenty-one years at sea', he smiles. 'We're making sure the view is looking good by bringing ships safely in. So the view is good for our community.'

THE harbour leaves its mark far beyond the high-water level; the influence is also there in the architecture.

On the ridge above the city is a cylindrical tower wearing a castellated crown. It looks like something from a fairy tale. You almost expect to see Rapunzel's hair tumbling from one of the windows. However, the tower was built in 1865, then raised in 1877 to peer over a growing town, as a navigation aid to guide ships into port. Further up the hill, at the highest point, is a white obelisk. It may point at the clouds, but the obelisk's reason for being lies in the harbour. This structure stands on the site of the first windmill in Newcastle. That windmill, with its four large blades scything the sky, served as a marker for mariners. When it was demolished in 1847, the seafaring community complained. To give sailors something to navigate by, the obelisk was erected a few years later. Over time, in the mouths of Novocastrians, the obelisk grew to be The Obelisk. We Novocastrians are fond of capital letters to denote something of local importance. So The Obelisk is the highest point on a hill called The Hill. Standing at the feet of The Obelisk on The Hill we could once look over to The BHP. The view from there is still panoramic and telling. You can observe the city spreading and climbing. Panning around to the east, any aspirations of The City seem to shrink, as our gaze goes past Nobbys and far out to sea, out to where generations of mariners have come from and return to.

Dotted over The Hill are historic houses with deep verandahs and towers that offered their former occupants views of the harbour and sea, so they could trace the comings and goings of their fortunes. Some of Newcastle's finest homes may not be built by the harbour, but their reason for being was because of the port.

Closer to the shoreline are more modest terrace houses where those working on and by the water lived. A stone's throw from the harbour at the eastern end of the city is the grand Victorian Italianate face of the former Customs House, where, from 1877, taxes were collected from ships' masters and, each day at 1 pm, the time ball dropped. These days, people while away time in the old Customs House; it is now a hotel.

Unlike the Customs House Hotel, many of Newcastle's inner-city pubs came into being because of visiting sailors. At any given time, there could be more than 1000 mariners visiting town, pouring money into the economy. The visitors helped make the harbour town multinational. For the crews on the ships were from all over the globe. It has been estimated that during the 19th century, as few as 54 per cent of merchant seamen on British ships were actually British.[28] From the 1800s into the early 20th century, you can imagine Scandinavians and Pacific Islanders, Russians and seamen from Asia, as well as mariners from Britain and its colonies walking the streets of Newcastle.

One of those mariners was a young apprentice, William Jones, serving on a sailing ship, the *British Isles*, when it slid past Nobbys to load coal in 1906. As Captain Jones wrote many years later in his memoir, *The Cape Horn Breed*, 'Newcastle was one of the most frequented sailing ship ports in the world'.[29] Another mariner visitor to the port in the early years of the 20th century, HC de Mierre, noted as he looked around the harbour, 'Never before had we seen so many sailing-vessels crowded so close together'.[30]

So popular was the port that ships and their crews often had to wait to load. Many ships were moored in the middle of the harbour, creating virtual stepping stones of masts and spars across the water. William Jones and his shipmates on the *British Isles* were in Newcastle for 80 days.

The crowded harbour and the delays to load created frustration. A renowned British master of ships in the final days of sail, WA Nelson, wrote in his logbook on arrival at Newcastle on 8 May 1904, 'We found the harbour as congested as ever, with idle ships waiting their turn to load. It looked like another long spell in port'. Captain Nelson and the crew of the sailing ship *Acamas* were in port until 3 August, a stay of almost three months.[31]

The age of sail had slipped its lines and left behind most other ports around the globe, but not in Newcastle. Its harbour remained a place out of time well into the 20th century, with sailing ships berthed along the Stockton shores, which was a blessing for the film makers of the convict saga, *For The Term of His Natural Life*. They needed sailing ships for their movie, and they found a fleet of them in Newcastle. In 1927, 'convicts' returned to Stockton, only this time they were film extras. When it was released later that year, *For The Term of His Natural Life* had its world premiere at the Theatre Royal in Newcastle.[32]

More than lighting up the big screen, Newcastle Harbour was a sight to behold on any given day.

'In its hey-day the whole harbour was a forest of masts and yards', wrote Stan Hugill in *Sailortown*.[33]

From that forest emerged the men of the sea, seeking pleasure on land. Newcastle's pubs were not only numerous but legendary. Hugill recalled how 'the pubs of Newcastle were known from Frisco to Liverpool'.[34] The best known was the Clarendon, but other sailors' haunts included the Westminster and one with a name that reminded the clientele what they were here for, the Black Diamond. In the pubs, they drank and brawled and were recruited for ships – whether they were willing or not. The practice of crimping, or shanghaiing, was rife in Newcastle, as ships' masters needed crews, any which way they could. So men were enticed aboard – or carried aboard, drunk and unconscious, only to wake up at sea.

The risk of being shanghaied didn't just lurk in a bar. Many sailors stayed at boarding houses while in port, and those establishments often provided an underhand crew recruitment service for ships. In a newspaper report in 1906, it was alleged that 70 per cent of the boarding-house masters and publicans in Newcastle were involved in shanghaiing.[35]

As the 20th century progressed, recruitment methods changed dramatically. Just near Customs House was a shed known by seafarers as the 'pick-up'. If a mariner wanted work, then he'd turn up at the 'pick-up' in the morning, scan the board listing ships needing crew members and, within hours, could be back out at sea. The 'pick-up' continued for many years, and it was a popular place, according to retired mariner Tom Jones, who grew up within a stone's throw of the harbour in the suburb of Wickham before embarking on a long career on ships. However, it became less and less needed, as there were fewer and fewer

Australian-crewed ships cruising in and out of the port, until they all but disappeared. During his many years of returning from the sea, the highlight of each voyage for Tom was seeing Nobbys on the ship's port side. He knew he was home. And then he'd dock in the heart of home, for ships were lined up at the wharves along the city's edge. The ships were part of the texture, character and excitement of Newcastle. And even if they didn't come from here, as Tom did, the crews were part of Newcastle life.

Living in the city as a child, historian Rosemary Melville saw sailors walking up the hill from the wharves. They would trudge past the shipping agents and owners in their finely built offices along Watt Street, heading to boarding houses overlooking the harbour. Others would stay closer to the waterfront, in the pubs or the brothels in the back lanes.

Those markers of a seafaring community have changed or disappeared. The shipping offices are now largely occupied by other businesses. Although one Watt Street building, coated in tiles of honeyed brown tones, is still adorned with the name, 'Union Steam Ship Company', spelt out in metal letters. Many of the sailors' boarding houses have been demolished or converted into grand homes. Perhaps the most stunning example is the former Coutts' Sailors' Home, established in 1882 in Newcastle East by the Reverend James Coutts, who wanted to give seamen a refuge from the temptations to be found when loitering in a port city. The former sailors' home is now a beautiful example of restoration amid other reminders of the city's maritime history, standing between Customs House and the former Earp Gillam Bond Store, which itself has been brought back to life as offices. So the historic sailors' home has been rescued, just as the Reverend Coutts wanted to do for its clientele back in the day. However, as the years passed, sailors no longer needed a home away from home in the harbour town. As shipping schedules changed, the amount of time they spent in port shrank from months and weeks to days and even hours.

Just as it has done in Newcastle for more than a century and a half, the Mission to Seafarers provides a semblance of home for visiting mariners from around the globe. But most of the 50 000 or so seafarers who pass through Newcastle each year have only a short amount of time to put their feet on firm ground, according to the Reverend Canon

Garry Dodd, the mission's senior chaplain. Many ships are loaded and heading for sea again in about 12 hours.

Unlike his forebear of the cloth, James Coutts, Father Garry and his team at the Mission to Seafarers aren't trying to save sailors with too much time on their hands in Newcastle; they're helping mariners make the most of what little time they have on shore.

Fifty years ago, when I was a child, I would hear groups of sailors walking along the street, speaking languages carried far from across the sea and exciting me with the possibilities of what lay over the horizon. Those sailors were part of my awakening to the fact that I belonged to a larger, richer world. It was one of the privileges of growing up in a harbour town. Yet the days of sailors ambling through the city have largely gone. The days of mariners congregating – and occasionally fighting (I once saw a hell of a brawl involving sailors outside the Blue Peter Hotel in Hunter Street) – have all but gone. Indeed, many of the famous sailors' pubs, including the Blue Peter Hotel, have gone as well. Instead, Novocastrians may grab a glimpse of visiting mariners quickly shopping for supplies or souvenirs before being driven back to their ship on the mission bus.

Today's sailors may be time-poor, but Father Garry reckons the city is poorer as well. Less time in port means less money spent by mariners, but there's a bigger loss for the residents of a harbour city.

'What the seafarers actually bring is a wealth of exposure to the world, to their customs and their cultures', Father Garry says. They want connection with the earth, and with others beyond the ship. Yet with so little time in port, they miss out on that, Father Garry says, and so do Novocastrians.

'We miss out on those connections, we miss out on being that conduit, to help them feel real again.'

What has changed Newcastle as a harbour town has been not just a matter of time. The issue is also one of distance.

In one respect, the activity of the port can seem very close, with the ships coming and going. As you stand in the heart of the city, at the end of the street, you will often see the great steel wall of a ship slide by. It is at once a disconcerting and exhilarating sight. In those moments, Newcastle isn't just a harbour town; it can feel like the harbour is *in* the town. The scale and impact of the port are right there before our eyes.

However, so much of harbour life has moved further away from the city. That movement has been going on since the 1800s, when much of the coal loading onto ships was transferred from the city's shore over to The Dyke at Carrington. But in recent years, the berthing of ships has gone further upriver, especially to the massive Kooragang industrial precinct shaped from a string of subsumed Hunter estuary islands. Rosemary Melville prefers the port of her childhood.

'I'd go walking with Mum, and it was a hive of activity because the ships were on this side of the harbour ... you could reach out and touch them. I had pieces of wool I picked up along the wharves.'

The warehouses and wharves along the waterfront slowly decayed, and the foreshore air was heavy with dashed hopes and fading memories. At the former Lee wharves, at the south-western end of the port, where everything from wool to frozen meat was loaded onto ships, there were only weeds and rust. Although this area had a European name redolent with sweetness, Honeysuckle, it had the look and stench of a wasteland. During the 1800s, there was a cemetery at Honeysuckle, before it was closed in the late 19th century and the land was resumed for a developing port. By the 1980s, it seemed Honeysuckle was once more being used as a graveyard, only this time for a key part of the city's waterside industry.

However, where Novocastrians saw degradation, the NSW Government saw an opportunity. That stretch of land by the harbour had the makings of a 'growth centre'. In 1992, the Honeysuckle Development Corporation was established to oversee the area's transformation. The corporation's charter was 'to coordinate the redevelopment of surplus government railway and port related land along four kilometres of harbour front'. Among the key objectives for the project was 'to make Newcastle's central business district an even more attractive place to live, work and visit'.[36]

What has risen from that weed-choked ground along the harbour are commercial buildings and residential blocks. Water – or the prospect of a harbour view – has drawn thousands into the heart of the city to live after many years of a declining population.

However, as you travel along Honeysuckle Drive, you find yourself in a growing chasm of cement and glass. The views to the harbour are limited to glimpses through the slivers of space between the buildings. Not that the recently constructed buildings encourage you to look at the gaps; your vision is tunnelled and channelled dead ahead. So when it comes to the placement of those buildings, the expansive views, it would seem, are primarily for those who can afford the waterfront apartments.

A few of those residents evidently would prefer harbour life to be seen and not heard. Harbour Master Vikas Bangia has received complaints from residents about ships' horns, although their number has dropped despite growing urban encroachment along the harbour. He says it is all about educating new arrivals and reminding them where they have moved to.

'I always say ports came first, before the buildings came in', Vikas says.

On the harbour's edge, threaded between the developments and the water, is a public promenade. There are a few concessions to the port as it used to be, with old bollards standing sentinel but serving no role other than jogging memories, for there are no ships to be held firm. There are also a few ornaments acknowledging the port as it is now, with sculptures reminiscent of navigational aids. However, those on the promenade and the harbour itself are kept separate, with few access points for those wanting to engage with the water beyond looking at it.

Some of the old buildings in the Honeysuckle precinct have survived, but the future of one is yet to be determined. In the final parcel of land waiting to be developed at the western end of Honeysuckle is a stone-faced two storey-building standing on its own on barren ground. This is the former Wickham School of Arts, built in 1882, for use by those living in the waterside industrial suburb. For years, the building has housed nothing and no-one. However, it holds links to not just the city's past but the nation's literary heritage. For in here was held the first meeting of the Starr-Bowkett Society, which would later become the Newcastle Permanent Building Society. Generations of Novocastrians have deposited their money there and have drawn part of their identity from the society's presence. Yet this lonely building holds value beyond words, and because of words. In 1884, Henry Lawson worked briefly in Newcastle, at a coach-painting business in Wickham. Desperate to improve his education, the teenage Lawson spent many hours in the Wickham School of Arts' library and reading room. The poet and short story writer's recollections of that time, written in an unfinished biography, have been set in stone in a secluded part of a nearby park beside the harbour. As Lawson notes, it was here in Wickham that 'I haunted the School of Arts still with an idea of learning before it was too late'.[37] Within a few years, Lawson's first poems were being published in *The Bulletin* magazine, setting him on a new course in life and, through his words, providing Australians with new insights into themselves and their country.

The former school of arts building has been restored, its classical façade gazing across a carpark towards the new harbourfront developments. Given its history, many want to see the building given a new purpose, perhaps even as a Henry Lawson museum.[38]

Other historical buildings in the precinct have been given new life. Newcastle Museum occupies the former Honeysuckle Railway Workshops. The brick buildings date to the late 1800s, and when you wander through the museum, amid artefacts and touchstones of Newcastle's past, the architecture helps give the exhibitions more meaning. Newcastle's story becomes visceral, rather than something to be simply looked at.

Nearby, on Lee Wharf, are two restored cargo sheds. The rest were demolished as the area was redeveloped. One of the sheds is now a hotel, and the other was, until 2018, the repository of more of Newcastle's story, and the city's connection to the sea. It housed the maritime museum. But the shed itself, a dignified assemblage of hardwood and iron, tells a compelling story because of the cargo it held, including the most precious of all: people.

For it was in here that about 13 000 people journeying from the Old World to the New in the years after the Second World War were processed after disembarking from their ship. The first of the 'migrant ships' docked at Lee Wharf in 1949. Another dozen migrant ships would cruise into the harbour, including S.S. *Roma*, which arrived on 18 December 1950, with 949 passengers who had journeyed from Bremerhaven in Germany.

One of the passengers on the *Roma* was Halina Paczynski. Halina was the four-year-old daughter of a Polish father, Zygmunt, and a German mother, Alina. They had made the long voyage, leaving behind their ravaged homelands, for one reason.

'We came here to start a new life in Australia', Halina says.

Halina's first steps in Australia were actually on wood over water. She and her family walked from the wharf into the cargo shed to go through immigration procedures and collect their luggage, and then they stepped out the other side onto a train, transporting them directly to the Greta migrant camp, an hour's journey up the Hunter Valley.

'It was hot, it was brown, but it had the most amazing flowers', was the four-year-old's impressions of her new home.

After almost two years in the camp, the Paczynskis moved to the Newcastle outer suburb of Cardiff, onto almost half a hectare of land, a purchase that was beyond anything Zygmunt could have even dreamt of in Europe. The Newcastle fringe, with the opportunity for more land, was popular with new arrivals. Halina says neighbouring Cardiff South was known as Little Poland.

As the family created a home on Australian soil, they worked hard to maintain their Polish links and language. Zygmunt was a founder and the first president of the Newcastle Polish Association, and helped establish language schools in the region. But speaking Polish – or any language other than English – in Newcastle in the 1950s was potentially asking for attention, or worse.

'You didn't speak your own language much because you were told to shut up, "You're in Australia now",' Halina recalls. 'People were quite vocal about it. They weren't always cruel about it; the mindset was that the quicker you learned the language and the customs, the quicker you'd adjust.'

The Newcastle of the past, bewildered by the European arrivals and often intolerant of their 'different' ways, is far removed from the contemporary city, Halina believes. She no longer experiences discrimination. Indeed, the post-war arrivals have helped create the more welcoming, more diverse and more interesting city that Newcastle has become.

'I think Newcastle became more accepting of people from different backgrounds, and they certainly wholeheartedly accepted the different foods! And that's still the case.' Halina often walks along the waterfront and is encouraged by the sight of people using the promenade. But she is not happy that the maritime museum was shut. Outside the museum was a Welcome Wall celebrating the port's immigration history, with the names of those who had arrived here, such as the Paczynski family's, on display. The wall has been in storage, along with many of the maritime museum's exhibits. For Halina, it feels as though Newcastle has erased a significant part of its past.

'It denies our identity', Halina says. 'If we don't have a past, we don't know who we are now.

'That's where it all started, it started at sea.'

For Halina Paczyinski, Newcastle Harbour is not just her starting place in Australia, it is her anchoring place. And at the centre of it all is the old shed. The building's stout walls cast long shadows across the wharf. Where a little girl once trod, finding her feet in a strange brown land after a long voyage, the older woman strides, secure in her place in the world.

'When I go anywhere near the harbour, I feel like I've come home', Halina murmurs. 'I know where I've come from, but this is home.'

Across the water from Honeysuckle, barely 100 metres away at Dyke Point, thousands of people, including some of those who had arrived on the 'migrant ships', once worked in the maritime industry. Over there used to be the State Dockyard.

The building and repairing of ships has been a part of harbour life since the early 1800s. A reminder of that bobs at Lee Wharf, with the meticulously crafted replica of the *William the Fourth* paddle steamer berthed there. The original was the first steamship built in Australia, taking shape on the banks of the Williams River, a tributary of the Hunter. The replica, built as a bicentenary project, takes passengers out on the harbour and back in time, giving them a sense of what the port used to be like.

And what it was like was a flurry of activity, not just on the water but along the harbour's edges. Shipyards and slipways were etched into the shorelines in earnest from the mid-19th century, contributing to what was 'a coally seaport', as a newspaper report stated, where, 'every third house sells slops or ropes or blocks of some of the many other articles required by those who go down to the sea in ships'.[39]

Shipbuilding became an even greater focus in 1942, with the opening of the State Dockyard. This was during the Second World War, when the building and repair of ships was seen as vital to the nation's survival. By the end of the conflict in 1945, the facility had built 23 vessels and repaired hundreds, including many that had limped into the harbour, bearing the wounds of war in the Pacific.

The State Dockyard was seen as integral to not just Newcastle but the nation in the post-war years. The NSW Minister for Public Works, JJ Cahill, declared straight after the war, 'I confidently prophesy that the Dockyard will play a significant part in the permanent establishment of Australian shipbuilding, which is essential both to the security of the Empire and the industrial development of our great Commonwealth.'[40]

For a time, the minister's words rang true. Down the dockyard's slips slid vessels that helped supply and transport the residents of an island nation, from Sydney Harbour ferries and fuel tankers to passenger ships for crossing Bass Strait, including the *Princess of Tasmania* and the *Australian Trader*. Although the harbour was reluctant to let the *Australian Trader* go. As the new ship cruised out of the port, it was grabbed by a mud bank, and tugs had to be called in.[41] Many more vessels were repaired at the facility. However, the dockyard struggled for years. Despite Minister Cahill's predictions, the dockyard closed in 1987.

Other markers of shipbuilding and repair slipped out of the harbour as well. The last floating dock, *Muloobinba*, which was moored just off the Carrington shore and cradling big vessels since 1978, was towed out of the harbour in 2012. Physically, the departure of the *Muloobinba* made that section of the harbour feel wider, giving more room for the growing role of recreation. After all, the Newcastle Cruising Yacht Club had set itself up on the opposite shore, with its marina hosting about 180 boats, from the historical to the ultra-luxurious. But symbolically, the loss of the *Muloobinba* makes the harbour feel emptier, as though a part of its industrial tradition and character has disappeared over the horizon. This area at the western end of the harbour may be known as the Marine Services Precinct, but the services are not how they used to be.

Shipbuilding moved not just offshore but upstream. A local boatbuilding family, the Lavericks, had established Carrington Slipways in the 1950s, providing a splash at the western end of the harbour, with the launching of ships. In the 1970s, Carrington Slipways headed up the Hunter River to Tomago. On the Carrington site, maritime work goes on. Multinational company Thales has operations there, doing a lot of Department of Defence-related work.

Along the Carrington shore, near where the *Muloobinba* was moored, it looks like a maritime retirement home. For sitting there in recent times have been vessels that used to be something else. However, quite a few in the motley fleet are taking on new lives. Among the vessels has been a former New Zealand Navy vessel, which has been renamed the *Ocean Recovery* and involved in environmental and maritime archaeological missions in the Pacific, and the camouflage-hulled *Steve Irwin*. The former flagship of the Sea Shepherd environmental group once stared down Japanese whalers amid the waves near Antarctica. For the past few years, the *Steve Irwin* has been dozing at the dock, having been bought – for $10 – and saved from the scrapheap by a maritime enthusiast. The ship has been used as a floating environmental education centre, as well as providing a museum of sorts, celebrating the *Steve Irwin*'s past life on the seas.

The harbour and its foreshores are not simply a repository of memories and of artefacts. However, a lot of land around the harbour is no longer used, or is waiting to be used. In an interview in 2022, Port of Newcastle's CEO Craig Carmody told me about half of the 777 hectares managed by the corporation was vacant. As well as trying to attract investment to do something with that land, the corporation is pushing ahead with its own projects to transform harbour land. It has battled for years to develop a major container terminal on a stretch along the southern arm of the Hunter River, where BHP's own 'Iron Ships' used to dock at the steelworks. Port of Newcastle has other big plans, including working on what it calls a 'clean energy precinct', with facilities to export green hydrogen and ammonia. Craig Carmody believes the port can also look to elements of its past for its future. He has asserted the city could once more be a place where ships come to be repaired and maintained. Others who work around the harbour say it would be ideal to have a superyacht maintenance facility here. That would bring the vessel's wealthy owners into the harbour, and more money would flow into the city. But with all of these projects, it's a case of getting the money here in the first place to turn plans and hopes into something that occupies the waterfront land.

If the harbourside land is developed, then Newcastle will be a much busier port. Newcastle Harbour Master Vikas Bangia says there is provision for more ships.

'The channel is not utilised to 100 per cent', Vikas says. 'It is at 52 per cent utilisation, so that really tells you we can definitely do more ships. As the Harbour Master I can say, "Bring more ships".'

Across the water from Honeysuckle, you can see more than vacant land, empty buildings and a sense of what used to be. Nestled in the indented shoreline known as The Basin, tugs come and go from their base, as they prepare to nudge and guide ships in and out of the harbour. Occasionally, the vessel entering is a cruise ship. Sixteen cruise ships visited Newcastle in 2024, bringing thousands of tourists to the city. A cruise ship is usually greeted with a blast of Fort Scratchley's guns, so the armaments once used to keep enemies at bay now provide an ear-ringing welcome. The cruise ships' passengers disembark at the Channel Berth on Dyke Point, amid the remnants of the State Dockyard. While there is a big 'Welcome' sign painted on a building and pointed straight at arriving ships, the passengers are not exactly stepping into the lap of luxury. There is no permanent cruise ship terminal. The plans for that were scuppered in 2019, after the state government's Infrastructure NSW withdrew funding. Many in the city had expected a terminal as some sort of return, after the NSW Government privatised the port in 2014 for $1.75 billion. Although a cruise terminal was not part of the privatisation deal, that emptiness on the waterfront is, in the minds of many Novocastrians, symbolic of how Sydney short-changes Newcastle. Not that the disembarking cruise passengers would see it that way; they just see no terminal and an expanse of undeveloped land. The passengers may well see hints of the port's history and charm, including the classical grandeur of the nearby hydraulic engine house, which was built in Carrington in 1877 to power the coal-loading cranes. And as they are bussed to the Hunter Valley vineyards or around to the city, the visitors may even catch a glimpse of Carrington's Seven Seas Hotel, which, for generations, has been popular with those working on or by the water. The Art Deco beauty has even starred in a number of films. So even though they would be made to feel welcome, whether by Fort Scratchley's cannon fire or by the regulars at the Seven Seas, the tourists would be well aware that they have cruised into a working industrial harbour. More pointedly, they have arrived at a coal port.

FOR more than 220 years, coal has been exported from Newcastle.

When the first load of Hunter coal was carried out of the river mouth in a barque bound for Bengal in 1799, it created history: this was the first commercial export from the British colony. But that shipment also set the pattern for the future port of Newcastle.

Ever since, ships have been loaded in Newcastle and set off over the horizon with Hunter coal in their hold.

In the days when convicts were still labouring in Newcastle's mines, loading coal could be painfully slow. As a journalist at the time noted, 'The coal is doled out in miserable thimblefuls and drawn about the wharf in wheelbarrows.'[42]

The thimbles have turned into mountains. Almost 150 million tonnes of coal were exported from the port in 2024. The mountains of mined coal form a range across the lowlands of the Kooragang precinct, presiding between the North and South arms of the river. Along the South Arm, there is a string of wharves and coal-loading facilities, constantly pouring the mountains through ships' hatches. In 2024, 1726 ships were loaded with Hunter coal.[43]

To those opposed to the coal trade, the bulk carriers are not just departing with crushed pieces of the Hunter's heart, they are also helping leave a hole in the soul of the region. What's more, they are contributing to a growing global climate crisis.

As a result, the harbour is occasionally an environmental battleground. For the best part of two days in November 2023, hundreds of floating craft milled about in the main shipping channel in what was called 'the people's blockade of the world's largest coal port'.

Protestors from near and far travelled to Newcastle, erecting a tent community in the Camp Shortland parkland near the harbour's entrance, and they lined up their kayaks along Horseshoe Beach, which is normally where people bring their dogs to run off the leash. This scalloped strip of sand is known locally as The Dog Beach.

But the Hunter-based environmental organisation behind the protest, Rising Tide, wanted to use this space as a beachhead in the battle against the fossil fuel industry and politicians, and to bring attention to the climate change issue, by stopping coal ships from entering or leaving the port.

The organisers, in the people's blockade handbook given to participants, argued the port was the single biggest contributor of greenhouse gas pollution in Australia.[44] But as one of the volunteer organisers, Zack Schofield, explains, that wasn't the only reason Newcastle Harbour was chosen for the climate protest.

'I reckon people will start to demand accountability more and more from the fossil fuel industry, and I think the public water of Newcastle Harbour is a fantastic canvas to expose that demand for accountability because it's such an open place', Zack tells me a couple of weeks after the 2023 protest. 'You can see what happens there and see the tension between the vast, vast ships that come out of here, and the many small craft placing themselves in the way of these monsters of industry.'

For Zack, the harbour is not just a battleground, it is home ground. He grew up in the inner-city suburb of Cooks Hill.

'The harbour was ever present, because we could hear the foghorns and ships' horns at all hours of a night. It was a place of intrigue and opportunity to imagine what was happening across the harbour, imagining the sailors on the ships, counting the ships on the horizon.'

As a teenager, Zack wanted to stop some of those ships, taking part in a blockade in 2016. Seven years later, the blockade had grown larger, because the stakes were higher, and, as the young law student explained, the climate crisis was greater.

'The continuation and expansion of the coal industry is at the risk of my future, and that of other young people.'

The atmosphere on the beach was carnival-like, with singers performing on a stage, and protestors forming human signs on the sand. Out on the water, however, the mood was more pensive, with the protest flotilla monitored by police vessels.

For 30 hours, the port was effectively closed. Zack estimates in that time, the blockade stopped eight to 10 ships, and about 500 000 tonnes of coal, from leaving.

The tension escalated on the Sunday afternoon when, after the authorised time for the blockade, protestors remained on the water. The police moved in and about 100 protestors, including Zack, were arrested.

As far as Zack is concerned, it was worth it. He views the blockade as his generation's Franklin Dam protest, 'a landmark struggle with global implications'. This environmental campaign is not only bringing attention to a global issue, but also to the need for change and transition in the region. Zack argues there have to be bigger taxes on the fossil fuel industry to help pay for Newcastle and the Hunter to move into a future that is not dependent on coal.

'We have the opportunity to be a global leader in showing what a bold transition can look like', he says.

'Newcastle's industry has been a source of pride in the past, and there's no reason why it can't be moving forward. It just has to be the right kind of industry.'

The port itself is seeking to change by diversifying what it handles. While a wide range of products are shipped in and out of the port, coal dominates, accounting for 95 per cent of the total trade volume in 2024. Port of Newcastle's CEO, Craig Carmody, reckons the demand for Hunter coal will remain for a time yet. The company's vision is that by 2030, 50 per cent of its revenue will come from non-coal sources, and that's what Craig is working towards.

'I'm in a position to help the world's largest coal export port to be something else', Craig told me in 2022.[45]

Zack Schofield has his own ideas about what the port could be.

'As a Novocastrian, I want to see the port become one of the world's largest renewables ports', he says. 'We have an amazing opportunity to develop the off-shore wind industry … If we can develop that industry locally, we can export renewables components from here.'

Yet others don't see off-shore wind as the future for this region. On the fringe of the people's blockade camp in November 2023 stood a solitary man with a placard protesting against plans for a wind energy project off the Hunter coast.

Zack says Rising Tide will continue to push for change. It organised another large 'protestival', as Rising Tide called the action, by, and on, the harbour in November 2024. This time shipping was only briefly disrupted, as the NSW Government had clamped down on the blockade. But Rising Tide hopes to stop the coal ships for good. Zack says the organisation wants an end to coal exports from the port of Newcastle by 2030.

And just as he did as a kid, Zack will continue to count the ships on the horizon, all the while agitating for them to stop carrying away Hunter coal.

'I know that a lot of my life, and the most significant parts of my life, will revolve around what happens around the port', he says. 'So I feel a sense of ownership and responsibility and I feel extraordinarily lucky to come from here and feel that responsibility.'

I'm arriving in Newcastle by water. Which means I'm seeing Newcastle at its best.

I'm on board the *Shinchi Maru*, a ship bearing the Japanese flag that is heading into the port to load 95 000 tonnes of coal. I'm following marine pilot Captain Stuart Noble, who has been working for the Port Authority of New South Wales in Newcastle for more than 25 years and in that time has helped about 6000 ships navigate their way in and out of the harbour.

Earlier Stuart and I had been gently placed on the ship's number three hatch, which serves as a helipad. The helicopter ride from Dyke Point to the *Shinchi Maru*, which was about four nautical miles, or 7.4 kilometres, off the coast, took a few minutes. The ship ploughs through a benign sea, with a swell of about 2 metres.

'When it's like this, it's fantastic', smiles Stuart. 'When it's rough, it's not so fantastic.'

Stuart introduces himself to the ship's captain, Nelson Sigua. Nelson is in charge of a crew of 20, all from the Philippines, and he stands on the bridge of a 240-metre long ship making its way to the harbour entrance.

Newcastle's cityscape rises above the striated, sea-sculpted cliffs, which tip down to the strips of beaches near the harbour entrance. While I'm gazing towards the land, Stuart is conferring with Nelson, studying the sea, and giving directions to the helmsman.

'Steer three one five, please.'

'Three one five', the helmsman replies.

When I ask Stuart what he does as the pilot, and how he works with the captain, he replies, 'His job is to manage the ship, and my job is to manage the passage'.

Back in 1820, one of Newcastle's earliest marine pilots, William Eckford, said it was difficult for ships to enter the harbour. He described it as 'a very dangerous harbour, on account of the shifting of the sands and the variety of currents caused by the passage between the mainland and the island called Nobbys'.[46]

More than two centuries on, Stuart Noble says it can be still a tricky harbour to enter. The challenges can arrive even before a ship reaches the entrance. Stuart explains the swell generally comes from the southeast, 'so on approach, it's directly on the side of the ship, so the ship gets pushed a bit that way'.

Three tugs are waiting at the entrance as insurance, just in case the ship needs to be nudged into the channel and away from the shorelines. But before we reach the tugs, we're at the mercy of the ship and the sea.

'If we get a failure [before the harbour entrance], there are no tugs to save us, and the rocks are awfully close on either side', Stuart points out. 'Also, we're at the highest speed we're going to be at any time. On approach we'll be doing about nine knots [almost 17 km/h]. There's a lot of momentum there.'

The *Shinchi Maru* glides into the harbour entrance. Stuart gives instructions to the helmsman, using two green leading lights in the distance as a guide. The lights are on the land, as are other navigational aids perched on towers along the foreshore and on the hill. These pieces of harbour life are all but unnoticed and unobtrusive to those going about their business in the city but vital to the safe navigation of those entering and leaving the port. After all, ships do not have a lot of space to play with in Newcastle. The main channel is only 183 metres wide. The *Shinchi Maru* is 43 metres wide. The breakwaters flanking the channel can feel awfully close.

To the left, Nobbys slides past, the lighthouse about the same height as the ship's bridge. To the right, poking above the northern breakwater, is the rusting prow of the wreck of the *Adolphe*, serving not as a navigational aid but a warning and reminder of what can happen. Not that Stuart Noble needs reminding of how treacherous this harbour entrance can be, and how quickly conditions can change.

'It's always there', Stuart says when asked whether he thinks about what can go wrong as he passes the *Adolphe* and the other ships' corpses buried under the breakwater on the Oyster Bank. 'And most of us have had experiences as well.'

Stuart recounts an incident many years earlier while bringing a ship in when the swell was huge. To complicate matters, one of the ship's anchors had accidentally dropped into the heavy seas and was uncontrolled. The captain was apparently concerned and ordered for the engine to be stopped. Stuart countered that by ensuring the engine kept going.

'If he had got his way and stopped the engine, there was only one place the ship was going and that was onto the northern breakwater. And that wouldn't have done anyone any good.'

A ship on the breakwater or stuck in the channel would not just be a potential maritime disaster. It would block the flow of trade and dollars in and out of the port, imposing pressure on businesses and thousands of jobs. Back in 1820 the colonial marine pilot William Eckford explained that in usual conditions, the weight of a ship's cargo could be no more than 100 tonnes leaving Newcastle, otherwise they risked being stuck. These days, ships could weigh 230 000 tonnes leaving the port, so if a vessel that heavy, and up to 300 metres long, were to become stuck in the channel, the impact would ripple far beyond the harbour.

As Stuart Noble says, 'Those kinds of things play on your mind the whole time'.

The *Shinchi Maru* follows the leading lights and pushes out rolls of white-flecked aquamarine towards the shores as it cuts down the middle of the main channel. Newcastle unfolds along the shore and up the hill. Whatever people are doing, however life is playing out in the city, they all stop for a moment to watch the ship go by. It is an imposing affirmation, cast in steel, that we are a harbour town.

'Most of the ports you go to around the world, the port is outside the city, it's seaward to the city, so the ships never go past it', Stuart muses. 'It's not unique but it's more than a little bit unusual for a city to sit here and have the entirety of the trade going past the front door.'

We slide past the Italianate tower of the former Customs House, its time ball suspended and waiting for its moment to drop, setting the clock on a harbour ritual. The building sits at the bottom of Watt Street. I see the lines of 19th-century and 20th-century buildings, many of them built for – or from the money of – shipping, lining the street, all the way up to where the road bends and the land tips once more into the sea.

Stuart notes where I'm looking and says, 'You can start at the top of Watt Street and drive the whole way down; there's a ship going past when you were at the top of Watt Street and by the time you're at the bottom, the ship is still going past'.

For Captain Nelson Sigua, the sight of Newcastle from the water is something he never tires of, even though he has entered and left this port up to 40 times during his 22 years on ships.

'A magnificent view', the *Shinchi Maru*'s captain says.

Over to our right, the Stockton Ferry bobs at its terminal, waiting for us to pass, so it can cross back to the city. Further along the harbour, the waters are often sprinkled with sailboats racing, while others skitter across the surface from the historical skiff club on the Stockton shore. Tour boats meander around the harbour while others carry visitors out to sea during whale-watching seasons. Before the sun even rises, kayaks, outrigger canoes and stand-up paddleboards slice the harbour's skin, passing the trawlers wearing their veils of whorling gulls, while along the shore, joggers find their rhythm and fishers plumb the depths with their lines. The harbour is a playground and an escape valve in a fast-growing city. However, it is also a commercial conduit. With the harbour playing so many roles, supporting so many interests, for so many different elements of the community, I wonder if it is big enough for everyone.

'I think absolutely it is, with the caveat we've all got to know our place in it', Stuart Noble says, before the marine pilot states another proviso, with a smile. 'However, come the time I need to use it, please get out!

'Even then, it's not a case of "you can't be there". You just have to be selective about where you are.' Which is good advice from a man who pilots ships up to three rugby league fields long on these waters.

As I look around, absorbing the view, I reflect how much my harbour view has been shaped and coloured by visual artists through the years. I think of the images of the convict artist Joseph Lycett. I think of the working harbour swirling and billowing to life in the paintings of Margaret Olley. Margaret may have lived in Sydney but she loved Newcastle. The harbour city left its mark on Oll, and, as a result, Oll made marks reflecting the harbour city. She saw beauty and vibrancy where so many others saw smoke and grit. In her eyes, Newcastle was a 'painterly city', as she once told me. But it was the harbour that changed her view of Newcastle.

Prior to visiting Newcastle for the first time in the 1960s, her impression was that it was a 'terrible coal-hole, smoky place'.

'But when the train turned and I started seeing all the wharves and ships, it gave me the same feeling as when I was five or six in Townsville. It had that same sort of feeling, that bustling thing of a port, which is always exciting.'[47]

Now, ahead of me, I see the work of Wonnarua and Anaiwan woman and insightful interpreter of the Hunter landscape and character, Saretta Fielding. Her observation of the harbour and the surrounding country flows across the 'Welcome' billboard at the former State Dockyard site on Dyke Point. She created that huge artwork.

Saretta explains she wanted to depict the beauty of the waterways and surrounding landscape, including a long yellow strip across the image representing the enormous Worimi sand dunes to the north of the harbour. In the water are circles, which represent the people of Newcastle.

The artist says that as well as serving as a welcome, her work underscores that Aboriginal people have 'lived and been prosperous alongside Country for many years'. She points out the 'Welcome' sign is only a few hundred metres from an ancient fig tree, known as the Tree of Knowledge, on the harbour shore at Wickham. The tree grows in an area where the Awabakal used to gather for corroborees. Saretta also notes that the purpose of the artwork aligns with the way Aboriginal people here have been for thousands of years. They are welcoming and inclusive.

When I ask Saretta to imagine how the First Nations peoples around the harbour would have responded when they saw the Europeans slide into the river for the first time, she replies, 'Putting myself in that place, it would have been like an alien invasion.

'It would have been bizarre.'

The harbour has featured so often in paintings and photographs and yet not so much in Australian literature. Perhaps because Newcastle Harbour doesn't possess the drama of Sydney's, for example, its waters haven't been turned into words. But the harbour does occasionally pop up. It features in the generational tale largely set in Newcastle, *Lovers' Knots*, by Novocastrian writer Marion Halligan. The novelist has one of her characters declare that it used to be the greatest port in the world, and it is described as being 'often beautiful'.[48] That same word, beautiful, is attached to the harbour when it makes a cameo in Tom Keneally's novel, *The People's Train*.[49] So the use of 'beautiful' by these two acclaimed novelists seems to undermine my theory about why the harbour is not a popular literary muse.

Dymphna Cusack, who would find fame as the co-author of *Come in Spinner*, was posted to Newcastle as a teacher during the Second World War. She later used wartime Newcastle as the setting for her book, *Southern Steel*. The harbour is featured in the novel, and Cusack's choice of words further erodes my theory. As one of the main characters returns to Newcastle by air, he is elated by the sight of his hometown, with 'the harbour sparkling between the winding shores of the estuary, its waters streaked with the purplish line of the river, the twin arms of Nobbys and Stockton enclosing it like the pincers of a giant crab'.[50]

At one point in *Southern Steel*, a character called Hoppy is looking at 'the busy harbour, the crowded foreshores' and declares, 'someone ought to write a book just about this place'.[51]

What a good thought, Hoppy.

The *Shinchi Maru* traces the channel along the Horseshoe, the stretch that bends around the point of Stockton, and Captain Nelson Sigua sees the 'Welcome' billboard.

'Very hospitable', Nelson says of Newcastle. 'I'm always made welcome.'

We turn away from the city and head upriver towards the Kooragang berths. Although BHP shut its massive complex on the vast tract of land over to our left in 1999, this stretch of water is still known as the Steelworks Channel. It is a stretch that takes Stuart Noble back to his introduction to a life on ships.

'I joined my very first ship here in 1979', recalls Stuart.

The 16-year-old cruised out of the harbour on board BHP's *Iron Spencer*. This was Stuart's first voyage of many, as he worked in the BHP fleet for 19 years.

As we approach the old steelworks site, Stuart conjures the days when this area was known as Port Waratah and the wharves were lined with BHP ships. At berths two and three, ships loaded the products made at the steelworks. At berths four and five were the ships bringing in the iron ore. At that site, now known as Mayfield 4, is where Port of Newcastle has planted the seeds for its container terminal. Upriver, Stuart recalls, was where chemical tankers berthed.

'I did pretty much the lot', Stuart says, as he gazes along the shore and over the clear fields where a steelworks once ruled, before he looks down to the water. He has noticed change there too since the steelworks shut.

'I think we should celebrate it's so clean.'

The steelworks 'might have been an economically valuable place, but it wasn't a nice place. It was dirty'.

The signs of a future energy source rest on the old steelworks land near the river's edge. Blades for wind turbines have been delivered by sea, waiting to be trucked inland.

However, we're crossing the river to where coal remains king. The *Shinchi Maru* is destined for the Kooragang 5 berth. The tugs nudge and push the ship into the berth, the effort stirring up the river bottom and swirling sediment into psychedelic patterns on the surface. Downriver, just over 4 kilometres away, is the CBD. I can see glimmering on The Hill, like an exclamation mark, The Obelisk. The colonial mariners would be relieved to know that, despite all the recent developments in the city, this navigational mark is still visible from the water.

Just 90 minutes after we landed on the ship's deck, the *Shinchi Maru* is secured at Kooragang 5. Eighteen hours later, with a belly filled with coal and sitting about 13.2 metres down in the water, she will cruise out of the port, leaving the security of the harbour for all the opportunities and terrors the sea holds, destined for Japan.

Captain Stuart Noble's assignment is complete. But the next assignment, the next ship loaded and ready to leave, is waiting. The work on the water never ends. And Stuart doubts it ever will, even when the coal ships disappear over the horizon for the final time.

He remembers when people used to say, 'If the steelworks go, Newcastle will die'.

'But Newcastle has thrived ever since', Stuart says. 'If coal goes, will Newcastle thrive? Something else will come along.'

While ever something else comes along, Newcastle will remain a harbour town.

Over at the Mission to Seafarers, where crews such as those on the *Shinchi Maru* go for their precious few hours on land, the Reverend Canon Garry Dodd believes we will continue to see the ships gliding in and out. However, seeing the ships is not enough. We have to see, and feel connected to, those on board.

'We are in a harbour city, but we're losing it, we're getting sea blind', says Father Garry. 'In the past, our eyes were open to the vessels and the seafarers, because many of us had family or friends working on ships or around the port, but we're starting to lose that connection, so we're losing sight of the people on board. Our vision is getting fuzzy.'

However, Father Garry also believes we will be resolutely a harbour city.

'As we change yet again, and the city reinvents itself, one of the things that will continue to inspire us is the vessels that come and go', he says.

IN their voyages in and out of the harbour, seafarers would notice on the tip of Dyke Point, where steel was once shaped into ships, the bronze statue of a young woman. The statue was commissioned in 1999 to commemorate 200 years of commercial shipping in the port of Newcastle. The woman appears to be pointing to where all the ships that cruise into the harbour will inevitably head once more: the sea. Little wonder then the statue is titled *Destiny*.

Perhaps *Destiny* is also showing Newcastle where its future lies, embracing and offering shelter to what comes in from the sea, and to continue looking out.

Just as the waters of Yohaaba provided a bridge between the lands of the Worimi and the Awabakal, they connect a harbour city and a river valley with the rest of the world.

In the harbour lie Newcastle's past and its destiny.

CHAPTER TWO

THE CITY'S HEART

WHILE on a speaking tour of Australia in 1895 to pay off debts, the great American writer Samuel Langhorne Clemens, better known as Mark Twain, stopped off in Newcastle.

He may have derived his pen name from his days of working on boats on the Mississippi River, with Mark Twain being a reference to two fathoms of water, but the writer didn't arrive in Newcastle by ship. He rode into the city's heart on a train.

While he was renowned, and sometimes derided by the literati, for being a 'humourist', and reviews of his speaking tour recounted how Twain had his audiences roaring with laughter, he was in no joking mood when he briefly visited Newcastle. He was in pain.

Mark Twain was on his way to perform in the Upper Hunter town of Scone, but a toothache compelled him to get off the train in Newcastle. He trudged up nearby Bolton Street to a dentist, who evidently dealt with the pain. In a 'thank you' note to the dentist, Twain wrote, 'I now depart on my journey in greater comfort than on my arrival'.[1]

Perhaps as a result of the dental work, Mark Twain purportedly tapped into his humour once more. He is attributed with having said that Newcastle consisted of a long street with a graveyard at one end with no bodies in it, and a gentlemen's club at the other with no gentlemen in it.

Twain's purported observation of Newcastle didn't feature in his written account of his speaking tour, titled 'Following the Equator'. Nor has the comment's source ever been found. Perhaps the alleged observation is like what Twain wrote about Australian history: that it didn't read like history, but like the most beautiful lies.[2] It might be a beautiful lie that Twain ever made this witticism about Newcastle.

But if he did, Twain's observation holds some truth about the city's layout. Newcastle has a couple of long streets running through its CBD, with the main thoroughfare being Hunter Street. At the western end, in the Honeysuckle area, there had been a cemetery. By the time Twain visited Newcastle, the cemetery had closed, but there were still bodies in it. As for the gentlemen's club, the gathering place for many of the city's rich and influential has been, since 1885, the Newcastle Club. Gleaming with varnished wood, starched with a strict dress code, and brushed with an air of cool repose piped in from another era and another place (perhaps St James's Square or Pall Mall in London), the Newcastle Club has been a consistent drawcard for gentlemen. Ladies, on the other hand, were admitted to membership only in 2002. The club's home has moved through the years, but in Twain's time it was on the corner of King and Watt streets.

Even if Twain never did make that comment, it tells something about Novocastrians that we have not only accepted he said it but quoted it liberally. It is as though we are just grateful that a famous American writer and performer even noticed us. Perhaps we should be insulted that Twain stopped in Newcastle only long enough for dental treatment, rather than stay and perform here. Scone got the entertainment; Newcastle got the pain.

What Mark Twain did write about Newcastle was brief, describing it as a rushing town and the capital of the coal regions. But that description doesn't have the Twain zing about it, so we go with the clever but negative quote. After all, not only does it *sound* more like something Mark Twain would say, it rings true to what Novocastrians have expected outsiders to say about Newcastle for generations.

From its birth, Newcastle was a place often scorned and even feared, a place to be avoided and to escape from. Never mind one long street running through its heart; Newcastle had one long seam of aversion running through its history.

The first Europeans to arrive in Yohaaba and explore the shores of what would become Newcastle may have made promising comments about the place, particularly its commercial potential for the colony, but that only encouraged its establishment as a human dumping ground.

No sooner had the first survey party to explore the lower reaches of the Hunter River returned to Sydney in June 1801 than Governor Philip Gidley King had ordered a group of convicts and a handful of soldiers to head north and begin mining coal. However, dissent and discontent soon festered in the mouth of the Hunter, and within months the governor abandoned the settlement.

In early 1804, however, strife in Sydney led to the settlement by the Hunter being brought back to life as a place of secondary punishment for prisoners. In the words of local historian John Turner, Newcastle was to be Sydney's Siberia.[3]

Among those shipped out of Sydney to Newcastle were Irish convicts who had participated in a series of attempted escapes and acts of rebellion, culminating in a showdown known as the Battle of Vinegar Hill on 5 March 1804. The uprising, around what is now the north-western outskirts of Sydney, was named after a battle in Ireland that had led to political prisoners being transported to Sydney, and some of those convicts were then involved in this second Battle of Vinegar Hill. The rebellion not only made the authorities in Sydney skittish, it was momentous. According to historian Lynette Ramsay Silver, it was 'the first European battle fought on Australian soil'.[4] The catchcry of the rebels had been 'Death or Liberty'. For many, it was death, with about 30 killed in battle, and more by hanging as punishment. For 34 rebels, liberty was pushed even further away, as they were exiled to the re-born settlement at Coal River.

Being sent to Newcastle didn't quell some of the rebels' bid for liberty. They formed plans to escape, which were uncovered, leading to further punishment, including time in double irons, floggings, and being exiled further within the place of exile, on Nobbys. Four of the six ringleaders were confined to the island in the harbour's entrance. Irish convicts based around Castle Hill even planned a rescue mission to Newcastle to help their compatriots escape, but that amounted to nothing.[5]

So Newcastle was, in part, founded because of the desperate acts of men who were willing to die for freedom. And that may well explain at least one source of the rebellious streak many Novocastrians take pride in claiming as part of their character.

For those passing through, the settlement could seem bucolic enough. Visiting botanist Robert Brown noted in 1804 how the infant town was taking shape on a gentle slope of a grassy hill.[6] But for those stuck here, Sydney's Siberia developed a formidable reputation.

'It was a hell of pain, despair and ugliness, a hell tucked out of sight', declared author Marjorie Barnard in her description of the penal settlement.[7]

It may not have been contained by high walls, but Newcastle was made to be hard to escape from. The instructions for the administration of the settlement stated, 'No person whatever whether civil, military or convict under your command is to be permitted to leave Newcastle, or to come to Sydney ... without the Governor's permission'.[8] To prevent visiting ships being stolen and sailed away, or prisoners stowing away, the commandant imposed a string of rules. Ships' crews had to deliver their sails and anchors soon after mooring in the harbour, and the mariners had to sleep on board. The settlement's inhabitants were prohibited from boarding any vessel without the commandant's permission. So the wider world was kept from those in Newcastle. What's more, even once a convict had done their time, it was hard to leave Newcastle behind and find a way back into society. According to Marjorie Barnard, 'a man who had been to Newcastle was marked'.[9]

Reading the colonial novel, *Ralph Rashleigh*, which is partly set in the convict settlement, you gain the impression that a man who had been to Newcastle was marked by the cat o' nine tails.

The title character is sentenced to Newcastle, where he is one of the 'luckless wretches' working in the 'old' coal mine near the harbour's entrance.[10] After toiling all week, on the Sunday, the convicts are paraded before the settlement's commandant, the King of the Coal River, and many of them are flogged for the most trivial reasons. The narrator recounts one incident where the commandant has six men lined up, each whipping the one in front as incentive to flog the one before him harder. At the back of the line, lashing away with a horsewhip, is the commandant. This bizarre and cruel scene, the narrator offers, 'may afford to the reader some slight idea of the state of affairs in Newcastle at that period'.[11]

However, fiction and reputation may have been taking licence with reality. In 1819, the British Government commissioned John Thomas Bigge to conduct an inquiry into the administration of the Australian colonies, and Newcastle featured when he toured the settlements. The commissioner heard from a range of people in Newcastle, from the commandant, James Morisset, to convicts. The inquiry was told Newcastle was undoubtedly seen as a place of punishment by the convicts, and Bigge concluded that flogging was inflicted with more severity than at the other settlements. But that hadn't always been the case.

'When I first came here in 1811 this place could not be called a place of punishment', William Evans, the assistant colonial surgeon at Newcastle, told the inquiry. 'There were great indulgences in everything and the labour was light.'[12]

Discipline had tightened, and, as the inquiry was told, the settlement was in far better order.[13] The stricter discipline raised some eyebrows. One of Newcastle's pioneering businessmen, the merchant and mariner John Bingle, recalled walking with Morisset around the settlement in 1821. He noted how the convicts stood still and every coal cart was brought to a halt as the pair passed.

'Perhaps it was necessary for the safety of the settlement that such severe discipline and punishments should be adopted, but to a stranger's eye it seemed very un-English', Bingle wrote.[14] Still, the discipline wasn't so strict as to stop a gang of convicts stealing the trading vessel Bingle's company had built in Newcastle in 1822.

While the Bigge inquiry heard how Newcastle had changed, it also learnt how the settlement had to change. The commissioner was told about inadequate buildings, insufficient food allowances, only one good well for water, and the incessant impact of the sand hills creeping into the settlement. Much of Newcastle, including the gaol and hospital, was built on sand. So the foundations often weren't stable. Despite that, or perhaps because of the shifting ground around and under it, Newcastle dug in and grew.

In the eyes of Governor Macquarie, at least, Newcastle had the makings of a neatly laid-out and clean town. In a visit to Newcastle in 1818, he attended a couple of services in the recently built church on the hill. Macquarie wrote in his journal about how he named it Christ Church. On Monday 3 August, Macquarie noted, 10 couples were married and 30 children baptised in the church, 'the first ceremony of the kind ever yet performed at Newcastle'.[15]

Just as the church physically presided over Newcastle, so did religion over the inhabitants' lives. As Governor Macquarie made clear in his instructions for the settlement's administration, every convict and soldier was expected to go to church each Sunday. Yet the church itself had sand at its feet and, according to a convict who helped build it, James Clohesy, its body was made of stone impregnated with salt water that, he believed, 'will moulder away by exposure to the weather'.[16] The building Clohesy helped build did moulder away. Within a decade, the church was not being used and its steeple had to be dismantled. But a new incarnation rose on the site.

More than 200 years on, the church still holds the high ground in Newcastle. In that time, it has been rebuilt and expanded, and so has its status, becoming Christ Church Cathedral, or, to give the building its full title, the Cathedral Church of Christ the King.

But the cathedral has also been threatened. The ground under it was mined for years in the quest for coal, part of the roof was torn off during a storm in 1974, and the building was shaken and damaged by the 1989 earthquake. Yet the cathedral stands, crowning Newcastle, its tower poking at the heavens and offering perhaps the city's finest viewing platform. Little wonder that seafarers arriving in Newcastle for the first time see the great brick building on The Hill and presume it is the castle that has given the city its name.

'It's a place people literally look up to, it is iconic in its current form on The Hill, and it symbolises more than an Anglican space', says the Dean of Newcastle, The Very Reverend Katherine Bowyer. 'I think the community owns the cathedral, it belongs to the community.

'People have said to me that there's no earthquake memorial in Newcastle, but I think the cathedral is that memorial because the community raised so much money for its restoration.'

More than being a place of worship, the cathedral is a war memorial. Through a series of archways on the cathedral's northern side is the Warriors' Chapel. In here, the loss and suffering produced by the

First World War have been carved into stone and cedar and poured into the treasures on display, including the Book of Gold. This book glimmers in the chapel's subdued light, for its covers are plates of gold. Much of the gold was donated by women, who slipped off their fingers the rings given to them by their men, now lying in the earth on the other side of the globe. Pressed between the golden covers are the names of Hunter Valley servicemen killed during the war. More than 2000 men were lost. It is a very thick book, and heavy. For the weight of grief is far greater than that of gold.

Christ Church Cathedral is also a place of celebration and joyous noise. It serves as a venue for the Newcastle Music Festival and hosts concerts throughout the year. It is a divine music venue in more ways than one, as the sounds of instruments and voices curl towards the vaulted ceiling and ricochet off the stone columns. When the cathedral's historic organ is played, the walls just about shudder as the space fills with sound. Yet, in a city whose soundtrack in recent years has been the cacophony of construction, perhaps the cathedral's greatest gift to Novocastrians is serenity.

The cathedral appears as a symbol of permanence amid change. But as Dean Katherine points out, it is also a harbinger of change. Dean Katherine is a part of that change – she is the Diocese of Newcastle's first female dean. What's more, she is the diocese's first Novocastrian dean.

'I'm really aware where the cathedral stands was a much higher hill, and when the hill was levelled, it's taken away some of the significance for the Awabakal and Worimi peoples', Dean Katherine says. 'I'm really aware we are a place that has been imposed on First Nations land. And, as a child of Newcastle, what I love is we have a working harbour in the heart of the city. I can see ships coming in and out, and it's part of the soundscape of the city. And I think that says something about who we are as a community. There's hard work – and it's often described as dirty work – and in a time of climate awareness we think about what it means to be a coal port and coal city, and the cathedral is a part of that. And we're a part of the struggle. We're immersed in the life of the city, and I'd be sad if we weren't a part of that.'

To maintain a connection between the harbour and the cathedral, in 2006 a group of architects proposed the construction of a 'stairway to heaven'. Some have compared the concept to the renowned Spanish Steps in Rome. The public staircase marching up the slope from the CBD would climb over the site of an old carpark, the brutal concrete structure for tyres making way for something grand for feet. Many years since the idea was proposed, this part of the city looks more like a stairway to developers' heaven, while the link between the harbour and the cathedral remains a concept only. All the while, as multi-storey buildings climb higher and creep closer to The Hill, Dean Katherine prays the city doesn't lose sight of the cathedral.

'I pray it will always have a place in the hearts of the community and the sight lines of the community', she says.

What Dean Katherine believes won't change is that the cathedral's doors are open to everyone to walk through, and that can be seen in the congregation. She has looked out and seen a snapshot of Newcastle during services: people in their swimwear, having wandered up from the nearby beaches, sitting beside heads of industry. In those moments, Dean Katherine has thought, 'You know, this is something wonderful!'

By 1823, Newcastle's days as a penal settlement were numbered. However, convicts had to stay on in town for many years, working on projects such as the building of Macquarie Pier.

Around the time it was moving on from being a place of secondary punishment run by the military, the regimen and rules imposed on the rag-tag population during the early convict years were applied to the streets of Newcastle. A young surveyor, Henry Dangar, had arrived to draw a ground plan for the town. Curiously, he referred to it as 'King's Town'. That didn't stick. But what he plotted for Newcastle's heart did.

Dangar imposed symmetry on a topography that resisted any sort of pattern. In his plotting of the town, he created a line linking the church on the hill through the market area to the harbour's edge. So Dangar had a 'stairway to heaven' vision almost two centuries before a similar idea was proposed. Dangar planned streets that sliced down the hill to the water, providing the stage for the theatre that remains not just the heart but the dramatic soul of Newcastle.

When you stand at the top of Brown Street, for instance, you feel your gaze being pulled by gravity down a slope so steep it compels you to just about hold your breath. Your vision whooshes between the trees lining the street, past historical terraced houses that lean into the incline. You finally exhale when your gaze slides onto flatter ground, through the commercial centre, across the reclaimed land and into the harbour. The view is thrilling, not just for what you see but how you feel.

For his efforts in harnessing, and exploiting, the drama of Newcastle's topography, Henry Dangar received an allotment with the sort of position and outlook people pay big dollars for now: at the eastern end of town, facing the harbour. Henry Dangar and his family would leave their mark on the community and landscape of not just Newcastle but throughout the Hunter Valley. Dangar's surveying laid the groundwork for large land grants in the valley. His own influence stretched beyond the Hunter, becoming one of the most prominent landholders in the colony. His surname remains attached to signs around Newcastle, including Dangar Park in the suburb of Mayfield. Dangar's legacy, however, is also impressed with every step we take in the centre of Newcastle, as we journey along the streets he planned.

As we walk those streets, we see how Newcastle has taken shape. In the stone and wood, in the cement and steel and glass, we see the reflections of economic booms and busts. We see architectural marvels and abominations, beauty and ugliness, function and ornamentation. We see people working and playing and living. We see ourselves reflected. The city is the sum of its buildings. And the buildings are the sum of us.

More than most, Brian Suters sees himself in the buildings of Newcastle. He was an architect for more than half a century, and, by his own estimation, designed more than 100 buildings in the area. He and his teams were involved in converting and preserving many more historical buildings. Among his many projects were the Newcastle East private and social housing development in the 1980s and the conversion of the former Honeysuckle railway workshops that now house Newcastle Museum. The life of Brian is in the face and soul of Newcastle.

Newcastle's dramatic topography and the way it has been built on appeals to his architectural imagination.

'It's quite unique', he says. 'In Europe, you see the villages. There's the church sitting on the top, and usually gathering around the base are the houses. If you look around Australia, Newcastle's the only one that has anything like that, as far as I'm aware.'

Brian was born in Sydney in 1937 but was raised in Newcastle, his mother's home city. He turned his love of drawing and design into a job, working for an architect in Newcastle East, looking out the office window at the ships leaving the harbour and dreaming of one day cruising away. His dream came true. Having won a travelling scholarship, he and wife Kay travelled to Britain, where Brian studied and worked on church architecture.

While he could have taken his skills and experience anywhere around the globe, Brian returned to Newcastle in 1964 on a mission. The city, he realised, was 'a fresh palette', and Brian combined his respect for Newcastle's setting and history with a modernist sensibility.

Brian has literally inhabited his creations. The Suters' former home on The Hill, a four-storey statement in concrete and glass, not only won a swag of architecture awards in the 1970s, it put the shock of the new into the historic suburb. The couple's latest home melds the past and the present. The front is an 1874-built worker's cottage, and at the back is a two-storey modernist 'cube' that offers not only views across the rooftops but a perspective of what is possible in building. To Brian, architecture is not so much about bricks and mortar but poetry and prose. In Newcastle, poetry exists on, and due to, the dramatic topography. Christ Church Cathedral, Brian says, is poetic, asserting, 'I think it's made a bold statement'.

Yet perhaps some of the city's finest statements are to be found by sitting in Civic Park. Just as poems do, this space holds symmetry and rhythm, linking some of Newcastle's most important and beautiful public buildings, which frame the park. And the city's architectural poet laureate, Brian Suters, has had a hand in many of them.

Civic Park is, in many ways, the centre of Newcastle. It is usually a space of relaxation and reflection, with meticulously tended flower gardens and mature trees casting long shadows over the paths and benches where office workers escape air-conditioned routine. Memorials to those who have served in war hold ground throughout the space, including an eternal flame flickering before a cenotaph at the park's entrance. This park hasn't always been a sacred space. For many years, while the park grew in size and staked out its place in Novocastrians' lives, it was sliced by industry, with a rail line running through it. Civic Park has also heaved with humanity, and often, hosting protest rallies, theatre performances, community markets, festivals, and rock concerts.

At the back of the park, set under a proscenium arch of steps, is a ballet of copper and water – a stunning fountain, a sculpture where jets of water firm into glistening curves and make metal look fluid. This piece of alchemic public art is, in part, thanks to Brian. Not long after returning to Newcastle, he worked on the fountain with artist couple, Margel and Frank Hinder. Margel Hinder, an acclaimed modernist sculptor, had won a design competition for the fountain, and she cited Newcastle's topography and elements of the city's built history among her inspirations. So for Brian, the fountain brought together three principles that would characterise his career and help shape the look of Newcastle: honouring the local environment, respecting the past and striving for something new. The fountain would be later named the Captain Cook Memorial Fountain, but in its look and vigour, it has Margel Hinder written all over it. The sculpture is considered her masterpiece. What's more, on hot days it serves as a de facto water park for kids. Dr Ross Kerridge, who was elected Lord Mayor of Newcastle in 2024, was a child when his parents brought him to the night-time official opening of the fountain in 1966. He recalls the park's lighting being dimmed except for the illumination in the pool, shining up on the arcing jets of water, triggering a collective sigh from the crowd. To Ross, that sigh was the sound of a community falling in love with not just a fountain but also itself, realising Newcastle had something that would prompt anyone anywhere to go, 'Wow!'[17]

Directly in front of Civic Park, facing and partnering the green space, is Newcastle City Hall, which was opened in 1929. Brian and his company are part of City Hall's history, having done redesign work on its interior. While much of the inside gleams with wood and marble, City Hall's stolid neo-classical exterior is what most people associate with the centre of Newcastle. The clocks set into the tower, which is built of Sydney sandstone, not only ring out across the city, they offer a sense of solidity to Novocastrians, as if assuring 'All is well'. That assurance has perhaps flown in the face of the fierier council meetings held in the chambers through the years. On the balcony at the foot of the tower, everyone from royalty to victorious sports teams have stood and waved at crowds. Novocastrians may regard themselves, and everyone else, as roughly equal, but they have enthusiastically thronged to Civic Park to stare up at distant figures on the balcony and cheer them on.

By virtue of its stately appearance, the building has starred in pictures, both still and moving. When Greg Pead, a former tyre fitter from the Newcastle suburb Cardiff, reimagined himself as independent film maker and artist Yahoo Serious, the young Novocastrian also transformed his hometown for scenes in his debut movie, *Young Einstein*. City Hall was a ready-made set, and movie-star glamorous, for Yahoo Serious and his joyously inventive hit film. Before he let his imagination run wild with feature films, Yahoo Serious marked the world he was from, making a documentary titled *Coaltown*.[18]

To the west of City Hall is NESCA House, which looks like a stunning Art Deco fortress when it was actually the headquarters of an electricity supply authority. The building was the creation of a young Sydney architect, Emil Sodersten, who designed one of Newcastle's most genteel and, for its time, tallest apartment blocks, Segenhoe, in the 1930s. The building stood out because Newcastle did not then have a crop of apartment towers. To the east of City Hall is a round building with exposed ribs of concrete. It was once the council's administration centre. However, it was widely called the Roundhouse or The Beehive, thanks to its recessed windows creating the impression of a honeycomb. An architect knows he is grabbing people's attention when they nickname a building. Which is why Brian is honoured by the names attached to the building he helped design in the 1970s. He calls the building's design '20th-century modern'. Although these days, 'The Beehive' is 21st-century luxury; it has been converted into a hotel.

The council has shifted its administration centre further west into a new glass-dominated building on one of the city's busiest intersections. The thinking is that the commercial heart of the city is heading west. But the move hasn't pleased Brian.

'That really breaks my heart. The Civic was the municipal centre.'

On the other side of Civic Park, facing City Hall, is the War Memorial

Cultural Centre. Built in the 1950s, the centre was crammed with just about everything considered 'cultural' in post-war Newcastle. The four-storey building, with its severe skin of brick and terracotta panels, housed the public library, the local branch of the New South Wales Conservatorium of Music, and the city's art gallery. Twenty years on, the art gallery moved into its own home next door in Laman Street, while musicians were given a dedicated space just up the road in a conservatorium that Brian was involved in designing. So words, images and music are still neighbours, even if the city's administrators have moved away.

Also along Laman Street, continuing the architectural poetry, are two churches. These buildings, in turn, have served as muses for a poet, as they appeared in a piece by Newcastle writer Paul Kavanagh:

> Two churches stand as if they made
> To speak, so clean their faces turn
> Toward each other to discern
> The style in which the other stands.[19]

The two buildings facing each other are the Baptist Tabernacle, with its face of an ancient Greek temple, and, across the road, above the south-western corner of the park, the Gothic-influenced, butter-brick Saint Andrews Presbyterian Church. Both were built in 1890, and both were designed by a hero of Brian and another architectural poet, Frederick Menkens.

Born in north-eastern Germany, Menkens arrived in Newcastle in 1882. The young man brought with him centuries of architectural tradition from his homeland, and the ambition and vision to apply it to a growing industrial port community. As a result, Menkens brought the look of central and northern Europe to the heart of Newcastle. He was, as Brian once wrote for an exhibition he organised to honour Menkens, 'a man who, perhaps more than any other single man in this area, has shaped our built environment'.[20]

More than shape it, Menkens adorned Newcastle's built environment, creating more than 100 buildings in the area. However, it is not the number but the look he applied to so many of his designs that continues to grab eyes and hearts. Menkens transformed harbourside warehouses into Baroque mercantile cathedrals. For a number of the entrepreneurs who commissioned him to design the warehouses, Menkens created mansions with classical and Italianate influences, and offices that added the mythological to the functional. For the Scott Street offices and auction room of brewery owner and wine merchant Joseph Wood, Menkens conjured an extravaganza in an Anglo-Dutch style, with a cast of characters in stone on the façade, including Atlas and Hercules. For another prominent merchant, John Hall, Menkens designed his imposing home, known as Shalamah, on The Hill. Those two structures are among a number of the architect's designs still standing in the centre of Newcastle, which makes it like an open-air Menkens museum.

However, Brian laments how many other Menkens designs have been lost, with buildings demolished or changed beyond recognition. During his own career, Brian tried to preserve a number of buildings designed by Menkens, including a restoration project for the former Earp Gillam bond store in Newcastle East. The reimagined 1880s warehouse served as Brian's office for a time.

When asked what he loves about Menkens, Brian replies, 'The strength of the man, and the conviction. He didn't tolerate half-baked solutions'. That conviction even led to prison. Menkens served a 12-month sentence after a dispute with an electrical contractor ballooned into a court case for slander, which the architect lost. Menkens refused to pay the damages, so off to gaol he went. While in prison, Menkens apparently continued taking on architectural projects. Menkens' commitment to his art, to creating beauty, even in the most testing of conditions, impresses Brian. Menkens is a man after Brian's own heart. And Brian is a man with Newcastle – and art – at heart.

But conviction, be it Frederick Menkens' or Brian Suters', has not been enough to resist the force of change tearing through the city's centre. As more and more developments rise ever higher, the visual appeal of Newcastle is diminishing, according to Brian.

The very look of Newcastle that makes it unique, in Brian's eyes, the way the town is gathered around the cathedral on The Hill, is 'being diluted'.

Brian's vision for Newcastle is clear: 'A city that respects the past, because we build our future on the past. So we want to retain that. We need to retain the character of it as one of the first towns created in Australia'.[21]

However, in a matter of seconds, what Newcastle had been, and where it was headed, threatened to fall into a crack when the city was shaken to its core.

In her novel set in wartime Newcastle, *Southern Steel*, Dymphna Cusack has one of her characters ruminating about Novocastrians.

'Most people had a fatalism who made their living from the mines or the sea, as Newcastle had done for more than a century before the steelworks came. They were used to disaster – it came only too often.'[22]

Yet few people were used to the type of disaster that arrived in Newcastle on 28 December 1989.

On that day, most Novocastrians were sauntering through summer. The tempo of life had slowed and was flowing languidly towards a new decade. Then, at 10.27 am, Newcastle was jolted out of its post-Christmas slumber. A rumble and roar ripped through the morning. Buildings shook and toppled. Roads and streets rippled and cracked. Some watched in bewilderment as teacups toppled off tables; for others, life as they knew it crumbled before them. It was as though the earth was trying to swallow the city. *Something* had just happened. But no-one knew what it was.

Some wondered if old mine workings had collapsed. Had there been an explosion at the BHP steelworks? Maybe it was a bomb.

It was an earthquake. The scientists charted it as a 5.6-magnitude quake. The impact on the city was, and continues to be, immeasurable. According to Geoscience Australia, the earthquake was one of the most significant natural disasters in the country's history.[23] To Novocastrians, the earthquake was one of the most significant days in their lives, tossing up shock and bewilderment, trauma and tragedy. For 13 people, the disaster took their life.

For Alan Playford, it was a day that changed so much, as he used his training and skills to sustain life. Alan had been in the NSW Ambulance

Service since 1974, and for more than a decade had been working as a paramedic. However, just after the earthquake hit, Alan was wearing not his paramedic's uniform but a fireman's. Alan also served as a fireman at his local brigade, and he had responded to an emergency call. As the fire crew drove from the suburb of New Lambton into town, Alan was stunned by more and more signs of damage. Alan knew this area so well. After all, he was a Newcastle boy. He'd grown up in this city. But this was a journey into the utterly unfamiliar and surreal. The scale of destruction leapt as the crew approached the suburb of Hamilton, close to the city centre. One of Hamilton's major thoroughfares, Beaumont Street, looked as though it had imploded and, as he gazed in the direction of the steelworks, a few kilometres to the north, Alan thought something catastrophic had occurred.

'The BHP looked like it had blown up', Alan recalls. 'It looked like an atomic bomb had gone off, with a cloud. I thought, "Wow, this is big!"'

A pager beeped, carrying the message that it was an earthquake. Alan couldn't believe it, still searching for other explanations, wondering if it was a mine explosion. Whatever the cause, the brigade captain reckoned Alan should swap uniforms. He would be needed as a paramedic.

Alan was dropped off at the nearby ambulance headquarters, which had been damaged. He changed into borrowed overalls and returned to Beaumont Street, where people were crawling out from under toppled buildings, while others were trapped in the rubble. In just a few blocks, Alan and his colleagues had counted 168 casualties. The number was staggering. The level of shock and injuries to be dealt with verged on the overwhelming.

'We're by ourselves and I thought, "How do we gather these people in?"' says Alan.

The paramedics tried to get the injured to sit on the kerb, creating an impromptu waiting room amid the ruins, while other emergency services workers and passers-by toiled furiously to free those still trapped. As Alan was working his way along the street, treating people, he was approached by a bus driver who offered to use his vehicle to transport the 'walking wounded' to Royal Newcastle Hospital in Newcastle East.

'So he ducked around the corner, brings his government bus up and we load all of these people on the bus', says Alan. 'He told me later that he got them singing all the way to Royal Newcastle.'

However, the hospital had also been damaged by the earthquake, and patients were being evacuated. A makeshift emergency centre was set up outside the hospital to deal with the rising torrent of injured being brought in by whatever means available – including by bus.

Alan was summoned to the city centre to help out at Newcastle Workers Club. Since the late 1940s, the club on the corner of King and Union streets had been the centre of entertainment in the city, hosting concerts, but it was also integral to the local trades and labour movement. Word came through that this pillar of Newcastle life had collapsed, with people trapped inside. The timing of the disaster could have been much worse. A sold-out concert, featuring Split Enz and Crowded House, was to have been held that night. Thousands would have been in the club then.

While the journey from Beaumont Street to the club was only a couple of kilometres, Alan felt as though he had been plunged into another world.

'It looked like Dante's *Inferno*; there was no fire but just this incessant concrete dust', Alan says. 'The fallout was like fog. I thought, "For goodness sake, it's a sunny morning, there can't be any fog!" That was a fleeting thought; quickly I thought that it was concrete dust.'

Alan and fellow paramedic Neville Grieve pushed through the dust into a nightmare. The floors of the club had cascaded onto each other, including the carpark. Alan saw cars teetering on the edge of slabs, rocking ominously whenever there was a shake. The paramedics shimmied down the steep slope of what had been a floor, listening anxiously to the twang of reinforced metal rods holding chunks of concrete suspended just near them. The twang marked an aftershock, and it was an alarm, warning the pair they were risking their own lives.

'Neville and I looked at one another and said, "Are we going to do this? We've got to ignore what's going on and just get on with it". And that's how we did it.'

Another colleague, Mal Martin, was already in the shattered pits of the club, and he directed Alan to where voices had been heard below.

Alan traced the voices to a trench in what had been the club's basement. There he met the man he considers the most remarkable person to have ever come into his life: Norm Duffy.

Norm had been in the club with his wife, Miriam, when the quake hit. And he was still with her, only Miriam was dead, lying beside him and covered in a layer of concrete dust so thick that Alan wasn't aware he was standing on her body. Miriam was among the nine who died in the workers club after it collapsed. There were two injured women beside Norm, and he had been talking with them, assuring them they would be rescued. In the darkness, pinned under rubble and breathing dust and dreadful uncertainty, Norm repeated a line to the women: 'We're all going to see the sun together when we get out'. The sun seemed a little closer when the paramedics arrived. Norm urged the rescuers to save the two women first.

'He said, "You just get them out first and I'll wait my turn". I said, "But I can get you more easily", and he said, "Take them".'

The women were hoisted out then, after quite a few hours, it was Norm's turn. Alan had to dig him out, all the while worried that when the rubble pinning Norm was finally removed, all the toxins in the compressed areas of his body would be released. Alan feared Norm would die. Alan's fears seemed to be realised. The bravest man Alan had ever met had a cardiac arrest as he was being lifted out. Alan believed Norm had died, only to discover his colleague, Mal Martin, had saved him.

As a result of what they went through together, Alan and Norm stayed in touch. For Alan, Norm's selflessness in the rubble has remained an inspiration.

'You know we think that Olympians are exceptional people, but there are those who live amongst us who are exceptional people, and Norm Duffy was exactly one of them.'

And so is Alan Playford. Through his long career, he has made a difference to, and saved, many lives. He has received accolades and awards, including a Star of Courage, and in Newcastle he is considered a hero. Alan personifies the best of Newcastle. Yet, typically Novocastrian, he brushes away the word 'hero'.

'I feel uncomfortable when they go to extremes and say that', Alan says. 'It's just your job, it's just what you've got to do. And if you stood back and you didn't do it, you'd be ashamed of yourself for the rest of your life. So you've just got to pin your ears back and set your course and stay with it and don't think about the things that are happening around, just concentrate on those you're trying to help. And there's your reward.'

THE 1989 earthquake's deepest aftershock was to be found in the expressions on people's faces. No-one in Newcastle could believe what had happened. No-one anywhere could believe it, as news of the disaster travelled around the globe.

I couldn't believe it when I was told by an old woman while standing in a field of snow on the edge of a village in the Japanese Alps. I was living in Tokyo at the time and was holidaying in the mountains. When the old woman asked where I was from, I told her Tokyo but added my home was in Australia. She asked where in Australia. I replied, 'Newcastle'. She started talking about an earthquake. I thought something was lost in translation, or that she was referring to Tokyo, renowned for being jostled, on occasion disastrously, by earthquakes. When I asked her if there had been an earthquake in Tokyo, she looked at me and said, 'No. Newcastle'.

The event that had threatened to shake Newcastle off the map had put my hometown on it, in the eyes of the world.

After trudging back through the snow, I phoned my parents' home in the suburb of Merewether Heights. Remarkably, my call got through and my father answered, explaining to me what had happened. The house was fine, sustaining only minor damage. A few items had smashed, including a sculpture I had loved.

Dad hesitated then said in a soft voice, 'Your friend Ulric died'.

Ulric Burstein was a brilliant musician and a generous friend. He had opened my ears and mind, and those of so many other listeners, to the majesty and beauty of orchestral and choral music. Ulric had grown up and studied music in New Zealand, and his formidable talent took him to London, where he studied with legendary conductors Sir John Pritchard and Sir Colin Davis. Ulric had performed at the Royal Albert Hall, a place I'd heard of because The Beatles had sung about it in

'A Day in the Life'. Ulric had conducted a symphony by some bloke named Bruckner. I'd never heard of Anton Bruckner, let alone his *Symphony No. 4*, until I met Ulric.

Music had given Ulric a passport to wherever he wanted to go on earth, and yet he chose to return to the southern hemisphere and bring all he knew, and all that he was passionate about, to Newcastle. I never asked him why. Nonetheless, he helped make Newcastle seem more cultural. He was the founding director of the university's choir and the founder of the Newcastle Conservatorium Orchestra. After years of appealing and persuading and convincing people that the region deserved its own professional orchestra, Ulric became the founding musical director of the Hunter Orchestra in 1985.

As well as helping the city become more cultural, Ulric Burstein helped a Newcastle boy feel a little less ignorant. When I met Ulric in 1988, I asked him what was the name of the classical music that sounded a lot like Eric Carmen's hit song, 'All By Myself'. Ulric could have patronised or dismissed me. But he didn't, even when I hummed him the melody. He replied that the music was from Rachmaninoff's *Concerto No. 2 in C Minor* and offered to lend me a CD, so I could hear the piece in full.

Ulric lent me a lot of CDs, and he would invite me to his small unit in a social housing complex, where he would play symphonies at death metal volumes late at night, all the while sharing his knowledge of the music and their creators and telling anecdotes about musicians he had studied and worked with. I was struck with wonder at the music, and at the patience – or perhaps selective hearing – of Ulric's neighbours.

Before I departed for Japan, Ulric took me to dinner and gave me a CD featuring Gustav Mahler's *Symphony No. 5*, with Sir John Barbirolli conducting the New Philharmonia Orchestra. I took that CD to Japan. And I was certain my classical music education would continue as soon as I returned to Newcastle, thanks to Ulric.

When the earthquake hit, Ulric was in Royal Newcastle Hospital, receiving treatment for complications from a major surgical procedure he'd had earlier in the year. As it was told to me, Ulric was among the patients evacuated from the hospital. They were taken to a nearby park, and even to Newcastle Beach. From there, on a clear day, you would swear you could almost see New Zealand. Ulric would never return there. He died.

Ulric was laid to rest in Stockton Cemetery, which is about a kilometre away from the Tasman Sea. While staying in Newcastle, this was the closest his remains could be to his birth country.

Every time I hear 'All By Myself', I smile and think of Ulric. Every time I listen to Mahler's *Symphony No. 5*, especially its adagio, I thank Ulric for all he taught me about music. And I wonder what I missed out on learning, and what the city missed out on hearing, because fate placed Ulric in hospital on the day the earthquake hit.

If he were still here, Ulric would have been bitterly disappointed the orchestra he worked so hard to help bring into being was disbanded. In 1985, when the Hunter Orchestra began performing, the organisation's chairman, Professor David Frost, said the ensemble was serving a population of about 500 000 people in the region. The Hunter's population is now close to 700 000, and yet there is no full-time professional orchestra in the city.

If that is frustrating to listeners, it is even more so for music creators. David Banney is an acclaimed composer, Director of Music at Christ Church Cathedral, and he was the founding artistic director of the Newcastle Music Festival.

He says the loss of the Hunter Orchestra had a devastating effect for both local audiences and musicians.

'It meant there was a complete loss of orchestral culture at a professional level, and that has never recovered', David says.

With Newcastle having the Hunter Orchestra when it was still a steel city, David says, 'you could see it as this incredible thing that went against the tide'. However, steel and classical music had been melded before the Hunter Orchestra even existed. In 1959, to celebrate the centenary of local government in Newcastle, the city council commissioned composer John Antill to write an orchestral work, which was titled *Symphony on a City*. The symphony's finale involved the striking of a large steel plate with a hammer.

The Hunter Orchestra was long gone by the time David arrived in Newcastle in 2001 to lecture in conducting at the Newcastle Conservatorium. He formed a new ensemble called the Hunter Sinfonia. Up to 60 musicians would play in the orchestra. However, the orchestra ended after a few years, David says, when there were changes in the teaching of music, particularly after the Conservatorium was folded into the University of Newcastle. David had found it harder to find the musicians to sustain an orchestra.

While Newcastle's population has grown, and it has become a wealthier city, he believes there is still not much of an audience for a full-time professional orchestra.

'I think there's still a fair bit of classical music happening, but it's all being done by visitors and local amateurs', David says. 'What's missing is the local professional stream. So I think people need to get energised to rebuild the tertiary music environment. We need to do that to keep the excellent young players who are taught here and then feed that into a professional music scene.'

'We're all going to see the sun together when we get out.'

The words Norm Duffy uttered to lift the spirits of his fellow survivors stuck in the rubble at the workers club seemed to be a motto for a city that had to climb out of the ruins.

In the days after the earthquake, the centre of Newcastle was a ghost town. Alan Playford still remembers the scenes of soldiers patrolling deserted streets.

'We went from that to slowly coming back to some sort of normality and picking up the rubble and cleaning up', Alan recalls. And he saw in the approach of his fellow Novocastrians echoes of Norm Duffy's words.

'I think there was a stoicism in the attitude of people, that we're going to get on with this and we're going to make this city better.'

While the city tried to make sense of what it had gone through, the earthquake and the mess it made provided material for storytelling. The stories of those caught up in the disaster inspired the dialogue for a play written by Paul Brown and the Workers' Cultural Action Committee, titled *Aftershocks*, which centred around the workers' club collapse. Author Peter Corris used the earthquake as a setting and a plot device in a novel from his Cliff Hardy private investiagtor series, titled *Aftershock*.

The main character offers plenty of observations about Novocastrians and the city. At one point, having seen some of the devastation caused by the shock waves that rippled through the sedimentary layers under the city, Cliff Hardy thinks about the big trees growing in Newcastle, sending their roots deep into the earth and holding on. In the private investigator's mind, that makes the historic city squatting on the surface 'seem very impermanent'.[24]

The impermanence felt pronounced after the earthquake. There was much wiped away, and a lot to clean up. About 50 000 buildings were damaged. About 40 000 of those were homes. Many were in such a bad state that 1000 people were left homeless. The earthquake's estimated damage bill was $4 billion.

The face of Newcastle was not only badly disfigured but lost some of its defining characteristics. Buildings that had been central to Novocastrian life for generations, from hotels to theatres, were lost. Many more historical buildings had lost features such as parapets and chimneys. So the wounds of the quake were marked by not just cracks in walls and piles of rubble, but by vacant blocks and missing architectural details.

To some, the push to rebuild the city came at the expense of reminders of its heritage, with a number of significant buildings being demolished. Historians Erik Eklund and David Andrew Roberts noted Newcastle had long been a frontline in the battle between the interests of heritage and development, and this escalated dramatically after the earthquake.[25] Yet to others, the rebuild was dragging on, and the wounds of the quake were left to fester. Many Novocastrians felt as though they were picking their way through a maze of rubble and red tape.

If the streets of Newcastle carried a sense of dormancy in the 1990s, it wasn't due to just the earthquake's legacy. Unemployment was well above the state average, spiking to 16 per cent, the city's industries were feeling the pinch, and Newcastle's heart was struggling.

For generations, Hunter Street was the aorta of the CBD and beyond. Beautiful architectural statements from the 19th century through to the later 20th century lined much of the street, reflecting the boom times in the city. The buildings housed businesses offering whatever people needed and desired. As a result, Hunter Street pumped with people. If Novocastrians wanted something, they went into town. And 'town' was

Hunter Street. Once they were in 'town', they stayed in town. Along Hunter Street, they could shop, dine and drink, see a show or movie, and while away time. For many years, commercial and residential life had been drifting out to the suburbs. When the earthquake struck, it seemed to only bolster the feeling that the city centre was dying. The east end stretch of Hunter Street that had been converted to a mall to attract more people was increasingly unpeopled. At the western end of Hunter Street was the former Latec House, an 11-storey building that had been the tallest in the city when it was opened in 1959. Now it was empty and vandalised, a monument to the rot creeping along Newcastle's main street. Along the waterfront, particularly in the Honeysuckle precinct, a mixture of government funding and private investment would gradually bring the area back to life. But just a couple of hundred metres away, on the other – or wrong – side of the rail tracks, Hunter Street had become a ghost of its former self.

Yet in every community, every generation, there are those who not only swim against the tide, they somehow turn the tide to flow with them. And so it was with Marcus Westbury. With his large glasses, sensible haircut and trim frame cloaked in conservative clothes, Marcus looks like a Novocastrian Clark Kent. Yet Marcus has been a Superman for Newcastle.

In his late teens, Marcus moved into the city from the suburbs, living in share houses in Newcastle East and Cooks Hill and on The Hill, suburbs that have since been gentrified to the point of unaffordability for students with dreams in their head but relatively little in their pockets.

'The city was in that weird in-between period', recalls Marcus, when he moved into town in 1992. 'It was relatively soon after the earthquake, the earthquake had broken the back of the city, but the city hadn't realised it yet.'

The future seemed bleak in Newcastle for Marcus' generation. At that time, youth unemployment in the city had climbed sharply.

'I used to joke I didn't know anyone who had a job', he says. 'On one level it was really despairing, on another it was a great DIY town. Newcastle, I think, was a really good place to try to do stuff.

'People good at something left Newcastle, and they left a vacuum, so you could do things in that vacuum.'

Marcus remembers wandering with a friend along Hunter Street, peering through dust-mottled windows with nothing on display in empty shops. Yet when the pair peered in, they saw opportunity. The friends were filled with 'a real weird sense of possibility', talking of establishing a media centre, art and craft galleries, anything that displayed how creative they and their peers were. They just needed an outlet. And here it was. Lots of potential outlets.

Marcus and a group of fellow students and artists pooled their money and rented a warehouse in Newcastle West. The creative collective had a space and soon, a name, The Octapod. Marcus had been mixing his love of words with work he had been doing at festivals around the country. He brought that experience back to Newcastle, helping found the National Young Writers' Festival, and that blossomed into a broader event called This Is Not Art.

In some ways, this was like a child of the Mattara Festival, the annual celebration of the Newcastle community that brought people in from the suburbs to cheer the parade inching along the city's streets, and to experience the carnival and exhibitions held in Civic Park. 'Mattara' is an Awabakal word for 'hand', which is what This Is Not Art was extending. Only its reach was way beyond Newcastle, bringing participants from around the nation. Up to 3000 people would be in the city, giving the locals a sense of what was possible in bringing life back to their city, and opening eyes to what was here. Marcus distributed a survey among the visitors and was a little concerned the response might be that Newcastle was 'a terrifying place full of scary bogans'. Instead, the general response was, 'This is amazing; I didn't know this place was here!'

Around the time Marcus organised the first of these festivals, the ground shifted again under Newcastle. In 1997, BHP announced it would be closing its Newcastle steelworks in two years. While BHP's local workforce had been shrinking for years, the thought of the steelworks closing was shocking. To many Novocastrians, by the time the announcement had pealed across the harbour from the steelworks into the city's heart, it sounded like a death knell for Newcastle.

Hunter politician Richard Face, who was the state member for Charlestown and the Minister Assisting the Premier on Hunter

Development, likened the reaction to BHP's decision to learning of a close relative dying of cancer.

'One has time to prepare for the inevitable, but when the end comes it does not stop the pain caused by the loss', he told the parliament.[26]

While politicians at all levels of government debated and argued about what could be done, what should be done, and – this was a long list – what had not been done for an ailing Newcastle, the cancer seemed to be spreading. Businesses and shops closed their doors, as jobs were lost and spending dwindled. The spiral intensified, as people left town for the sake of work, in the hope of a better future. One who left was Marcus Westbury. While he was coming and going, largely determined by work, he eventually ended up in Melbourne. But Newcastle never left Marcus.

When NSW liquor laws were changed, and small bar licences were introduced, Marcus returned to his hometown in late 2007, with the view to finding a property and opening a venue. He was shocked by what he found.

'I noticed how much the city was falling apart', he recalls. For someone living here full-time, it was like being the frog in the slowly heating water, hardly noticing the change, other than yet another shop closing. For Marcus, 'it was like seeing it in time lapse'.

'It had got to the point where no-one wanted to be the last business left when all the others were closing down, and you could almost see that happening, block by block.'

Marcus walked the blocks and counted about 150 empty properties in the CBD. Marcus figured that at least he had plenty of choice for a small bar space, except that of all the inquiries he made, he had the 'crazy, deflating' experience of receiving no replies. It seemed to him that inertia and an utter lack of imagination had moved into town. But he knew that there remained in Newcastle creative people who were willing to give something a go, if only they had the space and encouragement to try.

Newcastle was full of spaces, of lost opportunities waiting to be found, and Marcus had an idea to provide a platform for encouragement. Instead of being a festival director and small bar owner, he tumbled down a side path, becoming a de facto urban re-planner. He founded Renew Newcastle in 2008.

The organisation's philosophy was simple, tapping into the DIY approach Marcus himself had employed: 'Rather than work out what you want and get someone else to do it, find out what someone else wants to do and help them do it.'

A central idea for how Newcastle could be renewed and have a future lay in its past. And it was there for all to see, if you studied the finer detail. Marcus recalls looking at historical photos of the city, of crammed and crowded streetscapes. In the shadow of the grand and ornate buildings were small traders offering tailoring and footwear making. There were jewellers and bakers, butchers and even candle makers working from small, unpretentious shops, but the sum of their creation was a bustling, vibrant city. As Marcus wrote in his book, *Creating Cities*, 'Before the supermarket and the mega mall, the streets were for the bespoke and the boutique'. So those streets were 'places for creation as much as for consumption'.[27]

Marcus' plan was to make Newcastle's centre a place of creation. The empty spaces would be populated by people with ideas and a desire to show what they were capable of. With the help of a local legal firm, he devised a licensing agreement, where property owners would effectively lend their vacant spaces to small businesspeople and artisans. The tenants had space to create and earn a living, and the owners had their property taken care of.

The hoardings were prised from shopfronts, spaces were cleaned up, and in the display windows dust and debris were replaced with locally made products, such as jewellery and clothing. Marcus' plan for the CBD was happening. It was a place of creation once more, and perhaps the most profound creation was a new perception about the city itself. Marcus Westbury, his team, and those who invested their belief in the idea turned an organisation's name into an eyebrow-raising reality. This was renewing Newcastle.

Remarkably, this all began at a time when the world was sliding into a financial crisis and businesses were collapsing. Then again, the downturn the world was now experiencing, Newcastle had contended with for years. While so much of the world was staring at disaster, Newcastle was glimpsing hope. And the city found that hope within.

As Marcus wrote in *Creating Cities*, 'Newcastle has changed not by attracting new and cool people to it, but largely from bringing out the talents and the capabilities of the people who were already there'.[28]

At times, however, it seemed Renew Newcastle was simply delaying the inevitable, as major players left town. In 2011, David Jones vacated its iconic site in the city after more than half a century of trading. After yet another big plan for the CBD, a $600 million redevelopment project, stalled, the retailer had decided to get out. So one loss led to another. However, to Renew Newcastle, it was a fresh opportunity. After David Jones vacated the historic building on the corner of Hunter and Perkins streets, it became a warren of small traders and delightfully eclectic goods for a few years.

When he started Renew Newcastle, Marcus thought the organisation would gain access to 10 properties and be involved in about 30 projects. In the decade it was operating, it had about 80 properties and had been involved in about 270 projects.

Renew Newcastle was transformative, not just for many of its participants but for the city itself.

'There was a real shift from, "If you're going to do something, why do it here?" to a whole lot of things happening.'

The initiative also brought attention to Newcastle. The immensely influential travel publisher Lonely Planet placed Newcastle in its top 10 world cities to visit in 2011, referring to it as Australia's most underrated city. After that, Marcus had to deal with a constant stream of requests from travel writers, to the extent he felt like Renew Newcastle was the city's unofficial tourist bureau.

Suddenly, for the first time in a long time, people wanted to visit Newcastle. International tourists turned up in the city. In turn, Newcastle sent something new into the world. The city renowned for coal and steel began exporting an idea for urban regeneration. What Marcus Westbury and Renew Newcastle had done was studied and applied around the globe to varying degrees of success. To Marcus Westbury, even in the face of all the interest from far and wide, this remained an idea born in Newcastle, designed to help Newcastle.

'We were building confidence to live, work and invest in Newcastle.'

After years of crying out for more investment from governments, Newcastle received a new program, and a new word involving a 're-'

prefix. In 2015, the NSW Government launched its $650 million Newcastle Urban Transformation and Transportation Program. It was better known as Revitalising Newcastle.

Among the program's key objectives were to bring people back to the city centre and create new jobs in the CBD, aims that Renew Newcastle were already working at.

With so much public money and private investment coming into Newcastle through the government program, the CBD became an elongated construction zone. In the public eye, it was sometimes hard to tell the difference between Renew and Revitalising. As a result, Marcus would occasionally cop criticism for projects that were either changing the look of the city or the flow of life, or both, but were being done under the Revitalising Newcastle banner.

The more the Revitalising Newcastle project progressed, and the more millions of developers' dollars were committed to the city, the less visible Renew Newcastle's work became. For one thing, some buildings that small traders had occupied were now construction sites. The businesses in the former David Jones building, for instance, moved out to make way for a boutique hotel and residential development. The momentum and funding for Renew Newcastle were slowing. The organisation wrapped up in early 2019.

'There was a perception the problem we had set up for to solve had been solved', says Marcus.

But it had not been. And new problems arose.

The heavy rail line that sliced through the heart of the CBD, delivering train passengers to the East End, was removed, with a new terminus built at the western end of the city. The removal was meant to provide a better link between the city and the harbour, but it created an even deeper fissure in the community between those who wanted the rail line to stay and those who wanted it gone. The fissure was hardly repaired when some of the heavy rail corridor was sold for residential and commercial developments. A light rail system was installed along Hunter and Scott streets, linking the western end of the city to the east, and with the aim of 'activating' the city. However, the light rail construction led to massive traffic disruptions, diving trading conditions, and another wave of retailers leaving the CBD.

In terms of construction, Newcastle seemed to be rising from its grave, or at least from the shells of older buildings. Some historic structures were retained. For instance, the now-redundant Newcastle and Civic stations were repurposed, the Civic facility being converted into the city's tourist office. However, other buildings that had been part of Novocastrians' lives, and the look of the CBD, for generations were stripped back to little more than their façades. Multi-storey apartment complexes took shape behind, and over, those beautiful historic faces. The façade of heritage conservation looked increasingly flimsy and diminished as new structures reached ever higher.

Statistics tell how in just five years from 2016 to 2021, the number of high-density dwellings in the City of Newcastle increased by more than 2100. That constituted 10 per cent of homes in the city, a jump from 7.8 per cent just five years earlier.[29] In those dwellings were many more people. A 2021 summary report of the Revitalising Newcastle program concluded that there were 3244 new residents in the city centre, along with 7246 new jobs.[30]

But you don't need statistics to spell out the increase in high-density living in Newcastle. This was a city that had kept close to the ground. The highest point was the cathedral – the city's undisputed crown. Now the city, notably its western end, is studded with multi-storey towers. Newcastle looks as though it is becoming a vertical city.

As the commercial and administrative centre of Newcastle is moved further west along Hunter Street, away from The Hill and the tighter heritage-related restrictions of the east and onto the lowlands and former swamps, the cityscape is expected to reach even higher. As you travel away from the sea along Hunter Street, the sky is buttressed by cranes. And there will soon be more. At the western end of Hunter Street many Novocastrians didn't just shop but had ownership in the commercial well-being of their town, as customers and members of The Store (once again, there's that capital 'T' on the definite article, denoting an important local place). The Newcastle and Suburban Cooperative Society was one of the most successful enterprises of its type in Australia. The Store delivered items to customers, including transporting bread by a cart and a doleful-looking horse that continued to clip and clop its way along the streets well into the 20th century, and it had branches throughout the area. However, people travelled in from the suburbs to shop here. It was our emporium. The building even looked special, like a mercantile palace, with its bits and bobs of classical and Art Deco architectural styles. The Store's big display windows filled a consumer's eyes with desire and a kid's heart with excitement, especially at Christmas time, with its Santa and nativity scenes. As the shopping centres moved to the suburbs, so did the customers, and The Store closed in 1981. The building kept attracting some shoppers until the end of the decade, hosting a mercantile bazaar known as the Pink Elephant Markets, before the earthquake forced that to close and the building lay dormant. More than a quarter of a century on, the historic building was levelled, making way for a car park and planned residential development. At least something of the past remains. The developers have called their vision The Store.

A little further to the west along Hunter Street is a precinct known as Dairy Farmers Corner. For many years, this site, a milk and dairy products distribution centre, connected farmers of the Hunter Valley with the breakfast tables of Newcastle. The building's architecture spoke proudly of its purpose, with the central feature being a clock tower, erected in the late 1930s. The front face of the tower has a glass block frieze in the shape of a milk bottle. Bending around the clock on the side of the tower was an illuminated sign reading, 'Precious as Time. Dairy Farmers Milk'. But even more precious in early 21st-century Newcastle are development sites, and it seems not even time can stand in the way of progress.

Planned for this site are two residential and commercial towers that will be among the tallest buildings in the city. The clock tower is to be retained in the planned development. The local branch of the National Trust has referred to the clock tower as a rare remnant of industrial Art Deco style in Newcastle,[31] but it will look like a heritage molehill compared with the mountains of glass and steel shadowing it. Still, according to the development's marketing catchphrase, with Dairy Farmers Towers, 'A Landmark Is Reborn'.[32] The western end of the city gets another high-rise development, and Newcastle gets another 're-' word.

Yet for all the revitalising and rebirthing in the city, Marcus Westbury is seeing history repeating. Returning to his hometown from Melbourne is a journey that holds mixed emotions for him. He feels pride at seeing businesses that began through Renew Newcastle continue, but he is 'disappointed and depressed' to see buildings becoming empty and falling into disrepair once more. He was horrified by the state of the former Newcastle Mall shopping area, empty and trashed, until its demolition in early 2024.

'To go back and see some of the very sad buildings we took care of now smashed up, I'm disappointed in that', says Marcus. 'It's a depressing problem to see those empty shops back again.'

For too long, the mall, which was designed as a main retail artery in the city's heart, has been largely devoid of lifeblood. The ghosts of shopping past haunt the strip, tumbling and stumbling along the paving, wafting through the shells of heritage buildings waiting to be redeveloped and marketed as inner-city apartments. At the top of the mall, the former post office, a stunning early 20th-century creation sculpted and carved from sandstone, has lurched through two decades of decay and dormancy. The building has been sold and bought a couple of times, and there are plans for it to be restored and reused, with shops, a function centre and an Aboriginal cultural hub. But as of early 2025, the building has remained cloistered behind boards. Out the front, in Hunter Street, the sculpture of an Australian soldier stands sentinel atop a war memorial. The white marble figure was unveiled before the First World War was over, and the dreadful loss of local men was finally tallied. Through the years, past that war memorial, returned servicemen and servicewomen have marched to the cheers of the crowds lining Hunter Street. Protestors have paraded past here, advocating for change in their lives and our city. If only he could see, the soldier sculpture would have observed so much play out before him. But like him, when it comes to observing the inexorable march of time impacting one of the city's finest buildings, we seem to have eyes of marble.

While residential and commercial projects continue to climb behind the veneer of heritage retained on some sites, on others historical structures have been demolished to make way for the new. A 19th-century building at the eastern end of King Street, and purportedly the oldest timber building in Newcastle, was knocked down in early 2024, raising an outcry.

Marcus Westbury has been watching the continued changes to his former workplace, his testing ground, his hometown, from afar geographically. But in every other way, it all remains close.

'To see activity and investment and people living and appreciating the city again is a good thing', he says. But he reckons there's still room for the small in the city. 'There could still be schemes like Renew Newcastle. There's still a lot of unutilised space. You don't know if you don't try stuff. It would be sad if Newcastle went down a path or a formula where everything's predictable.

'There's something about Newcastle that works on the scale of someone who wants to roll up their sleeves.

'I really hope Newcastle values the dynamic where you can create things, start things and try things.'

THE layers of human experience have been gradually revealed in the heart of Newcastle, as developers prepare to build a new story on top of others.

A great part of that story, wherever you may be in the CBD, is that of the Aboriginal people.

As Worimi man, author and academic John Maynard says, 'Anywhere across the city, if you dug into the ground, you'd find something'.

And so it was in Hunter Street, near the corner of Steel Street, when the memories of dance hall days and rock concerts were scraped off the surface with the demolition of the former Palais Royale entertainment venue in 2008, and crews began digging.

Stratum upon stratum, generation upon generation, of evidence of the First Nations people's presence was unearthed.

The contribution of the First Nations people in colonial times also played out around here. Near this site was once the temporary home of the Reverend Lancelot Threlkeld, who arrived in Newcastle with his family in 1825. Threlkeld was working for the London Missionary Society and was on his way a little further south to establish a mission on the shores of Lake Macquarie. The Threlkelds were to be the first European full-time residents at the lake. But for about a year, as he waited for the mission to be built, he and his family lived in the government cottage in Newcastle.

Threlkeld soon learnt what sort of town he was living in. No sooner had some of the family's belongings been unloaded from a ship than a bunch of convicts commandeered the vessel and sailed off, which probably only confirmed to the missionary what he had written in his diary the day before; that in Newcastle, 'the most choice rogues are of course here'.[33] And not all the rogues were convicts. A group of soldiers filled with grog and anger towards civilians had roamed the streets one Christmas in the mid-1820s, threatening to cut open anyone they came across. One man was bayoneted and died.[34] So the Newcastle Threlkeld had arrived in was one filled with not just rogues but resentment and division.

Yet it was the people who would become known as the Awabakal who were Threlkeld's reason for coming to this part of the world. As he wrote in a letter from Newcastle about his mission, 'Our Object is first Christianise and Civilization will then follow'.[35]

From the outset, the missionary observed and recorded his impressions of the First Nations people. Threlkeld could watch them at close quarters. As he noted, they camped around his cottage and performed a dance to welcome the family.

'The Native camp which surrounded our habitation gave a cheerfulness to the scene at night in consequence of the number of fires kept up by the families at the front of their respective sleeping places, which were mere erections of boughs of trees, or sheets of bark placed upright supported by stakes', he wrote.

Threlkeld also came to understand the disruption and violence that the Awabakal had been subjected to.

'The blacks chose our place of residence for their new encampment, they having been so frequently molested by many of the prisoners of the crown who perambulated the settlement in the night for purposes that would not bear the light of day.'[36]

By the end of 1825, when he sent off his report to the London Missionary Society from Newcastle, Threlkeld had become not just a keen observer of the life and customs of Aboriginal people, he had also developed strong beliefs, and even stronger words, about what was needed, and what was lacking.

'If we, boasting of our superior light and knowledge, use no means to instruct and raise these wretched Aborigines from the depths of their misery, increased by our residence among them, where is our vaunted characteristic philanthropy? If those, who are accumulating wealth in the possession of this people's land, do not devote a portion of those riches for so noble, so just a cause, will not the cry of a brother's blood, occasioned too often to be shed through the thirst for wealth, encroaching on their native rights, ascend into the ears of him who has said, "For the oppression of the poor, for the sighing of the needy, now will I arise".'[37]

Being a man of not just faith, but of opinion, Threlkeld traded stern words with other figures in the colony, including some powerful ones, such as the Reverend Samuel Marsden. Yet he found a friend and collaborator, a guide and teacher, in an Awabakal leader, Biraban. This team would become immensely important not just in their time but for the recording of Aboriginal language and culture. Threlkeld was well aware that the doors to his mission would be built around language. As he wrote before even arriving in Newcastle, 'My first employment will be to Obtain the Language of the Aborigines without which it would be a mere farce to attempt anything under a Missionary establishment.'[38] And the person who would open those doors for Threlkeld was Biraban.

As a boy, Biraban had been taken to Sydney, where he worked for a military officer and learnt English. The British called him Johnny M'Gill. They relied on him to guide them through Aboriginal land, languages and cultures. Biraban was part of an exploratory party up the coast, to the area that would become Port Macquarie and the site of the penal settlement that would effectively replace Newcastle in the early 1820s. So Biraban was involved in moving Newcastle on from being a place of secondary punishment for convicts.

Biraban impressed those who met him. Governor Lachlan Macquarie recognised him as the king of the Awabakal. He was also portrayed by a convict artist, Richard Browne. While he was doing his time in Newcastle between 1811 and 1817, Browne did watercolour portraits of Awabakal and Worimi people, and more than 50 works have survived, including one of Biraban in a dance pose with his torso painted with ceremonial markings.[39]

Threlkeld came to Newcastle and Lake Macquarie to Christianise and 'civilise' the Aboriginal people, but it was Biraban who educated Threlkeld. He taught the missionary about his people's language and culture. Together they translated tracts of the Bible and prayers into the Aboriginal language. That may have helped Threlkeld bring Christianity to the Awabakal people, but it was another series of projects that helped bring the Aboriginal language to English speakers. In 1834, Threlkeld had published a book titled *An Australian grammar, comprehending the principles and natural rules of the language, as spoken by the Aborigines, in the vicinity of Hunter's River, Lake Macquarie, &c. New South Wales*. As well as explaining grammar, the book is a dictionary, translating Aboriginal words, phrases, concepts and place names into English, including 'Mu-lu-bin-ba, the name of the site of Newcastle, from an indigenous fern, *Mu-lu-bin*'.[40] While Threlkeld was noted as the author on the title page, and he went on to write other books on Aboriginal language, Biraban's knowledge and ability to bridge languages and cultures are there on every page. Biraban received official acknowledgment for his work. In 1830, Governor Sir Ralph Darling had presented Biraban with a brass plate as a 'Reward for his assistance in reducing his Native Tongue to a written Language'.[41] Biraban and Threlkeld's contribution went beyond the written word. The pair travelled to Sydney to interpret and translate in court cases involving First Nations people.

Threlkeld himself was grateful for Biraban's teaching, something he acknowledged in his writing. In a book about Aboriginal language published in 1850, Threlkeld had included a portrait of Biraban and wrote a preface titled, 'Reminiscences of Biraban'.

'An aboriginal of this part of the colony was my almost daily companion for many years, and to his intelligence I am principally indebted for much of my knowledge respecting the structure of the language', Threlkeld wrote.[42]

Threlkeld's mission work in Lake Macquarie had ended in 1841 because of 'the sad fact that the aborigines themselves had then become almost extinct'.[43] Threlkeld felt compelled to continue writing about the Aboriginal language for the same reason. As he wrote in 1850, at the end of his book about Aboriginal language, 'The Author trusts he has now placed on permanent record the language of the aborigines of this part of the colony, before the speakers themselves become totally extinct'.[44] Threlkeld's fears and prophecy were wrong. Almost two centuries on, the Awabakal people, language and culture are central to Newcastle life. But the 'permanent record of the language' remains a key reference, thanks to not just the Reverend Lancelot Threlkeld, but also to Biraban and his linguistic skills.

From the founding of the settlement, Aboriginal people were being pushed to the fringes. Joseph Lycett's paintings often suggested otherwise. The convict artist depicted traditional Aboriginal culture, with corroborees, hunting and night fishing highlighted in his work, as though the pattern of life had not been disrupted by colonisation. Lycett also portrayed in his paintings of the town British settlers and an Aboriginal man walking together, returning from what appears to be a hunting expedition. It has been suggested the figures depicted are James Wallis, Newcastle's commandant at the time and patron of Lycett, with a local elder, Burigon. The commandant hunted and fished with Burigon and, being an amateur artist, painted the Aboriginal leader's portrait. When Governor Macquarie visited Newcastle in 1818, he was entertained by Burigon and about 40 others, who performed a corroboree in 'high stile'. In acknowledgement of those who performed for him, Macquarie 'ordered them to be treated with some grog and an allowance of maize'.[45]

First Nations people's knowledge of the country was used by the colonial authorities to explore the land, and to track convicts who ran away from the settlement. Bungaree, an Aboriginal leader from further south who had been a member of the 1801 survey expedition of the lower Hunter River and had gone on to circumnavigate Australia with navigator and explorer Matthew Flinders, visited Newcastle as it grew. On one of his visits, Bungaree was involved in tracking down a runaway convict. But to come into contact with an escaped convict could be fatal. Bungaree's father was killed by three convict runaways from Newcastle in 1804.[46]

The tragic collision between convict runaways and First Nations people led to the death of Burigon in 1820. He was fatally stabbed in

Newcastle by a convict runaway he had caught. The convict was found guilty of murder and hanged. Wallis clearly missed his former companion and guide, writing about the range of emotions he experienced when remembering Burigon and all that the Aboriginal leader had done for him.[47]

They were being pushed ever further to the fringes by colonial expansion, but Aboriginal people continued to be part of town life. In 1827, when Lieutenant William S Coke was posted to the settlement, he wrote to his father, describing Newcastle as 'a small village crowded with convicts and savages and no ladies or gentlemen'.

In the letter to his father, Coke described some of what he had observed.

'I believe the natives are my best friends, we often witness battles between different tribes even in the village. They are very expert in throwing a spear as far as 200 yards.'[48]

What Coke observed and documented would fade from the streets of Newcastle. But the Aboriginal presence is there, in the heart of the city. It always has been. It is all around us, including beneath our feet.

When work began on the former Palais site, archaeologists undertook an excavation, uncovering thousands of stone tools and campsite remains. Dating of the artefacts indicated Aboriginal occupation stretched back about 6700 years. This amounted to the oldest evidence ever found of settlement in Newcastle.[49] The implements discovered suggested the site was used as a trading place, with tools being brought from far and wide to be exchanged here. In the layers closer to the surface were artefacts from the colonial era. So in the earth lay so much of the story of Newcastle.

The excavation report for the site declared that it held 'high to exceptional' cultural and scientific significance.[50] Yet the excavation report only came to light a year after that site of exceptional cultural and scientific significance had been built on. On top of all those layers of history and knowledge, a cornerstone of contemporary western life was constructed: a fast food outlet. Where Aboriginal groups once traded, the peckish could now feast on fried chicken in what has been trumpeted as the largest KFC restaurant in Australia.

While about 5000 artefacts were excavated and saved, so many more would have been entombed under concrete. Perhaps we'll never know how much was down there, as the excavation work was limited. The thought of what was lost has dismayed those devoted to the city's heritage. Gionni di Gravio, the archivist at the University of Newcastle, was reported as saying at the time that what happened with this site indicated Aboriginal archaeology was not treated with importance.[51]

As Novocastrians often do, as humans do, when faced with loss, they adapted and innovated. If we cannot literally see the archaeological site and the treasures they contained, then at least we can virtually. With many of the artefacts stored at the university, a coalition of Aboriginal leaders, historians, archaeologists and technological experts devised a way to put those objects back, and to take us back, in an initiative called the Deep Time Project.

Basically, the university has set up a 3D scanning facility to digitise the artefacts. Then those artefacts are virtually returned to where they were found in a holographic reproduction of the site. And, by wearing a headset, you can virtually head underground into the past.

At the invitation of the university's GLAMx Living Histories Digitisation Lab, I wore the headset and delved into that head-spinning, mind-blowing world. Like a surrealist diver, I descended through the ages, through the layers, floating through grid lines until I was about 6000 years back. Looking around, I saw a small stone floating like sunken treasure. Ann Hardy, the coordinator of the GLAMx Living Histories Digitisation Lab, encouraged me to use the control grips I was holding to inspect the stone. As I virtually turned the stone and used a magnifying glass to study it, a digital panel popped up to inform me I was looking at an 'amorphic stone artefact'. Returning to the surface, I felt simultaneously slightly disoriented and exhilarated. Also diving through time that day were local Aboriginal leaders, as they explored what their forebears had created, and where they had traded, worked and lived. As Peter Townsend, from the Awabakal Local Aboriginal Land Council, told me after his virtual reality experience, this was a very modern way of bringing Newcastle's cultural heritage to life.

The Deep Time Project is an Australian first. When the team members set off, as far as they knew, they were treading new ground globally, unaware of any other archaeological dig of this type that had been digitally recreated. To Ann Hardy, the project allows all Australians to learn more about Aboriginal culture, and to respect how rich that culture is.[52]

But inevitably the project also prods us to lament how much culture and history may have been buried or destroyed. For that 3D headset also opens our eyes to the stark reality of what is not just beneath the fast food restaurant's slab but under construction sites across the city. After all, as the archaeological excavation report for the former Palais site noted, the cultural landscape was likely to extend for several hundred metres (and perhaps further) to the east and west.[53] And there have been developments in recent years for several hundred metres in either direction. And there will be many more further afield in the city.

In 1997, the same year Newcastle was reeling from the imminent closure of BHP's steelworks and many were wondering who would want to invest here, Suters Architects prepared an archaeological management plan for the city. A raft of geographical and economic factors had impeded development in the CBD, much to the frustration of those who felt the town was stagnating, but that had allowed Newcastle to remain a 'substantially intact nineteenth century city above and below ground'. Archaeological surveys had indicated more than 177 sites that had connections to Newcastle's convict period, and it was estimated that 75 to 80 per cent of the CBD's land area was likely to hold archaeological relics. That estimate put Newcastle far ahead of Sydney and Melbourne, in terms of survival of relics.[54] At a time when so many were questioning what was next for Newcastle, right under its feet lay a resource that could provide one way forward for the city. For the conservation of the city's archaeological resource could feed not just knowledge and education, but could also nurture cultural tourism. That was something the city's council noted in its archaeological management strategy almost two decades later, in 2015.

However, with so much development in the city since that 1997 report was prepared, we don't need to wear a virtual reality headset to envisage how the archaeological richness of Newcastle has been impacted in recent years. Then again, maybe we do. Perhaps there is no other way to see what we have potentially lost.

Streets don't just carry vehicles. They cradle the passage of time. And so it is with Hunter Street. Along its flanks, we can mark change architecturally and socially, and on the road itself we have a sense of how we have moved with the times.

By the time Mark Twain saw it in 1895, Hunter Street had progressed from a raggedy string of tracks into a long ribbon of dirt, etched with tram tracks and cart wheel marks, and punctuated with horseshoe prints. When it rained heavily, Hunter Street became a quagmire. In the early 20th century, the road was given a harder skin, providing a platform for the rise and rise of the motor vehicle.

Newcastle's natural outline might have been defined by water, with the CBD effectively sitting on a peninsula, but the city itself was increasingly being shaped by, and for, the car. The corridors of old railways that had brought coal to the port from outlying collieries were resumed and turned into roads. As a result, there are a number of intersections that still look as though the planners decided to get creative with geometry. In 1950, the tram network that had linked the city to the suburbs and to the industries was dismantled, effectively shoved off the rails by motor vehicles, which quickly colonised that space as well. Roads were cut through green spaces, and buildings were demolished for parking stations. Even parks were turned into de facto car parks. The car was king.

In Newcastle, the car has been not just a mode of transport but a badge of identity. As a result, for many years, the city's main artery doubled as a show-and-go runway for the city's car culture. Gleaming pieces of metal cruised like sharks along Hunter Street, only there was nothing silent about their passage. Men and machines grunted and roared through town. They were desperate for attention, and they got it, from pedestrians, from the police, and from a local radio presenter and musician named Bob Hudson.

Bob had grown up on the NSW Central Coast, and he lived and studied in Newcastle in the 1960s. He lived above a hamburger shop – 'every young bloke's idea of heaven' – near the intersection of Hunter and Pacific streets, an area Novocastrians still call 'the top of town', a curious description given the entire length of Hunter Street is fairly flat. In the 1970s, Bob moved out of the city centre but retained a strong connection through music, as he played in a popular pub outfit, the Electric Jug Band.

During that period, Bob transposed his observations of life along Hunter Street into a song, which became a national number one hit and, in the city that was its muse, a phenomenon. Bob titled his composition 'The Newcastle Song'.

While the main drag may have been named back in the early 1800s in honour of former governor John Hunter, Bob's song gave new meaning to Hunter Street, as he outlined the 'very strange mating habits' of the young in Newcastle. In 'The Newcastle Song', the hunters are the young blokes in cars. And the cars in the song are described in meticulous detail. They are 'FJ Holdens/with chrome-plated grease nipples/and double reverse overhead twin cam door handles'. The men are 'sitting eight abreast in the front seat', leaning out of the car and trying to attract the attention of young women walking along the footpath or waiting outside the Parthenon Milk Bar. In the song, the young blokes, led by a character named Norm (or Normie), seem destined for a fight with a 9-foot bikie, who is with a young woman outside the milk bar. However, salvation arrives. The traffic lights change, giving the boys the opportunity to race off in their FJ Holden. As the chorus goes, 'Don't you ever let a chance go by, oh Lord'.[55]

Bob explained in an email that 'The Newcastle Song' 'contained an accumulation of stuff from living in non-Sydney Australia, including my time in Newcastle'.

'At that stage in our history, the idea that Australian performers could merrily take the piss out of ourselves was a part of our culture – hence Paul Hogan etc', writes Bob, who, like the city that inspired him, has changed direction markedly. In recent years, he has become renowned and respected as an archaeologist and academic at the University of Sydney.

'The song was largely composed/compiled/accumulated in Newcastle, but it owed a lot to life in any Australian town. I imagine that's why it touched a chord with people all over.'[56]

The mention of the Parthenon in 'The Newcastle Song' conjures another cultural marker of Hunter Street life: the milk bar. Many Novocastrians figure the little milk bars and cafes along Hunter Street sprouted after the Second World War, when the docking of 'migrant ships' in the harbour brought new cultures, new tastes and new ways of seeing to Newcastle. However, many migrants had made that journey long before the post-war years, and they brought the idea of the milk bar with them. In 1898, Angelo Bourtzos, who had travelled from the Californian goldfields to Newcastle, opened the Niagara Café in Hunter Street. This was an emporium of flavours, as Angelo, originally from Greece, offered a taste of the United States, with ice cream he made in the café, milkshakes and fresh pastries.[57] In the years ahead, Hunter Street, and the main drags of most Australian towns and cities, would be enlivened by the rise of the 'Greek café' and the 'milk bar'. They weren't just places to dine; they were places to be seen, which is made clear in 'The Newcastle Song'. Although perhaps the Parthenon Milk Bar came into being because of the song. I recall scouting Hunter Street after 'The Newcastle Song' was released, looking for this Parthenon Milk Bar. I saw plenty of other cafés and milk bars but no Parthenon. Sometime after the song, a Parthenon Milk Bar did pop up along Hunter Street in Newcastle West. I don't remember seeing 9-foot bikies outside, but I did notice young blokes who would have fitted Normie's description. And hotted-up cars did trawl past. But that was Hunter Street. That was Newcastle then.

Just as the number of milk bars along Hunter Street has dwindled, so has the car culture. For the motor vehicle has literally had to move aside to make way for public transport on rails once more. In a return to the past, tracks have been laid along the middle of Hunter and Scott streets for about 1.75 kilometres, with the installation of the light rail system. The project was part of the NSW Government's Revitalising Newcastle program, but the light rail's critics said its construction disrupted the flow of traffic and the rhythm of life along Hunter Street. Those who expected to be able to drive into the city and find a park for their car considered the light rail an imposition to their rituals on wheels, with only one vehicle lane in each direction and a speed limit of 40 kilometres per hour. Yet the city has gradually, if begrudgingly, got on board with the new/old way of getting around. Since it was launched in 2019, the light rail system has been growing in patronage, with about four million trips taken in the system's first five years, according to its private operator, Keolis Downer.[58] The red carriages humming through the city's heart have become part of Hunter Street life.

Others want to see cars pull back further in the CBD and provide more space for those on two wheels. They believe the way for the heart of Newcastle to move forward is the bicycle. One of those is Sam Reich. Sam is the president of the Newcastle Cycleways Movement and is a representative on a number of bicycling organisations, including the City of Newcastle's Cycling Strategy Working Party.

Newcastle is ideal for cycling, Sam argues, because of the flat terrain along much of the peninsula in the CBD, and to many of the city's suburbs. Before the car ruled in Newcastle, the bike was prominent in the city. It was how many Novocastrians got around. Sam mentions that the BHP steelworks had parking spaces for thousands of bicycles. A former employee of the nearby Lysaght steel mills recalled five big sheds to accommodate bikes, ridden by workers from as far away as Lake Macquarie.[59]

'So we have a very rich heritage for bicycling as transport in the city', Sam says.

For the sake of the city's liveability, Sam asserts, we have to return to that heritage. Bicycles should largely replace cars in the CBD. What's more, he says, that would free up a lot of land for buildings, including space that is presently tied to the motor vehicle, with garages and parking stations. Narrow streets are also being used as car parks. The city, and its ability to evolve, is constipated with cars.

'It's a narrow peninsula with high growth, and it simply can't support the situation where everyone in a family has a car', Sam argues. 'The requirements for dwellings needing a certain number of car spaces is being reduced, because it's been realised that's not sustainable and not supportable.

'I've seen people lobbying to increase the size of our parking spaces, but we're not making more land. So all of these influences are cramming together, and it's a bit of a tug-of-war over a finite resource of road space.'

Sam's views are shared by Steven Fleming, a Novocastrian who has been considered a world authority on incorporating cycling into urban design. He has advised city authorities, from Oslo to Singapore, on developing cycling-friendly infrastructure and attitudes.

When I first spoke with Steven in 2019, he said the car no longer had a place in Hunter Street, or on any other street in the city's heart. He argued the development control plans were out of date. Instead of having regulations requiring developers to provide car parking spaces, there should be a push to make the city centre car-free and improve public transport and cycling routes. Other, much bigger, cities had done it, Steven pointed out. Newcastle should do it.[60]

Five years on, when we speak again, Steven believes the city's centre should be free of motor vehicles, other than for essential access, such as transporting supplies. Most inner-city residents, he argues, will be car-free in the future – 'and it would be better if it was that way now'.

'As a city diversifies, the sprawl becomes untenable, and you can't have all these one-tonne steel contraptions driving around. It just doesn't work.'

In his book that explores building cities for bikes, *Velotopia: The production of cyclespace in our minds and our cities*, Steven composes a striking simile about Newcastle and other smaller cities that continue to rely on motor vehicles: 'Small cities with cars are like young adults with snack foods. Young people can't see the day coming when their habit will have clogged their arteries. People who live in small cities can't see how their habit of driving will soon clog their roads'.[61]

Sam Reich believes hope is pedalling its way into Newcastle.

'The bicycle is coming back, and it makes eminent sense in this city where you can get anywhere other than the far-flung corners in half an hour.'

To get anywhere, however, you need infrastructure. For the most part, cyclists have shared paths and roads with others. As the marketing of Newcastle as a 'lifestyle' city has taken hold, and people have put that catchword into action, the shared paths have become more crowded. Along the harbour front, where waterside workers once toiled, recreation is writ large, especially early in the morning and on weekends, as cyclists parry around pedestrians and joggers, all jostling for space. That same competition is played out beyond the western reaches of the harbour and along Throsby Creek. A shared path unravels along the creek's western bank, passing the former site of warehouses once packed with wool waiting to be loaded onto ships. All those symbols of a nation riding on the sheep's back have been replaced by a vast townhouse and apartment complex, and by a city getting active.

Many of those on bicycles are riding for pleasure, rather than commuting. To encourage more people to choose bicycles as a mode of transportation, Sam asserts the city needs more dedicated bike paths. He was involved in developing a proposal for Newcastle called the Cycle Safe Network, which, if funded by the state government, would provide more bike routes, encourage riding, and take cars off the road, reducing congestion. Yet when Sam last inquired, the report had not really gone anywhere. However, he believes the network plan has influenced both state- and local-government cycling strategies, keeping the idea moving.

The council supports developing a cycling city, and that belief has been converted into a few dedicated cycling routes. The CBD is partly covered by a cycleway, and it is being extended further to the west. The notion of more territory being shaved off the motorist's domain in the city's heart has been met with grumbling from some drivers and businesses, but, according to Sam, 'the idea of taking away a lane is often much worse than the reality when it happens'. To Sam's disappointment, the prospect of creating more cycleways in the city's heart along the former heavy rail corridor has been all but closed off and buried under building developments.

For the moment, as they wait for more of their own paths, cycling groups look to other changes to keep them, and pedestrians, out of harm's way. Reducing the speed limit to 30 kilometres per hour in some inner-city areas has helped, Sam says.

'Thankfully we've started with our baby steps that 30 kilometres per hour doesn't bring the world to an end, and making those kinds of shopping strips and pedestrian-heavy places is a good thing, it makes people feel good and improves the amenity.'

Yet there are many who have no desire to get out of their cars. And they want the cyclists to get out of their way. As Steven Fleming told me in 2019, there was a culture of entitlement among drivers. To change that point of view is like pedalling up the formidably steep streets climbing The Hill: it is slow going, energy sapping, and requires deep breaths to push on.

Steven Fleming reckons there will come 'a political tipping point' in Newcastle, where the people calling for fewer cars and better public transport and cycling options in the city will outnumber those advocating driving. When that happens, governments will respond.

Sam Reich believes change is not just possible, it is happening.

'We're not insisting that everybody ride', the Newcastle Cycleways Movement president says. 'Of course, not everyone can ride.'

But many more could, and that would make a huge difference to the city, and to our lives, according to Sam. It has been estimated that fewer than 2 per cent of short journeys, from 5 to 10 kilometres, are done on bicycle.

'If we could raise that to 15 per cent, it will have a marked and very identifiable impact on congestion, on parking. It will become a safer community in which to ride, people will see more people on bikes, and it will be normalised. It's normalised behaviour.'

And when that happens, Newcastle will need a new song. Instead of being in an FJ Holden with chrome-plated grease nipples, Normie can be pedalling a carbon-fibre mountain bike along Hunter Street. He will still never let a chance go by. This will just be a new opportunity for Normie, and for Newcastle.

CHAPTER THREE

PUB ROCK CITY

IF Mark Twain had visited Newcastle 80 years later than he did, surely he would have devised a bon mot about Hunter Street that involved beer and music. For this was the era of pub rock. This one long street measures about 3.5 kilometres. But on any given night in the 1970s and 1980s, it felt much longer, if you stopped at every hotel hosting a rock band.

Along Hunter Street alone, there were 15 hotels in the mid-1970s,[1] and many of them had live music. Then there were the nightclubs, such as the Ambassador (commonly called The Bass) and the cavernous hall with the gracious weathered face and the flash name, the Palais Royale (which, inevitably, was shortened to The Palais).

To attempt to see every band playing along Hunter Street was to embark on an odyssey into oblivion, with ringing ears your constant companion.

And if somehow you completed that quest, you could begin a new musical adventure in the pubs and clubs along King Street, down the inner city's lanes and along the cross streets.

You would be exhausted or deafened, or both, before seeing every band playing in town. Then you could do it all again the next night.

As Rick Pointon, who was a member of one of the biggest local bands of the 1970s, Benny and the Jets, says, 'Newcastle was considered a rock city'.

The steel city had been a rock city before the 1970s. As a young musician, Rick recalls one night in 1965 counting 25 bands playing in the inner-city pubs and clubs.

'It was jumping. Pubs on every corner, bands in every pub. Even back in the 1960s, I was playing five nights a week, six nights a week, more jobs than you could handle. The 70s were the same, and the 80s.'

No sooner was rock music born than Newcastle began embracing the makers of this exciting new sound. In the Marketown shopping centre in Newcastle West, those hurrying to buy what they need probably don't notice they are treading on music history. Stone stars are embedded in the pavement, and each is encrusted with the name of a performer. Some of the names have drifted into obscurity but quite a few are synonymous with the early days of rock and roll in Australia, such as The Delltones, Lucky Starr and Col Joye. This galaxy is beneath consumers' feet because the site of this shopping centre once held the Newcastle Stadium. The biggest acts from not just Australia but around the globe performed there, including, in 1957, a young Johnny O'Keefe and American stars Eddie Cochran, Gene Vincent and Little Richard, all on the same bill. The course of Little Richard's life, and that of rock music, changed while the singer was in Newcastle. The Hunter River may not have the same biblical significance as the River Jordan, but one of the early superstars of rock apparently had an epiphany while crossing the Hunter's mouth. He declared, while on the Stockton vehicular ferry, that he was quitting show business to serve God. According to Johnny O'Keefe, who was there and recounted the moment in a letter to Rick Pointon, when one of Little Richard's musicians responded by saying he should give away his jewellery, the star peeled off his rings and a watch and threw them into the harbour.[2] Little Richard subsequently ended his Australian tour early and returned to the United States to study religion. Somewhere buried in the mire at the bottom of Newcastle Harbour there may well be rock and roll treasure.

In spite of Little Richard's experience, or perhaps because of it, the stars kept coming to Newcastle. In 1966, Rick Pointon's outfit at the time, Second Thoughts, were booked to be the backing band for a string of artists performing at the Mattara concert in Civic Park. One of the headline acts was an emerging trio of brothers called the Bee Gees.

During their performance, the Bee Gees unveiled their new single, 'Spicks and Specks', now considered one of their classics. Rick says he and his band had been told to mime the song; the music would be supplied from a record played on the side of the stage. However, the record stuck, and the crowd was hearing 'where is the …' over and over. Rick wrote in his memoir, *Hey Rock 'n' Roll*, that Barry Gibb instructed the backing band to jump around to distract the crowd, and the three brothers joined in, waiting for their father to place the stylus in the right place so the song could go on. A loud screech ripped through the public address system, 'Spicks and Specks' resumed, and so did the career of the Bee Gees, rollicking towards global success.[3]

By the 1970s, Newcastle was, in the eyes and ears of the young, as much a city of rock and roll as it was steel and coal.

'It was a big music town, a huge music town that had a lot of cover bands, but there was also that important original music scene', says Gaye Sheather.

Gaye's life has been entwined with Newcastle's music scene. As a teenager and in her early 20s, the weekly gig guide was her Bible, and Newcastle's pubs and clubs were her churches. The nightclubs hosted a lot of touring acts, particularly from Sydney, so she would see Midnight Oil and INXS long before they dominated stages around the world. Many of these touring bands had a following in Newcastle before they even broke through nationally. The members of Cold Chisel have said Newcastle was one of the first places to support them. Then again, one of Cold Chisel's earlier songs was titled 'Shipping Steel', so their high-tensile, swollen-tonsil rock rang with familiarity in Newcastle.

'Those touring bands were like local bands, they played here often enough', Gaye recalls.

The hotels booked many Hunter bands who also drew a crowd.

'Places would get packed, so it would be a fight to get to the bar, a fight to get to the toilets, a fight to get to the stage', she says.

While there were more than 100 acts playing around Newcastle, she religiously attended concerts by a Newcastle rock and blues trio called DV8. They were her favourite band, as DV8 played music heard on the radio as well as their own songs, which they released on records that became hits locally. So DV8 could be heard on Newcastle radio, and as a result, were rock stars in their own town. They would play just about every night of the week, pulling large crowds. They were the kings of the packed pub in 1980s Newcastle. DV8's lead singer and guitarist, Greg Bryce, has celebrated, or eulogised, those days, writing a song,

'Rock 'n' Roll Town', which he and his band continue to perform in live shows. In the song Greg name-checks venues his band used to play: the Star Hotel, the Bel-Air, the Jolly Roger. Those venues no longer exist.

'They were the glory days of live music', Greg says. 'You can't go back in those places any more; all you can do is remember.'

Yet for Greg, 'Rock 'n' Roll Town' is not a lament.

'It's a celebration song of those golden days, and not just golden days for the bands.'

Greg recounts how at a recent gig a man approached him and talked about seeing DV8 at the Bel-Air. A woman walked up, and the man introduced her. 'This is my wife. We met there.'

So 'Rock 'n' Roll Town' is a portal to another time for all who hear it.

Gaye Sheather became part of that rock 'n' roll town, as the lead singer for a couple of bands. The male-dominated local industry was discriminatory at times. She recalls one venue where she was repeatedly stopped by security officers because they didn't believe she was in the band. Gaye resorted to walking in with musical equipment as proof, only to be told carrying her boyfriend's microphone stand didn't mean she would be allowed in for free.

'It was a misogynistic time, I hope we've moved from that a bit', she says.

Newcastle's rock music scene remained an abiding passion for Gaye. She studied it for her PhD at the University of Newcastle and then turned her research into a book, *Rock This City: Live music in Newcastle, 1970s–1980s*.

As Gaye points out in her book, the sheer number of venues and audiences who turned up each and every night meant musicians could keep themselves busy and, for many, could make a living from it. The scene was thriving and self-contained, and many bands were happy to stay and play here.

'For musicians performing in the pub rock era, it wasn't all about striving for national acclaim and commercial success', Gaye writes in her book. 'The unique mix of bands, venues and people in Newcastle created the perfect conditions for what became a special and healthy live music scene.'[4]

Yet in the pubs' beer-soaked carpets were planted the seeds for bands that would go far beyond Newcastle.

In the early 1980s, a bunch of schoolmates from Marist Brothers Hamilton played in a band called Aspect. They were watching those already on the pub rock circuit, learning and dreaming. At the core of Aspect was a teenage guitarist, Grant Walmsley.

In one of those symmetries of Newcastle that makes the place feel reassuringly small, Grant's parents were close friends of Greg Bryce's parents. So Grant was often around at the Bryce home and hanging out in the room of the DV8 frontman, listening to songs, watching Greg play guitar, and talking about two of their shared passions, music and surfing. Grant tagged along with Greg to DV8 gigs. As he watched the band transfix audiences of up to 1000 in the beer barns around Newcastle, Grant saw his future.

'I thought, "That's what I'll do". And I did. You could then.'

Aspect was soon playing four or five nights a week, building a following and earning money, all while the members were going to school.

'Newcastle was the best breeding ground', Grant says. 'We'd bought a truck and a PA [sound] system before we'd left high school.'

Being a covers band, playing other people's hits, you could work just about every night in Newcastle. But Grant wanted to play his own songs. That was harder to do in Newcastle and get regular gigs. There was an independent music scene in the city in the 1980s, with bands performing their original songs on smaller stages, including at a wildly surreal venue called Uptown Circus, which operated from the first floor of the historic Newcastle RSL Club. However, Newcastle was primarily a cover-version town, unless you already had songs on the radio. But you weren't going to get songs on the radio by playing only cover versions. To break that paradox, Grant was writing and recording and, through his mentor Greg's introduction, was getting advice from a fellow guitarist and producer, Mark Tinson. Mark had found success beyond Newcastle not once but twice, with his band, Rabbit, in the mid-1970s, and then Heroes. Both acts had recorded albums and toured. Heroes had enjoyed a massive local audience as well, with the band playing just about every night of the week. When Heroes called it a day, Mark had played with popular national acts, such as Swanee. So Mark could give

Grant a sense of what was possible not just in the recording studio but on the national stage.

'The best lesson I learnt from DV8 and Heroes was to get out of Newcastle', Grant recalls. 'Their thing was, "If you're going to do this, move to Sydney or Melbourne". Which you do had to do to be a national entity.'

As Mark knew, Newcastle's ability to provide big audiences and decent money could encourage a band to stay at home. As a result, ambition and talent could easily be contained and constrained within the city's limits.

'The advice I gave to younger bands to get the hell out of here was not because it wasn't a great place but because it was too comfortable', Mark says.

There was no constraining Grant Walmsley's ambition. As he kept practising, playing and songwriting, Aspect morphed into a new unit. Out front was still Grant's mate, a charismatic and endearingly cheeky bloke with long curly hair and a killer grin, Dave Gleeson. Other players joined the band. And the band changed names. They became The Screaming Jets.

The apprenticeship continued on stages around Newcastle, including a residency at The Cambridge Hotel on Hunter Street. The front bar was clotted with sweaty, sweary, happy humanity. The boys were making their mark. But they wanted to see what else was happening and what others were doing, to keep learning. And Newcastle on a Saturday night was the ideal classroom.

'We'd finish at the Cambridge, pack up and we'd walk. The first stop was the Family [Hotel] and look at original bands or bands doing their own thing, then you'd go across the road to the Palais and see the cover bands, and then you'd go to the Castle [Tavern], then to the Workers Club, then to the JR [Jolly Roger nightclub], then you'd go to the Lucky Country [Hotel]. And if you did a detour you could go to the Oriental or the Cricketer's Arms [hotels in Cooks Hill], and you could go to Fannys [a nightclub with a name that unfailingly raised outsiders' eyebrows]. And then onto the Great Northern Hotel. It was amazing.'

The Screaming Jets began venturing beyond Newcastle, heading down the freeway to Sydney and further afield. The band set up headquarters in a two-bedroom apartment in Kings Cross in Sydney. The Screaming Jets were treated like country cousins by some of the big-city bands, and they met resistance. Seared into Grant's memory is older people advising that no band got anywhere far from Newcastle, and that he should get a proper job.

'I remember hearing, "You'll never get anywhere",' he says.

That piece of cautionary advice, or put-down, became the catch line of a song Grant wrote with his band mates and rehearsed in a studio in the Newcastle suburb of Broadmeadow.

The song is titled 'Better'. The song is a guitar anthem that proved to be a siren call to a nation that fell in love with The Screaming Jets. In 1991, 'Better' became a Top 5 hit, and it ranks highly in listener polls for the greatest Australian rock songs.

The jubilation in the band's playing of the song and the defiance in the lyrics are seamed with a distinctly Newcastle tone. 'Better' is the soundtrack of the city as it was then, and of the people it produced.

'Our band had mongrel', says Grant. 'We had the songs, but we had mongrel. I think that's a real bonded Newcastle thing. We weren't a team of champions but we were a champion team. We were accomplished.'

The band strapped in for a long and heady ride, with hit albums and overseas tours. The Screaming Jets were not just champions of Newcastle, they were synonymous with the city. For a time, they were as big as the Newcastle Knights. They even shared the stage with the Knights in a massive concert in Civic Park, after the rugby league team won its first premiership in 1997. The connection between The Screaming Jets and the Knights, between Newcastle culture and sport, continues, with the team running onto the field to the strains of 'Better' at home games.

Grant left The Screaming Jets in 2006, but the band continues to record and tour. The sole founding member in the existing line-up is Dave Gleeson. However, Grant is still immersed in music, helping guide the next generation, and he lives in Newcastle.

However, he doubts Newcastle could produce another The Screaming Jets, because the times and music tastes have changed, and so has the city that spawned the band.

'You couldn't have the same band as us because we were a working-class band', Grant muses. 'Everything we got we had to work hard to pay for.

'My two grandfathers worked their whole careers at The BHP. You can't get much more Newy than that.'

THE best-known rock pub in Newcastle was the Star Hotel. This rambunctious concoction of bricks and booze was halfway along Hunter Street and in the dead centre of many people's minds as the place to go for fun. But it wasn't fun for everyone.

'I wouldn't have gone to the Star for a night out myself', says Mark Tinson. 'It sometimes felt a bit uncomfortable, a bit dangerous even.'

However, Mark was often at the Star. His band, Heroes, was one of the most popular acts at the pub, playing there three times a week.

'Because the band was popular, we had a full house. A full house being 100, 150 people. It was a great place to play.'

From the mid-1970s, the face of the Star was tattooed with band billboards and posters. This was the face of a rock pub. Yet the face didn't tell the full story of the Star. The pub had existed in one form or another since the mid-1800s, and it squatted on a large plot that stretched between Hunter and King streets, with a lane running along its side. The Star had developed into a gathering place for diverse cultures and subcultures. During the 1970s, at the pub's Hunter Street end in the front bar, seafarers would drink. In what was called the middle bar, members of the city's gay community would meet and watch the drag shows, with star performers such as Stella and Glenda. There had been other venues for members of LGBT+ communities in the city, and there would be more that would grow in popularity, notably Pipers in Newcastle West, but the Star remains legendary. Greg Jones, who visited the Star's middle bar from Sydney in the 1970s, recalls a perpetually packed place, where the performers danced on the bar.

'They could pick their way through the drinks', Greg says.

Beyond the walls of the Star, discrimination was common, and in daily life, discretion and care were usually required. But in the Star's middle bar, Greg recalls, the atmosphere was one of people being carefree. The bar wasn't just a refuge; it was a place to have fun.

However, near the end of the Star's life, the hotel was no longer a refuge. The publican made it clear he wanted the Star to go straight. Gay rights supporters from Newcastle and Sydney picketed the hotel, and many of the patrons and performers of the middle bar took their business along Hunter Street to Pipers.[5] That wound to the Star's reputation as a welcoming place to all was only an overture to the notoriety that would be imposed on it, courtesy of one wild night that began in the hotel's back bar.

This was where local bands played, packing the place.

'It was unbelievable', says Rick Pointon, whose band, Benny and the Jets, had a residency at the Star. 'I'm not comparing it to the Cavern in Liverpool, but it was one of those scenes that you couldn't explain. It was a freak of nature.'

At the Star, there were few distinctions. The stage tended to flow into the bar into the audience. Which meant the audience was frequently dancing on the bar and on the stage. The audience handed the band drinks, and the band could find itself in the midst of fights. However, according to Rick, there were few dramas.

'It was too crowded. You couldn't swing a cat. If someone mucked up, the crowd would shout, "Out, out, out", and the bouncers would get them out into the street.'

Bob Hudson, the writer of 'The Newcastle Song', performed at the Star regularly in the early 1970s as a member of the Electric Jug Band. He remembers a fight would break out occasionally.

'The bouncer had a tried-and-true technique for dealing with this', Bob recalls. 'He would wait until the fight died down and then chuck out the loser.'[6]

However, on Wednesday, 19 September 1979, drama spilled out of the Star, onto the streets of Newcastle, and then onto television screens around the world. It was the night of the Star Hotel riot.

It had begun as a wake. A week or so earlier, the licensees had been told by the pub's owner that the Star was to shut. The building was to be demolished.

In response, on the final evening, a large crowd crushed into the pub and the surrounding streets, apparently not in anger or sorrow, but for a party. Estimates for the numbers attending vary, but there were several thousand people in or around the pub. The band supplying the music for the final time was Heroes.

'It was absolutely electric', recalls Mark Tinson. 'You could cut the atmosphere with a knife, but it was an exciting, happy atmosphere. From the stage, we could see a sea of people.'

What the band didn't know is that the sea flowed outside, and it was about to be storm tossed. At 10 pm, the official closing time, police officers ordered the beer taps to be turned off and the band to stop playing. To grab the attention of Heroes' lead singer and guitarist, Pete de Jong, an officer shook the microphone stand and it hit the vocalist in the mouth, just as the band was finishing the song. As Mark remembers it, they were playing The Sweet's hit, 'Action', a title that would prove to be prophetic.

'It was a foolish move in retrospect', Mark says of the police's actions. 'There were only forty of them and thousands of partygoers.'

Pete told the crowd that 'the pigs have said you've got to go'. But the crowd didn't want to go. They didn't want the party to end. And they didn't want to lose their pub. As the Star's licensee Don Graham reflected, the young people felt as though they were having something taken from them.[7] Some were not going to let it go easily. At least, they were not going to let the Star simply fade away. It went out in a blaze of notoriety.

'We couldn't see much of what was happening', recalls Mark. 'We didn't realise anything was happening until a member of our road crew said "You should see what's happening outside!"'

What was happening outside was a rising wave of 'us and them'. Police vans pushing through the crowd were met with a rain of beer cans. Officers detained some of the projectile throwers, but others fought to free their fellow revellers.

Putting his faith in that old saying, 'music has charms to soothe a savage breast', Mark proposed the band return to the stage and play an encore. As Mark recalls, they played one of their own songs, one that would become associated with the riot, 'The Star And The Slaughter'. The guitar-driven song with the anthemic chorus had been written a year before the riot, so it had nothing to do with the hotel. However, the lyrics seemed to wrap themselves around the event, with talk of fighting in the streets and taking the town by storm to create a night people would remember.[8]

For a furious and frightening couple of hours, life seemed to imitate rock music. The mood outside the Star intensified when a group overturned a police car, with petrol spilling from its tank. In that moment, the Star's farewell seemed to swell into a riot. The petrol was ignited, and a couple of police vehicles were consumed in flames. When fire engines arrived, their hoses were used to not just douse the flames but to quell the rioters.

Gradually the crowd drifted into the night, the Star was closed, and a city was left to shake its head and wonder what happened. Civic leaders spoke of the damage done to Newcastle's image and reputation by the Star Hotel riot. The images of flying beer cans and burning police vehicles on the city streets stoked bemusement in faraway places, especially in Britain, where it was said that only in Australia would people riot over a pub closing. But closer to home, the riot fuelled shock, as Novocastrians went from wondering what happened to how it happened.

With the passing of time, and from his perspective on the stage, Mark reckons a host of reasons led to the riot. Some in the crowd felt angry the pub was closing. As there was no cover charge to see their favourite bands, it was a cheap night out for students and low-income earners. Many were there farewelling a venue that had meant a lot to them, and were not keen on complying when the police ordered them to go home. And it was about losing more than a pub. As one noted, the closure felt like the loss of your family.[9] Even accounting for all those reasons for the riot, Mark says, 'I don't think anybody expected it to happen'.

For Heroes, the hangover from that night was fame. Their name was emblazoned on the pub long after it closed, with the sign, 'Tonite: Heroes', pinned like an epitaph to the Star. And far and wide, they were known as the band who played in a riot.

'It was terrific for our career', says Mark. 'It did actually give us a national platform.'

Heroes were offered a recording contract – 'We got signed to that due to our notoriety from that event' – and they recorded a self-titled album. The opening sounds on the *Heroes* album is a cacophony of bottles smashing, people yelling and news reports from the Star Hotel riot, providing the introduction for the guitar onslaught of 'The Star And The Slaughter'. So from the very first song, Heroes acknowledged what they were known for.

The Star's last night – and the riot – became a point of recognition for many Novocastrians. Rick Pointon says the number of people who assert 'I was there!' is far greater than the estimated crowd.

'It's like people saying they were at Woodstock', he says, believing the crowd numbers are part of the myth of the Star.

Cold Chisel also immortalised the riot in its song, 'Star Hotel', but, contrary to another part of the myth, the band never played there.

While the rock music community lamented the loss of the venue, Mark Tinson reckons the riot left no lasting stain on Newcastle's reputation. What's more, being involved in teaching young musicians, Mark wonders how deeply ingrained that night is in the city's history.

'It's interesting to see, when you ask students, how often they *haven't* heard of the Star Hotel riot.

'It was just one of the dots on the history page.'

THE inner city of Newcastle could be a violent place.

One weekend night in the early 1980s, I was walking along Hunter Street with friends, heading to see a band, when another group of young men walked past. I suddenly felt my nose throbbing, as pain exploded behind my eyes. I was dazed and left stumbling on the footpath. I had been king hit.

My experience was hardly isolated. Newcastle had developed a dreadful reputation for alcohol-fuelled violence, especially late at night. As a result, in 2008, Newcastle became the guinea pig for tougher rules for alcohol service and hours of operation for venues.

What became known as the Newcastle Solution involved a ban on shots and cocktails late at night, and the imposition of earlier closing hours. No new patrons were allowed into a venue after 1 am, and everyone was out by 3.30 am.

It may not have been a 'solution', as the name indicated, but the lockout laws and restrictions led to a drop in reported assaults and hospital cases. Having had an effect in Newcastle, similar laws were applied to hotspots in other cities.

After 15 years, the laws were repealed and the restrictions lifted in Newcastle. As many argued, the city's drinking culture had changed. But so had pubs and the live music environment. Before the lockout laws bit into night-time Newcastle, there had been the crackdown on drink-driving, the rise of solo and duo acts instead of bands to reduce costs, and the impact of gaming machines. Then there was the ever deeper encroachment of the new urbanites. Thousands had moved into the new apartments built in town, but many didn't want to live beside venues thumping with rock music. In response to complaints, more and more venues had stopped booking live bands. And all the while, developers were looking for more sites, bringing more residents back into the city – but not to rock.

In 2023, the Cambridge Hotel, which was one of the last bastions of live music along Hunter Street and the proving ground for a battalion of Newcastle bands, including a young trio called Silverchair, was closed to make way for another residential development. The echoes of the glory days of pub rock seemed to be fading into nothingness, and with them, part of the character of Newcastle was going too.

The council is aware of the importance of entertainment in Newcastle. The city has the second largest night-time economy in the state, and to help invigorate the hospitality and entertainment sector, it has introduced a Newcastle After Dark strategy. Yet to those who once ruled the city when the sun set, it is as though the lights have been turned off.

'It's dead', Rick Pointon says of the inner-city band scene. 'It's more like a retirement village in there now.'

For the teenage Mark Tinson, Hunter Street, before it became his workplace, offered a rite of passage towards what, and who, he would be. He would catch the train from his home in Maitland then walk from one end of Hunter Street to the other, dropping into the music and record shops dotted along the way. Apart from the Muso's Corner instrument store, just off Hunter Street in Newcastle West, Mark could now walk that teenage pilgrim trail without stopping. As he says, 'It's sad'.

Grant Walmsley says he avoids Hunter Street 'like the plague'. On some weeknights, it seems everyone shares Grant's view; it looks as though plague and pestilence have torn along the street, ridding it of signs of life.

'I gave up on Hunter Street that long ago', Grant says.

These three alumni of the city's pub rock scene believe great musicians will continue to come through in Newcastle. But unlike in their day, when they had to have ambition to leave, there is little incentive to stay.

As to whether Newcastle can be a rock city again, no-one has an answer.

'Who knows?' says Rick. 'I can't see it, because I don't think people will be able to open venues in this situation. Some will keep going, and that's great. But where they were once on every corner, it won't be as common, or as often.'

WHILE Newcastle's pubs were renowned for being sticky-carpeted nurseries for rock bands, in a room at the back of the Clarendon Hotel in Hunter Street in the early 1980s, what took shape was a phenomenon that joyously defied the reputation of 'Steel City', the times, and all expectations. It was called the Castanet Club.

This was not so much a band as a collective, and what the Castanet Club staged was not so much a concert as a happening.

The Castanet Club's act was an amalgam of so much that had gone before in popular culture, from vaudeville and Las Vegas singers to television game shows, yet it was unlike anything that had been seen before, especially in Newcastle.

That this surreal and absurdist cabaret cavorted its way through a city pub only added to the joy of the Castanet Club. This was a subversive cultural revolution in plain sight.

In a city with a reputation for toughness, the Castanet Club felt as much like liberation as entertainment. The Castanets' happy and funny, frequently chaotic and proudly daggy performances and image led to ever-growing queues outside the back of the Clarendon. People wanted to be part of this happening, and they wanted to find themselves and be themselves – whatever that meant – in this most unNewcastle of cultural happenings in the heart of Newcastle.

Like its act, the membership of the Castanet Club was elastic and subject to change. Actually, such was the interaction, and the absence of walls, between the performers and the audience that everyone who attended effectively became a member of the Castanet Club. However, there were some core performers, conjuring characters who were simultaneously outrageous and painfully familiar.

Among them was Bowling Man, who was like an embarrassing uncle; the sad comedian Johnny Goodman; the take-no-prisoners older woman Shirley Purvis; Douggie the roadie, who, with his mullet and flanno shirt, looked like he'd just walked in off Hunter Street; and a singer whose voice was even smoother than his velvet suit, Lance Norton.

The crooner was brought to life by singer and actor Glenn Butcher. The Castanet Club may have looked and sounded like a reaction to life in early 1980s Newcastle, but Glenn says the ensemble happened because of Newcastle.

Many of the members found each other and cooked up ideas as students at the University of Newcastle, then a sprawling campus on the fringe of the city.

As Glenn says, 'Everybody brought their own ingredients to it. It was a heady cocktail'.

Newcastle, Glenn says, was the perfect size to allow The Castanet Club to come into being. The city was big enough to attract creatives, particularly to the university, but small enough for them to find each other. And the city was cheap, compared with life in Sydney. They could afford to chase their dreams and turn their ideas into an act.

'Looking back, they were happy times', says Glenn. 'None of us had money but it was fantastic. They were times of plenty.'

The Castanets made Newcastle feel like part of the wider world. Actually, one of their earlier initiatives involved hiring a bus, packing it with punters, and driving around Newcastle, using the city as a stage, all the while pretending it was a world tour. The Castanet Club did venture out into the world, taking its act into pubs, clubs and theatres, to the Adelaide Festival and onto a triumphant run at the Edinburgh Fringe Festival.

The Castanet Club called it a day in 1991, but its members continued to entertain and be part of Australian popular culture, performing in everything from films and TV sketch comedies to television game shows.

'It took us out of Newcastle ... and set us up for life', Glenn says.

Whether The Castanet Club was a product of Newcastle as it was then and something similar couldn't happen now, Glenn isn't sure. Although he is fairly certain the club the Castanets created out the back of the Clarendon couldn't happen now.

'You would be shut down. You couldn't have 200 people in a 100-person venue. And the parachute we had hanging from the ceiling! I don't think you'd get away with it any more.'

However, if a bunch of creative people get together, anything can happen. As The Castanet Club showed, despite the times and what people think of a place, something magical can happen.

For those seeking culture along Hunter Street in a venue other than a pub, there has been, since 1929, the Civic Theatre. This building is like some spell conjured along the street, an elaborate Georgian Revival confection, as dramatic and transformative as the performances that have been staged in its space. And for the best part of a century, just about everything has been staged at the Civic, from orchestras and rock bands to plays and musicals. Inside, the drama and symphonic splendour are not confined to what happens on the stage. The theatre's interior is an opera in architecture. The walls and the domed ceiling sing in a Spanish Baroque style, while statues and a delicately painted frieze demand your attention. A lot of the interior painting work was done by a First World War veteran and gifted artist, Emlyn Britton Dickson or, as he was better known, Ernie Dickson. Ernie had returned from Gallipoli and the Western Front with sketchbooks full of images, physical wounds, and an alcohol problem. There were stories of Dickson not being allowed off the scaffold while he was painting the Civic Theatre's interior, in case he slipped away for a drink. Life became more precarious for Ernie, but art allowed him to keep on living in the Newcastle and Lake Macquarie area. He put a roof over his head by painting gentle, and often exotic, landscapes on the interior walls of people's homes in return for accommodation in a back shed or stable. So people lived with an Ernie Dickson artwork, while the artist himself often lived out the back. Whenever I'm in the Civic Theatre, I think about Ernie. Those who knew him reckoned he painted to escape all he had experienced, trying to paint his way to happiness. In turn, his art, which is part of the joy of seeing a performance in the Civic Theatre, makes the rest of us happier. Sitting in the Civic Theatre and looking around at the ornate interior, it is hard to believe you're in Newcastle. However, if you haven't sat in the Civic Theatre, you are yet to experience something that is quintessentially Newcastle.

Neighbouring the entrance to the theatre is a much smaller, less ornate opening to another wonderland: the Civic Playhouse.

In this intimate space, the community has been able to peer into a magic mirror since 1979. Newcastle life has inspired theatrical art. We've seen our stories, our people, and elements of the city's life and our lives on the Playhouse stage. We have seen ourselves emerging from the darkness and stepping into the light. Plays about the Star Hotel riot, the 1929 Rothbury miners' riot, the 1989 earthquake and the rise of the BHP steelworks were among the historic events and landmarks that have inspired locally produced plays. These stories were often written by local playwrights, and the words were fleshed out by local actors.

What's more, the Civic Playhouse was home to our own professional theatre company, the first in regional Australia. The Hunter Valley Theatre Company (HVTC) was established in 1976, inhabiting different stages before the Civic Playhouse took shape.

As well as enacting our stories, the Civic Playhouse and the HVTC helped launch careers. Names that appeared on HVTC production notes became faces and voices known by the nation. One of those names is Jonathan Biggins.

Never mind being a 'triple threat', Jonathan is an actor, comedian, director, writer and singer. His face has appeared regularly on the stage and screen, to the point he is one of those 'Oh, I know him!' performers.

And at times, his face and voice have been barely recognisable as he inhabits other people, notably the public figures featured in the acclaimed Wharf Revue productions that Jonathan helped devise, and his portrayal of former prime minister Paul Keating in the stage comedy, *The Gospel According to Paul*. To paraphrase what Paul Keating said about the two main ingredients for leadership, Jonathan Biggins' career has been about imagination and courage. And it began in Newcastle.

Jonathan grew up in an artistic household in Cooks Hill, but close enough to the steelworks to see the plumes, reminding him what city he was in. As a boy, he was a member of the Christ Church Cathedral choir and attended the Young People's Theatre (YPT) in Hamilton, a magnet for creative youngsters. The YPT was an escape in an industrial city, yet the city provided the incentive and the grit for a creative person to chase their ideas.

'I think that was one of the beauties of Newcastle, you could do creative things, because no-one expected you to', says Jonathan. 'The attitude of "have a go, see what happens".

'Towns like Newcastle – and probably it's even still the case now – give you a greater chance to try your hand at something. It doesn't matter so much if it works or fails as it does in the bigger centres. That's the whole way we did things.'

The 'have a go' ethos helped bring about the Hunter Valley Theatre Company (HVTC). Jonathan acted in its productions as a teenager before joining the company full-time in 1981.

'When the HVTC started, that was a theatrical education you can't get any more', he says. 'You very quickly learnt a lot of professional skills, the value of hard work and collaborative creativity.'

Everyone did a bit of everything, giving shape to big visions on a small stage that could easily feel crowded. One night, Jonathan recalls, three Korean sailors wandered onto the Playhouse stage, apparently thinking it was a pub, and sat on the prop barrels. Confusion ensued, for the performers, the audience, and the seafarers. Yet the occasional stage invader wasn't the only risk with the Playhouse.

'It was always going to be marginal whether an auditorium that size could work commercially, but it kind of did,' reflects Jonathan. 'But through sheer hard work.'

One of the HVTC's early productions was *A Happy and Holy Occasion*, a coming-of-age story set in the Newcastle industrial suburb of Mayfield, written by a local teacher, John O'Donoghue.

In 2017, John told me he became aware of the importance of regional theatre, for telling the stories of communities to communities for communities, while living and working in Britain in the late 1950s. He reasoned the same could, and should, be done in Newcastle.

In the early 1980s, John wrote a play about a giant of BHP, the steel company's long-time boss, Essington Lewis. Or, as Jonathan Biggins describes it, 'a play about us'. John O'Donoghue's play, *Essington Lewis: I Am Work* turned into a staple of Australian theatre. It has been produced many times, transplanting Newcastle onto stages far and wide.

'Looking back on it, I was very conscious I was writing a play about Newcastle in Newcastle', John reflected. 'People would have said to me, "You can't do that in Newcastle". It could be done, and we did pretty well.'[10]

John, who died in 2022, was being modest. However, the play did not immediately find an audience. Jonathan Biggins was in the original production and remembers it wasn't until Australia's most famous playwright, David Williamson, saw *Essington Lewis: I Am Work* and praised it in the newspaper that the Playhouse filled up.

'We still needed the prophet from somewhere else to tell us what we were missing', Jonathan says. 'But that was the high point of the HVTC, a local playwright, local people, and it worked and showed people we were capable of doing it.'

The play not only opened Novocastrians' eyes. When *Essington Lewis: I Am Work* toured, it confronted people's preconceptions of Newcastle, showing the city could produce more than steel.

'We've been honing our craft and creating in a place where people don't imagine you do, but you do', Jonathan says.

While its members were treading the boards and turning heads, the HVTC was constantly tip-toeing across a financial tightrope. After threatening to topple a couple of times, the company effectively folded in the mid-1990s. The staircase leading to the theatre in the Civic Playhouse is like one long epitaph for the HVTC, for the walls are lined with fading posters from the company's productions, reminding us of what we have lost, and what we sorely miss. If it were a play, it would be a tragedy. Changes to government funding and, as Jonathan Biggins sees it, modern economic realities have made it very difficult for a regional theatre company to survive.

'We were just lucky to be there at a time when the stars aligned and we were able to take advantage of it. It's a shame people don't have that now.'

However, as he points out, it is not all bleak. He cites the success of touring productions pulling large audiences into the Civic Theatre, encouraging promoters to view Newcastle as a strong market. Smaller independent companies stage productions in the Civic Playhouse and even in the main theatre, the Young People's Theatre continues to nurture the next generation of creatives, and there are community theatres filling spaces with stories and wonder.

'There's still a scene, and that tradition of "make it yourself because no one else is going to make it for you", that is still there', Jonathan argues.

'We weren't being given these opportunities, we created them. We were filling the vacuum and that's a great incentive. You just need to get enough like-minded people to fill it. If there's a sense of nothing, something will grow.'

All the world's been a stage for Jonathan Biggins. But his world, as he knows it, was born on the tiny stage in the Civic Playhouse.

'You couldn't overestimate the importance of it, not just in the friendships, but my whole work ethic, what theatre can be and should be', Jonathan says. 'I've really survived a lot by creating my own work. You have to go out there and hustle. And Newcastle is a place, when we were growing up, you had to create your own fun, with any creative enterprise. I think you appreciate it more and you're better at it when it's not fed to you with a spoon.

'It's much better when you've got to kick against something and earn it, and growing up in Newcastle you can safely say you have to earn it. And that's guided me through my career.'

NEWCASTLE is only lightly populated with statues dedicated to its citizens. It is not that Newcastle hasn't produced some extraordinary individuals. What's more, the community is proud of those who have achieved great feats or done wonderful things. It is just that Novocastrians generally don't like placing themselves on pedestals, and they are reluctant to do it to others.

However, along Hunter Street, opposite the Civic Theatre and Civic Playhouse, is the bronze statue of the person who helped bring live theatre into those spaces: Joy Cummings.

Joy was Lord Mayor of Newcastle for nine years from 1974. She was Australia's first female lord mayor. And she is the first Newcastle woman to be immortalised in bronze.

The statue of Joy Cummings was unveiled in 2019, 16 years after she died. Her eldest daughter, Margaret Badger, reckons her mother would have been bemused by seeing her image cast in bronze and presiding over Newcastle's main street.

'I don't know what she'd make of it', Margaret says.

'Mum would have said, "Why not do a monument to the Awabakal people?" or something like that.'

Yet Joy's connection to local First Nations communities is cast in the statue, for she is holding a furled Aboriginal flag. Joy was the first lord mayor in the country to raise the Aboriginal flag above a city hall.

Joy was born in Sydney and moved to Newcastle as a teenager with her family, living in Newcastle East. Her first impressions of her new home were far from rosy. Everything seemed to be either chuffing out soot and grit or covered in soot and grit.

'She was really disappointed', says Margaret. 'Then she walked down to the beach and to the harbour, and she thought she was in heaven.'

After marrying a Coalfields man, Ray Cummings, just after the Second World War, Joy set up home in the industrial suburb of Mayfield, raising four children.

'By then she loved it', Margaret says of her mother's life in Newcastle. 'She even taught us to love The BHP. "There's the whistle, all the men will be knocking off, and coming home, and the next ones will be going in." We'd hear that whistle three times a day.'

As the lord mayor, Joy was praised for making Newcastle a better place. However, it was her concern the city was about to be made a lesser place that pushed her into local government. Newcastle council intended to cut down a line of old Moreton Bay fig trees in Islington, and Joy joined the push to save them. Only she fought to protect the trees from the inside, being elected to the council in 1968. The trees still stand along Maitland Road, their branches like a reassuring hug for those in the vehicles below. Yet, as an alderman, Joy lost the battle to save a section of Birdwood Park in the west end of the CBD, as trees were felled for road widening. She told her children she was ashamed of that outcome. And she foresaw what was coming to that part of town.

'She used to say the West End would be the high-rise area of Newcastle one day and there were few enough open spaces.'

When she was the lord mayor, Joy had a string of victories for the environment, for those who live in Newcastle, and for the power of transformation. Perhaps her proudest environmental legacy was her involvement in creating the foreshore park on former industrial land beside the harbour in the East End, a stone's throw from where she grew up and first saw the grime coming from the Zaara Street Power Station and railway yards. In a way, the park and the promenade on its edge are her statue. The popular waterfront path is named the Joy Cummings Promenade.

'She believed there was a lot that could be done to improve and beautify Newcastle', says Margaret. 'She didn't think being an industrial city ran against being beautiful.'

Having helped revive the Civic Theatre for live performances and encouraged the creation of the Civic Playhouse, Joy did more than provide a stage for actors. She fed them. With City Hall neighbouring the theatres, Joy would head over after council meetings with trays of leftover food for the thespians.

Joy's eldest daughter was one of those thespians. Margaret acted for a year with Hunter Valley Theatre Company. And one of Joy's granddaughters, Sarah Wynter, would pursue a career in acting, which would take her from Newcastle to Hollywood. She has starred in films and TV series, including *The 6th Day*, with Arnold Schwarzenegger and *24*, opposite Kiefer Sutherland.

Sarah lives and works half a world away from Newcastle, but the image, the influence and the character of Joy continue to guide her.

'My grandmother's portrait hangs proudly in my dining room', Sarah has written from the US. 'I have been telling stories about Grandma Joy to my three teenage sons since they were born. Her achievements and place in history inspire awe in them.

'She was, and remains, the strongest, most beautiful, fiercely loyal woman I will ever know. Her light shone bright over the Steel City, and her service to Newcastle has left an indelible mark.

'Her love for her family I will carry forever.'

In her time as Newcastle's civic leader, Joy Cummings notched up a string of firsts. But that wasn't important to her, according to Margaret Badger; not even being Australia's first female lord mayor.

'It didn't mean much to her', Margaret says. 'Other people were more impressed by it, saying she paved the way for women to be successful in the political arena.'

Margaret reckons her mother's greatest achievement was the way in which she connected with people. For her, this was a people's council, and, as lord mayor, Joy didn't preside over them; she was one of them.

Joy Cumming's time as lord mayor ended because of ill health. She had a stroke in 1984, soon after turning the first sod of soil at the foreshore park project. Four years later, when Queen Elizabeth II officially opened the park during Australia's bicentennial commemorations, Joy was sitting in the audience. They had met before, when Joy was lord mayor, not that she expected the monarch to remember her. However, as she walked past, the queen stopped and talked with Joy. After all, Joy Cummings was someone you didn't forget.

Newcastle hasn't forgotten her. What's more, the city doesn't need the statue to remind them what she did for the community. A walk along the foreshore, sitting in the Civic Playhouse, driving past the fig trees in Islington; the activities that are part of our lives are, in no small part, thanks to Joy Cummings encouraging Newcastle to realise what it could do – 'You can do anything' – and what it should have.

If she could see the city now, Joy would have mixed feelings, her eldest daughter reckons. Joy would have been saddened by the sight of multi-storey developments creeping closer to Newcastle East than she had imagined. She would have been disappointed to see so much of the harbour foreshore given over to private housing. She would have also been disappointed, but not surprised, by the demise of Newcastle Mall, which she had supported to slow the draining away of shoppers to the suburbs. But what wouldn't have changed for Joy, according to Margaret, is her love for Newcastle, and her belief in its future.

'She always thought it would have a future', says Margaret, 'no matter how the industrial side changed.'

EVEN though Newcastle was founded as a place of punishment, the settlement was a nursery for creativity. Perhaps that tough birth helped create that nursery.

In the ragged ranks of convicts were a few artists, including Joseph Lycett and Richard Browne, and among those guarding them were amateur painters. Occasionally they collaborated. Thomas Skottowe, the penal settlement's commandant from 1811 to 1814, turned his observations of, and curiosity about, his surroundings into words, writing a manuscript titled *Select Specimens of Nature of the Birds, Animals &c &c of New South Wales*. The manuscript was illustrated by Richard Browne. A later commandant, Captain James Wallis, was an enthusiastic painter, depicting scenes around the settlement. Wallis encouraged Lycett as an artist and worked with him on the plans for the first Christ Church. Wallis also patronised and worked with other convicts, as he indicated in a letter he wrote from Newcastle. The convict artists most likely helped Wallis with his own side project, a book of engravings depicting the scenery of the colony, which was published after he returned to England in 1820. Writer and curator Elizabeth Ellis, who has researched this period in Newcastle, noted that what Wallis had established in the penal outpost was a small informal art academy. She referred to it as the 'Newcastle academy'.[11]

The commandant patron and members of his 'academy' may well have played a part in producing an extraordinary record of the profusion of natural life in New South Wales and, whether by design or default, the remarkable store of artistic talent in Newcastle. James Wallis is believed to be behind the construction of a wooden chest as a gift for Governor Lachlan Macquarie and his wife, Elizabeth, in 1818. The result, known as the Macquarie collector's chest, is an assemblage of Hunter timber, including cedar and Australian rosewood, of drawers and hidden compartments containing hundreds of specimens of local fauna, flora and shells, carefully preserved and meticulously laid out in patterned brilliance, and of art believed to have been created in, and showing off, the Newcastle area. The chest contains a series of beautifully painted panels depicting Newcastle and Lake Macquarie. The paintings are believed to be the work of Joseph Lycett. Art may be the expression of a free mind, but the earliest colonial images from Newcastle are largely from the hands of those shackled to the penal system.

Art continued to sprout in unlikely places in Newcastle. In 1829, a businessman and naturalist, Alexander Walker Scott, took up a grant on one of the low-lying islands strung through the Hunter estuary. In the rich, damp earth on Ash Island, Scott established a renowned orchard. For his daughters, Harriet and Helena, the island was a muse and a studio, offering ceaseless subjects to paint and draw, from the tiniest insects to the blooms and leaves of plants. The Scott sisters' detailed and meticulous depictions of nature were used to illustrate books, including their father's study of butterflies and moths, titled *Australia's Lepidoptera and Their Transformations*. Through the years, the environment the sisters had once explored and wandered, depicted and loved was denuded by farming and industry. At least Ash Island still existed. Other Hunter estuary islands had been subsumed and clumped into the Kooragang heavy industrial precinct, as the inexorable tide of change crept up the river from the 1950s. In 1993, the environment of Ash Island was to be regenerated as part of the Kooragang Wetland Rehabilitation Project. The program involved planting thousands of trees and reinstating vegetation on the island. In helping to determine what to plant, the organisers and volunteers consulted the notes and images of the Scott sisters. Art was pivotal in bringing life back to the environment.

Closer to the city's heart, two of Australia's greatest artists were born. To the south of Civic Park is Cooks Hill, which is now one of the city's most desirable suburbs, with its historic cottages and terraces, tree-lined streets, and sprinkling of cafés and art galleries. Yet in the 1800s and early 20th century, this was a working-class suburb, and its homes were crowded with people trying to make do. While it was called Cooks Hill, the suburb was barely higher than the swampy ground that bordered it to the west. And what passed for a hill was precarious, comprising spare and sandy soil. So it could well have been Cooks Sandhill. Coal rail lines cut through the suburb, and industrial businesses were dotted through the area, including William Arnott's biscuit factory, which was established in the 1870s. Prior to that, he had a bakery in Hunter Street. Arnott's biscuits were popular among the seafaring community, so supplies were loaded onto the ships in port. By the end of the century, the name Arnott's would flow not just out to sea on ships but would be on everyone's lips around the nation. For a time, Arnott and his family lived in a large, two-storey home at Cooks Hill, and if he were to stand on his verandah, William would have been within sniffing distance of his biscuit factory. While the factory is long gone, the house, Leslieville, remains a landmark.

Just as Arnott was becoming a household name, a name that would become synonymous with 20th-century Australian art – Dobell – was coming into being. William Dobell was born at Cooks Hill in 1899, the youngest son of a bricklayer who helped build one of the suburb's finest buildings, St Andrews Church. While he drew at home, young Bill harboured desires to be a musician, and took piano lessons at a home in Laman Street. Many years later, the home of his piano teacher would be demolished to make way for Newcastle's first dedicated public art gallery, which, since its opening in 1977, has frequently exhibited Dobell's works. Dobell made his way out of Newcastle as a young man. He first lived and worked in Sydney. Then he moved to London to study and paint for almost a decade before returning to Australia and setting up a home and studio in Sydney, quietly building a career. Then, through just one painting, he was ambushed by fame. The public eye fixed upon both him and his art due to the furore surrounding his portrait of friend and fellow artist Joshua Smith, which won the 1943 Archibald Prize. The painting was at the centre of a sensational court case, as two other artists contested Dobell's work was a caricature, not a portrait, and therefore should not have won the prize. Dobell's painting was judged to be a portrait. But through it all, Dobell felt both he and his art were being judged and scrutinised, critiqued and torn apart, and it took a terrible toll on his health and self-confidence. To escape the controversy and his own celebrity, he moved to the family's weekender at Wangi Wangi, on the western side of Lake Macquarie, where he lived and painted until his death in 1970. However, Dobell used his celebrity to help his hometown. At the height of his fame in the mid-1940s, the artist lent his reticent voice to call for the long-delayed cultural centre to be built on the southern side of Civic Park, just a couple of blocks from where he grew up. As he met with city leaders, Dobell noted how 'wonderfully improved' Newcastle was, and he forecast it would become a beautiful city. But part of that beauty required the community to have its own cultural facilities and character.

'The creative power is here, and I am sure the need is felt', Dobell was reported as saying, declaring he would do all he could to help 'my city'.[12]

Despite the presence of Dobell's artistic power, it was not until 1957 that the cultural centre was officially opened, giving Newcastle's creatives a hub.

Just a month before Dobell died, Newcastle City Art Gallery, which was still housed in the cultural centre, staged an exhibition of the artist's recent works. By then, he was not only Sir William Dobell, but in the eyes of the gallery director at the time, David Thomas, the artist was 'God'.[13] The exhibition was a huge success. Dobell may have been the best-known artist in the land, whose works attracted big prices and even bigger interest, but he didn't want to be seen as 'God'. To those who knew him, he was 'Bill', not 'Sir William'. In Wangi Wangi, he drank at the pub with the local workers each afternoon. He enjoyed their company but he also wanted to be seen as one of the blokes. He had a talent that took him a long way and set him apart, but he worked constantly at not standing out or looking different. The man who was lauded and awarded for his ability to use a paintbrush as a scalpel, cutting through to the soul of a person in his portraits, was vague and evasive about his own life. In some ways, Dobell's public face was his greatest creation. It gave next to nothing away. To the end, he was, in many respects, a Cooks Hill boy, a product of his upbringing. He fitted in. But the sheer brilliance of his portraiture has ensured that Sir William Dobell continues to stand out.

Just a few streets from where Dobell grew up was the boyhood home of John Olsen. Born in 1928, John created art that brimmed with his personality. As a result, his paintings are not just wonderful landscapes, they throb and glow with ebullience and a hunger for life. Somehow John squeezed the light and heat of the sun, and his own ceaseless energy, into his paintings. His art makes you squint and smile. His paintings are vehicles of energy transference. Yet the world he was born into was about to tumble into the uncertainty of the Great Depression.

'They were very bad years', John told me in 2016, when I interviewed him for the catalogue essay of a major exhibition, *John Olsen: The city's son*, at Newcastle Art Gallery. 'Whilst my father had a job [with a clothing company in Hunter Street], there'd be scarcely a day where some man didn't come and ask to do some gardening or chop some wood.'

The sounds of an industrial city labouring became part of the little boy's world.

'I can remember clearly the shunting coal trains, "ch-ch-ch!"' he said.

Although John moved to Sydney as a boy, his imagination continually returned to Newcastle. Flowing into his work are John's memories of the harbour, of the great industrial sculpture of the steelworks, and of the Hunter River. But John didn't rely on memories alone; he would visit Newcastle, sketching harbour life or flying in a helicopter to trace the sinuous brown line of the river. He had not lived in Newcastle for many years, but he seemed to feel at home here. You can see it in his art.

'The sense of place is the procreator of a work of art', John told me.

When I spoke with John, he had just finished a major work, *King Sun and the Hunter*, that was to be unveiled at his exhibition in Newcastle. The river wended its way across the canvas, carrying John's impressions and emotions about 'home'. He called Newcastle a 'soul city'.

'To be a Novocastrian is an identity, and for those who live in Newcastle, it means something to them', John said. 'They know they're different – "Don't come your Sydney tricks here!"'

As John observed, 'for Novocastrians, identity is important. There's a kind of a stubborn will about it. They see themselves as being different.

'While ever they've got that, they've got substance. They don't belong in that Sydney myth.

'The Novocastrian ethic is "No bullshit!"' he says.[14]

Which is a summation of John Olsen's art, really. True feeling. No bullshit. Truly Novocastrian.

ON the corner of Laman Street and Hunnifords Lane, just a few minutes' walk from the childhood homes of William Dobell and John Olsen, is a brick building that began life in the late 1870s as a row of four terrace houses.

Yet it is best remembered as being the home of art in Newcastle in the second half of the 20th century. For this was von Bertouch Galleries, an institution almost as renowned and beloved as its owner.

Anne von Bertouch was a former teacher, author and passionate art collector, who had begun what is believed to be Australia's first commercial gallery outside a capital city. When Anne opened the gallery in a terrace house in Laman Street in 1963, the inaugural show was a statement in paint that Newcastle was more than an industrial city; it featured the works of eight local artists, including Dobell and Olsen. Anne's home and gallery were across the road from the four terrace houses. Which meant she had an unimpeded view of history rotting.

'By the late 1960s they were derelict, stripped of all dignity, beginning to give way at the ends and about to be demolished to make way for a nine-storey block of flats', Anne wrote in her biography of the houses, *What Was It? Before it was a gallery*.[15]

Anne was determined to save the terrace houses. She saw that mission as a way of saving herself as well. At the time, Anne was recovering from serious injuries sustained in a car crash. To affirm that this row of historic houses could be given a new lease on life galvanised Anne's own will to live.

'If it could be saved I too might survive and all might yet be well', she wrote in her book.[16]

Anne convinced the developer-owner to sell her Hunniford Terrace, as the building was known, and so began a five-year project to restore the houses and reshape them into her home and new gallery.

The building had an air of a mysterious past about it. As she was restoring the building, Anne would hear passers-by guessing or declaring what it had been. A monastery or a chapel. An inn. A bond store. Stables perhaps. All this speculation had given Anne the title for her book about Hunniford Terrace and the journey to save it. What's more, Anne gave the building – and Newcastle – an artistic hub unlike anything the city had ever seen. Not only did the big names of Australian art exhibit here, but Anne nurtured local creatives. So many of those local artists she exhibited continue to create and bring colour to the city. Anne welcomed not just artists but everyone and anyone through the arched entry to the gallery. Even a gormless young man, a boy really, who had lent his bike against her wall and peered through the entry.

Growing up in the suburb of Merewether Heights, I had a comfortable life, for which I remain grateful, but the subdivision, which colonised a coastal gum forest in the 1960s, felt too new and samey for my liking. I was in love with history and old things. The past is a foreign country, according to English novelist LP Hartley. However, I had only the dreams but not the means to get to that foreign country. So in order to experience the past, I would pedal to Cooks Hill, a journey of about 15 minutes. I would first visit the public library on the ground floor of the Cultural Centre, smelling the hall of books as if I could inhale learning, before heading into the Newcastle Region Art Gallery next door. I would stand in front of Brett Whiteley's sun-burnished landscape *Summer at Carcoar* and Dobell's *Portrait of a Strapper*, its subject with an elongated face and doleful eyes like a thoroughbred, and wonder how those artists did it. I'd slowly ride along the streets, their skin welted by the roots of the massive, and seemingly ancient, figs pushing through the bitumen, and I'd look at the rows of historic terrace houses. Finally, I would stop at von Bertouch Galleries and wonder, as so many others had done, what this place once was. To me, it looked medieval, like a castle, with its ornate iron gate guarding the entry. The gate was a work of art by sculptor Marcus Skipper, who had been commissioned by Anne. The corridor seemed to sop up the light, so it was hard to make out what the central courtyard was like. That lack of light only illuminated my imagination as to what this gallery-castle was like inside. I dared not cross the threshold, walk along the undulating sea of bricks that formed the corridor floor, and enter the gallery. That is, until the day I met Anne.

As usual, I had placed my bike against the wall and was standing in the entrance, when this lady emerged out of a side door and stood in the half light. I half expected her to tell me to get my bike off her building. Instead, what Anne said changed part of my life.

'Oh, hello. Are you going to come in?'

I entered the gallery. I wasn't just enveloped by the past restored but was in the midst of an artistic wonderland. I had found my place in the world. Or, at least, in the city. Off the main courtyard were little rooms and pavilions filled with paintings. It wasn't a castle but a picture palace. In the courtyard itself was a long wooden table and bench seats, where Anne would place food and drinks, encouraging visitors to sit and talk. As her close friend and long-time gallery manager, Gael Davies, told me, this place was almost like a community centre. Everyone was welcome.

Anne thought everyone should be more than welcome to view art. They should be able to afford to own it. She devised an annual exhibition called *Collector's Choice*, where the works of well-known artists, such as John Coburn, Nora Heysen and Arthur Boyd, were available at vastly reduced prices. The exhibition turned into a street party, as people queued outside, sharing food and wine, laughter and stories. The queues grew, and so did the reputation of *Collector's Choice*. Some slept in their cars for up to a week to secure the work they wanted, and simply to be part of the event. The exhibition that fostered a street party blossomed into a Newcastle institution. Anne von Bertouch's vision ensured people didn't just collect art but new friends. Anne made Newcastle not just a more cultural place but a better place.

Unbeknown to me, another young man was spending time in Cooks Hill as part of his own journey to find out who he was and where he was headed. His name is Nick Mitzevich, now Director of the National Gallery of Art in Canberra. Although for Nick, growing up on a property at Abermain in the Coalfields, his journey into town was not just about destiny and identity, but also one of necessity.

'I lived in the Hunter Valley, so Newcastle was the place you came to for important things', Nick explains. 'It was the place you came to shop, and to go to hospital. It was the place you came to for special things. When I was a teenager, I looked to Newcastle to go to the art gallery, I went to see movies in King Street, and I decided to study there.

'I remember the gallery was where I saw things that were in art books. *Summer at Carcoar. Portrait of a Strapper*. I felt like I was walking into important things there, it felt like art history.

'I can still remember today where all the pictures were hung.

'It wasn't until I started studying at uni that I heard the cliché that Newcastle wasn't a place renowned for art. That cliché never touched the sides for me. I think people like to categorise things. I think it was easy to say Newcastle was a city of sportsmen and steel. It was never my experience that that was it. I thought it was a lazy cliché that maybe wasn't relevant.'

As part of his journey away from clichés and into the embrace of art, Nick also wandered along Laman Street to von Bertouch Galleries. Yet it wasn't at the gallery where Nick had met Anne. He was first drawn into her orbit at the University of Newcastle, where he was an art student. Anne was attending the students' end-of-year exhibition.

'She walked in, and I thought, "Who is this eccentric, crazy woman!?"' recalls Nick. 'She was unlike anyone else. She was more eccentric and outrageous than the art students. I was drawn to her very quickly. She was quite comfortable in who she was.'

Anne's gallery was part of Nick's art education. Anne herself was integral to Nick's education in life, encouraging him to be who he is and to become what he wanted to be.

'Anne created an atmosphere where you could meet people', Nick says. 'Every time I went there, I always met someone interesting.

'She had this great conviction about culture, the environment and heritage, and community, and I loved seeing someone with such confidence about those matters. People were encouraged by [it].'

Just as Anne had done, Nick converted an inner-city building into a commercial art gallery in the late 1990s. In his own gallery conversion, Nick subverted the notion of Newcastle being a city where sport ruled by reimagining a former squash court complex.

After a few years running his business, Nick moved across the road, having been appointed Director of Newcastle Art Gallery. A significant early change was removing the thick curtains that shrouded the gallery windows, as though he was inviting not just the light but the community in. The art gallery and Newcastle could see each other and realise they were part of each other. He would host morning teas there, and one of his first guests was Anne von Bertouch.

'When you work within the cultural sphere of things', Nick says, 'it's good to have people around you contributing to it'.

Among those who worked with Nick was then Lord Mayor John Tate and his wife, Cathy. The trio were at the helm of a push to redevelop and extend the gallery, so that there was more room for art, and for the community. A design for a new gallery was proposed. After Nick moved on in 2007, a new plan for the gallery's redevelopment was decided upon. But that plan sat on the paper.

Instead, the city continued debating what sort of redevelopment it wanted, and if it wanted – or needed – a bigger gallery at all. Funding avenues dried up, and so did enthusiasm and belief in the project. The only thing that was building around the gallery was uncertainty it would ever be expanded. For a time, the council shelved the project. The vast majority of the 7000 items in the largest public art collection in regional Australia would remain out of sight, and a bigger Newcastle Art Gallery that reflected a growing and changing city would remain out of mind. Newcastle seemed determined to deny its rich cultural character and instead prove correct those who embraced the misconception that the city was full of philistines who had no interest in art, let alone any desire to have a larger gallery.

This was hardly the first time Newcastle had let time and opportunity slip through its fingers when it came to art. William Bowmore was a music and Latin teacher who arrived in Newcastle just before the Second World War. However, it was visual art for which Bill would become renowned. In the years after the war, he began amassing an extensive art collection, from Rodin sculptures and African masks to paintings by European masters. Bill Bowmore owned not just one of the most diverse private collections in Australia, but one of the most valuable. He had a beautiful house on The Hill overlooking the city, but what his home contained was worth much, much more. I recall as a boy visiting his house and being startled by a medieval suit of armour standing sentinel near the front door. Bill Bowmore's house was not big enough to contain his passion for collecting art. However, he seemed even more passionate about giving it away. He donated so much of his collection to institutions around the country, including to Newcastle's public gallery. What's more, he commissioned artists to create work that he gave away. Whiteley's *Summer at Carcoar* is a Bowmore donation. Bill Bowmore wanted much of his collection to stay in Newcastle, even buying the distinctive rounded-façade building at Bank Corner in Newcastle West to house the works. However, negotiations with the council about maintaining the collection dragged on and no agreement was reached. In the 1990s, Bill Bowmore and most of his incredible collection left town. Newcastle's loss was other cities' gain, as works found a home in state collections. The Art Gallery of South Australia celebrated its gifts by holding an exhibition and publishing a catalogue titled, in part, *The Fine Art of Giving*. For many Novocastrians, it might well have been called *The Fine Art of Looking a Gift Horse in the Mouth*. So for those with longer memories, the protracted hand-wringing and head-shaking in response to the Newcastle Art Gallery redevelopment project felt painfully, frustratingly familiar.

Ironically, while Newcastle couldn't get a bigger gallery to display its collection, art flourished in the most public way across the city. Buildings were used as massive vertical canvases for murals. The council even began a Big Picture Fest and declared Newcastle a street art capital.[17]

Galleries grew in the unlikeliest of places. Before Newcastle Police Station moved up the hill into its brutalist fortress on the corner of Watt and Church streets in the 1980s, it was sited in an imposing Victorian-era building on Hunter Street. The station had a lock-up; a complex of spare cells, including a padded enclosure, and an exercise yard with a ceiling of steel bars to prevent escapes. It is a dispiriting view even for a present-day visitor; you look up at the sky imprisoned. If the lock-up's walls could talk, they could recount a colourful history of Newcastle, from drunken seamen and Star Hotel rioters to hardened crims waiting for their moment in court. For a time, the former police station served as the Hunter Heritage Centre, and in 2014, the cells complex was reimagined as a contemporary arts space, where ideas and creativity can run free. It is called, quite appropriately, The Lock-Up. Yet in its past life, those detained in the lock-up created their own art. They etched graffiti into the stone walls, while in the women's cells, prisoners wrote messages with red fingernail polish.[18] These days, many of the exhibitions staged in the claustrophobically small cells and yard centre on social justice.

While art popped up in other places around the city, many were not about to let the idea of an expanded public gallery be abandoned. Novocastrians put their money where their mouth and faith were. A long-time gallery supporter, Valerie Ryan, made a $10 million bequest to the institution's foundation. That extraordinary act of private generosity, along with the many years of community fundraising, seemed to almost shame governments into re-engaging with the redevelopment project and provide funding. Finally, construction work on the gallery expansion, offering about two and half times the present exhibiting space and budgeted at about $40 million, began in 2022. True to Newcastle's character, initial work had to focus on ensuring the city's industrial past didn't devour the art. The site had to be remediated, with grout poured into the earth, because the gallery sits on top of an old coal mine. Watching all of this play out has been Nick Mitzevich. Rather than rue the time and opportunities lost, Nick takes a glass-half-full view of what has taken shape.

'Its new, bigger footprint can reflect the rapidly changing nature of the city. I'm enthused to see what happens.'

Although Nick points out it does reveal another aspect of Newcastle's character. The city is either an early adopter of cultural change, such as its embrace of pub rock in the 1970s and grassroots festivals in the 1990s, or it is very late to the party. And a prime example of the city dragging its feet is the redevelopment of cultural infrastructure. When you think about it in that context, he says, Newcastle is a city of extremes. Still, with the gallery, the redevelopment has become reality. Better late than never.

On the surface, Newcastle was arid ground in which to plant art. It was presumed to be that way since the settlement's founding. Despite that, or perhaps because of it, art has flourished. The roots are deep, and they have spread wide.

Newcastle artists have had a profound influence on how Australia has seen itself. Yet for many years, artists sought more fertile ground to develop, and for more eyes to see what they created. So they left. And if they didn't leave quickly enough, people believed their art suffered.

When the noted Sydney artist and author James Gleeson wrote about William Dobell, he mused that it was Dobell's misfortune to be born in Newcastle at a time when the nearest art gallery and art school were a hundred miles away. According to Gleeson, Dobell wasted time and his talent by staying in Newcastle until his mid-20s, before he was lucky enough to escape to Sydney.[19]

How the perspective has changed. In recent years, Newcastle has been enticing visual artists. Even with the city's rising property prices and buildings that were once considered ideal for cheap studio space being converted into expensive 'New York–style' residential developments, Newcastle remains more affordable than Sydney or Melbourne. And it is filled with muses, fostering ideas. It is no longer seen as a place you leave to become an artist; you can go to Newcastle to continue being an artist. Novocastrian artists have been returning, and artists from elsewhere are moving here. Indeed, Newcastle boasts that is has more artists per capita than any other Australian city.[20]

Among those who now call Newcastle home is the internationally acclaimed abstract artist Virginia Cuppaidge. Born in Brisbane in 1943, Virginia travelled across the globe to New York City in 1969. The young Australian embraced Manhattan life, working and living in a SoHo loft. While Virginia broadened her artistic horizons, New Yorkers focused on her work. Her deceptively spare and complexly restful paintings garnered many awards and admirers. Her work has featured in major exhibitions in North America and Australia. Yet in 2017, after the best part of half a century of living and working in New York, Virginia swapped the city that never sleeps for a city still waking up to its own possibilities.

Virginia was already familiar with Newcastle, regularly visiting her brother and his family, who had lived here for many years. So she knew where she was headed – and the destination excited her.

'Each time I visited, I really loved Newcastle, because of the size of the city and the friendliness of the people', Virginia says.

In her eyes, Newcastle hasn't been just a good place to live; it has been fuelling her art.

'I love the harbour, the ocean and the horizon line. I'm very much influenced by the horizon line.'

I wonder if she experienced culture shock in moving from New York City to Newcastle, but Virginia assures me she didn't.

'I didn't have to adjust dramatically because I liked it so much, and Newcastle was more laid back, which I think I needed. The only adjustment was not having access to a lot of art galleries and museums. But I had my fill, believe me, in New York!'

Virginia has found more than inspiration in Newcastle. She has found colleagues and friends. She points out that where she works, in a former light industrial warehouse at Newcastle Art Space (NAS) in the inner-west suburb of Islington, there are 25 studios. Creative enclaves, such as NAS, have sprouted around the edges of the inner city in former workshops, warehouses and industrial spaces, as artists have had to move out of the centre due to rising property prices and rents. Yet in the process, that shift has brought new life to old industrial sites and suburbs. Within those sites, both art and communities are created. The reimagined buildings, and what they produce, help Newcastle's reputation as a creative city.

Above all, Virginia Cuppaidge has found a home in Newcastle, declaring, 'I'm definitely going to stay here'.

Nick Mitzevich reminds me Newcastle has been viewed as 'an artist's city' long before it became fashionable to see it that way.

He refers to a Joseph Lycett painting of a corroboree at night in Newcastle. Lycett created the work about 1818, depicting dozens of First Nations people, their bodies decorated with art, dancing by moonlight. With *Corroboree at Newcastle*, the convict forger showed that First Nations art and culture were an integral part of this place and had been for a very long time. Through the act of painting, the convict forger also demonstrated that he too was a part of the continuing story of art.

'That work is an acknowledgment Newcastle wasn't Sydney's Siberia, or that there was nothing here', Nick says.

'It was never a cultural wasteland. It was never a land of milk and honey when it comes to culture, but it was never a desert either.'

As a young man in Newcastle, Nick rented a property on The Hill, overlooking the harbour. His landlady was Margaret Olley.

'I rented the garden flat underneath her painting studio', Nick says.

As she became better known and her work more and more sought after, Margaret invested some of her earnings in houses in inner-city Newcastle. But to Margaret, the richness of the city went well beyond bricks and mortar, which is why she regularly visited Newcastle to paint what she saw.

'She would look one way and see this bustling harbour', Nick explains. 'She would look another and see this extraordinary horizon, with glistening beaches. She would look another way and see this beautifully crafted heritage city, and another and see the modern city. There were all these elements she talked about. She loved the city for all its facets, and I love the city for all its facets.

'And culture and art is a very important facet of Newcastle.'

CHAPTER FOUR

CITY OF COAL AND STEEL

NEWCASTLE was founded to be exploited. The settlement's earliest European residents might have been convicts and soldiers sent to guard them, but the colonial authorities saw this place as more than a prison.

In 1804, Governor King made it clear to the settlement's first commandant, Charles Menzies, that the coal and timber in the area belonged to the government, and it wasn't for others to take those resources. That official view only became more entrenched as Newcastle dug in, and its commercial potential grew. When a later governor, Lachlan Macquarie, drafted instructions for the settlement's incoming commandant, James Morisset, in 1818, the first point he noted was, 'The principal objects in view on the original establishment of a post or military station at Newcastle having been to procure supplies of coal, timber and lime for the service of government, you are to employ all the means you are possessed of in the prosecution of these objects ...'[1]

The presence of so many resources, and a workforce in the convict population, meant that Newcastle was an industrial community from the outset. If you burrowed into the earth under Fort Scratchley, you could find evidence of that, with the remains of tunnels marking one of Australia's first coal mines in what was then known as Colliers Point. But you don't have to emulate the convict miners and take that risk to see proof of what Newcastle was from its first breaths. Instead, you can walk into an open space neighbouring the former Customs House, just near the harbour's edge.

In the area known as the Convict Lumber Yard, you can wander amid rusting slabs of steel and stone blocks pressed into the earth, outlining buildings long gone. This area is considered the birthplace of colonial industry in Australia. From 1805, it was used for the storage of coal, timber and lime, before these materials were loaded onto ships at a wharf built into the harbour. More than simply being used for storage, this area was also a manufacturing space. In the lumber yard, behind a log fence more than 3 metres high, convicts worked with timber and steel, making products for the settlement.

However, the reminders of the lumber yard and the convict stockade were eaten by a fire in 1851 and gradually sank in the sandy earth. In what seems like a tale of destiny, the convict-era remains were uncovered in the 1980s. The person who discovered them was none other than historian and university lecturer John Turner, who had done so much through his writing and talks to stoke interest in Newcastle's past. Although John did have a helper with this accidental discovery. John was taking his dog for a walk in the area. Apparently while the dog answered a call of nature, John followed his natural curiosity and had a look around what was then a vacant block of land, and he found a convict-made brick. And so began the journey that included a series of archaeological digs, uncovering what the years and the sand drifts had concealed. Hundreds of artefacts and the remains of structures relating to the convict days were found. Damaris Bairstow, a renowned archaeologist who worked on the digs, said in a 1989 excavation report that the lumber yard was the only known site in Australia retaining evidence of early convictism on a broad scale.[2]

Evidence of the convicts' toil and creativity in Newcastle is to be found not just in the ground at Newcastle but in libraries and words. Housed in the State Library of NSW in Sydney is the Macquarie collector's chest, a labyrinthine work of art crammed with references to Newcastle, and it may well have been crafted and assembled in the lumber yard. What's more, Australia's first dictionary, and the foundations of how we Australians talk, can be traced to one of those who worked and did time in Newcastle.

When we refer to our pants as 'togs' or 'duds', or to little ones as 'toddlers', or use that most Australian of words, 'swag', we are talking like convicts. The slang the convicts used was known as 'flash language', and the vocabulary they formulated to conceal meaning from, and confuse, those in authority has helped shape what we say and how we see ourselves.

And many of those words were transposed from the mouths of convicts and onto the page in Newcastle. The man who captured the flash language and turned all that slang into a dictionary was James Hardy Vaux, a well-educated convict who couldn't stay out of trouble. Vaux was a forger, fraudster and pickpocket, and he was transported twice from Britain to New South Wales. During his second stint, Vaux was found guilty of theft and was sent to Newcastle.

Unhappy to be doing hard labour in Newcastle, Vaux found a way with words to an easier existence in the penal settlement. When convicts spoke in their 'flash language', their gaolers and overseers did not understand what they were saying. Which, of course, was the point of the language. As a result, those in charge needed an interpreter. The commandant, Thomas Skottowe, called on Vaux to play that role, since he was bilingual, so to speak.

In 1812, Vaux proposed he write a dictionary, decoding the flash language and explaining the meaning of the words and phrases. The proposal was accepted. Vaux received a softer job while serving his sentence, and the authorities, and history, received a ground-breaking dictionary, the first of its type in Australia, that its author titled *A Vocabulary of the Flash Language*.

Another master of words, the author and journalist Kel Richards, wrote a biography of Vaux, titled *Flash Jim*. Kel told me that if Vaux had not been sentenced to hard labour in Newcastle, he doubted the convict would have ever written that dictionary.[3] So next time you are 'spinning a yarn', think of James Hardy Vaux, and of the role Newcastle has played in putting words in your mouth.

To historians, the discovery of the lumber yard site provided not just elation but relief.

'The unearthing of the lumberyard demonstrated that convict-era remains had not been entirely obliterated from the Newcastle CBD', wrote David Andrew Roberts and Erik Eklund in an article published in *Australian Historical Studies*.[4] Although the authors noted the report by Suters Architects from the 1990s, outlining how archaeological surveys had indicated much of Newcastle's CBD land was studded with reminders of its convict past.[5]

For a time, the lumber yard treasures were less at risk of being obliterated than buried under a building development. However, the site was saved, and it now serves as a tourist attraction, an outdoor education precinct, and an oasis in the East End, all the while exploring the origins of Newcastle as an industrial city.

The remains of the convict era offer the city a key to the future. As the Newcastle Archaeological Management Strategy of 2015 stated, 'The physical survival of archaeological remains of these buildings and structures will not only have the ability to demonstrate the way of life of the convicts, the civil servants and military personnel, but will also provide a much-needed focus for historical education and cultural tourism in the city and its region'.[6]

The archaeological digs at the lumberyard site revealed in the deeper layers the remains of implements used by First Nations people, underscoring that this was a place of industry long before the Europeans turned up.

The First Nations people recognised the value of coal, or nikkin, as they called it, for thousands of years. As John Maynard explains, the value was practical, with the Awabakal people using coal in their fires, and it was spiritual. John believes the Awabakal are the only Aboriginal group who have a Dreaming story about coal and its origins. According to the story, darkness was suddenly cast across the land. The darkness was due to a hole in a mountain, which blocked out sunlight. The people met and decided to cover the darkness across the ground. They used rocks and sand and cut down foliage to cover the thick darkness. They feared the fires deep in the ground would throw out more darkness, if the ground was not covered. After the ground was covered, generation after generation walked across the layers, pressing the darkness and deep fires together, creating coal.

'Whenever coal is burnt, the ancient fire is released', John explains.

John says the story seems to relate to a volcanic eruption, and its effect on the environment. To the south of Newcastle, at the coastal suburb of Redhead, there is an ancient volcanic plug in the seaside cliffs.

As the Reverend Lancelot Threlkeld noted in the book he wrote with the help of Awabakal leader Biraban in 1834, this area was called Kin-ti-ir-ra-bin.[7] John says the Awabakal also spoke of another volcano further up the valley, Ko-pur-ra-ba, which was the source of a brilliant red ochre used for ceremonial body decoration, and for painting.

The resource that was part of the First Nations peoples' lives and stories for so long brought the Industrial Revolution and its human emissions – convicts – to the shores of Yohaaba. There would be no more pressing of layers on the ground to cover the darkness and contain the fires within; rather the ground would be torn open and men would crawl into the darkness, extracting the rock that made not just fire but built fortunes and empires, and a city.

WHEN Newcastle's transformation from a penal and military outpost to a civilian town was plotted and planned, its future character and purpose seemed to be imprinted into street names. A number of key streets were named after engineers, particularly those involved in developing that marvel of industry, steam power. That marvel was tied to coal.

From the settlement's establishment, coal mining took place mostly around Colliers Point, chasing the seam exposed in the dramatic cliff face that marks the abrupt end of the CBD's eastern edge and the beginning of the sea. In 1817, a new mine was dug closer to the settlement, burrowing into what was called the Yard Seam, a reference to its thickness. By its proximity, mining was now in the heart of Newcastle. Benjamin Grainger, who was the superintendent of the coal mines, told the Bigge Inquiry in 1820 that up to 20 tons (18 tonnes) could be hewn each day by eight convicts in the mine. Others worked at bucketing the water out of the mine and transporting the coal by barrow to the shaft so it could be raised to the surface then taken by wagon to the wharf.[8] In 1820, about 3915 tons (about 3552 tonnes) had been mined and raised in Newcastle, with just over 3000 tons (about 2721 tonnes) being shipped out of the port. It was quite a jump from 1805, the year after Newcastle's foundation, when just 150 tons (136 tonnes) were brought to the surface.[9] However, for those working in the earth, it was an unhealthy environment. The miners' clothes were wet, and, as the Assistant Colonial Surgeon at Newcastle told the inquiry, 'The foul air that is breathed there produces spitting of blood and difficulty of breathing'.[10]

For the first 24 years of Newcastle's existence, the coal and its profits belonged to the British Government. However, in 1828, Britain handed the monopoly on coal in the colony to the Australian Agricultural (AA) Company. This was hardly the first demonstration of largesse for the AA Company. When it was founded in London in 1824, the company was granted a million acres (about 404 686 hectares) centred around the Port Stephens area, north of Newcastle. The company would also be handed a grant of 2000 acres (or 809 hectares) of land in Newcastle, which played a large role in how the town took shape, and what kind of community it would grow into being. That grant was heavily criticised almost half a century later by business pioneer John Bingle in his book, *Past and Present Records of Newcastle, New South Wales*. He called it a great mistake for this private company formed in England 'purely for agricultural pursuits' to have had the area's surface and mineral wealth handed to it, and to have 'our town hemmed in by them on every side'.[11]

The company quickly set out to find that wealth by cracking open the earth on a slope just above the town, with the 'A' Pit. These days on The Hill, surrounded by some of the finest homes and architectural statements in inner Newcastle, there is a small weathered plaque marking the vicinity of what was Australia's first privately owned colliery. The predominantly convict workforce mined the seam and loaded coal into wagons on tracks, marking it as the first railway in the colony. The coal was transported down the steep slope to the harbour to be loaded onto ships. By the early 1830s, a correspondent for the *Sydney Gazette* newspaper observed Newcastle was almost wholly possessed by the AA Company, with the company owning most of the land in the heart of town.[12] As a workplace, the company's mines received a rebuke in verse from the renowned convict poet, Frank McNamara, better known as Frank the Poet. McNamara was assigned to the Australian Agricultural Company, and when he was directed to work in the underground mines in Newcastle, the convict protested by writing a poem, 'For the Company underground'.

In stanza after stanza, McNamara outlines his refusal to work in the AA Company mines unless the impossible happened. He ends his litany with the lines:

> When the quick and the dead shall stand in array
> Cited at the trumpet's sound,
> Even then, damn me if I'd work a day
> For the Company underground.[13]

In McNamara's case, the pen is mightier than the whip, it would seem. He was transferred to an iron gang in Sydney.

The AA Company spread its presence above ground and under it with more pits around Newcastle and to the west of the town, at what would become the suburb of Hamilton. The company had the monopoly on coal – officially, at least – until 1847. However, other mines were operating in the region, including a small colliery on the shores of Lake Macquarie, established by the Reverend Lancelot Threlkeld, as he looked to coal to help fund his Christian mission. Perhaps subscribing to the aphorism that it is better to ask forgiveness than permission, Threlkeld had begun mining despite opposition from the AA Company and the government. After he made Lake Macquarie history by shipping the first load of coal from his mine to Sydney in 1841, Threlkeld had the support of the *Sydney Gazette*. The newspaper praised the quality of the coal and lashed what it called the 'disgraceful monopoly' held by the AA Company.

'Free citizens will never tolerate such an infringement of their rights and privileges', the paper's journalist wrote.[14]

In turn, more people tested the AA Company's monopoly, beginning their own mines. Among them was a Scottish family who would be synonymous with Hunter mining, the Browns. Ironically, considering what they would become, members of the Brown family had left their homeland and their former jobs as handloom weavers because the rise of steam power in the textile industry had pushed their method of work towards redundancy. They began their journey to being coal barons by mining on land James Brown leased at Four Mile Creek, near Maitland. It was an operation shaped by misfortune. One of James' brothers, John, died in 1846, when he was overcome by gas and fell while descending a shaft.¹⁵ The little mine was also targeted by the AA Company and the government. James had to go to court and was found guilty of intruding on the reserves of the Crown. Brown lost his mine, but the case helped push the AA Company's monopoly closer to ending. The New South Wales parliament was holding an inquiry into the coal monopoly. In August 1847, before the parliamentary committee's report was handed down, the AA Company had begun negotiations to end the agreement. The industry became more open, and so were the opportunities. While there was no dramatic surge in demand initially, according to historian John Turner, a coal rush developed within a few years. One reason for the jump in demand was another kind of rush – gold – on the other side of the ocean in California. Newcastle coal was shipped across the seas to help fuel the economic growth there. Turner quotes the well-known clergyman and writer the Reverend John Dunmore Lang observing the change in Newcastle Harbour, from being like a 'Dead Sea' to a place 'full of life and motion, flaunting with stars and stripes', a reference to 20 American ships loading coal in the port.¹⁶ But demand closer to home, in the Australian colonies, was also growing, including with the advent of steam navigation and, later, the railways. Coal was needed to get somewhere in and around the big continent.

At the forefront of riding coal's rising prospects were James Brown and his brother, Alexander. The brothers moved their operations and ambitions close to the coast, opening a mine on land at Burwood Estate, a few kilometres to the south of Newcastle, which was owned by another major figure in Newcastle's development as an industrial centre, Dr James Mitchell. As the Browns' Burwood mine reaped rewards, the brothers expanded into the maritime industry, including using their own ships to transport coal to new markets, such as China, the Dutch East Indies and North America. As John Turner wrote about the brothers, those voyages entitle the Browns to be considered as pioneers of the coal export trade.¹⁷ What's more, they imported new products on the return voyages, including sugar, rum and coffee from Java, believed to be the first time those goods were directly brought into the port. So the Browns were also precursors to Port of Newcastle's more recent efforts to diversify what comes in and out of the harbour.

Through lean times and rich, the family literally dug in. The first generation of J&A Brown had developed six collieries in the Newcastle and Lower Hunter areas, producing almost two million tonnes of coal. What was good for the region was also profitable for the Browns. A second-generation member of the family told a banquet in 1881, 'It had been the great business of the firm to advance the prosperity of Newcastle in every way because such prosperity meant their own personal aggrandizement and advance as well'.[18]

Newcastle coal was being shipped out into the world, and the world was viewing Newcastle through the prism of the black rock. When the Duke of Edinburgh visited Newcastle in 1868, the community welcomed the royal guest by erecting an arch of coal at the wharf. On Prince Alfred's itinerary was a quick tour of the collieries in the district.

The rise of Newcastle as a coalopolis was lauded.

'Some parts of history, they say, are "written in blood", but Newcastle can happily say for itself that the peaceful history of its extraordinary rise has been "written in coal"', noted the *Illustrated Sydney News* in 1889, apparently forgetting how the town began and its impact on the First Nations people.[19] However, the focus of the article was coal and wealth.

'The prosperity of Newcastle is indeed founded on a rock – the best kind of rock', the writer declared.

'Indeed, the prosperity of New South Wales could hardly have advanced so fast had Newcastle not been able to supply the very raw material of propulsion in exhaustless quantities.'[20]

In 1889, the year of that *Illustrated Sydney News* article, almost 2.1 million tons (about 1.9 million tonnes) of coal was shipped out of Newcastle. That was four times the volume exported just 20 years earlier.

Mines sprouted in areas around the harbour, working seams under the waters of the Hunter River estuary. This was known as delta mining. A later generation of engineers referred to the sinking of shafts at the delta mines as heroic, with workers pushing iron caissons through the sand until they hit bedrock.[21] The presence of tunnels snaking just under the harbour meant miners could hear the churn and thrum of ships passing overhead.[22]

By the end of the 19th century, there were more than 35 collieries in the Newcastle area, ranging from small operations such as Bayley's

Reward at Lambton, employing just three men, to collieries such as Burwood with 336 men underground. In all, more than 6000 men were employed in the local mines.[23] Even those who didn't work in the mines would have been aware they were in a mining community. The pits were in the midst of daily life. The AA Company's lyrically named Sea Pit, for instance, was between the coast and the streets lined with workers' cottages in Cooks Hill, and it remained in operation until 1915.

While coal was extracted in ever greater quantities from the Newcastle earth, entrepreneurs arrived to embed themselves here. Their names would become synonymous with industry in Newcastle. George Henry Varley, for instance, had established a coppersmith's business in 1886 to tap into the opportunities that the harbour and all the ships coming and going presented. The name Varley became prominent in Newcastle, reaching beyond the harbour into heavy engineering. In 1899, an engineer named Alfred Goninan arrived in Newcastle, with a desire to tap into the opportunities the coal industry presented, initially working on rail wagons and skips. Goninan's business grew, developing a range of mining equipment. Goninan convinced another entrepreneur, Henry Lane, to set up in Newcastle and manufacture rabbit traps, which were in huge demand because of plagues. The name 'Lane' is still found on hardware products, particularly locks. As for Goninan, in 1919 the company moved to a large tract of land at Broadmeadow, where, these days under the name of UGL, the workforce has continued to manufacture all manner of equipment for both industry and everyday life, notably rolling stock, including locomotives for coal haulage.[24]

One name that grew as the coal industry did was Brown. J&A Brown. The company continued to impress itself onto – and into – the landscape, into Novocastrians' lives and the character of Newcastle through the late 19th century and into the 20th. Never mind the reputation of Newcastle being just a worker's town. One of the city's best-known faces was that of John Brown. This face was not coal smeared but frequently crowned with a bowler hat. The son of James Brown would become renowned as a racehorse owner and shipowner, but above all he remained true to the family firm and was known as the coal baron. He would grow the empire, trying to make the company self-sufficient from the pit to the sea, owning collieries, ships and wharves, and rail lines. He embraced machines, pushing his operations to the cutting edge, but had a reputation for being antagonistic towards his men. He was bitterly opposed to unions, and in the face of industrial strife, he would stare straight back, waiting for the workforce to blink first. John Brown was very much part of Newcastle life and larger than life, playing the relentless capitalist, as historian John Turner noted.[25] When he died in 1930, Brown was referred to in the media far and wide as the most famous coal owner in the Commonwealth.[26] His funeral had an air of both solemnity and theatricality about it, attracting thousands to watch the procession as the coal baron's body was transported through the heart of Newcastle from his home in Wolfe Street to the railway station, where it was placed on a special train bound for the family vault in East Maitland. Crowds in Hunter Street brought traffic to a standstill. Among those paying their respects were miners, according to the *Sydney Morning Herald*, 'all eager to do reverence to the memory of the man who did more than any other to establish Newcastle as the Commonwealth's greatest industrial city'.[27] Although another media outlet reported that 'disgraceful scenes' were witnessed at the funeral, with 'morbid sightseers' snatching artificial flowers from wreaths, while others 'regarded the occasion in a holiday picnic spirit and brought hampers'.[28]

Even after he died, John Brown continued to be seamed in the impressions of Newcastle. In 'The Smell of Coal Smoke', Les Murray began his beautiful evocation of visiting Newcastle as a child with these lines:

John Brown, glowing far and down,
wartime Newcastle was a brown town

The industry of John Brown had also worked its way deep into Les Murray's family. The poet wrote about his dead grandfather, noting how 'his lungs creaked like mahogany with the grains of John Brown'.[29]

Mining and tragedy all too often share company. And all too often mining meted out death that was not as slow and insidious as 'black lung'. The tunnels under Newcastle would become tombs. The shock and terror that played out in the earth are carved into epitaphs on miners' headstones in historical cemeteries, from the city's fringe in the vast fields of the dead at Sandgate to the grounds of Christ Church Cathedral.

In the cathedral's cemetery, with its views over the city and the harbour to the sea, are the resting places of some of the city's powerful and influential in politics and business, whose names live on from the 19th century to the 21st in streets and suburbs; names such as Hannell and Tighe. Near those memorials is a simple headstone marking the memory of John Marland. Few may know his name, and it may not be found on a street sign, but John Marland left his mark in helping make Newcastle the place it was and still is. He was a miner. That was his living, and that's what ended his life. As his epitaph explains, John Marland died while at work in an AA Company pit on 21 January 1861. He was aged 38.

Below the epitaph is inscribed a verse:

As sprightely as the lark I rose
and hail'd the morning sun
before my daily work was closed
my precious life was gone.

Occasionally, there were mining disasters, resulting in multiple deaths. In 1889, the year the *Illustrated Sydney News* published that article extolling the virtues of mining, 11 miners were killed in a collapse at an AA Company pit at Hamilton. Three years earlier, the perils of mining under the water around Newcastle were tragically played out at a delta mine at Tighes Hill, a suburb within sight of Newcastle's centre and now in high demand for its historic houses. In 1886, under the houses, sand, mud and water from nearby Throsby Creek sluiced into the Ferndale Colliery after a collapse. A miner drowned, and others escaped by the faintest of breaths. One survivor, Henry Hargraves, recounted to a *Newcastle Morning Herald* journalist how his lamp was extinguished and, trapped in the darkness by sand and rising water, he thought he was sure to die.

'The water gradually rose to my waist, then to my chest, until it finally reached my throat', Henry Hargraves said. He managed to gasp at air by lying on his back then, finding his feet, made his way through the dark until he saw daylight and called for help. 'I have had two narrow escapes at mining in Staffordshire but I don't believe I was ever so near death as I was this morning.'[30]

The risks posed by mining had been a major factor in workers demanding better conditions and treatment. The days of compelling convict labourers to head into a pit had gone. However, the idea of fighting for something better had led to some convicts being sent to Newcastle in the first place. In December 1820, five convicts who had been transported for high treason were sent to Newcastle as soon as they arrived in Sydney from Britain. They were members of what was called the Cato Street Conspiracy. The group's members, which included tradesmen struggling due to industrialisation, were dismayed at the cost-of-living pressures so many contended with, and they blamed those in parliament for the widespread poverty and pain. The conspirators resolved to assassinate the British prime minister and his entire cabinet while they dined together in London, and this would mark the start of a revolution. However, the conspirators were given up, and five were publicly hanged, while five others ended up in Newcastle.[31] So the presence of workers agitating for a better deal has been part of Newcastle since its infancy.

With the gradual decline in the numbers of convict workers in Newcastle, the AA Company had brought out British miners for their operations. As more miners arrived from Britain, what they wanted to leave behind were some of the tough conditions they had endured in pits there.

One of those who had emigrated was James Fletcher. The Scotsman had been working in mines since he was a boy. He was involved in mining in Newcastle from the 1850s, but while he was hewing coal he also advocated for his colleagues' rights and better protection. Since the mid-1850s, local miners had created unions in their own workplaces. In 1860, when miners united to form their first district trade union, the Hunter River Miners' Association, James Fletcher was elected chairman. The following year, the first general strike in Newcastle was held, according to *Historical Records of Newcastle* of 1897. However, there had been earlier industrial disputes and flare-ups in pits, including the AA Company contending with a strike among its imported miners in the 1840s.³² The 1861 stoppage was on a much larger scale, with the *Historical Records of Newcastle* noting that about 800 members met in a theatre and resolved, 'That we, the miners of the Hunter River district, having from past experience become convinced of the necessity of the firmest bond of unity existing among us for the mutual protection of our rights and privileges as a class, do hereby pledge ourselves individually and collectively to unite together for that purpose'.³³

James Fletcher went from being a leader of miners to a manager of collieries. For a time, he owned the *Newcastle Morning Herald and Miners' Advocate*. And he moved into politics, first in local government as the mayor of mining communities Wallsend and Plattsburg, then he was elected to the New South Wales Legislative Assembly, representing Newcastle for more than a decade. An editorial in the *Daily Telegraph* in 1884 declared 'he has enriched the Browns and other colliery proprietors; he has advanced the prosperity of Newcastle as no other man has done; he has improved the condition of the miners; and in doing all this he had impoverished himself'.³⁴ After Fletcher died in 1891, the public raised the money for a statue, which continues to stand in the park named in his honour, a wedge of prime land overlooking Newcastle Beach. The statue of Fletcher, however, doesn't face the beach; rather, his gaze is fixed on the city he helped develop. It has grown beyond what James Fletcher perhaps envisioned. The view from the statue is now somewhat obscured by a barrier of high-rise apartment complexes, their occupants craning for a sea view. At the foot of Fletcher's statue is a plaque listing his roles and achievements. The plaque points out that the statue was erected 'to commemorate James Fletcher as a friend of the miner'.

Another mining union leader who emerged in the late 1800s was Peter Bowling. He had arrived in New South Wales from Scotland in the 1880s, working in collieries around Newcastle and increasingly becoming a strident and fiery voice for miners' rights. During a strike in 1896, Bowling lacerated the colliery owners, asserting they didn't deserve to have the welfare of the community at their disposal, and he believed the solution to fixing the industry and giving the worker a better deal lay in socialism.³⁵ During another general strike in 1909, Bowling, by then president of the northern Colliery Employees' Federation, was again at the industrial barricades, calling for direct action by workers.

He was arrested in Newcastle on a charge of conspiracy and sentenced to prison. He was released late in 1910, when Labor was voted into power for the first time in New South Wales.

Through the latter years of the 19th century and into the 20th, industrial relations see-sawed between strife and harmony. Relations between colliery owners and miners were fractured over profits, production costs and work conditions, before wounds were patched for a period. Long stoppages, dragging on for weeks into months, not only brought pits to a standstill, but money would dry up in the town, and the harbour would become even more clogged with ships waiting to be loaded. As the motto emblazoned on a Colliery Employees' Federation banner from the early 1900s declared, 'The pick is mightier than the sceptre'.[36] Although the sceptre, and the sabre, was occasionally raised and rattled against the pick. During a strike in 1888, a military camp with about 350 troopers and police was set up at Wallsend to protect non-union labour loading coal. Again in 1888, when tensions rose and about 1000 miners gathered to resist non-union workers at a pit in Adamstown, artillerymen, whose armaments included a large Nordenfeldt gun, were dispatched. The sight of military might rolling into an industrial dispute disturbed not just those who saw the gun but the *Newcastle Morning Herald*. The newspaper's editorial referred to the gun as 'death-dealing machinery' and argued the region had no desire to have democracy tested and be the first area in Australia 'to be experimented on by these interesting specimens of mechanism'.[37] Thankfully, there was no hail of bullets, just words.

These days, the mining union's headquarters are an hour's drive away from Newcastle on the edge of Cessnock. In the early years of the 20th century, coal mining increasingly moved out of Newcastle and deeper into the valley, onto what was called the South Maitland Coalfields. So the union's headquarters are where the heart of Hunter mining used to be, before it moved further up the valley, with the development of massive open-cut operations.

The union's president for the Northern Mining and NSW Energy District is Robin Williams. The son and grandson of miners, Robin first went to work in an open-cut operation in the Upper Hunter in the mid-1980s. From that experience, and his work with what is now called the Mining and Energy Union, Robin has an appreciation of what his forebears did, and what they achieved both in fighting for better conditions and simply staying alive.

'I, for the life of me, don't understand how those people actually survived in the early 1900s', he says, shaking his head. 'They didn't have safety gear, they didn't have working clothes, they had picks and shovels.

'Coal miners have always been at the forefront [of change], because there's been money in coal and multinationals in coal, and they wanted to make money at the expense of workers. And in the end, workers rebelled and said, "Hang on, we're not copping it any more".'

While the coal industry largely moved out of town a century ago, Robin believes miners – and the unions they formed – are still part of the Novocastrian character.

'If you've been involved in a lengthy dispute, it does change people, it does shape your character, it does shape the way humans interact with each other. People became more staunch, because of what [the companies] did. It was only the resolute strength of that collective grouping through unions that availed those people the ability to achieve what they did.

'And I think it did drive a mentality through coal miners, and then into the wider public, about being staunch and sticking up for yourself and fighting for your rights. You don't have to pick up arms and that type of thing, but people stood up for themselves, stuck up for themselves. A lot of those people didn't do it just for themselves, they did it for their family.

'I think a lot of that is still around Newcastle. I think people who live in and around Newcastle are pretty staunch, and they are prepared to stick up for themselves and uphold their rights, and I think that's been borne through the old coal miners of Newcastle.'

In the grounds of the union's northern district headquarters is a memorial wall, honouring every miner known to have died at work since the days of the convicts.

'As we sit here today, 1793 people have been killed', Robin says, while acknowledging the wall is more than likely not a complete list. Some of those killed in the early days may well have fallen through the cracks of history.

The lines of names, their ages, where they worked and the year they died cover more than 11 large panels. Some of those killed were boys. An R Irving, who died in a mine at Plattsburg in 1883, was aged just 11. Others had barely made it into their teens when they were killed. Others listed on the wall were in their later years when they were killed, such as a J McNaughton, who died in 1892 when he was 72. Reflecting the continued dangers of mining, the wall has a number of blank panels, anticipating more names being added.

For Robin Williams, to walk past the memorial wall and read the row after row of names is 'humbling, and sometimes you've got to hold back the tears'.

While the earlier days of the mining industry, and Newcastle as an industrial centre, were punctuated by strikes and strife, Robin is surprised the community was as settled as it was.

'You'd think, when you look at the fatalities, that we would have been more militant, less inclined to really do what the boss wanted. I think it was a different time. People dealt with things differently, and people needed to support their families.'

While mining had moved further afield in the 1900s, coal remained very much in Newcastle life. In 1947, the 150th anniversary of European arrival in Newcastle, the book *Newcastle 150 Years* was published to mark the occasion. One of the chapters is 'A city built on coal'.[38] In that year, according to the book, about 9000 men worked in 81 mines throughout the district. Most of the 6.8 million tonnes mined in the district that year were not exported. Unlike these days, with 149 950 823 tonnes of coal passing by Nobbys and sliding over the horizon in 2024, in the post-war years, 'The demand for coal by industries in Australia is so great that production is below demand'.[39]

In everyday life in Newcastle, coal was everywhere. It was in the cart delivered to your home, to be burnt in the fireplace and stove. It was in the air, in the tiniest but most pervasive of granules, chuffing out of factory chimneys, the funnels of ships and ferries, and the stacks of locomotives. It was there on the washing, on windowsills, on faces, and in lungs. Coal was in the blood of the city, and blood continued to be shed in mining it, prompting official responses such as the 1939 Report on the Royal Commission on the Safety and Health of Workers in Coal Mines.

While conditions improved, lives kept being taken. The memorial wall is testament to that. In the year the royal commission's report was released, at least 24 miners died. In 1947, the year *Newcastle 150 Years* proclaimed the city built on coal, another 24 miners died in the district. In so many ways, on so many levels through the 20th century, coal continued to provide the grit, the chiaroscuro, to the lives and the reputation of Novocastrians.

In contemporary Newcastle, the coal industry is dotted through the city. It doesn't seem as pervasive. You can catch a glimpse of it as you drive through the Kooragang industrial precinct, as the massive loaders looming with the appearance of a Jurassic creature convey products of the Permian period into the holds of ships lined up at the wharves like fledglings on a powerline, waiting to be fed. The sheer scale of all that coal stored at Kooragang to be loaded onto ships is better experienced from the air. Flying over the loading facilities, the rows of coal look like ploughed fields, only it has been vast tracts of land further up the valley that have been torn apart to access this black harvest. The coal is mostly brought to the port by rail. Back on the ground, you can see that supply chain on the move in rail wagons. And if you walk along the coast, you can see coal snaking between other rock layers in an escarpment, or you can pick up chunks of the black rock scattered along the shore, just as the first Europeans did, bewitched by what they held, and, before them, just as Aboriginal people did. And in the East End, you can see a stylised block of coal enthroned upon a monument, which the community erected in 1909 to commemorate 50 years since Newcastle's incorporation as a municipality, and to show just how far the place had come since 1859. By virtue of the rock crowning it, and the panels depicting mining and shipping, the monument also made it clear that the community owed the progress it celebrated to King Coal. The monument is all but out of sight these days, having been moved to a sliver of a park in Parnell Place.

However, the importance of coal remains set in stone in Newcastle, and the industry continues to seam through the city in ways that, like that monument, are barely noticed. It is there when the Newcastle Knights rugby league players run onto the ground in high-visibility jerseys for one round each season to acknowledge and honour the mining industry's support of the club. It is there on the livery of the region's rescue helicopter, with the logos of the mining union and the industry's representative body, NSW Mining. After all, that chopper has been the difference between survival and death for many an injured miner. And it is there in the workforce. Robin Williams says in 2024, the union's northern district had almost 9000 members, with a substantial number of them living, and spending their money, in Newcastle. In the late 1960s, author and journalist Alan Farrelly said coal was in the psyches of all Novocastrians.[40] More than half a century on, coal is still in Novocastrians' lives, but the mining union leader wonders if they are aware of it, or whether many are trying to bury it. Robin Williams believes that, broadly speaking, gratitude for what coal has done for Newcastle has ebbed away.

'Coal built the city, coal built Newcastle', he asserts.

'It's probably disappointing that people don't recognise the roots of the city. I think people should be indebted to coal, but people aren't indebted to coal. People now view coal as this dirty product that's killing the world.'

He feels some older residents who no longer believe coal is a good thing still acknowledge its links to Newcastle. But Robin feels many younger residents and some of those new to town see no link to coal and view it as 'a dirty part of Newcastle', and they hold the attitude, 'The sooner it's gone, the better off we'll all be'.

'And that's pretty disappointing.'

No sooner had the mining industry moved beyond the limits of 'coalopolis' than Newcastle became the centre of another product on which to build wealth and a community's identity: steel.

Newcastle became synonymous with not just steel but an acronym: BHP.

The Broken Hill Proprietary Company Limited was founded in 1885 and put down roots by the Hunter River 11 years later. The mining company acquired land for copper smelters. But in the early years of the 20th century, it realised the potential in converting its deposits of iron ore from South Australia into iron and steel. BHP chose to develop its steelworks on the stretch of riverside land known as Port Waratah.

The tract from which this giant would rise was unprepossessing. It was a swamp. At high tide, the land was almost a metre underwater; at other times, it was a swathe of mudflats and pungent pools. As a foundation for building for the future, Port Waratah looked underwhelming. Even members of the BHP board asked David Baker, the American steel expert brought out to manage the project's construction, many questions about building steelworks in a pond.[41] But where some saw a swamp, Baker foresaw a reservoir of possibility. He had recommended the site because it offered two key elements for the works: access to coal to fuel the plant and water frontage to ship ore in and products out.

In early 1913, work began, with thousands of piles being driven into the marshy earth to cradle the works. Beauty was sacrificed in the pursuit of industry. In 1868, a plan to establish the Newcastle Botanic Gardens on about 60 hectares of land on the site had been agreed upon. The *Newcastle Morning Herald* referred to it as 'one of the largest and most picturesque reserves for botanical gardens to be found in the colony'.[42]

However, when the NSW Government implemented the *Newcastle Iron and Steel Works Act 1912*, clearing the way for BHP's plans, any notion of gardens were swept aside as well. Where dreams of a Newcastle Botanic Gardens once flourished, massive pieces of machinery and plant were shipped in, as the industrial giant gradually rose from the marshlands along the Hunter River's South Arm. However, through the life of the steelworks, the river would take its revenge from time to time, flooding the plant, so that the great halls of fire confronted their mortal enemy, water.

When the steelworks were officially opened in a grand affair on 2 June 1915, the Governor-General, Sir Ronald Munro Ferguson, prophesied, 'The steel products of Newcastle will achieve a world-wide reputation'.[43]

The Newcastle steelworks were born in a time of conflict, immediately beginning production of materials for the First World War. From the new plant came rails for transport on the Western Front and munition steel for arms manufacturers.

Yet, according to historian Manning Clark, what the Newcastle steelworks were also producing was independence for Australia. The young nation was no longer relying on iron and steel from Europe and the United States, and that helped lay the foundations for political and cultural independence. But this was about even more than Australia learning to stand alone. In the furnaces and mills of the Newcastle plant, a new national identity was being fired and shaped.

'The Newcastle works were the dawn of a new era in the history of Australia, the material foundation for the end of that material backwardness and isolation which had condemned Australians hitherto to the role of second-rate Europeans. They held out the promise of an end to the sense of inferiority to western Europe, the end of the grovel to the English and the cultural cringe', Clark wrote in his mammoth *A History of Australia*.[44]

The steelworks also forged an identity for the town that hosted it, to the point that, through the years, it would seem as though it was the works hosting the town. While the works were putting steel into the backbone of a nation, Newcastle grew increasingly dependent on the works. Newcastle came to be Steel City.

The works were their own steel city. On the other side of the company gates were massive workshops and halls of industry, with names such as the coke ovens, the blast furnace, the open hearth plant, and the bloom mill. The works had their own power plant and water pumping station. Rail lines webbed their way through the 150-hectare main site, as the works had their own train system, carrying materials to and from the wharves, where BHP's own ships were berthed, and to the coal mines the company owned in the Hunter and beyond. The company was, for a time, the nation's biggest owner of ships and the largest miner of black coal. In the works' site by the river, but a world away from the spare and noisy halls filled with fire and steel and sweating humanity, was the main administration building, which has the look of a neo-classical Georgian mansion, or perhaps a London gentlemen's club.

From the outset, Newcastle felt a sense of loyalty towards the steelworks. The plant was known – and still is referred to – as The BHP. That definite article, perhaps more than any other in town, denotes the prominence and importance of the steelworks in the city and the region.

At times, one in 10 residents in the Newcastle area worked at The BHP, and tens of thousands more had jobs in associated industries. The BHP was not just the major employer, it was part of the community, ranging from the establishment of the Newcastle Industrial Benefits (NIB) hospital fund in 1952 to the building of public facilities. Even more than that, The BHP was virtually a member of many a Novocastrian family – families such as that of Aubrey Brooks. As Aub puts it, 'The BHP put sausages on the table'.

Aubrey began work at The BHP in 1961. He was following his father, James Brooks, who worked at the steelworks for 42 years, and his grandfather, James Massie, who was among the first working at The BHP when it opened, and he remained there for 37 years. Not that Aub wanted to follow his forebears through the steelworks' gates. He wanted to take up an apprenticeship as a butcher. But his father told him in no uncertain terms, 'You're going to work at The BHP. You start on Monday'. And so the 15-year-old joined the crowd of blokes getting on the bus for the steelworks, a boy among men, and he grew up quickly as a rivet cook in the rail wagon shop.

It was a workplace that ran on hard work and testosterone. Aub says the 100 or so working in the wagon shop were all men. That meant he had to endure the occasional initiation, such as being told he had to receive an inoculation for 'iron ore dust syndrome'. The moment he saw the massive needle his colleague produced, Aub bolted and hid at the bus stop. Yet change gradually seeped into the workshop. Aub recalls when a woman was first employed in the workshop. By then, he had worked his way up to a supervisory role. There were no facilities for a woman, so the new employee had to traipse to another part of the works to access a bathroom. Her job was to wheelbarrow away the metal shavings from underneath a lathe. A co-worker filling the wheelbarrow loaded it until it was so heavy the female worker couldn't lift it. Aub asked the worker why he did that.

'She's on the same money as me', the worker replied. 'She should be doing the same as me and working as hard as me. No mollycoddling.'

With that, Aub kicked over the wheelbarrow and told him to do his job and fill it up again – this time to the right level. More than once, Aub kicked over the wheelbarrow to make a point. And the point was that in the workshop everyone was equal. That message eventually got through.

'They ended up becoming good friends.'

According to Aub, among the employees were those who emigrated from Europe after the Second World War and, later, from Asia. When the post-war migrants arrived from Europe, they were presented with a 'welcome' booklet by an organisation called The Good Neighbour Council of NSW. In the booklet, the council pointed out the biggest employer in Newcastle was BHP, and that job seekers could obtain an application form in whatever language they spoke.[45] Also in the steelworks' workforce were Aboriginal employees. Long before BHP arrived on the scene, First Nations people, through their language, seemed to forecast what would be built beside the river. This area was known as Tirrikiba, which means 'place of fire'.[46]

Author and academic John Maynard recounts a conversation with Robert Smith, who, with his brother William, had established a highly successful and barrier-breaking employment contracting company in the late 1960s. As young men, the brothers moved to the Hunter, chasing work opportunities by helping repair damaged rail lines after the 1955 flood disaster had torn through the valley. The brothers provided similar work opportunities for other Aboriginal men and women when they established Smith General Contracting. At one stage, the company employed 130 men, with about 70 per cent of the workforce being Aboriginal. The BHP steelworks were one of Smith General Contracting's biggest clients. Robert Smith told John Maynard about his first visit to the steelworks. He had expected to confront racism. Instead, he was welcomed.

John Maynard, whose grandfather was the founding leader of the Australian Aboriginal Progressive Association, says, generally, Steel City was welcoming.

'I'm not saying it was a non-racist Utopia, but there was a degree of acceptance', John says. He cites another story Robert Smith told him.

When Robert had just arrived in the Hunter and was working on the railways, his colleagues invited him to the pub. Robert was concerned about the publican's reaction to an Aboriginal man in the hotel. That had been a problem in the past. The publican gave him two schooners for free as a welcome. However, he was worried when a police officer walked into the pub. Robert thought, 'I've got to get out of here'. His workmates called the 'Sarge' over, and the officer asked Robert, 'Who might you be?' Robert introduced himself, and the officer extended his hand as welcome. According to John, Robert wondered, 'Where am I? I must be in Hollywood!'

Based on his own experience in the workshop, Aubrey Brooks says racism was rare.

'I don't think it would have been tolerated.'

But The BHP was a dirty, noisy and potentially dangerous place. Even so, there was a time when one of the rites of passage of a Newcastle education was a school excursion to the steelworks. I recall following a guide through a section of the works with my classmates, watching men prodding at glowing metal like heroes taking on monsters, and staring at molten streams snaking past. It must well have been a stroll through hell, exciting but frightening as well. What was wondrous to a school kid was deadly for some employees. The first worker died before the steelworks were even officially opened. A trade assistant was killed in the final days of 1914, and on New Year's Day, 1915, another name was added to the fatality list. That list kept on growing through the works' 84 years of operation, with about 194 dying in work-related accidents.[47] In Aubrey's time at The BHP, about two dozen workers died on the job, and he lives with the memory of seeing colleagues killed or badly injured.

'I've seen some terrible things there', he murmurs.

Through the years there was also industrial strife, with strikes and dismissals. The works – along with the entire city – soared and tumbled in response to global booms and busts. In the early 1920s, during a recession, BHP shut down large sections of the Newcastle works and slashed its workforce from 5500 to just 840 for about nine months. This action decimated household budgets, and it gnawed at the city. After all, the steelworks' furnaces had been like beacons to those seeking employment, with the area's population swelling by about 16 000 in the 1920s. With the downturn, many lost opportunities for regular work and, according to historian Sheilah Gray, thousands of families were pushed close to starvation.[48] While the industry recovered in the early 1920s, at the end of the decade The Great Depression rolled in, wiping away demand for iron and steel, and jobs, once more. However, by the end of the following decade, the Newcastle plant had grown to be the biggest integrated steelworks in the Commonwealth. Other industries associated with the works, including ventures that BHP had either founded or invested in, such as Lysaght Brothers & Company, Rylands Brothers and Commonwealth Steel sprang up around the city. The industrial giant of Newcastle was becoming, as BHP called itself, the big Australian, supplying the materials for a nation. As BHP's legendary managing director and champion of the Newcastle works, Essington Lewis, wrote in 1935, 'The value of steel for all purposes of peace or war is heightened in proportion to Australia's distance from her partners in the Imperial Commonwealth'.[49]

That value, and the importance of Newcastle, was further heightened when the Second World War broke out in 1939. As Australia armed itself, the nation relied heavily on the Newcastle steelworks. In the course of the Second World War, the works provided steel for the manufacturing of guns, ships and tanks. Associated industries also manufactured materials for war. Rylands, for instance, had produced the net that ensnared one of the Japanese mini-submarines that snuck into Sydney Harbour and launched an attack on 1 June 1942. The war led to a radical change in the industries' workforce as well. With so many men enlisting in the services, thousands of women entered factories for the first time to continue manufacturing what was needed.

BHP produced not just the materials but the man to oversee a large slab of the war effort. Essington Lewis was appointed the nation's Director-General of Munitions and Director-General of Aircraft Production. Before those government appointments, Lewis had been preparing the company, and the nation, for war and greater self-sufficiency, encouraging Australia to stockpile raw materials and proposing to build ships in Newcastle.

The pivotal role Newcastle played in Australia's war effort meant it had to be protected. The city was defended by a ring of military installations, including forts, air and naval bases, and thousands of servicemen and servicewomen. Steel City had become Fortress Newcastle. The 'fortress' came under siege, and the steelworks were in the sights of the enemy, in the early hours of 8 June 1942, when Japanese submarine *I-21* fired a volley of shells on Newcastle. As one of the main targets, the steelworks could well have been easy to see, if the star shells had burst in the right place. A young serviceman, Lieutenant Ken Robin, was on board the minesweeper HMAS *Allenwood*, which was berthed in the harbour. He was woken by the shelling and saw the river washed by the brilliant white light of a star shell. But he noted the range was wrong and the star shells burst to the seaward side of the steelworks, so nothing of importance was illuminated.[50] Even so, it appeared the Japanese found their mark. A shell did land near the works but it didn't explode. That 5.5-inch shell is now exhibited at the Fort Scratchley Historical Society's museum, sharing a display case with the singed and tattered parachute of a star shell from that fateful night in 1942. But as the historical society's president, Frank Carter, points out, if that shell or the others fired from the Japanese submarine had exploded in The BHP, it would have not just damaged the steelworks, it would have dented the war effort.

In the post-war years, the steel city within Steel City grew. By the mid-1960s, the works had produced about 308 million tonnes in the course of its life. The BHP, wrote author and journalist Alan Farrelly then, supported Newcastle's industry on its shoulders. According to Alan, beyond the industries BHP was associated with, there were 1393 factory establishments in the Newcastle region, employing 45 389 people.[51] And the steel city, and all it fed, was destined to grow larger. With the Hunter River's string of little islands disappearing and being reincarnated as the Kooragang industrial precinct, as a means of at least partly solving the problem of where to next build factories in Newcastle, the plan, Alan Farrelly wrote, was for The BHP to duplicate itself and create new steelworks on the reclaimed land.[52] Kooragang was ugly, but the promise it held for Newcastle was beautiful.

The city fed its hopes for the future into the steelworks and out would come our dreams in the form of money, security and identity. In a way, it was like feeding your hopes into a monster. When you travelled along Kooragang and looked across the river, you could glimpse the fires in the soul of the place. That's where the blast furnaces were. Sometimes at night, the Newcastle sky would glow as though something apocalyptic had gripped the heavens. But it was just something to do with the coke ovens, or slag being dumped, or gas being burnt off. The sight of flames and heat was part of living in Newcastle. It didn't make you feel warm, just grounded. Occasionally, there would be complaints about pollution from the industries, and the scrim of smoke and steam and soot that would be smeared across the city's skyline could impede our view. But that was okay. We, as a city, had invested our view in The BHP, and if it was impeded, and all we could see was our world, and the future, through the haze of industry, that was all we needed to see. We could see our future in the haze.

But then our future got hazy. In the early 1980s, The BHP employed more than 11 000 people. Things seemed great in Newcastle then. But, soon enough, not in the wider world. A global recession pushed down demand for steel. I recall at my high school, many of the boys had planned on an apprenticeship or traineeship at The BHP. In 1981, there were 1150 apprentices, along with another 590 trainees, at the steelworks. But as the downturn gripped the steelworks in 1982, my schoolmates had doubts about what they would do in the future. What was happening in the playground was being played out across the city. As Richard Face, a Hunter parliamentarian and the NSW Minister Assisting the Premier on Hunter Development, later reflected of that time, 'everyone expected BHP to be there forever and that everybody would have a job there'.[53]

We didn't know it then, but the community was on a long ride to the closure of BHP Newcastle. At least it was not all down. There were times of hope, sometimes constructed by policies, such as the Hawke Government's Steel Industry Plan in the mid-1980s; at other times a feeling of 'we're all in this together', when the vast patchwork of unions associated with The BHP signed a landmark development agreement, and then there were the times when the market climbed and so did profits and hopes. In the mid-1990s, the company had been talking about changing its method of steel-making and investing in new equipment for Newcastle that would take the works into the 21st century. For those displaced by change, the NSW Government and industry were involved in a group with the optimistic title, the Beyond 2000 Committee.

Then, on 29 April 1997, everything changed. BHP announced what some had felt was inevitable, what many had believed was unthinkable.

The Newcastle steelworks were to close in 1999. There was to be no beyond 2000 for the works.

In halls and parks, around office desks and dining tables, across the city and the region, people gathered to protest BHP's decision, and to wonder what the future held. A union leader expressed what many were experiencing, saying the imminent departure felt like there had been a death in the family. In response to BHP's announcement and the worry and uncertainty coursing through the Hunter, politicians served up promises of support and volleys of accusations. The NSW Premier at the time, Bob Carr, stood on the steps of BHP's Newcastle administration building and told the throng this was a boardroom betrayal.[54]

That word would be rolled out often, as state politicians from both sides described how Hunter people felt about the steelworks' imminent closure. They debated what each political party had done, what they hadn't done, should have done, failed to do, of future opportunities, of opportunities past, and opportunities lost.

Amid the criticisms he raised about the company and the Liberal Federal Government, local Labor parliamentarian Richard Face tried to keep it positive in NSW Parliament, declaring, 'I have lived in the Hunter all my life and I know that the Hunter will survive. They wear it tough in the Hunter'.[55]

During the same debate, the Member for Newcastle, Bryce Gaudry, argued BHP had been built on the efforts and loyalty of Newcastle workers and that the company had 'ratted' on not just those workers and the city, but on the state and the nation. The Labor MP argued the company had to do more for Newcastle.

'BHP must pay back what it has taken from the city', Bryce Gaudry said.

Yet what many Novocastrians felt was being taken was the very soul of their community. The 'steel' was being taken from the city. How would you pay that back?

However, others foresaw Newcastle becoming something else. During the debate, Member for Coffs Harbour, the National Party's Andrew Fraser, declared he was a proud Novocastrian and said the city could be better promoted as a tourist destination.

'Tourism provides the potential to create jobs and to give Newcastle a new image of a place to go for a weekend away – not the image of smoke, dust, dirt and hard yakka', Andrew Fraser told parliament.[56]

In September 1997 in Federal Parliament, Senator John Tierney, who was a member of the Liberal Government, talked of the resilience of the Hunter, and pointed out that while the loss of jobs would hurt, the region was already economically diverse. All of the Hunter's eggs were not in the steel basket.

'What people do not often realise is that BHP is not really the biggest employer in Newcastle; it is actually the Hunter Area Health Service, followed by education, BHP, and a very wide range of wholesale and retail outlets', John Tierney told the Senate.[57]

In reflecting on this period a few years later, researchers and authors Phillip O'Neill and Roy Green noted that BHP's decision was a blow to the region, and to manufacturing in Australia, but the diversification of the Hunter's economy was already well advanced. At the time of the announcement, BHP had 2500 direct employees and another 800 on contract, amounting to less than 1.5 per cent of the region's total workforce. The academics said the Hunter Valley was arguably the nation's most diverse, skilled, well-endowed and socially cohesive region.[58]

Novocastrians had become used to hearing words of reassurance by then, as if words could salve the wound of the loss of jobs, and the loss of identity.

During a visit to the Hunter in July 1997, a few months after BHP's announcement, Prime Minister John Howard had found hope, optimism and forward thinking. He acknowledged the 'difficult circumstances' of those facing retrenchment, 'but the most important message that should go out of the Hunter Valley to people all around Australia [is] that this region has an enormous amount of fight left in it, this region has an enormous future, this region has a capacity to live beyond the BHP phase and this region has a capacity to regenerate and be better than ever in the years ahead'.[59]

Yet there was a gulf between what politicians had to say and how those at The BHP felt. Aubrey Brooks recalls that initially the response among many of his workmates was one of stoicism, with some even being jovial. Official planning for a different future picked up pace. Retraining programs were implemented, and governments spruiked, and put money into, industry diversification. BHP invested in the city, including contributing to an industry and technology park upstream from the main works, which was to be called Steel River. Yet Aubrey recalls as the final day, 30 September 1999, crept closer, the mood generally slipped. He was receiving calls from workmates, asking, 'What are we going to do, Aub?'

BHP worker Dan Boyd later expressed the bewilderment and disbelief many were experiencing in a poem titled, 'The Gravy Train Doesn't Stop Here Anymore'. As he wrote in one stanza:

> We took pride in our steel, it doesn't seem real,
> That no furnace will enter our life.
> Our daughters and sons knew we put on the runs
> At the Works when danger was rife.
> Now we've got to be mild, although we are riled,
> And suppress all our anger and fear
> Steelmaking has died, our hands are now tied,
> We solace in grumbling and beer.[60]

On the morning of the closure, the *Newcastle Herald* declared on its front page that after 84 years of The BHP and its steelworks in the city, there was hope for a new dawn. But for Aub and many of his workmates, it felt like the end of life as they had known it.

'It was the saddest day. We were trying to man up.'

Aub later wrote about that final day. With a lump in his throat, he shut the wagon shop where he had worked for 38 years, then he prepared to walk out of the main gates for the final time with 'my boys'.

'Their heads were held high but inside their hearts were broken and shattered, their lives would never be the same', Aubrey wrote. 'Some moved on, some retired, some never made it and some never worked again. After employing people for 84 years, BHP was gone. Newcastle would never be the same.'[61]

Standing outside the gates, watching the men walk out, gazing at their faces and sharing the thought that Newcastle would never be the same, was John Tate. John's own life was undergoing dramatic change, for he had just been elected Lord Mayor of Newcastle. He was to be the leader of a city uncertain of its future.

'When the gates shut I was there', John recalls. 'I looked in the faces of the people, they were walking past me, and I got inspiration from that. They weren't "This is bad", they weren't glum, they were going somewhere. That was inspirational. I didn't know them, but there was inspiration in their faces, and aspirations in their faces and their eyes. They were heading somewhere.'

Where they – and the city itself – were heading, not even the new lord mayor knew. John says he had no answers initially for the media when asked what the city's future was.

'I kept hearing from interviewers, "This is the end of Newcastle, isn't it?" I'd reply, "We'll cope with this, we'll survive. We'll get on. We'll get through this". I didn't have the answer at that moment.'

By the end of the day, John resolved, 'I'm not going to cop this any more'. So when asked what would Newcastle do now, he talked about its tourism potential. John no longer wanted anyone to associate the words 'Dirty Newcastle' with his hometown. He understood why people thought that. Anyone driving north along the Pacific Highway, the main east coast thoroughfare, could see, from the top of the ridge at Highfields, the city of Newcastle and its patchwork of suburbs. For drivers, it is like the curtains have been pulled back from the windscreen. These days it is a stunning view. In 1999, less so. For on the horizon were the BHP steelworks and other industries, their stacks pumping out emissions. When that sight filled drivers' windscreens, it reinforced many people's view of Newcastle. As a result, they were determined to go nowhere near 'Dirty Newcastle', and they kept driving north.

'That reputation was real', says John. But he wanted to ensure that in the years ahead people would no longer be able to say that about Newcastle. The air would clear on what the city could be, even if it wasn't clear then.

As for Aubrey Brooks, he wasn't sure where he was heading. The company had retained him to keep an eye on things at the steelworks. But he couldn't bear the silence. He was spooked by the ghosts of what this place had been, and what the works had meant to him. Aub lasted less than a day before quitting.

The ghosts are still there in that vast tract of land that became an industrial graveyard. After the works closed, many of the structures on the site were demolished. Like great beasts, the mills and the factories, the furnaces and the workshops groaned and roared as they were imploded or torn down, creating clouds of polluted dust. A remediation program for the site was implemented, attempting to clean up the ground and the river that had absorbed so much pollution from the works, or at least to cap the damage that had been done through the decades. With the stacks toppled and no more steam and smoke chuffing into the sky, the air around the city became clearer. Yet those chuffing stacks were, in the eyes of many Novocastrians, exclamation marks of reassurance that all was well and that they had a secure job. Now that had been blown away, as surely as the sea breezes had scrubbed clean the heavens. You could now see unpolluted skies and uncertainty arcing over the old steelworks site.

Before the works were even dead, all manner of ideas for the site were proposed. The University of Newcastle looked at the possibility of using the administration building and surrounding land as a campus. Heritage groups had wanted many of the buildings retained, perhaps as an industrial theme park. There were even suggestions the site could be turned into a film studio. After the company had handed over the steelworks site as part of a deal with the state in 2000, successive governments had their own designs and desires for the land. The day after BHP made its fateful announcement in 1997, WEJ Paradice, the CEO of Hunter Valley Research Foundation, said this prime waterfront land could not sit idle. However, he pointed out the challenge was to bring new life to the land.[62]

Despite all the ideas and intentions posed and floated, that challenge has so far proven too much. A quarter of a century after the steelworks closed, much of the site remains barren, a wound on the landscape, reminding us what the city has lost, and that, with this key piece of land at least, we haven't been able to move on. Just as Aub discovered on his final day as a BHP employee, we're all living with the ghosts. The city remains haunted by that land.

Dismayed that the site remains largely unused, Aubrey has his own ideas as to how the former steelworks land should be used.

'I'd like a steelworks put back there. A modern steelworks, with apprentices.'

Aubrey would like to see an industrial park established on the land, and for the main administration building to be brought back to life, perhaps as an exhibition centre or museum, so that people can remember the steelworks and those who worked here.

Even after The BHP shut, there was still some steel-making in Newcastle. However, it has dwindled further. In early 2024, the end of an era arrived at the suburb of Waratah. The Molycop mill announced it was restructuring its steel-making operations. After more than a century of steel-making on the site, no more steel would be produced there. The mill had begun operating amid farms and cottages in 1918 as the Commonwealth Steel Company, or, as it was commonly known, 'Comsteel'. After the announcement, Tony Callinan, from the Australian Workers' Union, reportedly declared that was the last of the steel makers in Newcastle. As a result, Newcastle would lose its badge of being a steel city.[63]

To Aubrey Brooks, that badge was effectively handed in a quarter of a century earlier. Not that he lives in the past. As he says, a little ruefully, Newcastle is a good place to have a coffee, but it is not Steel City any more.

'Newcastle's moved on. And a lot of people have moved on for the better. But we lost our heritage, we lost our history.'

And you can hear the longing, the pain, in his voice when he says, 'We've lost one of the greatest assets Australia ever had. And I still don't know why. I don't know why'.

Aubrey has seen his former workmates at reunions, and he sees them still in his dreams. The BHP has long gone, but in his head, Aubrey once more populates that barren ground, making something of it. Just as those tens of thousands of workers did, Aubrey performs a kind of alchemy. Only he doesn't turn ore into steel; he turns memories into dreams.

'I dream about it often. I dream about being in the blast furnace. I remember going around on the locos, talking to the blokes, having a giggle.

'The dreams aren't nightmares. Just reflections of the past.'

IN its 84 years of operation, and even after it closed, The BHP produced not just iron and steel products but also artistic inspiration. The aesthetics of the ugly and the noisy provided creative souls with ideas and perhaps a challenge.

The results could be compelling. Through the years, visual artists repeatedly captured the angles and the moods of this vast industrial sculpture. Have a look at the sketches of the steelworks at its most productive by renowned mid-20th century artist Robert Emerson-Curtis, or at the images of George Gittoes, depicting the humanity amid the machines, which he created during a residency in Newcastle in the late 1980s. Even from a distance, the steelworks were a siren song for artists, drawing them in. In her paintings of the city around the harbour, Margaret Olley would often include the steelworks, their stacks pumping out steam and smoke that scumbled their way across the canvas. For Margaret, the attraction of the steelworks was more than visual.

From her place up on The Hill, Margaret could hear The BHP humming and pulsing, especially at night. Those sounds, she told me, were reassuring.

'That pulse was like how a baby feels a heartbeat, it was like being close to the mother, close to the heart. You could hear it pulsing, throbbing.'

During her nocturnal wanderings on The Hill, Margaret revelled in the juxtaposition of sounds, listening to the rumble of the ocean to the east and, to the north across the river, the thrum of industry.

'Go out to the lavatory at night and it was pulsating!' she said, the words chopped up by that mischievous laugh of hers. 'A throb!'

Other artists reacted to The BHP's presence in, and enormous influence on, the community. Birgitte Hansen, who was renowned for her public art and murals, produced a social realist work titled, *'B.H.P.' Behind Huge Profits*, which depicted a Hogarthian crush of tired-looking women and children. Birgitte Hansen was later commissioned to paint a series of works documenting the life of the Newcastle plant.

Those paintings were part of a diverse cultural initiative called The Ribbons of Steel festival, which the company staged in the lead-up to the Newcastle works' closure. In effect, art was being used to soften the pain, or perhaps release it, for a community that felt rejected. And rather than art responding to industry, industry was very much in the art. What's more, the art was forged and staged in the cauldron of industry, with the steelworks becoming a performance space. The festival's events ranged from a choir comprising steelworkers to a ballet of forklifts. In many ways, the performances merely continued and echoed the drama and visual spectacle that had taken place in the works for more than 80 years. After all, steelmaking is industry as theatre.

Because of that theatre, the eye of the lens and the vision of Australia's best-known photographers had been trained on the Newcastle plant throughout its life. Max Dupain caught the angles of machines, the flash of light and glowering molten steel in his black-and-white photos of the works for the city's 150th anniversary commemoration book. In 1963, David Moore took perhaps the most iconic photo, depicting the relationship between the steelworks and the city. The photo shows two boys on bicycles riding away from the industrial leviathan, which is consuming the landscape and the sky. Even as it lay dying, the steel complex provided a compelling photographic portrait subject. Murray McKean was a BHP staff photographer who took a series of stunning studies of the works as buildings were demolished and torn down. Murray had a clear picture as to what he wanted to photograph, and why.

'Just to remember it. There were photographs of it when it was constructed, and this was my version, or vision, of how it came down.'

The great craters and gaping holes in the corpses of buildings, the mountains of crushed concrete and twisted metal, the toppled towers and gutted furnaces in Murray's photos amount to so much beautiful destruction at a place once dedicated to production. In a few of the photos there are solitary human figures, usually dwarfed by the demolition taking place around them, so, just as it was when the works were running full tilt, the men are effectively in the machines. Yet mostly the images are unpeopled, with only hints that humans once roamed this part of the land, such as a discarded safety helmet on a pile of metal, and goggles and gloves hanging limp in a locker.

Murray spent two years photographing the steelworks as it gradually disappeared, shooting hundreds of rolls of film. As stark as the contrasts may be in the images, they don't compare to what the photographer himself was experiencing.

'As a BHP photographer, it was a sensory overload when the place was fully operational. The smells, the sounds, were just incredible', Murray recalls. But when he was there alone with just his camera, wandering among the ruins, 'all you could hear were the pigeons'.

'It was the most remarkable experience I'd ever had.'

He found photography subjects in the unlikeliest of places. A piece of metal that had been there for more than 80 years had around 20 coats of paint on it, and when Murray peeled back that paint, he was struck by the vibrancy and play of colours.

'I used to call them my opals', he says. 'The combination of rust and colours has given me some remarkable images.'

His favourite image is of the wreckage of the blast furnace, which had just been toppled, with a tiny figure standing before it. To Murray, 'it looked like an animal and a trophy hunter'.

'It was the saddest feeling looking at it, thinking about the people working on it, and finely tuned to produce quality steel for Australia and overseas, and now it was a wreck. That photo is in my stairwell, and I look at it every day.'

Also fossicking for gems in the ruins was renowned Melbourne-based artist Jan Senbergs, who happened to be in Newcastle on a creative residency when the steelworks were being demolished. Jan did a series of drawings on site, capturing the structures, or what he called 'wonderful sculptures', before they were torn down. Even after they were toppled, the buildings had a sculptural quality, as Jan's drawings lyrically show.[64] Just as Murray McKean's photos are, the images of Jan Senbergs are both works of art and historical documents, invested with both poignancy and beauty.

Amid the clanging and the clamour of 84 years of steelmaking, there was music. Actually, the music was in the clanging and the clamour. As Aubrey Brooks said, the orchestration of hissing and banging, of machines roaring and whizzing, of locomotives chugging and whistles sounding was all music to him.

Music came from the steelworks' community too. Many fine musicians worked at The BHP, and it was the birthplace of ensembles as colleagues became bandmates. Just a year after the steelworks came into being, a brass band was formed, with the musicians largely coming from the workforce. After performing and competing in eisteddfods in the Hunter's coal communities, the Newcastle Steelworks Band set off on an international tour in 1924. In the process, the band would help challenge preconceptions that Australia was an artistic wasteland. A string of astonishing performances in three prestigious competitions in Britain earned the band its world-class reputation. At the British Empire Exhibition in Halifax, competing against some of the best-known ensembles in the land, the band from the small industrial city at the bottom of the empire took out top prize against all expectations. As a result, the Newcastle Steelworks Band was the British Empire champion. Next up, it participated in the British Open brass band championships in Manchester. An estimated 30 000 people turned up; many attended expecting to witness the downfall of the 'colonials'. But again, the band defied expectations, winning the title of British Open Champions. The Australians made history as the first overseas band to take the crown from the British. The band then performed in a contest comprising 130 ensembles at the Crystal Palace in London. It was considered the world championships for brass bands. The Australians didn't win, taking third place, but their playing won over the crowd, with reports of wild applause and hats and programmes thrown into the air in appreciation. In all, during its UK tour, the Newcastle Steelworks Band played 50 concerts, released recordings, and earned the respect of British audiences.[65]

The influence of the steelworks band has flowed through the generations. In 1924, one of the band members on that historic tour was William Norman Morgan, an apprentice electrician at The BHP. Norman, as he was known, played the E flat horn. Exactly a century on, his grandson, Justin Body, followed in Norman's wake to Britain. Justin journeyed to Scotland to perform at the Royal Edinburgh Military Tattoo after being selected from hundreds of musicians as one of the bagpipers in the tattoo's pipes and drums band.

Justin was all but destined to be a bagpiper. Both his parents played the instrument. While he is a Novocastrian, Justin recalls the music of Scotland always reverberating through his home. However, growing up, Justin rarely heard any stories from his grandfather about his grand tour. That was typical of a Newcastle person. As Justin says, 'You don't go big noting yourself. He was just a person who loved music'.

It was only just before Justin set off for Edinburgh in 2024 that he was shown his grandfather's scrapbook, the record of a young man's adventure snapped in a series of black-and-white photos, with leaflets and flyers from the venues that the steelworks band played resting between the pages, and with descriptions of each image, each memory, written in Norman's hand.

So into Edinburgh Castle each night, Justin carried the memory and the inspiration of his grandfather, and what it means to be a Novocastrian – then and now – and how far it can take you.

'We're just all hard-working people. We have a good work ethic.'

As for what Norman would make of his grandson being part of the Royal Edinburgh Military Tattoo, Justin replies, 'I think he'd be very proud, but he'd probably want me to play a trumpet, not a set of pipes'.

The steelworks have been pressed into the words of writers through the years, including in Dymphna Cusack's novel *Southern Steel*, in which both industry and the city glow. The production of steel changes lives, for better and worse, in the novel, and it gives life to the city. Cusack had her character and steel company employee, Keir Sweetapple, describe the presence of the works in the 'untidy, smoky city' that he loves as the 'sign and seal of Newcastle's existence'.[66] Through her words, Cusack makes the industrial romantic. Her stay in Newcastle as a teacher may have been brief, but Cusack seems to have fallen in love with the creative possibilities of the place, or, at least, what could be extracted from it.

Just as steelmaking can be seen as industrial theatre, Newcastle playwright John O'Donoghue literally turned industry into theatre with a couple of his works. It was his *Essington Lewis: I Am Work* that forged the feel of steel and the spirit of a place, along with the ambition of a man and a company, into a compelling piece of drama. From industrial strife portrayed as a boxing match to folk songs about the rise of the steelworks from the ground, and lifting workers from a life underground, *Essington Lewis: I Am Work* has The BHP and Newcastle dancing across the stage. As one of the steelworker characters, Taffy Williams, sings of his life and the place he had worked at since it began, 'And I never thought we'd both come this far'.[67] Yet it all comes at a cost. In Taffy's case, it was a leg, lost in an industrial accident in the rolling mill. Then again, as the character of Essington Lewis points out, 'Life's a rolling mill. You come in one shape and go out another'.[68] Taffy, and Steel City, would come to learn the painful truth of that aphorism.

Perhaps the best-known melding of industry and art to emerge from Newcastle has been the foot-stomping brilliance of a former fitter and turner, Dein Perry. Dein used his feet to turn how people saw Newcastle on its head. But he did it by taking the Steel City image, and his own experiences as a Novocastrian, and reshaping it as a dance spectacular known as Tap Dogs.

Dein grew up riding motorbikes through the bush near his home at Charlestown, playing football, and waiting till he could finish school and learn a trade. With his mother's encouragement, he had also been learning tap dancing and performing in competitions since early childhood.

To be a boy who danced at a Newcastle western suburbs high school was tantamount to shuffling into disaster. But after he performed, just to please his mother, at a school concert, everything changed for Dein. He gained the respect of the boys and attracted the interest of girls. Even so, he saw his future on a factory floor rather than before the footlights. At the end of Year 10, he took up an apprenticeship as a fitter and turner at a Newcastle engineering company. That inevitably took Dein into the steelworks, with the engineering firm contracted to do work in The BHP. As a Novocastrian, Dein knew the role of heavy industry in the city.

'The one thing that struck me about Newcastle, growing up, was it was like paradise at the beach, but then you could look over the hills and you saw all this *Mad Max* landscape', says Dein.

Dein wandered back onto the stage as a teenager, when the Hunter Valley Theatre Company hired him to perform in *West Side Story*. That experience gave him itchy feet to return to dancing and prompted him to leave factory life behind.

'I was trying to change my life, I wanted to get out of [industry], and the only other thing that I knew that I was good at and trained in was dancing.'

He was invited onto a Saturday night television variety program on the ABC to perform a tap-dancing routine.

'I remember when the ABC show was aired, the next day when I walked into work, all the workers lined up and did *Swan Lake* for me in their overalls', Dein laughs. Many years later, that moment would inspire a scene in Dein's film, *Bootmen*.

It was now the early 1980s, and with the economic downturn and less work at the steelworks, Dein was laid off. He worked for his father's trucking company for a time but was dreaming of a life back on the stage. He wanted to wear tap shoes, not work boots. However, he ended up wearing both.

To pursue dancing, Dein knew he had to leave Newcastle. He worked on a production at a casino in Hobart, then in musical theatre in Sydney. Landing a principal role in *42nd Street*, Dein was bitten by the tap bug once more. In 1991, he began developing an 'industrial' style of tap, and formed an ensemble called the Tap Brothers.

They performed the musical *Hot Shoe Shuffle* in Australia and London's West End, where Dein earned an Olivier Award for his choreography. The ABC asked him to come up with a clip for one of its programs, which Dein suggested filming in an old factory.

'Once we got that setting, it seemed ridiculous to wear patent leather tap shoes in there, so we got some boots and put tap shoes on them', recalls Dein. The clip was titled 'Tap Dogs'.

That was the birth of the Tap Dogs ensemble and show, placing muscly dancers in a factory setting, with heavy machinery and tools, forging elements of a Newcastle steelworker with a classic Hollywood musical performer. Top hats and tails were out, replaced by singlets and Blundstone boots. However, the idea of taking tap into the factory can be traced back to his apprenticeship.

'When I was a fitter, especially at night on dog watch, I used to work on this huge machine called the floor borer. It's like a big milling machine. It makes the sound "Koonk! Koonk" – basically it's a backbeat for music. And that used to go through my veins all the time, working there.'

For his industrial tap, Dein used actual machines to provide the rhythm and the character. He wanted to use not props, but 'a real lathe, or a real compressor or a real jackhammer to make it real'. Dein Perry and the Tap Dogs were taking the feel and character, the grit and energy of Newcastle out into the world. One of the productions was even called

Dein Perry's Steel City, which toured Australia and was staged at Radio City Music Hall in New York City. Suddenly all the qualities for which Newcastle had been derided were being celebrated by audiences and critics in theatres far and wide.

'For me, it was just putting those two elements together. You've got a complete and utter steel city, steel environment, and then you've got this art form, and those two had never been put together before.

'Everyone goes, "a genius move", or whatever, but for me, it was just what I knew. I knew both worlds, and so it was just an obvious thing for me. You've got to have a point of difference ... and for us that was a massive point of difference.'

Having incorporated the rhythms and sounds of industrial Newcastle into his art, Dein then wanted audiences to see his hometown. In 2000, the stage productions morphed into *Bootmen*.

Dein's life and art are threaded through the movie. *Bootmen* is about Sean, a steelworker who wants to be a tap dancer. Declaring he can't make a living tap dancing in this town, Sean heads to Sydney to join a production, but clashes with the troupe's leader (played by Dein). Sean returns to Newcastle and the steelworks, even though he knows it holds no security any more. Sean establishes his own blue-singlet-and-boots tap dancing troupe, and he uses his workplace as a rehearsal studio and stage.

Life presses deeply into art in a scene where the foreman announces the steelworks are to close in three months. To raise money to help his workmates, and to find a way out of grief because of a family tragedy, Sean and his Bootmen stage a stunning benefit show in a machine shop. Sceptics and critics join the cheering crowd, and, for one night at least, the sounds of machinery, heavy rock and amplified tap boots echo through the dying steelworks.

For Dein, the timing, and intertwining of art and life in Newcastle, was extraordinary. The steelworks had only just shut, so he could use the site as one big movie lot. He also wanted to record the site for posterity, 'before they knocked it down', including shooting scenes in the engineering shop where he used to work. Filming in the dormant and deserted steelworks was both disconcerting and reassuring: 'Well, it said to me that I'd made a good choice in getting out of the business'.

Rather than just record what was about to go, Dein was also keen to showcase what the city had, what it was, and what it could be. So there are many luscious shots of the beaches and the harbour, of the Stockton Ferry and the ocean baths, of the Civic Theatre and the Seven Seas Hotel in Carrington. There is a loving acknowledgment of his family, with the players in a rugby league game at Stockton wearing the sponsor's name on their jerseys – Des Perry Transport – as a coal ship glides by in the background. The Screaming Jets' founding guitarist, Grant Walmsley, plays a part in the film. And the director wears his love of the Newcastle Knights in *Bootmen*. Tony Butterfield, the former Knights front rower and a hero of the club's first ever grand final win in 1997, has a cameo role, and the team's home ground features in a couple of scenes.

'I've always loved the Knights. I put them in the movie, I made sure they were in the movie, I made sure we shot at the stadium. We wrote a scene deliberately to be in the stadium.'

So *Bootmen* feels faintly biographical and proudly Novocastrian. Released at a time when many were reading the city its last rites, the film is a stunning statement that Newcastle was brimming with life and energy. In the film's final scene, when the Bootmen perform an encore to the rapturous audience, the troupe pushes over a line of steel beams, as if the performers are dancing on the grave of the steel industry. Yet it doesn't feel like a funeral. It feels like young Sean, and the city, has been reinvigorated. By the time the end credits roll, and the producers express their thanks to the last of the BHP workers and the people of Newcastle, anything seems possible.

There may be a lot of him in the shows he created, but Dein has a very different energy. He is serene and humble, with a gentle voice. It is a long time since he danced on stage, but he continues to oversee Tap Dogs, which has been performed in dozens of countries to more than 12 million people. For most of his adult life, Dein has resided in Sydney, but so much of him continues to live in Newcastle. He is here often, visiting family, and to work. His production company is involved with the Knights' home games, so we catch up and talk just before he heads over to the stadium.

Across the road from the Newcastle West café where we meet is a dance studio, Perry on Parry, run by his younger sister, Renae. Dein's daughter also teaches there sometimes. His imprint is never far away in this town. On the studio's roller door is the image of two boots. Dein points out they are his boots.

'I'm still a proud Newcastle guy and Novocastrian, and people who know me or who've heard of me associate me with being a Novocastrian and Newcastle, and I'm really proud of that. I love that they say, "Oh, you're that tap dancer guy from Tap Dogs", and they say, "Where are you from?" I say, "Newcastle", and they say, "Yeah, of course you are. You're from Newcastle".'

NEWCASTLE is no longer seen as just a labour town economically, but politically it remains, largely, a Labor city.

Despite all the changes in Newcastle, and to Newcastle, with many industries having shut or declined, some things remain true. And when it comes to the Australian Labor Party, it seems many Novocastrians remain true believers.

As of mid-2025, all the members of parliament representing Newcastle at the state and federal levels of government are from the Labor side of politics.

'I think it's ingrained and rooted in the city', muses the mining union's Robin Williams. 'It's a working-class city, it's a coal port, it's a coal city, and it's still attached to the coal industry that's now moved further up the valley. And I think that some of the things that do cut through are some of those stories by the people who are still around, that this is a working-class city.

'It is still a Labor-type city.'

Since Federation, voters in the federal electorate of Newcastle have elected only Labor candidates to represent them in the nation's parliament. And they have voted for the same person time and again. From 1901 to 2001, Newcastle had only four MPs. Entwined with loyalty to the party has been family. David Watkins, a former miner and the first federal MP for Newcastle, was in office until he died in 1935. He was succeeded by his son, David Oliver Watkins, who remained the local member for 23 years. Allan Morris, the federal Newcastle

MP for almost 19 years from 1983, is the brother of Peter Morris, a former member for the neighbouring seat of Shortland and a Hawke Government minister. At a federal level, Newcastle is still considered a very safe Labor seat.

For the NSW Parliament, the electorate has chosen someone other than a Labor politician a couple of times in the past century or so. In 1988, independent candidate and local businessman George Keegan was elected the Member for Newcastle, and in 2011, there was a momentous shift, with the Liberal Party's Tim Owen winning the seat. But in both cases, the motivation was primarily about Newcastle voters punishing the state Labor government of the time, rather than booting out the local representative. So it was not so much personal or local but giving Sydney a serve.

Robin Williams reckons that desire to 'give it' to Sydney still shapes a lot of politics in Newcastle, and it continues to be part of what it means to be a Novocastrian. If our character were to be scanned, we'd notice there is a sizeable chip on our shoulder.

'I guess the good argument we hear all the time is that Newcastle gets left behind, and that Sydney gets everything, that we don't get anything. I think that does resonate with people, that we are being left behind.'

Novocastrians can cite a long list of examples of where they feel the city has been short-changed. Perhaps one of the biggest issues is that of coal royalties. Coal is the salt rubbed into the wound gaping around that chip on the shoulder. Many Novocastrians, and those further up the valley, complain they live with the consequences of mining, and the Hunter provides billions of dollars to the state economy through royalties from coal exports, and yet the region gets comparatively little back.

Prior to releasing the 2024 state budget, Treasurer Daniel Mookhey acknowledged the Hunter deserved more, and that the region made a significant contribution to NSW. However, the Treasurer pointed out the coal royalties derived from the Hunter being dug up belonged to everyone in the state.[69]

Robin Williams says there is justification for Newcastle and the Hunter feeling short-changed.

'For the amount of money produced as a result of coal, those areas all the way down to Newcastle have not seen the benefit of the industry that's impacted them.'

At the local government level, Labor has not had such a clear ride in Newcastle politics. Since 1948, when the title 'Lord Mayor' was instituted for the City of Newcastle's leader, there have been five Labor representatives but also a string of independents and representatives of the Citizens' Group. In 2024, Labor's Nuatali Nelmes was voted out as lord mayor after almost 10 years in the role. She was replaced by former ALP member and Novocastrian anaesthetist Ross Kerridge, standing under the banner of Our Newcastle.

Our Newcastle promoted itself as a group of independents, determined to put the 'local' back into local government. Our Newcastle argued that 'local government is not a place for divisive party politics'.[70] The argument seemed to strike a chord with voters, who value what 'Newcastle' means to them, even more so than what Labor is perceived to mean to Newcastle. So while some read the 2024 Lord Mayoral poll as indicating many voters were dissatisfied with Labor, it says more about how the electorate feels at the local level. What motivates voters is a question many feel they have little control in influencing, let alone answering, at state or federal elections, but it holds great power at council elections: What's best for Newcastle?

John Tate asked a variation of that question himself when he stood for lord mayor in 1999. John had been an independent councillor since 1980. By the late 1990s, he was frustrated by what he saw as the negativity in the council chamber, and he believed that was shaping the mood in the city. He felt it was dragging Newcastle down. He thought, 'This city is better than that'.

'Somebody had to stand up and say, "It's a good place, it's a place where you can live and work and enjoy. Don't put it down". That's why I threw my hat into the ring.'

John Tate would go on to be the longest serving lord mayor of the City of Newcastle so far, remaining in office until he retired from the role in 2012.

Having become the lord mayor as the BHP steelworks was shutting, John saw his role as building confidence and self-belief in a city where both had taken a major hit. He approached that by concentrating on what Novocastrians do have: a sense of place, and a strong identity.

The council installed new signs identifying each suburb, underscoring that Newcastle is the sum of many communities and characters. Restoring identity was one thing; making the city look in the mirror and be proud of what it saw was another.

'What was a challenge was that the place looked tired and not cared for in many instances', John says. 'What I put a lot of emphasis on was to get the place looking tidy and spick and span. Fix the fences, fix the roads, clean the lawns.'

He wanted the impression of Newcastle to be, 'They care about this city'.

'I think we did achieve that.'

While he was a popular lord mayor, John missed out twice on being elected to state politics. In 2007, Labor won with its candidate, former local television newsreader Jodi McKay. But John Tate came close. Then, in 2011, he was lost in the maelstrom of Newcastle voters teaching NSW Labor a lesson by electing a Liberal representative. In some ways, that blip in the city's voting habits is closer to what John Tate believes would be good for Newcastle. If a seat seems winnable by either major party, that is good for the electorate. The city would not be taken for granted by either those in power, or by those seeking to win over voters. John didn't take those two results personally. Being a Novocastrian, he knew bigger issues were at play at the state and federal levels. Labor, he acknowledges, has been good at tapping into local issues with its network of branches. And in council, local is what counts.

'I didn't worry about the politics. I was elected by the people. They expressed their opinion, and I served the people. That's how I survived.'

If John Tate's thinking about Newcastle's political preferences is correct, we are not so much a Labor town as a 'local' town.

'The only explanation I can offer is that local-level people want to talk to people locally,' John says.

'I think we see ourselves as people of purpose, of honesty and integrity; people who are prepared to get in and have a go.'

CHAPTER FIVE
SURF CITY

If you wish to dive into the heart of being in Newcastle, and yet feel far removed from the city, head to the beach. If you were to swim in a straight line, City of Newcastle has about 11 kilometres of coastline, from Glenrock Lagoon and Burwood Beach in the south to part of the great ribbon of sand along Stockton Bight in the north. So there is plenty of sand for everyone, even if it may not feel like it during summer holidays.

The beach is a place of both land and sea, and yet it belongs to neither. It is, as the Newcastle-born author and historian Greg Dening called it, a space of transformation, and of crossing.

Dening studied the peoples and cultures of Oceania, and he noted that to them, the beach was a sacred and unresolved space where things could happen and be made to happen.[1]

Living in Newcastle, we are people of the ocean, and the beach is where things happen for us. The beach is where we have seen ourselves as something more than the descendants of industry. Here our skin has been made sheeny not by sweat and toil but by the surf and sun oil. The beach is our temple, our place of communion. It is our playground, our place of hedonism. The beach is where we go to escape and lose ourselves. It is where we go to find ourselves. We shed our clothes and any pretensions to reveal ourselves. And to be a Novocastrian is to be nakedly unpretentious.

As much as anything, a Novocastrian is a beach person. Our reputation might have been forged by fire and steel, but our character has been shaped by sand and water.

The beach has been, for thousands of years, where culture and identity have been sculpted, where food and stories have been collected, and where a sense of place has been nurtured. The Awabakal and Worimi have given names to landmarks, including the beach itself. As Biraban and Threlkeld recorded, the beach is wom-bul.[2] The First Nations people have given names to the life pulsating and swaying through the fibrillating light in the shallows and on the pocked rock platforms, or gliding and gambolling beyond the breakers, from the minuscule to the leviathan. They have even given names to the coalition of time and emotion, as experienced on the beach. The word for 'dawn' is ngo-ro-kan.[3] You can almost feel the sun rising out of the sea in the sound of those syllables.

On the beach, time means nothing. And yet it is everything. With every breaking wave, every gust of wind, every shifting grain of sand, there is change. The beach is bringing change to Newcastle itself. It is the space of transformation for how the city is perceived. Slowly the surf is eroding preconceptions about Steel City, washing away the memory of all that entails, to leave lying on the sand a glistening visage of a place to visit, to relax and chill, and in which to live. The beach is bringing a new wave of admirers.

As Novocastrian board rider and filmmaker Phil Avalon says, 'Newcastle is a surf city'.

But the beach hasn't always been seen as a place of crossing, of identity, of transformation. In the eyes of the early European arrivals, it was largely to be avoided.

In the instructions Governor Lachlan Macquarie gave to the incoming commandant, James Morisset, in 1818 for the administration of the settlement, he wrote as his 36th rule, 'Some lives having been lost by persons bathing on that part of the beach where there is a heavy surf, you are to caution all persons against bathing in any other place than on the beach within the harbour to the westward of the wharf'.[4] Ironically, Macquarie, in his enthusiasm for building public works, also helped create a popular beach. The construction of Macquarie Pier scooped up sand and banked it along its eastern edge. What took shape was Nobbys Beach.

Those in Newcastle seemed to keep their distance from the beach many years after Macquarie's instructions had waned. In the mid-1800s, JF Mortlock, who was from a well-known family in Cambridge and was transported to New South Wales in 1843, toured the colony after his release. In his memoir, Mortlock observed of Newcastle that it was 'curiously situate[d] on the inner side of a hilly point; not a single house in the town possessing a view of the ocean only three hundred yards behind them'.

'To enjoy the cool sea breeze, the inhabitants must surmount a gentle rise.'[5]

Even in the early colonial days, others saw the beach as one of Newcastle's greatest assets, especially in unshackling itself from its reputation as a 'purgatory' for the twice-convicted. In a letter to the editor of the *Sydney Gazette*, written in October 1829, the correspondent rhapsodised about Newcastle, outlining in more than 3000 words why it was better than Sydney.

'A resident here experiences less of ennui than the resident of the capital – the fitful gushes of the healthy ocean breeze, the leapings and sallying to and fro of the sportive fish in the first shooting of the morning beams, the eddying airy whirls of the eager sea fowl in quest of their tiny prey, and the tranquil aspect of the brightening loops and windings of the river among its dusky islands and sunny beached bays, presenting also in their quiet beauty a charm which even the most moody minds could not resist.'[6]

This correspondent conveys what people now want, and are willing to pay handsomely for, in Newcastle. Unlike what Mortlock observed, any rise, gentle or otherwise, any trough or dune, is studded with some of the most expensive real estate in Newcastle, as the inhabitants seek not just the breezes but the views that reach out to the waiting coal ships and over the horizon. They are no longer merely million-dollar views; the top beachfront homes sell for much higher than that.

Dave Anderson has seen change just beyond the sand since the early 1960s. Although he has observed the change along the sand as well, whenever the tide turns or the wind shifts. Dave is a well-known surf reporter and sublime photographer, as well as being a life member of Merewether Surfboard Club. Dave is as rusted on to Merewether as anything metallic in the seaspray-coated suburb. He has lived near the beach pretty much all his life. His parents bought a house in the early 1960s a few hundred metres from Merewether Beach for a few thousand pounds. They bought the house Dave lives in about 50 years ago for a fraction of its worth now. Not that Dave is planning on selling, let alone moving out of Merewether. For him, the house is not an asset. It's home.

Not far from Dave's house, along the street that faces the sea, with only a retaining wall between it and the sand, built to effectively stop the street toppling onto the sand, is what is known as Millionaires' Row. In the streets behind, bungalows and miners' cottages have been progressively knocked down for townhouses and apartments or houses that colonise just about every square centimetre of the allotment's sandy earth. Merewether is the home of quite a few of the city's rich and well-known, including musicians and Newcastle Knights players – and those who have done very well from the surfing industry.

'Gone are the days when a group of guys who loved surfing could move in and rent a house', laments Dave.

Yet real estate prices haven't barred Novocastrians from the beach. You don't need to live in a beachfront mansion to enjoy the cool sea breeze, and the community of the coast. You don't even need to get your feet wet or sandy.

For a 6-kilometre stretch along the coast, from Merewether to Nobbys, is a walk known as Bathers Way. That very name suggests a pilgrimage, something almost religious. Which it is to many. By following the concrete trail set down over sand dunes, gentle rises, and breath-stealing headlands, thousands replenish their souls, and often their dog's as well, on a daily basis. If you wish to see the face of Newcastle in all its complexity and diversity, journey along Bathers Way. Not that those walking or jogging, skating or chasing the dog will see you; for all those beach pilgrims are too busy huffing and puffing, talking animatedly, or glancing sideways at their constant companion, the water. People don't come to Bathers Way to be seen. They come to be with the sea. They're consumed with looking out, or within, so they're really not interested in seeing you. But what you will see is the portrait of contentment in face after passing face. This is the face of Newcastle at its happiest.

For many, the pilgrimage leads to an area skirting South Newcastle Beach, where the path cuts between the sea and the escarpment. Millions of years of the earth's life are presented in the rock face shadowing you. A dyke, molten rock solidified, pushes for the surface, cutting through layers of sandstone and coal, providing a clue to the pressures and violence that have helped create where we stand. After wet weather, the face weeps, with water trickling out of the deep past towards the sea. As you look up at the serrated edge of the escarpment's top sawing at the sky, you can see scant evidence of human settlement. A couple of light poles poke above the rock face and into the space. The scene looks like a Jeffrey Smart landscape painting. Yet this walk isn't just about rocks from deep in time but also from far across the sea. A little further north along Bathers Way, where the escarpment folds down to Newcastle Beach, there is a historic rock wall. Many of the materials in the wall are metamorphic rocks called gneiss, believed to have been quarried in Brazil and carried to Newcastle as ships' ballast.[7] Back at the South Newcastle escarpment, the remains of Second World War observation posts and gun emplacements are pressed into the rock face, a reminder that not so long ago, servicepeople stared out to sea, searching for threats. Now along Bathers Way, people stare out to sea, watching surfers or gazing out further at the archipelago of ships, which glitter at night, reminding us in the prettiest and most subtle of ways that another community is out there. Perhaps that community of seafarers is staring back at us, waiting to rejoin us on land. As the Mission to Seafarers' senior chaplain, the Reverend Canon Garry Dodd, reminds us, 'Wherever you are around Newcastle, you can see the horizon, and you can see a seafarer.'

And those moments near the coast or on the beach remind us we are more than a harbour town; we are part of a seafaring world.

The greatest distraction from the sea at South Newcastle is the skate park, as people on boards and wheels beetle and whizz about the bowls and curves. It is frenetic and seething with energy, like the ocean after a Southerly buster. Indeed, during the reconstruction of the skate park and this section of Bathers Way between 2020 and 2024, storm-lashed seas did their best to devour the work site, gobbling up work deadlines and budgets. Which, of course, is also the blessing of the sea and why we're attracted to it. The sea eats time.

Bathers Way may be built to encourage active movement along the coastline, but by its very placement, one of the great pleasures it offers is the opportunity to slow down and observe. On the northern edge of

Bar Beach, where the land swells and rises, as if trying to imitate what the sea is doing, is a lawn offering an uninterrupted view south along the coastline. On a clear day, with a breeze rinsing your imagination and the sun sprinkling diamonds in your eyes, you can almost see Antarctica. Not quite, but anything seems possible, and everything seems right, as you sit on the slope and watch people and, during the migration season, whales pass by. For out there is the Humpback Highway, with tens of thousands of whales heading north to have their calves then, a few months later, south with their expanded family. To see a whale breach, splintering the sea into spume, only adds to the feeling that Bathers Way offers something close to a religious experience. This patch of lawn is particularly popular at the end of the day, when the procession of headlands to the south hardens and the sea blends into the approaching darkness. The distant hill marking the eastern edge of Merewether Heights ignites into a fairyland, as the lights go on in houses and the beams of vehicles driving along the appropriately named Scenic Drive slice the slope. Way off to the south, a ray from the Norah Head lighthouse skitters over the headlands and wheels through the night. Just in front, along Bar Beach, birds whorl and dip in the soft illumination of lamps, which also spatter puddles of light on the sand that glistens with the remnants of each retreating wave. This lawn serves as more than a viewing platform; it is also an outdoor dining venue. People bring picnics or unfurl from butcher's paper freshly cooked fish and chips, attracting squadrons of squawking seagulls. Others back their utes or vans up to the lawn's edge and set up for their meals on wheels with a view. Just behind the lawn is a large car park. While it may be aesthetically ugly, that car park so near to the beach offers what passes for a miracle in any city: free parking. Apart from around Newcastle Beach, there is no charge for parking at the city's coastal hotspots. Perhaps that perpetuates the idea of Newcastle being a car city, but at least it means one less cost for people to get to the beach.

As you sit on the lawn, looking along Bar Beach towards Merewether and beyond, if life doesn't seem as near to perfect and as far from care as possible, then wander over to the small memorial standing sentinel on the grass. As the stone life buoy resting at the foot of the memorial indicates, this was erected by the Cooks Hill Life Saving and Surf Club, which has patrolled Bar Beach since 1908. This was one of the original surf life saving clubs in Newcastle, and among the first to be formed outside of Sydney, in response to a spate of drownings along the coast. However, it wasn't the sea that claimed the lives of those commemorated with the memorial. The nine names etched into the stone belong to surf club members who died while serving in the First World War. The siting of this memorial, overlooking the beach that these young men would have known so well, could not be more beautiful, or more poignant. Life, and its loss, is also memorialised in St John's Anglican Church at nearby Cooks Hill. The sandstock brick building, consecrated in 1860 and the oldest standing church in Newcastle, held the funeral of local surf swimming champion Ray Land in 1949, after he was killed by a shark at Bar Beach. While shark attacks had occurred every now and then along the Newcastle coastline and lurked as a constant threat in beachgoers' minds, the public outcry following Ray Land's death prompted the installation of shark nets off the beaches between North Stockton to Catherine Hill Bay by the end of 1949.[8] The nets have remained, spurring debate between those who believe they provide protection and a sense of security, and those who want them gone because of the indiscriminate damage they do to marine life of all kinds.

The marine life provided food and the opportunity for gathering for First Nations people for thousands of years. The convict artist Joseph Lycett had evidently ventured beyond the bedraggled little settlement he was confined to and found himself on the sea shore, recording the rituals of the Aboriginal people. He painted fishers spearing in the shallows and diving for lobsters. Another Lycett work depicts groups feasting on a whale washed ashore at what the Europeans would name Bar Beach.

North of the lawn overlooking Bar Beach, the land rears into a headland that has a sheer face, time-trampled and crumbling. Here the land tumbles off the cliff and into the rock-speckled sea. Peering over the edge, even on a calm day, there appears to be something unsettled, even violent, swirling just below the surface. According to the Reverend Lancelot Threlkeld, the area below the cliff was known as Yi-ran-na-lai, or the place of falling rocks. Contemporary Aboriginal leader and author John Maynard refers to it as the singing cliffs.[9] But that 'singing' could carry a perilous tune. Threlkeld wrote that the beach below the cliffs could be a dangerous place, with stones and rocks above dislodged by the 'concussions of air' from the human voice.[10] He noted that while walking at Yi-ran-na-lai, his Aboriginal language collaborator and guide, Biraban, along with others walking with them, had warned him to be silent. The missionary asked why he had been hushed.

'This elicited the tradition of the place as being a very fearful one, for if any speak whilst passing beneath the overhanging rocks, stones would invariably fall as we had just witnessed', Threlkeld later wrote.[11]

On a gale-lashed night in July 1884, voices would have been raised and panicked at the foot of the cliff. They would have been fearful not because of what could come from above, but because of the power of the sea. The *Susan Gilmore*, a sailing ship that worked the trans-Pacific coal run, had lurched into trouble while heading to Newcastle from Sydney and, in the storm, was being pushed ashore. The barque missed the rocks gnashing at the water's edge and was driven by the waves onto a stretch of sand. After daylight arrived, Newcastle's Rocket Brigade rescue crew arrived, firing a line over the stricken ship, allowing everyone on board – including two dogs, a cat and a canary – to be winched safely ashore. The wooden wreck was destroyed by Mother Nature but the ship's name remains on the sand. The place is known as Susan Gilmore Beach.

Along the cliff top, treading lightly over the land's edge, is a pedestrian bridge that has become one of the most popular places in Newcastle. If Bathers Way is a pilgrimage, this is the temple on the climb to its highest point. This bridge is part of a 450-metre-long stretch known as Newcastle Memorial Walk. This stretch is a place of animated chatter from walkers and joggers, of 'oohs' and 'aahs' from visitors and photographers pointing their cameras towards the cetacean show along the Humpback Highway, and of quiet reflection.

Newcastle Memorial Walk was officially opened at the going down of the sun on 24 April 2015 to commemorate, the following day, the centenary of the landing of Australian and New Zealand soldiers at Gallipoli, and the founding of the ANZAC tradition.

The opening was the end of a long journey for renowned Newcastle restaurateur Neil Slater. Neil had made a name along the harbour's edge with his seafood restaurant, Scratchley's. The building looks like a sleeker incarnation of the warehouses that once lined the harbour front, only this one has a face of glass but still has its feet in the water. As a result, every dish is served with water views and often the awesome sight of a steel wall sliding past the table, as a ship enters or leaves the port.

In the late 1990s, Neil was a member of a council tourism committee and was heartened to hear about plans for a coastal walk, which would become Bathers Way. He figured the crowning glory of the route would be the hill, since it would allow walkers to never lose sight of water. However, he was told the route would follow Memorial Drive, the vehicular road cut into the hill and blocking sea views to the east, as there was no budget for a section over the hill.

'This is typical Newcastle', Neil thought, 'settling for second, third best'.

Not that he had the time to do anything about it, for he was not only running Scratchley's but was trying to realise his vision of a restaurant on Nobbys headland, a vision that ultimately foundered. When that plan fell over, his attention turned back to a walking track over the hill. Basically, one of the main reasons he wanted that walk to be constructed is because he was sick of being told 'no'.

'I'd had eight years of Nobbys.'

In 2010, with state elections not too far away, he invited politicians and candidates to accompany him on a walk. He had one taker, Tim Owen, the Liberal candidate for the seat of Newcastle. Neil figured he needed something more to convince a politician of what he was thinking. He needed a plan on paper. With a limited budget for conceptual drawings, he contacted renowned architect Barney Collins. Barney drafted the plans for free. Neil had something to show Tim Owen by the time they went for their walk into a dream.

At this point, Neil imagined sculptures dotted along the route, to highlight that Newcastle was not just the home of great views but talented artists. Then it was pointed out to him the walk could serve another purpose. Memorial Drive was named in honour of First World War soldiers. For Neil, it was 'a light bulb moment'. Not only did the walk have a focus but the project had a time frame. It could be ready in time for the centenary of the Anzac landings at Gallipoli. So the opening date had to be on or before 25 April 2015. And Neil noticed that focus tended to smooth out political tensions and sceptics: 'You can't really argue with the ANZACs'.

The terrain itself almost shapes a connection to the first ANZACs. The time- and weather-sculpted ridgeline, the wind-blasted vegetation clinging tenaciously to the stony crust, and the serrated edge of the escarpment etched into the sea below are reminiscent of the landscape along the Gallipoli peninsula, where the Allied soldiers landed and fought in 1915.

In the meantime, the near-impossible political slog for Tim Owen had arrived at an improbable moment. He had been elected Member for Newcastle in the 2011 poll. The city turned its back on tradition and Labor. On a two-candidate basis, Owen secured 52.6 per cent of the vote, defeating the incumbent Jodi McKay. The Liberal Party had conquered a mountain, winning over Newcastle for the first time in a NSW election. However, as far as Neil Slater was concerned, never mind the mountain; there was still a hill to climb. The journey towards the Memorial Walk continued.

Neil recounts how Tim Owen had approached BHP to gauge the industrial giant's interest in the project, as 1915 was not just the birth of the ANZAC legend but also of the Newcastle steelworks, and the steel produced there had been rolled into the war effort. BHP contributed to the Memorial Walk. The city council, with property developer Jeff McCloy as the lord mayor, voted to fund the Memorial Walk as well. Government departments and local businesses lent their knowledge, experience and services to the project.

'Everyone rallied. It was part of the Newcastle ethos: "We're all in this together"', recalls Neil.

'The whole project was a case of "100 per cent in" once we got past the conceptual stage.'

Yet prior to the Memorial Walk's opening, political and meteorological storms swirled through Newcastle. Tim Owen and Jeff McCloy had been caught up in an Independent Commission Against Corruption investigation into banned political donations in the lead-up to the 2011 state election. Both resigned from public office, and the voters of Newcastle had returned to the polls to elect new representatives in state and local government. The voters returned to familiar ground, so by the time of the official opening, there was a Labor lord mayor, Nuatali Nelmes, and a Labor state member for Newcastle, Tim Crakanthorp.

In the days before the opening, an east coast low skulked in and smashed Newcastle. As if the Memorial Walk needed another metaphor tying it to the battles fought a century earlier, the new landmark on the hill copped it with high winds and sheets of rain. However, council workers had the site cleaned up by the opening.

The Memorial Walk crowning the hill can be seen from many parts of the inner city, and the helix-like stainless steel that garlands the bridge gleams in the sun. Looking up the hill from Bar Beach, you can see the walkway marching determinedly through the coastal heath up the headland. Driving along Memorial Drive, you can look up and see 'ANZAC' imprinted along the bridge's rails. And when you walk along that platform, there are plaques with information about Australia's involvement in the First World War, and a steel artwork depicting Diggers, and etched into the rusting skin are the family names of thousands of Hunter Valley men, women and boys who served.

The Memorial Walk leads to the highest point, known as the Strzelecki Scenic Lookout, named after the Polish geologist and explorer best known for naming mainland Australia's highest mountain, Mount Kosciuszko. Pawel Strzelecki's research into the colony's coal deposits in the 1840s influenced the development of the industry in the Hunter, which is why there is a commemorative plaque at the top of the hill. The plaque is on the western side, so if you wander over to the east, you're not so much thinking about a figure from the past and staring over the city and suburbs largely created by, and still lying on top of, coal; instead, you are gazing at the seeming endlessness of the sea, watching ships at anchor, waiting to enter the port, and, in most cases, to load coal. The enormous size of that trade is reduced to marks on the horizon, such is the overwhelming scale and beauty of the sea. As you stand here, you may be turning your back on the city, but it is this view that helps make Newcastle feel magical.

Neil Slater now rarely walks along the landmark he helped bring into being. He is moving at a pace faster than walking, pushing onto new dreams, new projects. But he feels proud to see so many people using it. After all, the view south from the Memorial Walk now rivals Nobbys as Newcastle's selfie central. When I mention to Neil that the Memorial Walk is perhaps the most embraced public project in Newcastle in our lifetime, he agrees, but adds a caveat.

'I guess I could answer "yes", but the sad thing is there aren't more public projects that have happened to compete with it.'

So more than the Memorial Walk being an attraction to residents and visitors, Neil Slater hopes it is a symbol of what Newcastle can be. He wants it to be a fillip for Novocastrians to realise who they are and what they deserve. And what they deserve is not second or third best. Once Novocastrians realise that, he argues, so will politicians at all levels of government.

'If you say, "That's all we deserve", they say, "That's all we'll give". We've got to look within and not ask for me – it's not *Oliver Twist* – but say "We deserve more".'

ON a map, beach names are spaced out along the outline of the coast: Nobbys, Newcastle, Newcastle South, Bar Beach, Dixon Park, Merewether, Burwood.

However, in the mind of a board rider, there is a horde of names for surf breaks. If they were to be placed on a map, Newcastle's coast would be crowded with names. By Dave Anderson's count there are more than 30 breaks between Nobbys and the spot near Glenrock Lagoon, or to give it the surfers' name, Leggy Point. A few of the names have historical references, such as Smelters, recalling a copper smelter built in the dunes south of Merewether in the 1850s, and Tank Traps, apparently marking where some of the concrete obstacles, placed along beaches in the event of a Japanese invasion during the Second World War, were dumped when peace returned. Other breaks acknowledged locals, such as Pogo's, named after printer and Merewether resident Reg Pogonoski. According to Dave, Reg Pogonoski was accorded the honour of having a break named after him because he allowed surfers to use his garden hose to wash their boards. And at least one name makes you wonder why you would surf there in the first place: Shark Alley, near Newcastle Beach.

The sum of these breaks is a surfer's paradise.

'Between all these breaks, you can just about surf somewhere in any wind', Dave says.

However, amid all the names of local surfing spots, perhaps the best known is Merewether.

Merewether may share its stretch of sand with other places, namely Dixon Park and Bar Beach, but it effectively holds the beach in the minds of people up and down the coast and across the seas. As beautiful as the southern end of this strip of sand is, and the conversion of the old surf club's house into a restaurant and café brings in the crowds, the source of Merewether's reputation lies just off the beach. The waves that rise and curl over the rocks and reefs just off the shore have been the training ground for generations of surfing champions, and it has helped nurture and fuel a fierce pride and sense of local identity. Such is the pull of this stretch of surf, Dave Anderson asserts (perhaps tongue in cheek) that those who call Merewether home don't even know other beaches exist.

The suburb that is now synonymous with surf came into being because of mining. And Merewether could well have been named Mitchell. Its European origins rest in the mid-1800s with a seemingly indefatigable multitasking doctor, James Mitchell. Doctor Mitchell didn't just practise medicine but was heavily involved in business and colonial life. He was a founding member of the Australian Club, a member of the Central Committee of the Australian Immigration Association, and a director of the Australian Mutual Provident (AMP) Society. He also poured a lot of his energy into Newcastle's growth. Mitchell wanted to get the place on the move, being a director of the Hunter River Steam Navigation Company. He established a tweed factory at Stockton, and two weavers he employed were the future coal entrepreneurs James and Alexander Brown. He was a property investor, owning farms and rental cottages. Mitchell also became involved in politics, becoming a member of the Legislative Council in 1855. The focus of so much of his world was the property he bought by the coast just south of Newcastle, a place he called Burwood Estate.

The estate was a cauldron of industry. On his stretch of land at various times there was a tannery, the first in Newcastle, on the banks of Flaggy Creek, and salt works and the copper smelter close to what is now known as Burwood Beach. To transport ore to the smelting works, Mitchell had a tunnel dug through the coastal landscape. For the tunnelling, a couple of thousand tonnes of coal were dug out, and he stored that on his land, waiting for the lifting of the Australian Agricultural Company's monopoly on the black rock. He lent his voice to opposing that monopoly, arguing it held back Newcastle's development. It also held back Mitchell's own ambitions.

More tunnels were dug under his estate to transport coal mined on his land. The rail lines carrying the coal converged at a place called The Junction on the estate. However, for the coal to reach the port, coal from Burwood Estate had to be carted around land owned by the AA Company. Even after the monopoly ended in 1847, the AA Company would not permit coal from Burwood Estate to be carried across its land, so a special act of parliament finally gave Dr Mitchell right of way.

James Mitchell would later have a closer association with the Australian Agricultural Company. In 1860, his daughter, Augusta Maria, married Edward Christopher Merewether, who would soon become the General Superintendent of the AA Company. Merewether would advise his father-in-law and eventually took over the management of Burwood Estate.[12]

The name 'Burwood' remains in the area, including on the façade of a historic hotel, and Mitchell's name can be found on signs for a street and a park. But it is the son-in-law's surname, Merewether, that has been impressed onto maps and memories. Mitchell had one son, David, who turned a private family fortune substantially earned from coal into books and public knowledge. David Scott Mitchell was more than a bibliophile; he was obsessed with collecting anything word-related about Australia that he could get his hands on. And with his money, Mitchell could get his hands on everything. His mansion in Sydney was, in effect, a house of paper. The books and documents he owned numbered in the tens of thousands. Mitchell bequeathed his collection, along with an endowment, to the trustees of the Public Library of New South Wales. And so we have the Mitchell Library, that magnificent sandstone-faced repository of knowledge and memory, sited in the heart of Sydney but, in part, built on Hunter Valley coal.

If he were still alive, David Scott Mitchell would have had in his collection the writings of Marion Halligan. The acclaimed novelist and short story writer was a Novocastrian, born in 1940. Long after she left Newcastle, Marion continued to play along the beach and in the sand dunes of her childhood, through words. Newcastle, particularly the Merewether area, features prominently in her novel, *Lovers' Knots*. One of the main characters, Veronica, who has grown up in Merewether, has revelled in looking at the water, and immersing herself in it. She loved 'the violence of swimming in Merewether's long unsheltered surf, with rips to drag you out and breakers to dump you'.

Veronica was intrigued how, at 5 o'clock, the beach emptied and the light changed.

'The sea mist blew in and hazed the land, the late sun shone low and it was very quiet, like walking through a nimbus.'[13]

The basic cottages that hold the sandy ground in Marion Halligan's prose and sheltered generations of miners and their families have been replaced by larger, gleaming homes. The source of the area's wealth, and its irresistible lure, no longer lies under the houses' foundations but in the view out of the windows.

However, the beach remains the home, workplace and playground of surfers, including some of the world's best.

The rider who put Merewether on the world surfing map is Mark Richards. Born in 1957, Mark had been introduced to surfing by his father, Ray, who swapped from selling cars to surfboards, when he realised how this sport, and culture, was growing in Newcastle.

Mark's surfing style, with his arms stretched out as he tore apart waves, earned him the nickname 'the wounded seagull'. His incredible ability and his competitiveness earned him four consecutive world titles, from 1979 to 1982.

Yet the man who was indomitable on the water was, and remains, softly spoken and gentle on the land. Mark surfed all over the world but always returned to Newcastle, and to his home break of Merewether. As well as being a champion rider, Mark developed a successful surfboard-shaping and manufacturing business. His boards were emblazoned with a logo featuring his initials in a Superman-like symbol. Off his board, he was more like a Clark Kent, with a bashful nature yet a welcoming face that burst into a smile quickly and often. But we Novocastrian kids viewed him as a Superman. Even those of us who were hopeless surfers. Especially those of us who were hopeless surfers.

I recall a moment in the summer of 1980. I was staggering up Merewether Beach like a newly born calf, having just displayed about the same level of dexterity as one in the sloppy surf, and feeling a certain shame and humiliation at not being able to ride a board. After all, I was from Merewether Heights, just up the road from the beach, so I presumed proximity would have given me the skills to at least stand on the board, even for a few seconds. I might as well have grown up in Alice Springs or on Mars. The sense of shame only deepened when I looked up to see the world's greatest surfer walking towards the water. And he was looking at me. I hung my head. As he passed, Mark said something to me. I don't know if I even heard it properly then, and I don't remember the actual words now, but I do know Mark Richards was softly encouraging. However, not even the world champion surfer could persuade me to get back on a board. That was the last time I attempted surfing. That is, until I enrolled for a lesson in the summer of 2018, in the lulling and forgiving surf at Nobbys. But the Merewether influence had followed me to this more protected break. My tutor was a new-generation champion whose home break was Merewether, Philippa Anderson.

Philippa emigrated from South Africa to Australia with her family in 2003, when she was 12. She had left behind a home opposite the beach in a small town near Port Elizabeth, and all her friends. The only consolation for Philippa was that the place she was headed for also had beaches. Only the family was living 40 minutes' drive inland, with relatives at Maitland. So each day for the first couple of weeks, the Andersons would drive from Maitland to surf at Newcastle Beach. Then after a fortnight or so, Philippa's father, Rod, suggested they drive south over The Hill and see what was there.

'We were coming down towards Bar Beach and saw that stretch, and my first impression was, "It's absolutely beautiful"', Philippa recalls. 'It wasn't like home, but seeing that stretch of waves ... "Woah! Look at this whole other world just over the hill!"'

The Andersons moved to a property at Cooks Hill, then to Merewether. All the while, the surf helped Philippa settle into her new home. As she puts it, surfing helped her through the tough times, helping her build resilience, a quality she would need when pursuing a career on the board.

Philippa noticed she was hardly the only woman surfing, and she didn't cop discrimination or sexist comments as she paddled out at Merewether. It was a welcoming place.

'That comes back to Newcastle and the people here, they just want to go out and have fun.'

In the surf at any given time at Merewether, she says, there can be both professional and recreational surfers, including older riders who have been part of this beach for decades, and they all find space for each other on the waves. The 'warrior vibe', which bristles with aggression and can lead to violence (that Philippa has seen overseas), is not present on this beach. Rather, 'It's such a happy vibe'.

If Mark Richards showed what was possible in the board-riding world, then the board-riding world saw what was possible in Newcastle with the staging of Surfest. This event, first held at Newcastle Beach in 1985, attracted the finest surfers from around the globe. More than being a surfing contest, this was a massive community event, demonstrating the ties between the beach and the town, as thousands of spectators packed onto and along the beach each day.

Surfest, Philippa says, pushed people to see Newcastle differently; that it wasn't just a steel city, it was a surf city.

'I think Surfest helped change that, showcasing the amazing waves.'

One of the festival's key events is the Surfest Indigenous Classic. For more than 25 years, First Nations surfers from up and down the coast have come to Newcastle to compete and bond. Helping organise and taking part in the Indigenous Classic for many years has been Gumbaynggirr and Dunghutti man and fearless surfer Stan Moylan.

Stan enjoys the competition – 'I don't have a competitive bone in my body, but I love having a go' – and he cherishes the sea. For Stan, entering the water is about more than going for a surf.

'It's like a feeling of charging the batteries', he says. 'A sense of cleansing. I like to go on the outgoing tide and sit there, and that takes your worries out.

'And there's definitely a connection. A connection to the land, to the ocean, to the spirits, to the old people.'

Stan has been surfing for more than 40 years. Growing up at Toronto by Lake Macquarie, he would catch the train to Newcastle and walk to Nobbys with his board. All these years on, Stan still heads to Nobbys first, sometimes to surf, other times to simply touch the water; each and every time to connect.

'I go to the rock pools, and I splash myself', Stan explains. 'For protection and cleansing, to let the old people know I'm there.'

Surfest founder and revered Newcastle character Warren Smith has nicknamed Stan 'The Patient Hunter' because, rather than paddling after smaller waves, he is content to wait for the big one to come along. Not that Stan is really waiting for something; out there, he is in the moment, in his element.

'To be at peace with the water and the waves.'

The official status of Surfest as a competition has changed through the years, and so has the venue, but the crowds have continued to come to the beach. Among the spectators in its earlier years was a young Philippa Anderson, who couldn't believe she could get so close to champion board riders as they emerged from the water.

Within a couple of years, in 2009, Philippa was one of those champion surfers. As a 17-year-old, she took out the women's title at Surfest. What's more, she achieved that at her home break, because Surfest had been moved to Merewether.

Since then, Philippa has continued to surf in competitions around the world. She is also helping train the next generation of board riders in Newcastle, with her own surf school. And whenever she can, she gets in the water at Merewether.

'That's my home now. It's my favourite break, and it has an almost amphitheatre set-up. You can sit there on the steps. But what's nice is the waves that break at Merewether are really world class.'

In 2009, Merewether was officially recognised as a National Surfing Reserve. As the commemorative plaque notes, 'You can surf Merewether's waves any time, any tide, any swell, any wind and any size'.[14] Merewether was also recognised for its environmental quality and shoreline, and for the community, heritage and culture attached to the surfing. But at the centre of it all are those waves. If the conditions are right, Philippa says, you can enjoy a 40-second ride. And those waves just keep coming. Yet so does change.

By being on the water, and through the students attending her surf school, she has seen more and more women and girls riding boards. And that doesn't just mark where the sport is heading; it is another indicator of what kind of city this is.

'I was standing at South Bar [Beach], and there were four girls in the water', recounts Philippa. 'And a long-time recreational surfer, who I recognised, was having a shower and counting them. He said, "There's a lot of girls in the water. How good is this!?" To hear him talk positively about that, I thought, "We're on the right path".'

Perhaps this little surfing postscript is an indicator what kind of city Newcastle is as well. Before my surfing lesson with Philippa, when I learned to stand and deliver (for a few glorious seconds), I texted Mark Richards. After all, as Philippa had discovered during Surfest, in Newcastle, surf gods are not distant beings. They walk among us. They're one of us. So I had contacted Mark, asking him whether he had any surfing tips. The four-time world champion took the time to reply, offering some points to remember. The first I didn't need reminding about: that surfing is a thousand times harder than it looks. He also offered advice about regular practice, board size and starting off in small, gently breaking surf. In the final point, Mark emphasised what surfing was all about. Fun. In fact, to use his term, surfing is funner than shit.

Which could just as easily be applied to many aspects of life in this surf city, really.

In Newcastle's early days, the sea – in the eyes of some – could seem like an escape from the restrictions of life in a penal settlement. Around the time Governor Macquarie visited Newcastle in 1818, a correspondent for the *Sydney Gazette* noted that from Christ Church on The Hill he could see 'the boundless ocean, with its rolling waves, far below'.[15]

Although that boundless ocean only made many convicts feel even more confined in their open-air prison at Newcastle. Perhaps that is why a prison for housing those working on Macquarie Pier was built on a rise overlooking Newcastle Beach. The ocean views could remind the convicts they were going nowhere.

What could not be so easily contained was the beach itself. The clearing of vegetation along the coast, in part to keep an eye on prisoners, meant the sand dunes constantly migrated towards the penal settlement, threatening to bury buildings. Little wonder Newcastle East was known as Sand Hills. Sand encroachment remained an ongoing issue for those along the coast, as the beach crawled into nearby suburbs. The sand drift covered roads and crept into properties. Fences were erected to stop it, but that was unsuccessful. In 1887, the colonial government passed the *Sand Drift Reclamation Act*, encouraging the planting of trees and shrubs to stabilise the sand.[16] So, in effect, the resolution acknowledged that removing so much vegetation had caused the problem in the first place. More and more of the sandy terrain was capped not with trees and shrubs but buildings, as suburbs grew. However, the sand drift still happens. After a big storm, sections of Shortland Esplanade, skirting the coast from Nobbys to Newcastle Beach, can look like a sand track.

As well as the ability to imprison, the sea offered the possibility of healing. The rhapsodic Newcastle promoter and letter writer to the *Sydney Gazette* in 1829 outlined not only the joys of exploring the shoreline but also the therapeutic qualities of the sea:

> The peninsular situation of Newcastle gives a more thorough exposure to the sea breeze from a greater variety of points than any other sea port town that ever can be founded along this coast, therefore, as a summer residence for valetudinarians, to whom the equable temperature of the sea air and sea bathing may prove beneficial, it is predestined to rank foremost in the Colony, its fine shelving and well sheltered sandy beaches pointing it out as if formed by nature for the purposes of a fashionable watering place – to rank in fact as the future Brighton of New South Wales.[17]

The colonial government may not have envisaged Newcastle as a seaside resort, but it did site the settlement's hospital along the stretch where the prison had been. That hospital grew into the city's health hub. Royal Newcastle Hospital (RNH) presided over a swathe of land overlooking the beach; some of the wards had rooms with a sea view, and the facility was scented with salt air. Yet eventually the region's health focus shifted to John Hunter Hospital, built on high ground amid suburbs and the bush to the city's west, and many of RNH's fine brick buildings were knocked down in 2008, replaced with multi-storey apartment complexes. Other former hospital buildings that remained were also converted into luxurious accommodation.

Despite the instructions and warnings from the colonial authorities about the perils – physical and moral – posed by the beach, people still stepped onto the sand and waded into the water.

In the 19th century and early years of the 20th, there was a ban on bathing in the sea in view of public areas during daylight hours to maintain 'decency'. However, some ignored or defied the daylight bathing restrictions. The forbidden pleasure of the sea was too great a draw. And the law could hardly block the adventures of youth.

Audley Reay, a council officer who wrote about his boyhood in the late 19th century in a book titled *Memories of the Hunter and Newcastle in the Eighties*, recalled swimming with his friends 'behind the Hospital', at Newcastle Beach, 'in the nude until 8am'.[18]

Once the restrictions were lifted, the popularity of the beach grew, increasing the number of drownings and heightening the need for surf life-saving clubs. By 1908, the city's first surf life saving club was formed to patrol Newcastle Beach. However, the first demonstration of surf life saving techniques on the beach was given by members of the Manly club. A number of Sydney's beaches had already established surf life saving clubs. A large crowd had gathered around the amphitheatre-like edges of Newcastle Beach to watch the demonstration, which became frighteningly real when a whale boat was flipped over by the large surf. Some of Newcastle's own rescuers, including the crew of a butcher boat, plucked the whale boat rowers out of the sea. Along the Newcastle coastline, at Stockton, Merewether and 'The Bar', other clubs soon sprang up.

While the surf has been made safer, with the mantra, 'swim between the flags' one of the few rules that now apply on the beach, for others the seeming endlessness of the ocean, and what may be there under the surface, means they are happy to keep their pleasure contained to the pools and baths that rest on the lip of the continent.

These swimming places, hewn and engineered on the rock shelves along Newcastle's coast, are almost as spectacular as what time and nature have created. The earliest of the ocean baths and pools are almost as old as Newcastle itself.

As the commandant of the penal settlement, Major James Morisset had convicts carve an ocean pool, not for public safety but private pleasure. The pool cut into the rock shelf at the foot of a cliff below what is now called Shepherds Hill was known as the Commandant's Bath. Yet through the years, that name of authority was washed away; the Commandant's Bath became known as the Bogey Hole. After the council took over control of the Bogey Hole in 1863, it was opened to the public. Or, at least half the public. It was a males-only domain. By law, public bathing was segregated by gender, and women were not permitted to swim here until 1911. To accommodate the growing demand for bathing areas, the council enlarged the Bogey Hole in the 1880s. By the end of the 19th century, a correspondent in the local newspaper was declaring it one of the finest swimming baths in NSW, perhaps Australia. And all these years on, in the opinions of many Novocastrians, that assertion clings to the Bogey Hole as tightly as the Bogey Hole clings to the city's edge.

The presence of the Bogey Hole means it is possible to be simultaneously connected to the city's convict past, while experiencing a sense of unbound freedom. What's more, it seems apt for this to be referred to as a hole rather than a pool or baths, for, standing above, you can see its irregular shape, having been cleaved from the rock. The hole looks very much part of the coastline.

The steep stairs offer a dramatic descent to a platform, where you can leave your towel. Or you can just stuff it into a crevice in the rock face. Plunging into the pool, you feel released. You are cocooned by the work of convicts but immersed in the sea. The hole is not deep, and it is easy to touch the bottom. The floor is rough and uneven, and the sides are covered in marine growth, so it looks and feels like a rock pool.

The Bogey Hole is a communal place, a place to gather, to celebrate life and the sanctity of water.

Newcastle's Greek Orthodox community holds its Blessing of the Waters service at the Bogey Hole each year on the Sunday after the feast of the Epiphany. On a summer's day, a scrum of young people dives in and thrashes the water in a desperate bid to be the first to retrieve a cross thrown into the pool by a priest. The service has been held at the pool for more than 60 years, and the Blessing of the Waters is an affirmation of the community's role in Newcastle, as attendees pray for the city's wellbeing, and for the welfare of seafarers.

On a very hot summer's day, when I plunge into the Bogey Hole, the water feels like a blessing. And on days like this, the hole is a broad church, drawing a diverse crowd. The Bogey Hole is very much an 'in' place for tourists, and the tourists are in the hole in force on this day, having a grand time. Major Morisset would have been disgusted. I chat with a Canadian who has been living in Victoria. He is visiting Newcastle to attend an ice hockey tournament. Bobbing in the tepid waters of the Bogey Hole, his homeland seems very far away. He points to the left, across the sea, and says it's that way to Canada, implying the connecting nature of water. Although he does observe that the water here is probably a little warmer than way over there.

On the sea side of the pool is a chain rail, as if the platform is tethered to the land, like a convict work gang. Standing on the rock shelf, grasping the chain, you very much feel as though you're teetering on the edge of the continent, as you look along the coastline, counting the headlands nudging into the Tasman Sea, then you turn and look at the escarpment looming over the pool, and a hang glider drifts over.

It may be set in rock, but the Bogey Hole's appearance constantly shifts, according to the moods of the sea and sky.

One morning, after heavy rain has seeped through the layers of the cliff into the water, the Bogey Hole looks muddy. Yet a group of older women assure me, 'It's like swimming in a dam'. I pass.

When the winds are howling from the south and east and shoving the sea against the coast, the waves hurl into the rock shelf and send spume into the sky. It rains onto the hole and kneads the water, swirling patterns on the surface and opening fantails of froth. When the sea enters the pool, it brings all its uncertainty and potential for tragedy with it. People have died at the Bogey Hole. Thomas Henry Jones, otherwise known as Harri Jones, a Welsh poet and academic who had moved to Newcastle, wrote in one of his works how he had itched 'for the griefless hills of the sea'.[19] He was buried by those hills. Jones drowned at the Bogey Hole in January 1965. Fellow Newcastle poet Norman Talbot composed an elegy to the lost man of verse, titled 'The Seafolding of Harri Jones', in which,

> The sea runs low & ceaseless as a wolf in a cage
>   to the edge & back.[20]

However, the threat the sea holds doesn't keep some away; it only draws them closer, to play with the wolf. On a wild summer's afternoon at the Bogey Hole, a bunch of boys stare the sea in the eye – that is, when the sea isn't spitting into their eyes – by standing on the edge, holding onto the chain and absorbing the bash and froth of the waves. Every now and then, a wave pushes one of the boys into the pool. The water explodes with whoops and squeals of delight. Staring down the sea at the Bogey Hole could well be a Novocastrian rite of passage. Audley Reay and his mates did something similar more than a century earlier. In his memoir, Audley wrote that the Bogey Hole was 'always the best place for a dip but dangerous in bad weather'.

'When the tide was very high and weather rough it was a most delightful place if you could get safely in and out – to a moderate or indifferent swimmer it was hard to get out without a few scratches from the rocks.'

Audley and his friends also clambered around the cliff face to look at the wreck of the *City of Newcastle*, a steamship that had come to grief in 1878 before it could reach its namesake. 'The remains of her boilers and engines were still visible', Audley Reay wrote, recounting how he would swim in the sea near the wreck.[21]

The boys also swam at The Soldiers' Baths, to the south of Nobbys Beach and at the foot of Fort Scratchley. They had been constructed for those stationed at the fort. However, 'baths' is perhaps too grand a word; as Audley describes the construction, it was 'simply a half circle of rocks to prevent undertow and keep out sharks'.[22] Further south was another enclosure the boys would not have been allowed to swim in – the Ladies' Baths.

The coastline doesn't so much march south from The Soldiers' Baths but meanders over a rock shelf profuse with life glimmering and swaying in the pocks and bowls the surf has carved out and filled. Just beyond the shelf in the swell there is an explosion of life as well, with surfers skittering across the waves at a place called the Cowrie Hole. The coastline then nudges into an Art Deco edifice the colour of creamy butter and garnished with blue columns and geometric patterns. The structure, built in 1922, outlines its purpose in the bold lettering imposed on the butter wall: OCEAN BATHS. Like a film set, the pavilion is but a backdrop for the real action. For this is the Newcastle Ocean Baths. Behind the fancy façade are two pools that are like a later generation of the Bogey Hole, for their origins were carved and hammered out of the rock shelf more than a century ago. After years of talking about the need for new baths to keep the public safe from the surf and sharks, work began in 1912. These baths were to break new ground. They were to accommodate mixed-gender bathing, marking a loosening of public decency laws. The-then Griffith Ocean Baths, named after the NSW minister who stumped up money for the project, opened to huge crowds the following year, even though work was not complete. In 1915, the Hawaiian Olympic swimmer and pioneer of surfing, Duke Kahanamoku, visited Newcastle and gave a demonstration in the baths. Generations of swimmers, from champions to the joyously flailing, have done laps in the Big Kahuna's wake ever since. On the stepped stand sheltering the northern pool sun lovers have lounged and stretched out. Although at the 1913 unofficial opening, there was no patience for those who desired to indulge in sun bathing; the inspector told them to keep to the edge of the water or move on. As a newspaper report declared, 'The ultimatum quickly chocked all attempts to bask in the sun'.[23]

These days, the concrete steps soak up the sun as hungrily as the lounging bathers do, and the play of light and shadows looks like a painting. Actually, many a painter and photographer has made art of the place and moment.

While there used to be an admission charge, the baths are free and open to all. Except when big swells breach the wall and the baths become an extension of the surf. The sea is the only one doing laps on those days.

What has also splashed around in the baths through their long life is the occasional controversy, from complaints about the water quality to protests about changing the pavilion.

The baths have a group working to protect them and ensure that they remain a place of community and simple pleasures. The Friends of Newcastle Ocean Baths Incorporated has about 60 members. One of them is Dianne Newman, who travels from near Kurri Kurri, more than half an hour's drive away, to the baths a couple of times a month. She points out that her doing that demonstrates the baths' attraction reaches beyond inner Newcastle.

'It's such a beautiful place, and it's an experience like nowhere else. It's more than the physical environment, it's a social environment. There are the regular swimmers, but also the waders and the walkers.

'People from all walks of life go there, and they develop social networks.'

The Friends of Newcastle Ocean Baths has spoken up about elements of the facility's upgrade. Members want to retain open-air change rooms, for example, and they oppose any suggestion of the baths becoming a money spinner. As far as Dianne is concerned, the baths must remain free of charge. After all, the Friends of Newcastle Ocean Baths regards this as the people's pool.

'Because it's free, people respect it. And it doesn't impose additional costs on people. We should stick with the original purpose of the baths, which is bathing and recreation.'

Much to the delight of the group, and many others who use the pools, in 2025, the Newcastle Ocean Baths were officially listed on the State Heritage Register because of their cultural, social and architectural significance.

Just to the south of the baths is another enclosure known as the Canoe Pool, its wall originally designed to offer the area some protection from the sea. Beside that enclosure was a circular construction called the Young Mariner's Pool. Built in the 1930s, this pool contained not just the sea but the entire world, for in the Young Mariner's Pool, a map of the world was shaped from concrete. The continents rose out of the water, and the countries of the British Commonwealth were painted red, while everywhere else was green. Anyone who waded in here could have looked down and seen a part of the world, but in the 1940s, a little boy named Bob Miller looked into the pool and saw his future. It had already been a day of wonder for Bob. Before reaching the pool, Bob had stood on the beach and stared out to sea. He hadn't been long in Newcastle, having moved from the bush to live with his grandparents in an old terrace house in the city. The sight of so much water reaching to the horizon, going on until it became sky, amazed him. Then he got to stand on the edge of the world. He watched other boys sailing their model boats, in the pool. From that moment he started thinking about designing boats. Bob began messing about in actual boats while living in Newcastle, including sailing a 16-foot skiff on the harbour. In the years ahead, that boy would not just change his name to Ben Lexcen, he would change the course of yachting history, designing a boat with a revolutionary winged keel. The boat was *Australia II*, which won the America's Cup in 1983, seizing the prize from the United States for the first time in the competition's 132-year history.[24] So the gentle influence of the river and the sea that embraces Newcastle and nurtured young Bob Miller helped lead to the moment after the America's Cup victory when then-Prime Minister Bob Hawke jubilantly told the nation that any boss who sacked anyone for not turning up to work was a bum. Somehow even Bob Hawke's choice of words seems like a product of Newcastle. And never was a facility so aptly named as the Young Mariner's Pool, considering who and what Bob Miller would become.

If the joy of Newcastle Ocean Baths plays out behind a façade, there is no such cover for the historic facility at Merewether (as long as you look past the brick changing rooms). Devotees of the Merewether Ocean Baths proclaim these as the largest of their type in the southern hemisphere.

While there was another pool at Merewether a little to the north, constructed in 1926 and gradually eaten by the seas, the baths that hold so much water and devotion these days took shape at the back end of the Great Depression in 1934–35.

The stairway to heaven here in Merewether descends rather than ascends. The stairs negotiate a treacherously steep slope, past the changing rooms. On the steps, outside the brick building, used to sit a huddle of burnished blokes, dressed in only swimming briefs and looking like ancient Roman Stoics, but with a life attitude and relaxed conversational style that suggested they were more devotees of Epicureanism. As a result of their presence, this part of the stairway was known as the Steps of Knowledge. The steps lead to two large baths. The one closest to the 'shed' is known as the kids' or 'small' pool, because it is relatively shallow. Beyond it, reaching towards the sea is the 'big' pool. It is 50 metres wide and, like the kids' pool, 100 metres long.

The kids' pool I know well. It holds both memories and submerged fears for me. As a little boy, I was dragged screaming into the pool for swimming lessons. I laboured through the torrent of tears to become sufficiently proficient to graduate to swimming in the big pool. It looked more adult, with its rows of numbered diving blocks worn along its edge like a castellated crown. I enjoyed diving off those blocks, feeling the invigorating cold grip me. Yet I quickly lost interest after making a splash. I never have had the patience or the stamina to do more than a few laps. Which is why I look on from the outside with admiration at the community of slow-stroking devotees of the baths, who greet the sun and affirm life each day.

In that community are Steve and Sylvia Watson. Steve and Sylvia have been together for more than half a century, having met as teenagers. They both grew up in Merewether, and their connection to these baths is even more time-honoured than their relationship. Steve was brought here for swimming lessons after he scared his family, dashing towards the sea as a small child. Sylvia also took her first strokes in these baths. She was brought here for lessons, because a neighbour thought the little girl whose parents had moved from war-ravaged Latvia to start a new life in Newcastle needed to know how to swim. Both learnt from an icon of the baths, Alice Ferguson, a local woman who taught generations of kids to swim by threading their little bodies through a tyre tube for flotation and telling them to get paddling. Alice Ferguson also taught me to swim. Even through the tears and the terror, I remember her as a kindly presence.

Sylvia doesn't swim every morning as she works, but Steve does. The daily dawn swim is a blessing conferred on the retired.

'It's a wasted day, if you don't swim', says Steve.

As a young man, Steve was a champion ocean swimmer, ploughing beyond the breakers off Dixon Park. Open swimming has become very popular along this coastline, with more and more people embracing the vast opportunities of the ocean. Off Newcastle Beach is a group called the Sandrays, whose members regularly share their kilometre or so swim with a pod of dolphins that treat this stretch as their playground. Occasionally, the migrating whales venture in close enough for the Sandrays members to hear their keening calls and the splash of their tails on the undulating surface. Yet these days, that's not for Steve. He finds comfort in the baths.

Steve swims a kilometre each morning, stroking out 10 laps lengthways in the small pool. Swimming may be among the most solitary of pursuits, with your body cocooned in water, leaving you with only your thoughts for company. But Steve finds company each morning before he reaches the lip of the baths.

'By the time I get changed and I'm stepping into the pool, I've probably spoken to 25 people. No big conversation, and I might not know their names, but it's a smile, a wave and a greeting. That's what Merewether is.'

In stripping off, Sylvia says, people are open and vulnerable. They rely on each other's kindness, and they bond. At the baths, wearing nothing but a pair of togs and a smile, you see Newcastle, and its humanity, at its most welcoming.

'It's inclusive', Sylvia says. 'Maybe not immediately. But you're seen, and you're included.

'The baths are a social leveller. Swimming at the pool, people greet each other, no matter from which walk of life you've come. It's those moments at sunrise when we're all just people. It's a very fair place, it's very equal. You're sharing the baths.

'The baths give you that village-type feeling.'

For some, the baths seem too good to be true, or to be free. Steve recalls being approached by a group of Italian tourists, asking him where they paid to swim. He replied there was no charge, just jump in. The tourists were stunned.

For Sylvia and Steve, the baths don't just affirm life but their love for each other. Whenever they are here together, before they swim, they share a saltwater kiss on the side of the baths.

'The baths are part of our relationship', says Sylvia. 'It's like a catalyst.

'The baths leave a person feeling exhilarated. And whatever issues or problems people arrive with, they are starting the day the right way.

'It's a place of optimism and hope.'

The baths are also a place of reconnecting, of finding a part of yourself in the water.

When Brydie Piaf moved back to Newcastle after many years away, she headed for a place of her childhood.

'The way of anchoring myself to the city after being away for so long was going back to Merewether Baths and making a project for myself.'

The project was photographing the baths, and the community they create, each weekend. Brydie amassed a series of stunning portraits and waterscapes. Yet through her lens, she not only captured light and moments but also a sense of self, and of belonging.

'As soon as I walk down the steps, I feel such a comfort', she says, 'seeing familiar faces and familiar swimming styles. You can often identity swimming styles from a mile away.'

The pool visits led Brydie to an exhibition and book of her photographs, *The Sunrise Swimmers of Merewether Ocean Baths*, in 2018. And they led to her being a better swimmer. When she began the project, she could barely swim 50 metres. Now she regularly swims 2 kilometres each session. She has found her rhythm and breath. And, through the camera and swimming, she has found friends in what she calls a kind and multi-generational group. Brydie also feels connected once more to her hometown through water.

'If there's a celebration to be had, I go to the water, if I have something that's grieving me, I go to the water. When I'm not there, I look forward to going there. It's a life force.'

THERE's something in the water that is a creative force as well. Just as Merewether has been a nursery for some of the world's greatest surfers, it has been a muse for artists and writers, filmmakers and musicians.

Artist Shay Docking transposed her observations of the area into compelling images on paper and canvas.

Born near the sea in Victoria in 1928, Docking had moved to Newcastle in 1958 with husband Gil, who had been appointed the first director of the city's art gallery. After initially living by the beach, the couple moved onto higher ground, into a home at Merewether Heights, with tree-filtered views of the coastline. Docking loved depicting the harbour and the geometric shapes of the buildings and heavy industries around its shores, but she was also inspired by the escarpments and cliff faces, the waves and the rocks, and the calligraphy of trees silhouetted against the sea. That inspiration turned into visual poetry, as Shay Docking portrayed with expressionistic vigour the natural beauty of the Newcastle coastline. Yet the beauty is not just skin deep. Her art digs below the surface to create works that seem to reveal the bones and soul of the landscape. Shay and Gil Docking were only in Newcastle for a few years, but all these decades later, whenever I look at the cliffs and the jagged sculptures of fallen and sea-gouged rocks along the Merewether shore, I see a Shay Docking artwork.

Around the time Shay Docking was capturing the coastal landscape with pencils and paint, a young Novocastrian named Phillip Holbrow was surfing along the Dixon Park and Merewether stretch. Phillip grew up in Merewether, and the beach had been part of his life since he was a very small child. His father, a seafarer on a BHP ship, would surf a longboard. Occasionally, Phil's father would plonk his son on the front of the board, much to the concern of some onlookers. Phil began surfing at 14, although his first foray into the waves was a failure. As he paddled out at Dixon Park, his board sank. He bought a new board and persisted, pursuing the passion of a lifetime, forging a bond with surfing mates, and laying the bedrock for another love: making movies.

While surfing was a big part of Phil's life from a young age, so were the arts. His father sang part-time in a big band, and his mother was a teacher who loved violin and piano and had a cosmopolitan outlook. Phil's mother decided that the language of conversation at the dinner table was to be French. There would have been few households in 1960s Newcastle where French was spoken, let alone by choice because it was 'cultural'. Young Phil had to learn violin, but he exchanged that for a guitar, an instrument that was a hit at beach parties. His interest in the arts, Phil concedes, was 'kind of weird in a steel city, but I was never harassed because of it'.

The journey from Merewether to movie-making was meandering. As a young man, after serving in the army, Phil took on a range of jobs. One of those jobs was in a fashion house, where a colleague told him he should be modelling. He did and quickly became one of the nation's most in-demand and looked-at male models, especially when he took his clothes off to be a centrefold. He also attended acting classes and was cast in television dramas, movies and advertisements. The TV ads and modelling work had brought Phil back to Newcastle, and to the hugely popular local television station, NBN (Newcastle Broadcasting New South Wales) Channel 3.

By the time he was travelling to Newcastle from Sydney for work, he was well-known – but as Phil Avalon. The name change was due to an appearance on a television dating show. For the show, Phil had taken on the name of a northern Sydney beach he surfed at, rather than adopting the name of his home break. Yet even that didn't lead to any harassment back in Newcastle. Phil says there was no sense of the tall poppy syndrome in Newcastle; rather it celebrated his success.

'Whenever I went back to Newcastle, it was part of my DNA, catching up with my surfing mates, going to the pubs and night clubs.'

Phil's fame soared in 1977 with the release of a film he produced, wrote and starred in titled *Summer City*. With that film, Phil catapulted a couple of other young actors into the limelight, Steve Bisley and Mel Gibson, with both going on to star in *Mad Max*.

Summer City was an enormous success. Phil Avalon had assured his future, but he did so by dropping in on his past. *Summer City* was a coming-of-age film that brought to the big screen the Australian surf culture. Yet the muse lay close to home for Phil.

'*Summer City* was set in the 1960s, in the experiences I had growing up in Newcastle, and I think we got it right on that film.'

Phil wanted to film *Summer City* in Newcastle but the city had changed so much since his boyhood, he ended up choosing a location 45 minutes south. Many of the scenes were filmed in and around the then-somnolent coastal mining village of Catherine Hill Bay.

However, in the years ahead, Phil did head back to Newcastle beaches, occasionally for filming, and often for inspiration. When he wrote the script for *Sons of Summer*, a sequel of sorts to *Summer City*, Phil wanted to film it in Newcastle. But this time it wasn't the city's changing face that ruled out filming there; it was a question of the budget. It was cheaper to film at the Gold Coast, where Phil lives these days.

But he continues to return to Newcastle, and to the siren call of the beach, particularly the Merewether-Dixon Park-Bar Beach strip. He has come back to surf. He comes back to remember. And he comes back to marvel at what is here, and what we have.

'Because of those beautiful beaches, and the breakwater, and you've got the river at the back door, it's a unique city. It rates up there with the Gold Coast.

'It's not promoted like the Gold Coast, but it should be.'

THE beach is not just a place of crossing but an ephemeral space. Nothing stays the same from one wave to the next.

The beach, therefore, is a place where you don't expect to see monuments. After all, monuments have an air of permanence about them. They are symbols of a certain time set in stone, steel or glass.

Yet on the promenade overlooking Nobbys Beach there is a monument to an extraordinary moment in Newcastle history. Actually, it is a sculpture, painted red to stand out like a navigational aid or a ship's hull and titled *Grounded*. This sculpture/monument is a bent piece of steel that looks as if it has fallen out of the sky or has been washed up by the sea. Which, in a way, it has.

The monument includes a piece cut from the rudder of the most famous piece of flotsam or jetsam to have ever come to rest at Nobbys Beach, the bulk carrier *Pasha Bulker*.

The rudder was retrieved by veteran marine salvage expert Bill Johnson, who was tasked with removing the massive artefact from the reef just off the beach. Yet Bill was already well acquainted with the *Pasha Bulker*, because he had been involved in the massive operation surrounding the 225-metre-long ship after it was pushed ashore by monstrous waves and gale-force winds on what has become known as Black Friday. On 8 June 2007, a super storm smashed Newcastle, and the sea brought havoc to the beach.

'When that blow came on, we were working at the dockyard', recalls Bill. 'We could hear the *Pasha Bulker* on the radio before she ran aground.'

Like the *Pasha Bulker*, Bill Johnson had been built for the water. He had grown up by, and playing on, Lake Macquarie, before heading to sea from Newcastle Harbour as a deck boy on an ageing steamship, the *Time*. He was aged 15. The seas had taken Bill around the globe and into a career towing vessels across the surface, surveying and dredging waterways, and salvaging what the depths tried to claim. He had done everything from working on the construction of the Sydney Harbour vehicle tunnel to being part of a crew in the Solomon Islands helping renowned ocean explorer and the discoverer of the sunken *Titanic*, Dr Robert Ballard, on a documentary about Second World War shipwrecks.

Bill had seen ships drift into disaster along the Newcastle coastline before. In May 1974, the dark turmoil of an east coast low had pushed a Norwegian bulk carrier, MV *Sygna*, into Stockton Bight and onto the beach. The 53 000-tonne ship's back was broken; a crack was riven through the hull. When the seas lulled, Bill accompanied the harbour master on board the great steel lump on Stockton Beach and recalls seeing the aft end flooded, as it sagged into the sea.

While the front half of the *Sygna* was salvaged, the stern section remained firm in the sand. The wreck became a tourist attraction, a camping spot for the gamest of fishermen, and a totem of the sea's power. Time and tide gradually stripped the *Sygna*, the wreck rusting away in the breakers, yet it grew in the minds of Novocastrians as a symbol of that dreadful night in 1974, which became known as 'the *Sygna* storm'.

Thirty-three years on, Bill Johnson feared history would repeat, as he listened to the radio and realised the *Pasha Bulker* was not the only ship in strife.

'There were other vessels looking as though they were going aground along Stockton Bight. Ships slowly snuck their way out.'

But the *Pasha Bulker* was pushed aground. As Bill and his team were already in the harbour, helping secure the floating dock, which had broken free in the storm, they were given a new, and incredibly challenging, task. They were asked to go out in their tug in the 8-metre waves to place buoys around the stricken ship to create an exclusion zone.

When Captain Stuart Noble turned up for his shift as a marine pilot at the Port Authority of NSW base, just a few hundred metres from Nobbys Beach, he was struck by the sight of the ship.

'It was right there. You couldn't miss it. It filled up the view.

'It was only a relatively small ship, 225 metres. But you put that on the beach there and you get some concept of how long 225 metres really is. And how high it is too.'

In a stunning display of bravery, Westpac rescue helicopter crews had battled the winds and massive waves to winch the 22 seafarers on the *Pasha Bulker* to safety. The storm passed, and water drained from the flooded streets that filled once more with cars and people. Many headed for Nobbys to see the ship on the beach. And even then, seeing wasn't believing. As a result, the ship on the beach was framed in thousands of camera viewfinders, and images raced around the globe. Perhaps for the first time in its ancient history, Nobbys was upstaged as the best-known landmark in Newcastle. The most famous, and possibly the most shared, image of the *Pasha Bulker* was taken by Newcastle professional photographer Murray McKean.

'I went down there, like everybody else, and everyone was corralled around Nobbys. Being a commercial photographer, you look for another angle or view that others don't think of', Murray says.

He looked around and spied the ideal viewing point: the top of the Christ Church Cathedral tower.

'I took a long lens, took a couple of shots and took them home.'

Murray's main picture showed the ship looking not just out of place but almost out of perspective, its red-hulled form gobbling up everything else around it, like a ravenous giant. Everything on the land, all the earthly concerns of the figures darting about, seems Lilliputian in comparison to that ship.

'It may have been an art director's dream to have all those colours together, but it was frightening to look at the size of it. The long lens flattened it out and gave the scale of it. That was my goal, to give some perspective to it.'

Murray sent the picture to a couple of colleagues, then 'the image was off the leash and the rest is history'. Murray's image has become iconic. Despite that, some still can't believe what they are looking at, asserting the image has been altered, an accusation that deeply hurts the professional photographer. But the image has also been lauded. It is *the* picture of what is called the *Pasha Bulker* storm.

'That shows the magnitude of the ship and the situation. And it could have been worse. If that thing had leaked, it could have been an environmental catastrophe.'

While the crowds gathered to watch, the authorities and experts tried to work out how to get the *Pasha Bulker* off the beach. Bill Johnson had been put on stand-by to place an apron around the ship to contain any major oil spill. Thankfully, he wasn't required to do that, but Bill was close enough to hear to the storm of opinions on how to free the ship. And after two attempts to get it back to sea, there was a growing tide of belief that the *Pasha Bulker* was going nowhere.

After 25 days aground, it was third time lucky for the *Pasha Bulker* and salvage crews. On the evening of 2 July, the ship was refloated and slid back into deeper water. Bill was on the beach, watching the *Pasha Bulker* retreat.

The ship was inspected offshore before being brought into the port. Bill and his crew accompanied her with the oil apron, just in case there was a spill. The *Pasha Bulker* had left a souvenir of where she had been grounded. The bulk carrier's rudder had snapped off and was on the reef. Bill was given the job of recovering it. His team located it in about three metres of water. So the depth wasn't the issue; the conditions were. Waves were breaking on the reef. The crew had to wait for calm weather. What's more, the rudder was much heavier than expected. It weighed about 24 tonnes. The team had to use a large crane erected on a barge to prise the rudder out of the reef. Finally, after a string of attempts, Bill had secured the rudder and was towing it into the harbour. Once the massive artefact had been transported to a metal yard at Kooragang, a small piece was cut from the rudder, and that was incorporated in the sculpture at Nobbys Beach.

Bill occasionally passes the red sculpture on the shore, but 'I don't give it much thought'.

'I thought the whole thing [rudder] should have been up there.'

The sculpture, and Murray McKean's photo, are not the only legacies of the *Pasha Bulker*'s unscheduled visit. Newcastle Harbour Master Vikas Bangia says policies and procedures for ships approaching and leaving port were reviewed and changed.

'We learnt a lot after that. The technologies have increased, the engagement with the ships, we start monitoring ships well in advance, we look at the weather forecasts. So we have controls in place to avoid situations', Captain Bangia says.

As a result, he is confident another ship won't end up on Nobbys Beach.

'We, as sailors and captains, always want water under our hull, not sitting on sand.'

ALONG the coast are a few green havens that are cherished by Novocastrians.

At the south-east edge of Newcastle, between Merewether Heights and Dudley, is a tract of land that has held off the encroachments of suburbia and sloughed off most of the layers of development and industry that once besmirched it.

The Glenrock State Conservation Area is about 550 hectares of dramatic coastal landscape, riding over hills and into valleys, and through subtropical vegetation, creeks and waterfalls. This place offers the delicious delusion that you are in the middle of nowhere when, in fact, it is a stone's throw from the everyday. Homes are just over the rise. When you're in Glenrock, you feel so far from, yet you are so near (about 5 kilometres) to, the centre of Newcastle.

At the heart of the reserve, and just a sand barrier away from the sea, is an elongated lagoon. For thousands of years, the Awabakal people camped by the lagoon, which they called Pillapay-kullitaran. Middens located around the lagoon's shores indicate the importance of this area as a food source. In the next valley to the north, the Awabakal quarried rock that they fashioned into tools, which were highly prized and traded. The Yuelarbah Track that carries hikers through the park is believed to have been part of the Aboriginal trading route. A form of camping continues near the lagoon. On the southern shore is the Glenrock Scout Centre, which was established in 1932.

Early colonial visitors relished the beauty of the area, especially when looking down the valley to the lagoon and the sea beyond. In 1842, the renowned Prussian naturalist and explorer Ludwig Leichhardt had gazed down that Valley of the Palms, as he referred to it, and raved about the luxuriant vegetation. It was that kind of perspective that gave the area its English name, for it reminded visitors of a rocky glen.

Yet no sooner had the Europeans washed up on the beach than they saw the potential to exploit the area. In 1791, a crew of convict runaways led by Mary and William Bryant are believed to have landed on the beach near the lagoon during their epic voyage of escape from Sydney to Timor. The Bryants are attributed with 'discovering' coal in the colony, since they used lumps of the black rock picked up around the lagoon to light a fire. Never mind that the Awabakal had been using coal for many generations. James Martin, a member of the convict crew, later wrote that they reached the area believed to be at Glenrock after two days' sailing from Sydney and found the 'fine' burning coal.

'There remaind 2 nights and one day and found a varse quantty of cabage tree which we cut down and procured the cabage.'

Martin recounted meeting Aboriginal people, who had approached the group, and he declared, 'The apperanance of the land appears much better here than at Sidney Cove'.

'Here we got avarse quantity of fish which of a great refreshment to us.'[25]

Half a century on, when the lagoon was part of James Mitchell's Burwood Estate, the pursuit of coal ramped up, with miners burrowing into the earth under Glenrock. The trains that hugged the coast, carrying coal to the port, transported picnickers to the lagoon during holidays. So industry and recreation each found its spot around the lagoon. Rusted reminders of those days poke out from the sand, for along the beach are sections of track, and the remains of wagons' undercarriages lie in the dunes.

Mining denuded the environment at Glenrock, but ironically, it also helped protect it from residential development. Long after the collieries had closed in the valley, much of the land remained in the hands of mining companies. So when the Glenrock State Recreation Area was gazetted in 1986, the land was free of homes. But it was hardly free of the scars and wounds of human intervention.

For many years, the Glenrock area had been treated as a dump. Motorcycles and four-wheel-drive vehicles tore along the beach and up the valleys, scouring the earth and adding to erosion problems. The creeks carried pollutants down the valley, and sewage washed onto the beach. The growing city was defiling its own jewel. Just to the north of the lagoon was an outfall pipe pouring effluent from the Burwood Beach sewerage works into the sea.

Even so, Glenrock remained a place of inspiration and escape, including for local boys. The creeks and valleys hold so many of my memories. Growing up in Merewether Heights, I would rock-hop down Flaggy Creek. My mother would take me and my brothers bushwalking there, and we'd picnic by a waterfall along the creek. I would ride my bicycle along the tracks snaking through there, skirting around dumped cars and rubbish, and I camped with mates by the lagoon. We even splashed around amid the effluent off Burwood Beach. We'd laugh at each other when we emerged from the surf with something disgusting matted in our hair.

The effluent is now pumped further out to sea, but the Glenrock area still has its issues. A newspaper article from 1933 extolling the wonders of Glenrock for visitors noted the lagoon 'is a fine swimming hole'.[26] The signs around the lagoon and beside Flaggy Creek, which feeds it, tell a different story these days, as the influence of suburban living leaches into the water and runs down the valley. The notices warn of sewage outflows and urban contaminants, so 'swimming is not advised'. However, the area has been gradually restored, and not just by government agencies working in the conservation area. Community groups who use Glenrock, such as mountain bike riders, have helped clean up the bush and establish proper tracks. Glenrock is now a major mountain biking destination, attracting thousands of riders on any given weekend.

As a National Parks and Wildlife Service ranger once told me, in the face of so much demand for coastal areas for development, to have a coastal conservation area in the midst of a city is so lucky. At times, we have cursed our luck with Glenrock, but now we realise what we have, and how much it has enriched life in Newcastle.

The individual who has arguably brought about the greatest transformation and rejuvenation in Glenrock, and helped us turn luck into opportunity with this patch of earth, is John Le Messurier. A retired deputy director of environmental management at Newcastle City Council, John is a passionate and celebrated gardener. So much so that the popular ABC program *Gardening Australia* named him the national Gardener of the Year in 2018. Nowhere are John's green thumbs more evident than in the grounds of the Scout camp at Glenrock, where he has been a volunteer gardener since 1976.

'This was barren, and there were coal chitter dumps', he recalls of the landscape then. 'It wasn't good. No top soil.'

He was told it was unlikely he would be able to get anything to grow in Glenrock's degraded earth. John saw that as a challenge worth taking. He, with the help of other volunteers, has enriched the soil and placed in that improved earth thousands of native plants, some of them growing into towering trees, such as red cedar and kauri pine. The legacies and scars of the mining days are still evident; a strip along the shoreline marks where the rail line used to be. However, even it has been covered in green, with lawn growing on it.

'I just love everything here', he says, smiling broadly.

Suddenly the smile shrinks ever so slightly as John squints at the tangle of vegetation before him.

'I can see a few weeds in there. That's no good. I've got to do something about that!'

A FEW kilometres to the north of Glenrock and tumbling down the slope from The Hill to the sea is another piece of green magic largely conjured by a man who mixed art and life until one was indiscernible from, and unimaginable, without the other.

You get to walk all over his work of art, which is just how Alfred Sharpe (or Sharp) designed it.

Before the multi-talented Mr Sharpe created the park, the earliest colonial arrivals allowed reminders of home to graze on this land. While leading the first survey party in 1801, Lieutenant Colonel William Paterson wrote to Governor Philip Gidley King, telling him of the excellent grass growing over the hills, and similar to those back in England where sheep fed. As a result, Paterson wrote, he named the site Sheep Pasture Hills. In time that piece of high ground would come to be known as Shepherds Hill. Yet, like every piece of earth around here, the hill already had a name and served a purpose. The First Nations people had named it Khanterin. Major Morisset walked these hills, following a 'pretty walk'[27] he had created that came to be referred to as the Horseshoe to reach his private bathing pool, the Bogey Hole.

By the 1850s, Newcastle's leaders wanted the land set aside as a public reserve. Their appeals to the colonial authorities led to the creation of the reserve. At the end of the 19th century, the Newcastle council had resolved that the upper portion of the reserve should be landscaped and manicured. The council awarded a contract to artist, designer, environmentalist and enthusiastic writer of letters to the local newspaper, Alfred Sharpe.[28]

Born in England, Sharpe migrated as a young man to New Zealand, where he developed a reputation through his painting, and his love for, and advocacy of, the natural environment. Sharpe voyaged across the Tasman Sea in 1887 to join his brother in Newcastle. Somewhere along the way, he had dropped the 'e' from his surname. In Newcastle, he was 'Sharp'. What he did bring was his desire to paint, and to fight for the environment. Both frequently intersected in the works Sharpe created, such as the descriptively titled *The last dying remnant of the grand ti tree forests, between Adamstown and the Glebe*, and that watercolour underscored the artist's belief that this area should have been reserved as a park.[29]

In his letters to the *Newcastle Morning Herald*, Sharpe bemoaned the lack of parks and trees in the industrial community, and that there was no public art gallery. He argued an art gallery was needed to show landscapes depicting the local natural beauty, 'ere those beauties are wiped out by the exigencies of the local coal industry and the spread of population'.[30]

While he could do little about the art gallery issue, other than convert shop fronts into temporary exhibition spaces for his works, Sharpe did turn words into action in creating more recreation spaces around Newcastle. He designed parks in Islington, Wickham and Hamilton, but his major work would be the reserve on The Hill.

In reporting on Sharpe being awarded the design of the Upper Reserve or Hill Reserve, the *Newcastle Morning Herald* declared it hoped for more than a park.

'We trust now the council have a definite plan to work to, that the laying-out of the park will progress by leaps and bounds, and that before long the reproach of Newcastle – that of being a community totally blind to natural beauty and perfectly indifferent to the squalor of their surroundings – will be done away with, and that we will be able to point proudly to our parks in disproof of it.'[31]

Sharpe may not have been able to wipe away that reproach, but he gave Novocastrians a beautiful space by the sea.

Sharpe loved trees, and he wanted to plant a cherished New Zealand species, the pohutukawa. He did plant these flowering trees in the reserve. However, he was disgusted that locals were cutting their blooms to display in their homes. The park is now dotted with trees offering shade and protection, with the predominant sight being copses and avenues of Norfolk Island pines.

In the heart of the park is a rotunda, built in 1898 and surrounded by lawn. Both the rotunda and lawn have been used through the years for everything from brass band concerts to weddings, from civic ceremonies to family picnics. When national cricket hero Victor Trumper visited Newcastle in 1903, he was welcomed with a ceremony in the rotunda, and he was presented with a commemorative art work, known as an illustrated address, that the man who designed the park had created. Designing and creating illuminated addresses for dignities was a source of income for Alfred Sharpe.

In the gully below the rotunda, where Sharpe envisaged a series of dams to collect the run-off and create water gardens, flower beds were constructed. Named Garside Gardens, the rows of beds bloom with colour a couple of times a year. It may not have been what Sharpe wanted, but the burst of colour in the gully, juxtaposed against the wedge of sea that can be viewed from here, brings joy. A stone wall that curves in a horseshoe shape, tracing the road wending through the park, protects the flowers in the garden from the elements. Seen from above, the gardens hold the shape and the profusion of colours of a stained-glass window, as though it has blown out of Christ Church Cathedral, just over the hill, and landed here in the valley.

Sharpe often wandered to places shaped by nature. After all, as his letters to the newspaper indicated, he was repulsed by the rubbish in the tree-bare streets and the sewage washing onto the beaches. In response to walking in the Merewether and Glenrock Lagoon area, Sharpe had composed a poem titled 'A Day in Burwood Glen', in which he leaves behind the 'city's bustle' to immerse himself in the environment:

> Sweet is thy calm, O Burwood!
> Far up thy lovely glen,
> In the Dryad-haunted bowers,
> Far from the haunts of men.[32]

More than a century on, people head to Sharpe's creation not so much to escape the haunts of men – it is too popular for that – but to relax and enjoy the theatrical views. It may have had its name changed in 1911 to honour Edward VII, but the coastal park has always remained close to the heart of Newcastle, both geographically and in a deeper sense. However, 'sweet calm' could not always be found in the park. From 1951, the park's serpentine road doubled as a motor sports track. For many years, an annual event, known as the Mattara Hillclimb, was held in the park. Thousands would line the route from near Newcastle South Beach to Shepherds Hill to watch the cars roar by.[33]

Motor sports were moved on from King Edward Park in 2015, although vehicles can still drive through a section of the reserve. Some who are experiencing 'van life' park along the edges and spend a night overlooking the sea for free. While motor sports left the park, they controversially roared into the city centre from 2017.

A leg of the Supercars Championship was to be staged in the city in an event called the Newcastle 500. These cars that could push towards 300 kilometres per hour and with engines that squeal at house-shaking levels were to race on a street circuit. The circuit would track past Newcastle Beach and Nobbys, along the harbour foreshore – where, for decades, lovers of hotted-up cars had congregated and revved on a weekend – and through the historic Newcastle East precinct, straight past apartments and heritage-listed houses. From a marketing point of view, this sounded like a dream, showing to a large television-viewing audience Newcastle at its most photogenic. This event would wipe away the idea Newcastle was a steel city; rather visitors and viewers would see it as a surf city, a harbour city, and a historic city. Even if it did further impress into some people's minds that this was a car-obsessed city, its inhabitants still driving around with Normie and his mates from 'The Newcastle Song'. However, to those opposed to the idea of cars racing through the streets, the Newcastle 500 sounded like a nightmare.

'It did have an audience, and a lot of people had a good time, there's no question about that', says Christine Everingham of the car races. 'But they also brought a lot of grief.'

Christine is a Newcastle East resident and a retired academic. She is also a prime mover of the Sandhills Community Garden in Newcastle East, helping convert the landscape from what it once was, as the name suggests, to a flourishing haven in the historic precinct. As a member of the Newcastle East Residents Group, Christine didn't like her neighbourhood being changed into a car-racing circuit. More than speaking up against the Newcastle 500's location, she also shaped those words of protest into a book that she co-authored, titled *Wrong Track*.

Christine believes the council and the state government foisted the event onto the city.

In an opinion piece published in the local newspaper just before the inaugural race, Jeremy Bath, then the interim chief executive of the City of Newcastle, talked about the pride of Newcastle hosting this event and how the city was buzzing with excitement. He saw the races and the coverage they would attract as shining a long-deserved positive light on the city.³⁴ Yet those opposed to the car races felt they did not open their city to the world but locked many out.

'I love Newcastle East, and the whole area was barricaded off to the public for nearly nine weeks every year. People couldn't get in', argues Christine.

What's more, residents and local businesses were locked in. Trade was disrupted or dried up, Christine says. Roads were closed, temporary fences and barricades were erected, grandstands and bridges were built, and trees even felled, as the organisers moved in and the inner city was converted into a race track for the three-day event.

Those in favour of the races were at loggerheads with those against. Others asserted Newcastle East residents were acting like NIMBYs (Not In My Backyard).

'It's so hurtful for people to say we're the NIMBYs', counters Christine. 'We're not keeping people out. We want people to be able to come in!'

Based on the figures released, the initial Newcastle 500 was considered a major success, attracting about 192 000 people over the three days. The cars and crowds returned the following year, and in 2019. Yet what also returned was the controversy and local opposition. After three years of competition were lost due to Covid-19 restrictions, the final race was held in 2023. Supercars had indicated it wanted to extend its stay in the city for another five years. A council-commissioned survey found a majority of respondents didn't want the deal extended. In October 2023, it was announced the Newcastle 500 would not be held in 2024, and so far the race cars haven't returned.

Christine Everingham is delighted opponents' voices were heard.

'It was a tremendous fight, and I think it showed the Newcastle people as being feisty and being able to stand up to power when it counts and not being taken for granted.'

Christine hopes the Newcastle 500 remains a memory. She urges governments and organisations to opt for smaller events that embrace the area's qualities and character rather than extravaganzas that consume the city.

'If we want to bring tourists into the city, we want to keep them here, having a lovely environment they can enjoy. This is our vision.

Place making. Local. Events that are good for local businesses, events that local people can participate in. It's a different sort of vision. It's about the place belonging to the people.'

IN Newcastle, people play not just on the sand and in the waves, but they have created sports fields by the sea.

Across the road from Bar Beach is the oval with echoes of another age in its name, Empire Park. On this patch of grass growing out of sand dunes, Newcastle Rugby Union put down roots in the 1920s with a match between GPS Old Boys and Novocastrians. Like the grass at Empire Park, rugby union has had to hold on tenaciously and accept its battles in this league-mad city. Still, for those courageously rucking and mauling on at Empire Park, the consolation for their game's comparatively fringe reputation is proximity to the sea.

Perhaps the most distractingly stunning view that comes with a sports field is to be found north of the harbour on the shores of Stockton Beach, just near the surf club. Lynn Oval offers a view north along the great strip of sand unfurling along the edge of Stockton Bight towards Port Stephens, and to the east is nothing but sea and sky. How a player could concentrate on their game of cricket or footy here is beyond me. Still, the park reminds us that life is not all fun and games and spent staring out to sea. On the edge of the oval are gateposts, their stone faces etched with tragedy. They hold the names of 11 men who, in the course of a few days in December 1896, died from inhaling poisonous gas in the mine that once burrowed under Stockton.

The beach itself has been the scene of trauma and riven the community. Stockton was in the headlines after the sexual assault and murder of a local teenager, Leigh Leigh, in 1989. She had attended a birthday party by the beach at Stockton North. Her body was found in the dunes the following morning. The events and impact on the community of that night were woven into a work of fiction by Maitland-born, Oscar-nominated playwright and screenwriter, Nick Enright. The play was adapted into a film, *Blackrock*. While the tragedy is set in a fictional suburb, Stockton people felt it was about their community. Stockton feels self-contained at the best of times, but *Blackrock* was seen as tapping into the worst of times. When the film makers arrived in Stockton, many in the community did not want them there and made it clear they were not welcome.

The area has made its mark on literature too; the rhythms of life and death, the changing of the seasons, the constantly shifting nature of the sand and the waves, as observed along Stockton Beach, flow through a series of stories under the title, *Down the Breakie*. Written by William Olson, the stories chart the journey of a Stockton boy during the Depression years leading into his adulthood and the Second World War, as he shares snippets of his relationship with his home area, particularly along the breakwater, or the breakie, and the beach that curls out to the north of that great assemblage of rocks and wrecks.

The coastal strip at Stockton offered shelter in the years after the Second World War. The remains of the artillery battery, built near the harbour entrance to protect shipping and the steel city from Japanese attacks during the war, provided a makeshift home for local families when housing was tight when peace returned.

Yet the beach that has defined and sheltered Stockton, that has provided it with a playground and held its secrets, is disappearing. The seas are taking away sand and gnawing at the edges of the beachside community, threatening properties and cornerstones of Stockton life, even the surf club. In response, more and more infrastructure and money, and sand, have been poured in to protect lives and livelihoods from toppling into the sea. The community has rallied, forming groups, staking out a presence on social media with a 'Save Stockton Beach' campaign, and lobbying governments at all levels for more help.

From his perch at the bar at the Boatrowers' Hotel, where he enjoys a daily beer, Reg Inglis can't see the beach (the perspective from the pub is of the river and the bank that once hosted sailing ships from around the globe). But he does have an opinion about what is causing the erosion problem: the breakie.

'While ever that breakwater is out, we're losing the battle', says Reg.

The breakwaters have been there for a long time, offering a safer passage for shipping and the enormous trade they carry. But what is good for shipping has created an issue for Stockton. This feat of engineering has interfered with the sea's ability to replace what it takes away, with tens of millions of cubic metres of sand washed from the southern end of the beach over the years. So the problem grows as the beach shrinks.

Reg was born close to another beach, Merewether, in 1937 but has lived in Stockton since he was five months old. However, that is not long enough to give him immunity from some gentle ribbing in the pub that he isn't a real local. Reg played on the beach when he was a kid and, as an adult, he built a shack further along the beach at a collection of huts in the dunes that is known as Tin City. Once an unofficial camp for the homeless during the Depression, Tin City was transformed into an off-the-grid fishing and recreation village. And 11 shacks seemingly floating and bobbing in a sea of sand have looked sufficiently surreal and post-apocalyptic to attract the eye of filmmakers and photographers through the years. Yet it was the presence of too many cameras, with tourists four-wheel-driving over the dunes to Tin City, that convinced Reg his little place of solitude for beach fishing was no more. In addition, there was the work of resisting the constantly shifting sand dunes trying to devour his shack. If only that sand could migrate south. Reg loves this stretch of beach, which is why he is dismayed to see the southern parts being eaten away. He laments how short the walk is now across the beach. And he is sceptical of management plans to bring in sand from offshore or from the Hunter River to stem the impact of coastal erosion.

'They can bring in as much sand as they like, but until they knock off the end of Stockton breakwater, there's going to be trouble. But that's a big enterprise, with the shipping.'

While Reg is talking, behind him a ship glides up the Hunter River's South Arm, heading for the coal loaders. Only half a kilometre to the east of the pub, on this narrow tonsil-shaped peninsula dangling in the mouth of the Hunter, the sea incessantly nibbles at the sand.

Yet the beach continues to be a siren for big money. Along Stockton's beachfront, older houses are being bought for eye-watering prices. And many of those houses are being knocked over to build grand piles of brick and glass. Never mind what the future might look like; the views from these beachfront homes are stunningly all-consuming.

While water has defined the very shape of the ground Stockton stands on, it has also acted as a moat for the community. It has provided protection for Stockton's identity. Ships no longer line its shores and the little slipways have long disappeared, but it still feels like a maritime village. Novocastrians make jokes about taking the Stockton ferry 'overseas'. But to Stockton residents, it is no joke; they are their own people, with their own ways. Stockton may be in the City of Newcastle, but Reg explains that Stockton is not a part of Newcastle. He sees the stretch of harbour between his home and the city as separating, not uniting, the two communities. As a kid, Reg had to cross the harbour to attend high school. High school-age students in Stockton still have to make that journey. The community has no public high school; they go to Newcastle High. But, Reg says, that doesn't make him a Novocastrian. Didn't then, doesn't now.

'We were always Stockton kids. We're from Stockton.'

Never mind the seas taking away the beach, beware of too many outsiders – and that includes those from across the harbour – moving in and changing Stockton.

'I don't think we're a part of Newcastle. If I want to be a part of Newcastle, I'd go over there. I'd rather stick with what we have here.'

Reg is not alone in his view. Many who live in Stockton see their place as different to everywhere else.

In one part, Stockton is the sum of everywhere else. Along the riverfront, on the community's western side, is the Ballast Ground, where sailing ships from around the globe would disgorge bits and pieces of faraway places before loading coal. Among the ballast dumped was the rubble from buildings in San Francisco destroyed in the 1906 earthquake.

For visiting seafarers, Stockton could feel a world away from where the action was in Newcastle. Stockton's most northern berth was known to sailors as 'Siberia' because it was so far removed from not just the town but the ferries that could transport them there. Yet to its residents, that sense of isolation has always been one of Stockton's greatest assets.

Until the construction of Stockton Bridge, this place must well have been an island. But even after the bridge opened in 1971, with a quicker road journey to Newcastle, that didn't mean everyone in Stockton felt more closely connected to the city. And that is still the case for many Stockton residents, including Reg Inglis. They are Newcastle's castaways.

Not that they need rescuing. If you ask Reg, whenever he looks across the water to the city, it is Newcastle that needs rescuing.

'In my book, you're looking at high-rises! We used to look across and be able to see the town hall clock. I reckon they've wrecked it. They're building more and more, higher and higher.'

Reg sips his beer and shakes his head.

'Who wants to be over there?'

CHAPTER SIX

CITY OF VILLAGES

EVEN in the way it has grown, Newcastle has roughly charted its own path. Unlike the trajectory of many cities, Newcastle has not so much spread outwards from its centre but inwards from its suburbs. Many of those suburbs began life as villages.

Newcastle was stitched together into a city council from 11 municipalities and sections of two shires in 1938. When Greater Newcastle was created, it was the largest local government area in NSW. But in effect, Newcastle was a patchwork of small communities.

The names of many of the villages sound as though they were transplanted from Britain: names such as Lambton, Wallsend, Wickham and Jesmond.

On the surface, and in the lives of their residents, there may have been reminders of somewhere else. But the reason for the villages' existence, the reason so many had come across the seas to the colony, lay under their feet. These were coal villages, sprouting from the soil, often in a rag-tag way, in the clefts of hills or along the flood plains and on the fringes of swamps, wherever companies created a mine.

In the late 1850s, the Australian Agricultural Company was giving shape to a Newcastle community whose name told of its purpose. It was known as Borehole. At the time, the AA Company's superintendent, Arthur Hodgson, noted that 'nothing can give coal proprietors greater command over their men than having them located on the spot and rooted to the soil'.[1]

In a sense, Hodgson was right. Men and their families did become rooted to the soil, and as a result, villages became communities. When mines closed and coal proprietors moved on, the residents often remained. It may have no longer held a living, but the soil, and what had grown out of it, provided a sense of belonging.

For the villages had become not just communities but home. The mine's whistle was replaced by something deeper in the soul, regulating the rhythm of life. There were shops for the necessities, which became places to exchange small talk and learn the ways of the village. There were schools for the children, and institutes and guild halls for self-improvement for the adults. There were parks and reserves to play in, hotels in which to lose yourself, and churches in which to reflect on what happened in the pub.

To improve living conditions, and in many cases realising they couldn't rely on the mining companies to do that, the villages joined into larger communities, forming municipalities. From among their own, the residents elected aldermen to agitate for what they needed, such as better roads and drainage to stop the low-lying areas becoming quagmires. Yet the coal companies' influence and legacy remained, even in place names. When the settlements around Borehole were incorporated in 1871, the name given to the new municipality was Hamilton, in honour of the Australian Agricultural Company's governor, Edward T Hamilton.

When the Scottish Australian Mining Company of London established a colliery about five kilometres from Hamilton, Thomas Croudace, the engineer who oversaw the project, named the mine Lambton, after his birthplace in England. The colliery gave a name to the village that grew around it, and because of it. The area had been providing a home long before the miners arrived in the 1860s, with the Awabakal people drawing water from Ker-rai, the creek snaking through the low-lying ground. That ground was progressively filled, with some of that land being groomed into what would become Lambton Park. The park was then, as it is now, a flourishing social hub for not just Lambton but areas further afield in the city. Before it was proclaimed as parkland in 1887, part of what was known as The Commonage was used for hastily erected homes, with miners making shelters by making do with whatever they could put their hands on. Living near, or on, ground prone to filling with water after heavy rain posed health risks. In 1890, after the park had been proclaimed, it was reported in the *Sydney Morning Herald*, 'The necessity for a recreation ground of this nature had made itself apparent by the fact of so many deaths occurring through typhoid fever, produced by the close proximity of the houses in the vicinity. Since the ground had been utilised as a park and public recreation ground, Lambton might be classed now as one of the healthiest localities in the world'.[2]

The park became more formal through the years, with a cricket ground installed, the planting of gardens and, in 1890, the construction of a rotunda. Set like a precious stone in this space, the rotunda has been a stage for brass bands and politicians, as it was at the structure's official opening, a grandstand for sporting events, an impromptu picnic shelter, and a gathering point for industrial meetings and rallies. Industrial strife was part of Lambton life; a miner's strike had pushed back the rotunda's official opening.

The miners had constructed their own gathering places in Lambton. In the late 1860s, a group of Welsh miners quarried stone and constructed the Bethel Independent Chapel, and they did this work usually after finishing their shifts in the colliery. The chapel the Welsh built with their hands still stands in Dickson Street. On a tablet set into the rough-hewn stone sings the lyrical language of the chapel's makers, the words carried across the seas from Wales' valleys and mines.

The presence of that rustic chapel in Lambton is also an indication of the richest stratum to be found in Newcastle's mining villages: neighbours and friends. Places were, as they still are, defined by the people. You didn't want to leave a place, otherwise you left a great chunk of yourself behind. And when you did leave, it was often for the community.

During the First World War, thousands signed up from the mining villages in the Hunter, and from the factories and offices around Newcastle. They served not just the King and the Empire but also their community. No sooner had war been declared in August 1914 than local men went off to fight. Across the ranks, from the Light Horse and infantry regiments, from the artillery to the engineers, Newcastle and Hunter men were there. And when those ranks were thinned in the course of the war, Newcastle and Hunter men were lost. As the focus of the fighting for Australians turned from Gallipoli to the Western Front, the nation's military forces were reshaped and recruiting drives redoubled. The 35th Battalion was formed in Newcastle in December 1915. Since most of its recruits were from the Newcastle area, the battalion became known as 'Newcastle's Own'. The battalion was heavily involved in pivotal and brutal battles on the Western Front, including in the mire and terror of Passchendale on 12 October 1917. Of the 508 men from the 35th who took part in the battle, only 90 were left unwounded. Less than a year later, in the fight around the French town of Villers-Bretonneux, the 35th sustained casualty rates of nearly 70 per cent.[3] By the time the war had ended, it is estimated about 11 000 Newcastle and Hunter men and women had served. More than 2000 were killed. Many more lived with wounds, physical and mental. The contribution to the war effort was enormous. The impact of lives lost or shattered by the war was inestimable. And that was all brought home. Who families lost, and what the community was denied, is encapsulated in the short life and death of Captain Clarence Smith Jeffries. A Wallsend boy, Clarence had followed his father's career path, becoming a mining surveyor. He was also a soldier. At the time he left for active service, Clarence was working for a mine on the Coalfields. He served on the Western Front in the 34th Battalion, which comprised many Hunter men and was known as 'Maitland's Own'. Clarence was involved in the heavy fighting at Passchendale on that dreadful day of 12 October, leading a bombing party and taking out machine gun posts under a barrage of enemy artillery. Clarence would later be awarded the Victoria Cross, the highest military honour, for what was termed his most conspicuous bravery in attack. But that most conspicuous bravery led not just to the VC but to a grave far from Newcastle. He was killed in action, a couple of weeks before his 23rd birthday. After the war, Clarence's father travelled to Belgium to search for his son's grave. He found his boy's resting place. Clarence Jeffries would never return to Newcastle, but he is honoured in his hometown. His Victoria Cross was presented to Christ Church Cathedral, and a housing estate in Adamstown is named after him.[4]

While Clarence Jeffries could never return to the community of his birth, others have never wanted to leave. Thomas William Moore, or Billy, has stayed put in Wallsend for more than a century. Billy was born close to the main drag of Nelson Street, in 1922. His hometown was anchored to coal. After all, Wallsend had been created as a mining town on land owned by one of the Brown coal barons. The Newcastle Wallsend Mining Company was a major employer in the area, with its pits pocking the terrain, and it shaped the character and texture of the town, from the middle of the 19th century into the 20th century. There was also a pit known as the Co-operative Colliery, which was initially run by a group of miners. Before a rail line reached Wallsend, coal was carried on punts and lighters down Ironbark Creek and the Hunter River to Newcastle. The waterways were also used to transport supplies to the township.[5] Even when the main pits shut, and more and more men travelled to the heavy industries closer to town for work, Wallsend remained a mining town in spirit, rambunctious and lively with 30 pubs, by Billy's count.

Some men still mined for a living, with little operations scrabbling into the earth just beyond town. Billy refers to these little pits as 'rat holes'. As a boy, Billy accompanied his father into the bush, helping him cut timber for use at props in the rat holes.

As a teenager, Billy had to join the daily flow out of town for work, with a job at Commonwealth Steel, where he stayed until he retired, apart from a couple of years serving in the air force during the Second World War. Throughout his career, Billy returned to Wallsend each day to live and play. Billy's passion was soccer, or football. It was a popular sport among the miners, many of whom had emigrated from Britain, and it had been played in Wallsend and the surrounding communities since the 1880s. Not far from Wallsend, in the mining village of Minmi, Scottish workmates became team mates in 1884. The Minmi Rangers are credited with being the first football club formed in Northern NSW. John Maynard, who has written extensively about the history of local football, has pointed out that the Minmi Rangers came into being before many of the world's most famous teams, including Liverpool and Arsenal.[6] A string of teams popped out of the ground around Newcastle, such as Hamilton Athletic, Burwood United and Wallsend Rovers. These teams were effectively born in the pits, and the home grounds were often just near the collieries where the players toiled. As Billy explains it, 'Miners go to work, come home and play football'.

By the time Billy was playing the sport, Wallsend Football Club was a powerhouse, and there was a competition ladder filled with other local teams.

'Soccer was real big. So many champion players. I wasn't one of them!' offers Billy.

He played for a smaller outfit known as Summerhill, and the team's home ground was a paddock on the edge of town. Coal had its place in the competition. Billy shows me a team photo from 1952, when Summerhill were the undefeated minor and major premiers. Amid the young men, with crossed arms and proud expressions, sits Billy with a trophy before him. It is the prize the team has secured, the Joint Coal Board Trophy.

Yet the coal industry also subsumed Billy's field of sporting dreams. Summerhill's ground was buried under hundreds of tonnes of ash from the nearby Gretley Colliery, which was one of the last mines to be operating in the Wallsend area.

Wallsend had its own council from 1874, but when Billy was a teenager, the municipality was swallowed up by Newcastle. From a Novocastrian's point of view, Wallsend was a part of Newcastle, but on the fringe. When the trams began running from Newcastle to Wallsend in 1887, it was proclaimed in the local press as historic, because it was the first tramway laid outside Sydney. An estimated 20 000 spectators turned out for the official opening. The tracks effectively connected the community to Newcastle until 1949, when the Wallsend trams stopped. Even so, to those in the city, Wallsend seemed distant. It was referred to as 'World's End'.

However, in the years since, the world has come to Wallsend. The former municipal council chambers is now the Newcastle Mosque, offering a place of worship for some of the estimated 2800 Muslim residents in the City of Newcastle. In Nelson Street, there are Asian grocery stores, with the perfume of spices dancing with the scent of beer drifting from the historical pubs that have survived since the miners drank there. One of the pubs, just across from Nelson Street and over the ghosts of the rail tracks, is called the Colliery Inn.

The legacy of the mining town remains, from the old cottages in the back streets to the bust of Wallsend's first mayor and miners' advocate, James Fletcher, standing sentinel beside a rotunda dressed in elegant wrought iron. Billy Moore doesn't see much evidence of the mining town he grew up in, and he feels Wallsend has lost some of its vibrancy.

However, to him this has never been 'World's End'; Wallsend has always been Billy's world.

Or as he puts it, 'Wallsend's always been Wallsend'.

THE signs and scars of the collieries that simultaneously built and undermined Newcastle have largely been covered. They have been converted into residential and business estates, parks and ovals, and old coal rail lines have been coated with bitumen and turned into roads. The Gully Line, for instance, is the name of a former colliery railway that cut through the villages from Charlestown, but these days is used to mark a busy traffic intersection.

Beyond names, the suburbs' mining heritage has a presence in our daily lives. The old mine workings impact what is built, and how, around the city. What is underneath has to be taken into account. Every now and then, the ground opens and the past threatens to swallow the present. For example, the Wallsend Diggers Sports Club was forced to close in 2023, when a sinkhole opened under its bowling greens. To teach young Novocastrians about subsidence, we have Maurie Mole.

Maurie Mole is an animated character wearing a high-visibility vest and a miner's lamp on his helmet. Maurie was developed for the state's Mine Subsidence Board, later called Subsidence Advisory NSW, to warn of the dangers when the ground moves and opens. And Maurie has had a song for the Newcastle kids to learn, with the lyrics telling them 'If you see a hole, don't think you're a mole. Walk in the opposite direction and report your detection'.[7]

Newcastle kids are used to following orders given by cute animals on the screen. For decades, a character named Big Dog has appeared at 7.30 each night on the NBN television channel to coax boys and girls to go to sleep. When the female narrator softly says good night as Big Dog (actually a person wearing a furry suit) is tucked into bed, that tolls another day over in Newcastle.

WHILE mining created villages that became suburbs, the rise of heavy industry in Newcastle shaped villages within suburbs.

Even after it wound back mining in the Hamilton area, the Australian Agricultural Company devised a way of making money from its land. In the early 1900s, the company released some of its holdings around Hamilton to be transformed into a 'garden suburb'. In its promotional booklet for the subdivision, the company noted Newcastle was taking interest in itself and caring about its appearance. The plan was for this suburb to fit into that new Newcastle, by presenting home gardens as the prominent feature. In effect, the soil that once helped bind the worker to the AA Company's mines would now sprout plants. A legacy of the company's plans is embedded on the edge of Learmonth Park, with a couple of sandstone pillars wearing the AA Co's seal and the words 'Garden Suburb' impressed into the plate. Yet there is another legacy in the surrounding streets, which are lined with beautiful homes and meticulously planned gardens.

In the years after the Second World War, many of those who emigrated from Europe to work in the heavy industries settled in and around Hamilton. The new arrivals created their own version of a garden suburb, teasing from the soil in their backyards vegetables and herbs that would excite the Novocastrian palate. The main thoroughfares of Hamilton, particularly Beaumont Street, were transformed. What brought reassurance and comfort to members of the migrant communities, as they installed reminders of where they had come from, offered the taste of the new for many Novocastrians. Cafes and delicatessens served food that Newcastle people initially struggled to pronounce but increasingly couldn't put into their mouths quickly enough. As Pina D'Accione, whose name was behind one of the most popular delis in Hamilton, once told me, customers would enter the gastronomical Aladdin's Cave, intrigued and wishing to learn more about Italian food and ingredients, pointing and asking, 'What's that? How do you use this?'.[8] At tables along the footpath sat men drinking coffee and scenting the air with cigarette smoke and snippets of languages rarely heard before on the streets of Hamilton. While it gained the nickname of 'Little Italy', Hamilton was home to people from many parts of Europe, and to non-Europeans as well. A Chinese–Australian family, the Mooks, had arrived in the 1920s and set up a renowned fruit and vegetable shop in Beaumont Street. Yet it was in the years after the Second World War that the cosmopolitan and polyglot atmosphere of Hamilton grew richer.

Much of the suburb's transformation was due to a network of friends and neighbours from the Old World, from an Italian village called Lettopalena. Nestled in the mountains in the Abruzzo area, Lettopalena was pulverised during the Second World War and occupied by German forces. After the war, recovery was slow and opportunities were thin, and many of the villagers left. More than 100 migrated from this one Italian community to Newcastle in the post-war years, as word spread through letters home that work and opportunities were available in this Australian industrial city. So many made the journey to Newcastle that this community within a community had its own name: the Lettesi. These days, it is estimated there are a couple of thousand descendants in the Newcastle area. As one of those descendants, well-known musician Leo Della Grotta, says, there are more people with Lettesi blood in Newcastle than there are in Lettopalena.

One of the post-war arrivals was Leo's father, Antonio. Born in 1931, Antonio Della Grotta voyaged to Australia in 1952. After trying his luck in South Australia and the canefields of Queensland, Antonio headed to Newcastle, because he heard 'BHP was here, Com Steel was here'. In other words, there was steady work. He arrived on New Year's Day, 1953. The day of fresh beginnings. Antonio was only 21 and spoke very little English.

'I was too young and naïve', says Antonio, as he points at a picture of a mountain village holding pride of place on his lounge room wall. It is a picture of Lettopalena. 'That town there, there was nothing there.'

Yet what he found in this steel city initially was resistance. On the night of his arrival, Antonio went to the suburb of Islington, just across the rail tracks from Hamilton, where he saw a fight between 'Australians and the newcomers'. Not that the confrontation overly concerned young Antonio.

'To us, me and my friends, it [Newcastle] was new, it was much better compared to Lettopalena. We were happy because we made a move. We were lucky to come here.'

Like so many others, Antonio found security and a sense of community in Hamilton. But it was not like home. There was no café like the places he had known; just a Greek milk bar. And what was part of everyday life in Lettopalena was scarce in Newcastle. If Italian migrants wanted pasta, they had to make it at home, and olive oil could be bought only at the pharmacy in small bottles. It was marketed as a medicine rather than as an ingredient for cooking. So, to obtain enough to cook with, Antonio Della Grotta bought a case of olive oil at a time.

With his earnings as a labourer at the BHP steelworks, Antonio bought a house just beyond Hamilton, at Broadmeadow, and worked at 'fitting in'. He saw his goal as assimilating as quickly as possible.

'I was always interested in learning the language, and I always try to find people. I'd say, "If I say something wrong, will you correct me? Because I need to be correct".'

Antonio's ability with English opened the next door for him after a back injury meant he could no longer work at the steelworks. He became a community leader, helping build bridges between Italians and others in Newcastle. Later, when the Lettesi formed an association, raising funds to support each other, Antonio headed that as well.

While Antonio worked at becoming 'Australian', Beaumont Street progressively transformed into 'Little Italy'.

'Don't forget, it was also Little Greece, Little Yugoslavia', corrects Leo. 'But the Italians were the most numerous. We were the most represented ethnic group there.'

Antonio shrugs and says, 'Where else would I go?'

Yet where Antonio and other Italians went, Novocastrians followed.

From barbers to deli owners, from cafes and restaurant operators to music teachers, the post-war arrivals, and the Lettesi, in particular, brought the colour and flavours and languages of the Mediterranean and the Adriatic into Newcastle.

'If you wanted to see a European, you didn't go to Merewether', says Leo. 'You went to Beaumont Street, Hamilton.'

For many Novocastrians, their first experience of Europe was in Beaumont Street. It is where eyes were opened, tastebuds bloomed and minds broadened. Newcastle became a more interesting city because of what Beaumont Street had become. The transformation shifted beyond

Beaumont Street, from suburb to suburb, as the Lettesi and other groups moved further afield. In 1968, the Della Grotta family moved from Broadmeadow to North Lambton.

'We were the only Della Grottas in the land of Smith and Jones', says Leo.

Wrenched out of his village of friends and relatives in Hamilton and Broadmeadow into the world of white bread, Leo, on the cusp of becoming a teenager, felt dislocated.

'It was like a microcosm of what Dad had gone through', Leo reflects. 'But after a week, I never looked back.'

What changed Beaumont Street dramatically was the 1989 earthquake. Buildings and lives were damaged and lost in the disaster. As the strip was rebuilt and restored, Leo recalls Beaumont Street was rebranded, trading on what had been there for many years.

'After the earthquake, it was marketed as a cosmopolitan centre. Before then, it was just Hamilton.'

Yet by then, many of those who had made Beaumont Street what it was had moved out. And that would continue. One of the biggest indicators of how a place and community had changed was a building about halfway along Beaumont Street. It was known as the Italian Centre. Founded by a religious order, the Scalabrini Fathers, but built with the toil and resources of the local Italian community, the centre opened in 1966. More than being a portal for pastoral care, the centre was a social and cultural hub for the Italian community. What's more, the centre projected the influence and significance of this community to the rest of Newcastle. However, in 2002, the centre was shut and the building sold. 'Little Italy' was increasingly part of broader Newcastle.

'"Little Italy" has died because the Italians are not there any more', says Antonio. 'There were so many young Italians in Beaumont Street. Now there isn't. We've all grown old!'

'There's a handful of Italians', adds Leo. 'Really to call it "Little Italy" now would be a bit of an insult to the other guys, other nationalities.'

Many of the Lettesi may have moved beyond Beaumont Street, but the impact of Lettopalena, and those who left the Italian village to begin a new life here, is literally imprinted in Hamilton. In James Street Plaza, 'Lettopalena' is stencilled on the concrete. Antonio Della Grotta is proud to see the village's name acknowledged there. But Lettopalena is much closer to home for Antonio. Below that picture hanging in the lounge room of him and Rosina, the childhood sweetheart whom he married in 1955, is a map of the area around Lettopalena. It is as though Antonio does not want to lose direction, to ensure that he can always find his way back there, to his past, should he need to. And there are times, he admits, when he still feels a little lost between two worlds, between the past and present, between his home of the first 20 years of his life and his home of more than 70 years. He has, on occasion, felt like a visitor over there and a migrant here. But mostly he feels like he belongs to both worlds. For he is a product of both.

'My heart is still ticking because of that', he says, looking at the picture of Lettopalena on the wall. Then, in describing what Newcastle means to him, he says, 'It's my home'.

And by making it his home, Antonio Della Grotta and thousands of others who have embraced two worlds have helped make Newcastle somewhere to call home for the rest of us. As Antonio's son reflects on how Newcastle has changed, he draws a distinction between the place and the people.

'Geographically, how you navigate the place has changed', Leo says. 'Culturally, you think how diverse it was. Now it's a monoculture, but it's a culture made up of all these other cultures. Before there were bubbles; now it's one.

'It's not monochrome, it's vivid colour. We've forgotten black and white. This is now the norm.'

BEFORE the steelworks and other mills colonised swathes of land along the Hunter River in the early 20th century, the community that became known as Mayfield was studded with farms. In the 1850s, a German immigrant, Peter Crebert, cultivated orchards and a vineyard, producing the first commercial wine in Newcastle, and he also developed much-admired gardens. Other emigrants moved to the area to farm, and the neighbourhood was referred to as Germantown. In the later part of the 1800s, some of Newcastle's wealthiest and most influential citizens also moved to Mayfield. One of them, John Scholey, named not just his house but his subdivided land 'Mayfield'. And so a suburb was named. Mayfield House was just one of the grand homes that occupied the high ground, gazing over the river flats towards the coast, and across the undulating landscape to Newcastle. It was far enough removed from the industrial character of the town to retain relatively clean air and a sufficiently bucolic atmosphere. The area attracted not only the wealthy to live but visitors. As well as Crebert's gardens, there were the Crystal Palace Gardens, apparently inspired by the London landmark. These gardens had horticultural and zoological displays, along with the attraction of a large banquet hall, a skating rink and a dancing pavilion. As the Crystal Palace Gardens' owner declared in an advertisement, they were 'the Favourite Resort of all Picnic Parties, Captains, Seafaring Men and Visitors to the district generally'.[9] But then the industrial character moved into Mayfield. The gardens and farms were ploughed in under factories and workers' homes. When the British galvanised steel manufacturer John Lysaght established works in Newcastle in the early 1920s, tradesmen and their families emigrated from the firm's base in Bristol to work at the new mills. Lysaght effectively created a village within Mayfield, building homes for employees. The streets were named after places back in Britain. Novocastrians gave the enclave its own name; they referred to it as Pommy Town. An early resident of Pommy Town, William Claridge, recalled streets of sand straggling down to Mayfield's shopping strip, literally half a world away from the rain-slicked cobblestone streets back in Bristol. In the vicinity were market gardens tended by Chinese-Australians, and a little community hall with the grand name of the Lysaght Institute. As well as bringing their trade skills to Mayfield, the British workers also carried their love of football. Lysaght United was formed, and that grew into Mayfield United.[10]

Since the closure of the BHP steelworks and other nearby industries, the character of Mayfield has changed dramatically. The suburb once considered working class and a little rough is now a beacon for those seeking a home with some history, and a place with character. Mayfield has streets full of historic homes, from former workers' cottages to the mansions on the hill. And the suburb is populated with character and characters. Mayfield also has a celebrated multicultural atmosphere. Just off the main strip, around the corner from the tallest building in the suburb and a monument to what many in Mayfield once did for a living, the Ironworkers' Centre, is the Sultan Fatih Mosque. It is commonly referred to as the Mayfield Mosque. While the red brick building attracts worshippers to Mayfield, members of the mosque take their faith beyond the suburb to break down barriers, via a cup of good coffee. The mosque has a mobile café.

On a sublime weekend morning, the Mayfield Mosque's coffee van is parked along the harbour foreshore, about 5 kilometres from its base. The service counter is open and dispensing free coffees to passers-by. Yet this van isn't so much about the coffee; it's about the conversations it starts. I see a young man wearing a broad smile and a T-shirt that reads, 'I'm a Muslim. Ask Me About Islam'. I stop to ask him about his life in Newcastle.

His name is Muhammad Zaid Sarwar and is originally from Pakistan. He has been in Newcastle for more than two years and works in IT.

I ask Muhammad Zaid what is the purpose of the coffee van, and he replies, 'To tell the people of Newcastle that peace is everything. If you are peaceful, if you're happy, if you're lovely, everything is good'.

By and large, he has found things to be good in Newcastle. He considers it a beautiful place – 'I feel the fresh air' – and his favourite destination is the beach. Although he has not learnt to surf yet. Muhammad Zaid says he has found ethnic and cultural diversity in the city.

According to the 2021 census, 25 015 people living in the city had been born overseas. That figure represents almost 15 per cent of Newcastle's population. Of that number, 5903 had arrived in Newcastle in the previous five years.[11] They have come to study, to work, or to seek what has been denied them, or lost to them, in their homelands. Stability and security.

Standing out front to greet asylum seekers and refugees in Newcastle has been Sister Diana Santleben, Dominican nun and a ball of energy and perpetual emotion.

The Newcastle Citizen of the Year for 2017 established Zara's House, a centre for recently arrived refugee women and their families. It is a place where they can develop their English skills, as well as improve literacy in their own language, and share their stories and talents. Above all, as Sister Di explains, Zara's House has an open door to ensure everyone feels welcome in Newcastle. She also hopes it helps the broader community embrace refugees and asylum seekers. Sister Di explains she often asks people, 'How many refugees do you think come to Newcastle each year?'

'I have never got [an] answer that was even close!'

She offers the correct answer: 'About 100 if you average them out. But most people say two or three thousand. So it's not an economic issue, like the housing issues that we have here around this town. They are not caused by migrants; they're caused by lack of government thinking and capitalism.'

Zara's House is in Jesmond, an old mining suburb between Lambton and Wallsend. Jesmond has hosted a large component of Newcastle's refugee population, mainly because of its relatively affordable housing. The centre is housed in an old Anglican church, Saint Margaret's. After Sister Di spearheaded the successful community fundraising campaign to buy it, she felt guilty when she saw the cross still crowning the building.

'Do we get up there and take the cross off? Like, nuns getting up and taking a cross off, it's a bit rude!' Sister Di recounts in her voice that bubbles with a joy of life, a joy that just about seeps out of her skin. She seems more like an excited kid than a septuagenarian nun. 'Anyway, I was thinking this, and I came out next morning, and there had been a thunderstorm and the cross had been blown off the top of the church. We never took it off, God took it off!'

Sister Di moved to Newcastle from Sydney in 2005 to find more time to garden, and to slow down a little. She knew the city well, and had written about the long connection between it and the Dominican sisters. Soon after the nuns established a convent here in the 1870s, they set up Australia's first Catholic school for the deaf at Waratah. For generations, the community helped keep the school going.

'It was a Catholic school but everybody loved it and looked after it', Sister Di says. 'So we had this enormous treasure, and I think this is why I really understood, when I came here to Newcastle, what I could do in Zara's House, because I saw the people of Newcastle do exactly that.'

When asked to list the nationalities of those who use Zara's House, Sister Di launches into it.

'We have Eritreans, we have Somalis, we have Egyptians, we have Sudanese, we have South Sudanese, we have Liberians ...'

It isn't long before she has passed a dozen nationalities. The words and nations keep coming, a passionate fusillade fired from a champion of social justice.

In welcoming refugees, Sister Di reckons Newcastle is doing 'a pretty jolly good job'. Through Zara's House, the women and their families are finding a home in Newcastle. Just as Sister Di has done. And she has handed over the daily running of Zara's House to Farida Baremgayabo and Mary Amponsah.

Farida, originally from Burundi, arrived from South Africa as a refugee with her husband and three children in 2012. She had very little knowledge of Australia and had to research on social media where she was headed, but she was pleased by what she found in Newcastle. She liked the city's smaller scale but also its diversity, attending the mosque at Wallsend.

'People of Newcastle are kind; it's a welcoming city.'

As well as helping run Zara's House, Farida is a mother of seven – 'I have four Novocastrians!' – and she intends to stay.

'I belong to Newcastle', Farida declares. 'I'm a local. It's my hometown.'

Mary is from Ghana and came to Newcastle to study. Like Farida, she uses 'welcoming' to describe her impression of the city. Mary tells a story about when she arrived in 2016, and a woman approached her to offer directions to the university and then showed her the way.

Which is pretty much what Mary does these days for others arriving in Newcastle. She sees the challenges for many trying to navigate their new life with limited English. However, she believes it is a good place to take on that journey.

As for her own journey, 'it's really hard moving out of Newcastle'.

'There's that sense of community in Newcastle', Mary says. 'I feel that more than anywhere.'

As for Sister Di, she now has more time for her permaculture garden and chooks at her home in the western suburb of Maryland, not far from Zara's House, where she continues to help. Sister Di proudly declares she is a 'Westy'. Above all, this former Sydneysider sees herself as a Newcastle person 'to my bootstraps'.

'I consider Newcastle about the most perfect small town/big town that you can have.'

WHEN the Great Depression reached Newcastle in force, the economic downturn decimated any sense of security for many. Thousands of casual workers in the industries and the mines had been dealing with a precarious living at the best of times; now at the end of the 1920s, with little or no work, there were scant pickings. Thousands more around Newcastle lost their jobs, as companies slowed down or shut their gates. To put a roof over their heads, and with no other option, some of those unemployed and their families made something out of next to nothing. Camps and so-called shanty towns appeared on the fringe, or in the midst, of the town and suburbs, often on public land.

Dwellings were constructed from whatever could be scrounged, from hessian bags and kerosene tins to old water tanks and even disused tram carriages. If it could keep you dry and offer a modicum of privacy and a hint of dignity, then it could be a home. A few of the communities were formally planned, such as the Diggers' camp in Newcastle West. As the name suggests, the residents were largely returned servicemen. But most of the communities sprang up and grew as desperation demanded. In the harbourside suburb of Carrington, many of those who had formerly worked on ships or the waterfront set up camp at a reserve nicknamed Texas. Around Waratah, a suburb close to the industries, there was a community known as Tramcar, with men living in carriages, while at the local salesyards, dozens of people lived in former pigsties. And out in the bush near Jesmond was a community with the ironically glamorous name of Hollywood, where facilities were few. Residents had to carry water to the camp.[12] Their waste disposal chute was an old mine shaft.

While reports at the time carried descriptions of homely comforts, such as gardens, and a dedication to cleanliness and order, this was a hard existence, particularly for children and women. Celebrated Newcastle writer and activist Vera Deacon, who was born in 1926, spent her early life in Mayfield. As the Depression took hold, Vera's father, a steelworker who was badly burnt on the job, moved the family to one of the islands in the Hunter estuary for a more sustainable life. However, at the height of the Depression, the family moved back across the river, as her father chased work. They lived in unemployment camps, making a home for themselves in Mayfield West amid others desperately seeking work and trying to get by. Vera's family kept up appearances of having a home, built mostly from what could be found and collected, all the while trying to ward off the hostile looks and criticism of those who didn't appreciate having camp dwellers in their suburb. Many years later, when she wrote evocatively about her years as a 'camp' kid, Vera surmised those seemingly safe and secure suburbanites were driven less by narrow-mindedness in criticising their unemployed neighbours than by a fear that they too could easily end up in a camp, if they lost their job. Vera wrote how her parents' daily lives were ruled by the search for food for the family. That quest ruled young lives as well. She told of how a Sunday treat was to eat dripping cake baked in a camp oven. The kids devised a game to see who could take the longest to eat their slice of cake. There was no prize as such, just the prolonged pleasure of making the cake last. Everything was scarce, with a glaring exception, as observed by Vera. Babies seemed to be in plentiful supply.[13]

The Great Depression was imprinted on the soul and character of Vera Deacon. Her childhood helped make her the extraordinary woman she would become. She devoted her life to fighting for equity and fairness. But more than write about it and agitate for it, she strove for fairness by constantly giving to those in need, or to make Newcastle a better place. Vera was dedicated to giving. She gave what money she could to the University of Newcastle to develop its archives and local history projects. She gave her time and energy to wetlands rehabilitation projects along her beloved Hunter River, which she considered 'a mother' for how it had nurtured her. She gave her opinion and organising ability to social justice campaigns, and to the Communist Party of Australia, of which she was a long-time member. Yet, as I said at her memorial service in 2021 after she died at the age of 94, Vera didn't just believe in 'sharing' as a political or ideological concept. She lived it. Hers was a life to be shared. The city of her birth gave something back to Vera. She had been made a Freeman of the City of Newcastle in 2019. Or, as she told people, a Freewoman. But even with that accolade, she used it to give credit to everyone but herself. Above all, Vera gave love and joy to Newcastle, and to everyone she met. She didn't want to see anyone go without, especially when it came to love and joy. So in those years that took so much from so many in not just Newcastle but around the globe, the Great Depression, in many ways, gave Newcastle Vera Deacon.

The years of deprivation that played such a formative role in Vera Deacon's life also galvanised what was already part of the Novocastrian character: a willingness to demand, and even battle for, something better, and to protest what seems inadequate or plain wrong. In June 1932, when a group of police attempted to evict an unemployed worker and his family from a rented house in Tighes Hill, the battle lines between the authorities and the dispossessed were drawn. Members of an organisation called the Newcastle Citizens Anti-Eviction Committee, formed by political groups and unions along with those from the community, had picketed the house. The demonstration swelled, as word spread, with trade union members and the public bringing the estimated numbers in the street to about 1000 by the time the police inspector arrived to serve the eviction order. The protest flared into what has been called a riot. The police and some of the demonstrators faced off and a fight broke out. According to newspaper reports, some of the picketers armed themselves with tools and pieces of wood. At least seven officers and more than a dozen protestors were injured, with some of those hurt lying on the road. Word of the confrontation spread far. The *Canberra Times* carried a report, stating, 'The riot, which only lasted a little more than 10 minutes, was remarkable for its violence', and that afterwards, the house's 'walls and floor were bespattered with blood'.[14] Thirty protestors were arrested and initially charged with riot. In the court, the judge said the case was unusual in Newcastle given that, in the face of the existing hardships, people were law-abiding, which reflected the greatest credit on the residents. While 20 of the defendants were acquitted, another 10 had to face a second trial, but ultimately no-one was convicted.[15] But the riot did feed Newcastle's reputation as a place where people literally fought for their rights, and it was impressed into not just local folklore but print, with Dymphna Cusack referring to the episode in her 'Newcastle' novel, *Southern Steel*. Yet historian Sheilah Gray, who researched and wrote about the impact of the Great Depression on Newcastle, noted that in June 1933, after the worst of the Depression had passed, 62 per cent of male workers were still earning less than the basic wage. She took those figures, along with other indicators such as the shanty towns, as confirmation that the suffering during those years was on a scale rarely, if ever, experienced before in Australia. 'That being so', Sheilah Gray wrote, 'the passivity of the community is remarkable'.[16] Or perhaps, as the community has demonstrated time and again, it was resilient rather than passive.

What the Depression years also developed among those who lived in Newcastle's makeshift communities was compassion. Author and historian John Maynard has written how non-Aboriginal Novocastrians in those camps experienced something many Aboriginal Australians had lived with for a long time. As a result, John believes, these camp residents gained a greater understanding of, and compassion for, the issues facing Aboriginal people. Those experiences, the historian argues, helped shape Newcastle through the years. John draws a line to 1993, when the city's council consulted with the local First Nations communities and presented a commitment to the Hunter's Aboriginal people. The commitment acknowledged the pain of loss experienced by Indigenous Australians and resolved that Aboriginal people and the wider community would work together 'for a treaty or other instrument of reconciliation'.[17]

In Newcastle during the Great Depression, some extraordinary talent was born and nurtured. One of the earlier makeshift towns had grown near Adamstown, another 19th-century mining village that had outgrown itself. The Depression camp clinging to Adamstown had been set up by the Australian Workers' Union to help those needing shelter as they sought and hoped for a job in the industries. But hope all too often took the shape of a shack constructed from logs dragged from the nearby bush and whitewashed hessian bags. A little boy named William, or Bill as he liked to be called, would look at those shacks, but his imagination was creating pictures. Bill had been born in 1934, and the economy was gradually recovering, but even so the Depression had left its mark on people who were still forced to call the most basic of dwellings 'home'. Not that Bill's home was much more substantial, by his description. His family lived in a tin shack in Adamstown, before moving to a nearby community, New Lambton, where Bill observed more constructions by people trying to get by with whatever they could get their hands on.

'It was a hard life, but as a kid it didn't seem like a hard life', Bill told me in 2013.[18]

Young Bill was interested in art, and the sight of people carving out a space for themselves in or near the bush held references to the kind of painting he admired. He particularly liked the so-called Australian Impressionists, artists such as Tom Roberts and Arthur Streeton, who cast a new light on the bush, and our place in it, in the late 19th and early 20th centuries. And just as those artists shaped Bill's early interest in art, so did the wildlife in the bush. He loved birds, seeing that flash of colour through the trees.

'I was born in the bush, I loved the bush, I bought books when I could about birds, and had a small library. I would sketch birds as well.'

In the years ahead, those two passions – art and birds – would coalesce for the self-taught painter. Before then, as a young man in Newcastle, Bill worked as a window dresser for a department store in town, then as a display manager for a menswear store. At night he painted landscapes, which he entered in local competitions and exhibitions. His art and ability were mentioned to another William, Dobell, and Australia's best-known artist invited the fledgling painter to his home and studio at Wangi Wangi, about 36 kilometres away, and offered advice and encouragement. Dobell's advice remained fixed in his memory, and his art practice.

'Learn to draw, draw when you can and you must be able to draw before you can carry on and do these other wondrous things that people do.'

Bill did go on to do wondrous things, combining the majesty of nature with the beauty of art. His name is synonymous with wildlife art. William T Cooper illustrated landmark books on wildlife, particularly birds. His paintings led to sold-out exhibitions internationally and awards and accolades from around the globe. In a documentary about the artist, *Portrait Painter to the Birds*, the great wildlife documentary maker David Attenborough described Bill as one of the greatest artists ever to work in this field.[19] Bill had lived by, and lived up to, another piece of advice Dobell had given him: 'Find your own way'. Through his art, and following the flight of birds, Bill Cooper had found his own way from Adamstown to the heights of natural history painting.

Many years after the Great Depression, the pressures of life in Adamstown made their way onto the screen in *The Love Letters from Teralba Road*. This sad but sweet 1970s film is about a relationship in trouble. The main character, Len, is from Newcastle. He is violent, and his wife, Barbara, has left him. He is living at his mother's house, a fibro workers' cottage, similar to the houses that once squatted on large blocks, with a street out the front and a night cart lane out the back, throughout Adamstown. Len writes letters filled with the words of longing and love he struggles to say to his wife. As she weighs up resuming the relationship, Barbara makes it clear to Len she doesn't want to live in Newcastle. The inspiration for the script, and the title of the film, came from a cache of old letters that writer and director Stephen Wallace, who was from Newcastle, found hidden in a drawer in his rented unit in Sydney. The letters had been written years earlier in Teralba Road, Adamstown. If Len were to return to Teralba Road and walk through Adamstown these days, he would be lost for words, and perhaps Barbara would like what she saw. Most of the miners' and workers' cottages have now been either renovated and remodelled or wiped away, as blocks have been entirely colonised by large homes or medium-density developments.

During the Great Depression, charity began at home, and assistance arrived largely from within the community. Organisations such as churches helped where they could, unions had relief funds that were in high demand, and people supported each other. In some ways, that idea of the community helping itself flowed through the years to the NBN Telethons. The local television station used its studios to produce a marathon variety show, which was a massive fundraiser. The telethon's incessant soundtrack was ringing phones, as the public dialled in to speak with a soap opera star, newsreader or musician on the other end of the line and pledge money. The telethon was more than just a major community event on the Newcastle calendar. From the 1970s to the early 2000s, it raised about $18 million for projects such as cancer treatment services. It was as though the telethon not only tapped into Newcastle's generosity but an attitude of, 'If no one else will help us, we'll help ourselves – and we'll have fun doing it'.

At the time of the Depression, local councils, often in coalition with the state government, set up work relief programs, offering part-time employment to men to help them get by. They constructed drains and roads, parks and baths. The legacy of those projects remains part of life in Newcastle. In places, that legacy is cast in concrete. Around Merewether and Adamstown, for instance, the monotony of bitumen suddenly gives way to a tract of stone-stubbled concrete. The road looks more characterful, and the journey feels rougher, as the grit and texture of the Depression-era surface bite into the tyres. It is as though the spirit of those who poured the concrete is giving us a shake to remind us what they had to endure.

Creeks were straightened and sculpted into a network of drains. These canals that criss-cross suburbs, stitching one community to the next with concrete, were designed to carry storm water to the river and the sea. This process of turning Newcastle's creeks into drains had begun many years before, to improve public health by washing potential problems away. And during the Depression, building infrastructure was one way to contend with the unemployment problem.

Famously, the engineering works of men were no match for the force of nature in June 2007, when the storm that pushed *Pasha Bulker* ashore at Nobbys dumped up to 300 millimetres of rain in the creeks' catchment areas. The drains network was flooded, water poured over the concrete lips and into vehicles, homes and lives. Suburban houses became islands in an archipelago of desperation or, worse, silt traps filled with sodden and ruined possessions. However, during dry times, the network of drains has been a playground and bike path for a few generations of kids, and it served as a path of wondering leading to words for former Newcastle bookshop owner and author, Mark MacLean. He and his dog, Jambo, walked along the drain that still bears the name of Styx Creek, carrying the pair below the surface, in more ways than physical. The drain's purpose may have been to quickly transport stormwater out of suburban lives, but it encouraged Mark to slow down, and to observe the minutiae of life, from the detritus washed or thrown into the canal to the wildlife that hangs around the drain. Just as a waterway seems to flow from the past to the future, Mark noted the shards and glimpses over the concrete of dead industries, whose corpses lay beside the drain, and he mused on where the city, and all this stuff it created and disposed of – including into Styx Creek – was headed. Mark poured his observations into a blog and a book, titled *A Year Down the Drain*. Despite the book's title, Mark posed a lyrical argument for considering this waterway as a creek rather than a drain, especially when he saw fish in the shallows or birds swirling above the water or resting on the booms designed to stop litter flowing downstream. Down there in the drain, or creek, Mark found himself in a place of contentment, especially in those moments when he came across the turning of the tide on the concrete bed. In turn, through his writing, Mark has opened more eyes to what Styx Creek is; not a conduit for getting rid of all that we don't want but a portal to everyday magic. This drain is a road to adventure, and it is just about in our backyards. Then again, many a kid with a bike already knew that.

Steven Fleming was keen for more of us to get on bikes and follow the stormwater drains/creeks. Years ago the designer and champion of bicycling mapped the land in Newcastle and looked at what could be potentially used as cycleways. What grabbed Steven's attention were stormwater drains and former coal rail corridors webbing their way through the suburbs. Steven devised what he called the Newcastle Waterway Discovery Loop, linking existing cycleways by creating tracks beside the drains and along the rail corridors.

'It ties all these loose ends as you approach the city', he says.

Steven even led a bicycle tour along the 'canals' to demonstrate what was possible in Newcastle in bringing those in the suburbs into the city without having to drive. But he also concedes that at the moment those reimagined cycling routes will probably remain stormwater drains and rail easements.

'Suburbs are still "car land" and will remain so while there's a way to power the things. It's not going to change in a hurry.'

Still, there has been some change along the 'drains' of Newcastle, as people gradually come to see at least some of the waterways as not a discharge channel or refuse point but as a creek. Along Throsby Creek, boardwalks and pathways have been built, and mangroves that were ripped out many years ago are reviving, providing nurseries for fish that languidly cruise amid the reeds, while birds roost in the trees and bob and pick their way through the shallows. And it is not just the wildlife returning. So are people. The waterways that repulsed them for so long, due to the actions and disregard of those before them, are now attracting them. They are drawn to the water to be reminded how to not hurry, to go with the flow. It is not quite how Mark MacLean foresaw it as he looked at his ugly/beautiful place down the drain and imagined what it could become, with all manner of water features and natural attractions.[20] But it is getting there.

As Steven Fleming says, the suburbs are 'car land'. The suburbs came into being, in no small part, because of the car. The villages they were transformed from were largely self-reliant, but those living in the suburbs have largely relied on the car to get anywhere. The car may have played a large role in Newcastle culture, but, in many ways, it throttled the inner city. For businesses followed people out to the suburbs. In 1947, when the rise of the car was taking hold, the book *Newcastle 150 Years* declared that Hunter Street 'has always been the hub of retail business' and mentioned how many suburbs had their own 'small editions of Hunter Street'.[21] But within a couple of decades, it was Hunter Street shrinking and suburban shopping centres growing amid housing estates. Many could walk to their shopping centre, although most didn't – they tended to drive. The centres were attached to massive carparks, which only expanded through the years as people became even more vehicle dependent.

When it came to furnishing your home in the suburbs, one name prominent in Newcastle was that of John Peschar. John had a string of discount stores, yet he hadn't chased customers into the suburbs in pursuit of a deal. He founded his retail kingdom in the suburbs.

At more than two metres tall, John stood out in more ways than just height. He was known as 'Big John', and he was good at attracting attention. In one newspaper photograph, 'Big John' had his feet on the desk and was holding two pistols, ready to take on retail prices.

'Big John' had grown up in the Netherlands wary of guns. Adriaan Johannes Peschar, or Hans, was about 12 when his homeland was invaded by German forces during the Second World War. For five years, he lived on his wits; his education focussed on survival. When the war ended, he embraced freedom and the possibility of going anywhere he chose. In 1950, Hans moved to Australia, a country he knew very little about, to be an agent for the sale of prefabricated houses. The big man arrived in a vast country, one he saw filled with opportunities. Hans moved on from sales to fruit picking and other farm work before landing a job as a commercial salesman in North Queensland. When Hans applied for the job, his prospective boss suggested he change his name to something that sounded less German.

'I said, "Look, if I can get the job, you can call me anything". They said, "How about John?" and I said, "That's fine".'

John moved to Newcastle for work in 1956. His wife Pamela, who he had met in Cairns, wanted to return to Queensland as soon as possible. After all, what greeted them was not a patch on the tropical north. John describes his first impressions of Newcastle as being 'a BHP town, and it was smoky and industrial'. He told his wife to give it 12 months and they would head home. Yet the Peschars experienced what so many before them, and so many since, have: the character of Newcastle gets into your soul.

From what John learnt about selling, from his affinity with people, and fuelled by a desire to be his own boss, he and Pamela began their own hardware and home goods business in a small shop in the suburb of Gateshead, about 15 minutes' drive south of Newcastle city. He saw his best hope of a good business lying in the suburbs.

'I remember when I was thinking a plan out, I knew I had to get out of the main street and be on my own.'

As well as choosing the right location, out where people lived, John figured the word that would help his business grow was one not often heard then in retail: discount.

'When I first got in, I was the only one who gave big discounts; by the time I sold, 25 years later, they [retailers] were all discounting.'

The customers quickly thronged through the doors of the little shop, so he had to take on bigger premises, still on the fringe of town, in the suburb of Mount Hutton. As word spread that if you needed something for the home then Peschar's was the place, John opened more stores, including in the Coalfields and the Central Coast.

'When I started I thought I would appeal to poor people so they could save money. But in actual fact, most of our clients were business people.'

Not everyone welcomed John's approach to retailing. As he was pulling so much trade out of Hunter Street, a number of businesses in the city complained to their suppliers about this newcomer discounting items. In response, some suppliers sought out John to ensure he stocked their products. He also came up against a union on one occasion, because his delivery drivers were not members. That was easily resolved. John spoke with the union official and paid for his drivers to join.

While he owned the business, John knew the importance of being out on the shop floor with his employees, treating them as equals.

'You don't come in as the manager; you come as one of them and sit alongside them. And that attitude is very Novocastrian, I think. They don't like this pyramid thing. And it works too. If you treat them well, they treat you well.'

Employing conversation and negotiation, showing respect and not aggression. What worked so well for John Peschar in life and business in Newcastle were skills that had saved his life on more than one occasion in the Netherlands during the war. Late one night, after curfew, he and a young neighbour were cycling back into their town with vegetables they had collected from outlying farms when they were stopped by two German soldiers, their rifles pointed at the teenagers. Rather than try and run, or resist, the boys talked with the soldiers. They saw under the soldiers' helmets the eyes of two other teenagers. They kept talking until finally the two young soldiers conferred and told the boys to be on their way. In those incredibly tense moments, John developed his approach to life, and the mantra for good living: 'Let's have a talk about it'.

John has been more than a man of words, and of his word. After selling his business, he was chairman of NBN television, and he has been actively involved in community organisations and campaigns, including the restoration of Christ Church Cathedral. He can see the results of that effort from his apartment. The man who made his money in the suburbs has, for many years, lived in the heart of the city that has dramatically changed since he arrived in the mid-1950s. As John says of himself, 'I really do feel like a Novocastrian'. He has been watching more and more people moving up the freeway from Sydney, and from far and wide, to Newcastle. He hopes the city doesn't grow too large and become overpopulated. But for those who do move to Newcastle, he hopes they will be welcomed and brought into the community, just as he was. In that way, we can continue to talk and get to know each other. To John Peschar, that's what sells Newcastle.

'This is the charm still of Newcastle that you go down the road, and there's always somebody you meet who you know. That's us. You don't have that in big cities, but [you do] here in Newcastle. It's an overgrown country town.'[22]

THE car may have reshaped Newcastle, physically and culturally, but it didn't get its way everywhere. In a few places around the city and in the suburbs, major thoroughfares cut across rail lines. Novocastrians have largely determined their travel patterns and itineraries to accommodate the gates coming down and having to wait for a train to pass. The rail crossing that Novocastrians have little time for is the one on the border of Adamstown and New Lambton South. The Adamstown gates are a hair-tearing aspect of modern Newcastle living. Actually, the gates have goaded generations of Novocastrians. For the best part of a century, there have been plans and proposals for vehicles to go over and even under the rail lines. But here we sit, as if we have all the time in the world, and often. For the Adamstown gates seem to be down very regularly, because the line carries both passengers and freight, including long, painfully slow coal trains heading to and from the port. As motorists fume in the queue of vehicles snaking ever longer through Adamstown and New Lambton South, their anger tends to be directed not so much at King Coal but at the successive state governments who benefit from billions of dollars in royalties from the black rock, yet can't do something about the crossing. For many, the gates symbolise Macquarie's Street's attitude to Newcastle. The big guys benefit, while we're stopped in our tracks. There is a Facebook page called 'I Hate Adamstown Gates'. Even the financial institution Newcastle Permanent has featured the gates and a long queue of vehicles in one of its advertising campaigns, with a patiently waiting driver smiling at the camera and acknowledging he was there for the long haul. For many Novocastrians, it is not just outdated infrastructure that stirs up frustration behind the steering wheel. When the state government ripped up the heavy rail line from Wickham to Newcastle, a consolation to motorists using Stewart Avenue, one of the busiest roads in the area, was, 'Well, at least we won't have to sit there any more, waiting for a train to pass'. And they don't. Now they wait for the light rail carriages to beetle by like red rags to a bull. That's progress.

Just as much of the urban flow in Newcastle was inwards, so was the popular cultural influence. Many of the bands that populated the pubs of inner-city Newcastle began in garages and bedrooms in the suburbs. The bands graduated from there to the local hotels. Before random breath testing, before the creation of 'VIP rooms' populated with pokies that devoured auditoriums and customers' spending money, suburban pubs were, on any given night, rock and roll palaces. The Bel-Air Hotel at Kotara used to advertise itself as 'Rockin in the Suburbs'. But the live music scene spread beyond the suburbs. The pubs were petri dishes for musical talent. The rock city was largely a product of the suburbs.

What those rock and roll pubs also bred were a fierce loyalty among audiences and a sense of community. As Gaye Sheather, who chronicled the peak of Newcastle's pub rock scene in her book, *Rock This City*, recalls, the pubs and the acts they booked were markers to guide you through your nights and weekends.

'Your weekend would revolve around where you were going, and what bands were on. I'd just go through the gig guide and drive to wherever my favourite bands were playing.'

In the suburbs, there were also recording studios. These contained spaces in the unlikeliest of places captured the sounds of both local acts and those from further afield. The Whitlams, who would go on to be one of the biggest independent bands in Australia, are synonymous with Sydney. They were a product of another thriving pub rock scene in Sydney's inner-west and later would have huge success with their somewhat tongue-in-cheek paean to the harbour city, with the title, 'You Gotta Love This City'. However, this resolutely Sydney band recorded their first work, *Introducing the Whitlams*, in Newcastle. The band recorded the mini-album in early 1993 at Skyhigh Studios at Jesmond.

Having been sent up the highway to the studio by the band's record company, The Whitlams' frontman Tim Freedman arrived at Jesmond in his Kingswood packed with musical equipment and anticipation.

'It was the first good studio we'd recorded in, so it was exciting.'

As Tim remembers it, the studio was above a Chinese restaurant and conveniently close to the suburb's shopping centre. During recording breaks, he would head over there for donuts. And musical inspiration was no match for an act of God in the studio. The Whitlams had finished a recording session and were driving back to Sydney when a power surge during an electrical storm had wiped a few seconds from the mini-album's opening track, 'The Ballad of Lester Walker'. Producer Rob Taylor phoned Tim and his bandmate Stevie Plunder to turn the Kingswood around and return to Jesmond to re-record the missing piece.

When the mini-album was released, The Whitlams would frequently play at the University of Newcastle, only a stone's throw from the recording studio, and they would venture into town, playing a late-night gig at a Hunter Street hotel.

'It was a late-night town then,' recalls Tim.

Some years later, when the band was one of the biggest acts in the land, Tim received a request for 'You Gotta Love This City', his song about Sydney, to be used in a car advertisement in Newcastle. As Tim said to me during an interview in 2024, 'People going, "I know that melody!"? It's because you saw the Newcastle Holden ad 20 years ago'.[23]

Tim Freedman has long and deep connections to the Hunter. Forebears on his mother's side of the family settled around Maitland in the mid-1800s. And he simply likes Newcastle.

'It was the first place that took the band to its heart, outside of the suburbs of inner Sydney. It accepted us, and we became part of the scene.

'So it's no wonder how comfortable I am there.'

By the mid-1990s, the age of pub rock was waning in Newcastle. Yet out of the dying days of that era, and out of a suburban bedroom, rose the most successful band yet formed in Newcastle: Silverchair.

All three members of Silverchair – singer and guitarist Daniel Johns, drummer Ben Gillies and bass player Chris Joannou – grew up in Merewether. Chris Joannou pointed out in the book he co-wrote with Ben Gillies, *Love & Pain*, that the genesis of Silverchair was very much a local affair, with everyone able to walk to each other's places and all going to the same schools. The Joannou family owned a local dry-cleaning business and lived behind the shop, so Chris' memories of his early life were of a house smelling of freshly pressed linen.

Aided by living near the beach, Daniel, Ben and Chris loved surfing. Yet from the outset, Silverchair didn't create surf music. It didn't even sound like a product of Newcastle; rather, with its grungy guitars, Silverchair's music had echoes of Seattle.

The band had formed as a four-piece, with the school boys calling themselves the Innocent Criminals, before becoming a trio. In Ben Gillies' bedroom, flanked by a Led Zeppelin banner and a Doors poster, the band members wrote their own future, with a song titled 'Tomorrow'. In 1994, 'Tomorrow' won a song contest, and so began the phenomenon of three teenagers from Newcastle grabbing the ears of the globe.

'Tomorrow' was released as a single, and it was at the top of the charts in Australia for six weeks. The boys were celebrating Ben's 15th birthday at Pizza Hut when they were told the song had reached number one. They didn't really care. They wanted to eat.

In 1995, the band released its debut album, *Frogstomp*, which went on to sell millions of copies worldwide, including climbing into the Top 20 in the United States. The trio toured extensively, all the while doing homework.

Suddenly, in a city that neither cuts down tall poppies nor hero worships, rock mania throbbed and wailed in Newcastle, as fans sought out the three boys at school, at home, at the beach, anywhere they could. Newcastle is not a big enough place to hide, especially when you're that famous. And, as Chris and Ben recall in their memoir, when you are that famous, you can expect fellow Novocastrians to keep you in check. Some began calling the band Nirvana in Pyjamas, or worse. Novocastrians celebrate those who do well, and people were proud of Silverchair's success. However, you're expected to keep your feet on the ground, which would be very hard when you're a kid on a rocket ride to the stars.

While the rest of the world clamoured to get close to these teenage rock stars, in Newcastle, it was possible to get a souvenir of their success. While dropping clothes in to be dry cleaned at the Joannou family business, my father mentioned to Chris' grandfather that one of his grandsons loved Silverchair. When Dad returned to pick up the clothes, Mr Joannou handed him a Silverchair poster signed by the three members. Silverchair may have been a big deal, but Newcastle was still a small community.

More than being proud of Silverchair, many in town at that time considered the band as the sound of hope. Silverchair reminded Novocastrians that the city was still capable of producing something the rest of the world wanted. The year the band released its second album, *Freak Show*, the city was told BHP was to close. By the time Silverchair was touring for its highly successful third album, *Neon Ballroom*, the steelworks were about to shut their gates. Silverchair was a success story in a period when Newcastle felt it had few to tell. The media was talking about the death of Steel City, but it was also fascinated that this was the town that spawned Silverchair. The success of those three kids gave some gleam to a bleak time.

Chris Joannou was moving too fast, too busy touring and recording, to feel the drag of a city clinging onto the band's coat tails. What's more, he did what many young Novocastrians did around that time. He left town.

'I moved away from Newcastle when I was around 21, so I missed a lot of that', Chris told me in 2017.[24] 'But I still came back fortnightly because my family was here. As the years went on, I just found this whole new appreciation [for Newcastle], and you could sense there was this thing bubbling below the surface, and it's really like someone's scratched it, and it's all just happened.'

By 2011, Silverchair had effectively split. So had the brotherhood. The three mates from Merewether who had been through so much together were riven. While the other two went on to other musical projects, Chris Joannou saw the end of Silverchair as the end of his career as a musician. He moved back to Newcastle. He was returning home.

'I think any person you ask who has been born and bred in Newcastle, even if they've moved away and still don't plan on coming back, they still call it "home". It is a very treasured kind of place. Novocastrians are extremely passionate people.'

When Chris returned, it wasn't as a rock star wanting to live on past glory. He wanted to be one of those scratching what he felt was bubbling below the surface. He saw a changing city, and he didn't want to be just part of the change, he wanted to contribute to it. The life of Chris Joannou and the life of Newcastle were entwined; both were transforming.

In the building where his parents had opened a laundromat and dry-cleaning business in Newcastle West some years earlier, Chris imagined creating a social and creative hub. The question Chris asked himself was, 'How do we engage on multiple levels under one roof, and [with] all my personal interests as well – music, food, arts, community engagement, people?' He answered those questions with the space he and his business partners opened in the former light industrial building in 2014. It was many things to many people – a restaurant and bar, and a music rehearsal and performance space. There was a record shop next door. The hospitality complex was named The Edwards, after the English anthropologist and author Sir Edward Burnett Tylor, who was renowned for his theories on cultures, and how they evolve. If he were still alive, Sir Edward would have found rich material to write about in Newcastle West. The Edwards was a shining example of an evolving culture in a part of town that had been down at heel and, as a result, downtrodden.

The Edwards was embraced, not only as a place to grab a drink or food, but to gather and create something, from a community choir to a ukulele group. And what was happening in The Edwards was sprouting through the town in 2017, in Chris' eyes.

'It's a lovely transition for the city. We're still bookended by coal and industry, yet down the other end now is this whole creative [aspect] and tech design, innovation, arts, music, and then we're filling out everything in between.

'Looking further down the track when this part of town is heavily developed and people are living in apartment blocks everywhere around us, as people do in New York, they should be able to walk down from their building into the place next door where they had dinner last night and do their ukulele lessons.'

Chris' foresight was sharp. Newcastle West has been growing denser and reaching high with apartment developments. Yet no one could foresee what happened to The Edwards. As Chris explained in *Love & Pain*, one reason he established it was to replace Silverchair, and to have a sense of control. In 2018, his creation was destroyed by a fire. Chris had rushed from his home at harbourside Carrington late at night only to witness everything he had built burning down. It devastated him. And, watching the news reports and reflecting on my conversation with Chris, I felt devastated for him, and for the town. It felt typically Newcastle. Someone builds up something, something that means a lot to so many in the town, only to see it ruined. But Chris' response was also Novocastrian, one of resilience. He and his partners rebuilt The Edwards.

The day after the hospitality hub reopened in 2019, Chris began a course of chemotherapy. He had been diagnosed with cancer. The treatment worked and he was cleared of the disease. In 2022, The Edwards was sold, and Chris moved with his family to Coffs Harbour. Soon after, he was back in Newcastle, having been flown down for emergency surgery after having a heart attack. In 2023, while visiting Newcastle, Chris felt unwell and needed another stent put into his heart. Picking him up after the procedure was former bandmate Ben, who had moved back to the Hunter. Chris and Ben had patched up their differences and repaired their friendship years earlier.[25] Yet Silverchair's brotherhood of three was not reunited. The triangle was not yet complete.

For many years, Daniel Johns had a beautiful home at Merewether Heights, overlooking the city, the coast and the landscape of his childhood. Yet it was a childhood interrupted. As he has talked about, Johns has had a difficult relationship with fame. It has demanded so much of him, and taken so much from him, particularly any hope of anonymity. Especially in his hometown. The house had been a creative sanctuary for Daniel. He wrote on social media in 2022 how he recorded the bulk of his solo album, *FutureNever*, in his home, taking the chance as well to publicly declare his love for his hometown. Yet I imagine that mansion on the hill, which I occasionally visited as a kid in the 1970s because it was then owned by the family of a school friend, also provided a luxurious bulwark from the outside world. For a reluctant rock star, Newcastle must have seemed so near, yet so distant, from up there. However, the home where music was born has gone. In 2025, Daniel Johns had the house demolished, with plans to redevelop the site. I guess sometimes the greatest view can be made even greater.

Novocastrians no longer wonder whether Silverchair will reform. It seems unlikely. But there's always 'Tomorrow'.

In early 2025, The Edwards, the business Chris Joannou had co-founded, shut. Even though Chris was no longer part of the business, yet again I felt for him, and for the town. When I reflect on my conversation with Chris all those years ago, I think about what he prophesied for Newcastle, and how the city would be viewed. I hope Chris' prophecy proves right.

'I think in ten years' time, people will take this as a benchmark of what a city can do and turn things around.'

THE physical heart of Newcastle may be in the CBD, but many Novocastrians would argue that the community's spiritual heart is located about 5 kilometres away on low-lying ground at Broadmeadow. And what flows through this particular heart is coloured red and blue.

For here is the city's stadium, the home ground of the city's two professional football teams, the Newcastle Jets, which plays in the A-league soccer competition, and the National Rugby League side, the Newcastle Knights. Both teams wear red-and-blue uniforms.

The stadium is a structure of imposing proportions. It has the angularity and rawness of an industrial structure. The cantilevered roofs over the grandstands give the impression of the gaping mouths of monsters, just waiting to devour something. What this place devours, and is nourished by, is the passion and loyalty of a community. And the crowds eat up what goes on in here.

The first incarnation of the stadium was built in the late 1960s, rising from the site of a former aerodrome. Among the famous pilots to use the strip were Charles Kingsford-Smith and Amy Johnson, who, just days before her visit in 1930, had become the first woman to fly solo from England to Australia.[26] The strip was also the base of Newcastle Aero Club, with members' planes serried across the field like a crop of dreams. So this once-marshy soil was impressed with human ambitions and achievement long before sportspeople sprinted onto it. Queen Elizabeth II officially opened the stadium in 1970. It was bestowed with a grand title, the Newcastle International Sports Centre.

Yet this place has always been about more than sports. When Prince Charles and Princess Diana visited Newcastle in 1983, about 40 000 schoolchildren packed into the stadium to wave at the royal couple as they were paraded around the ground in a Land Rover. When Newcastle was trying to find its feet after the 1989 earthquake, culture and community embraced on the sports ground, with the staging of a massive rock concert to raise funds and the city's mood. On 18 February 1990, nine of the country's biggest acts, including Midnight Oil, The Angels, and the two bands that were scheduled to play at the Newcastle Workers Club the night of the earthquake, Split Enz and Crowded House, performed in the stadium for a crowd of about 42 000. Across the front of the stage was a banner indicating that even after a disaster, Novocastrians retained their sense of humour. It read, 'It's Everybody's Fault!!'

Other massive outdoor concerts have been staged at the stadium, with Elton John, Pink, and Paul McCartney performing. That the city was able to attract the world's biggest music stars, particularly a Beatle, to perform was met with not just excitement but gratitude. In the lead-up to the McCartney concert in October 2023, a mural was painted on a wall at one of the busiest intersections in Newcastle West. The work, painted by one of the city's best-known artists and illustrators, Mitch Revs, is a burst of pop colour that references songs by The Beatles,

Wings and McCartney, from 'Yellow Submarine' and 'Penny Lane' to 'Band on the Run'. On his way to the stadium to perform, Paul McCartney stopped by the mural for photos and to give it his blessing with the stroke of a brush, painting smiley faces and writing his initials. Long after the legend left town, the mural has remained, grabbing attention and reminding people 'Paul was here!'

The stadium has also been used for smaller events, hosting memorial services for well-known Newcastle people or serving as a starting or finishing point for charity events. The Newcastle International Sports Centre had a name change and these days is known as McDonald Jones Stadium. Sports may have disappeared from the name, but certainly not from the ground

Newcastle has always been mad about sport. Sport reigned long before this area was called Newcastle. The Awabakal people loved competing and playing, be it with spear throwing or in the water. As Aboriginal leader and author John Maynard points out, the early colonial arrivals, such as the Reverend Lancelot Threlkeld, were impressed by the Aboriginal people's athleticism and games.

The new arrivals brought their own sports and a reminder of where they had come from through what they played, particularly with soccer, or football. The village teams played each other, competitions grew and, through the generations, champions were created. As John Maynard, himself a former first-grade soccer player, points out, Newcastle has produced many international footballers. Among the greatest players produced in this city is Cheryl Salisbury.

Cheryl was the captain of the Matildas, the women's national team, from 2003 until she retired in 2009. She played in four World Cups and represented Australia at two Olympics, including at the Sydney games in 2000, when she scored Australia's first ever goal at that level. In all, she played 151 games for her country. She was acknowledged internationally. Cheryl was named twice by the game's controlling body, FIFA, in the Women's World XI squad. For the prizes and awards she has received, Cheryl would need more than a trophy cabinet; more like a large gallery. Her name is already in galleries. In 2009, she was inducted into the Australian Football Hall of Fame. A decade later, she was inducted into the Sport Australia Hall of Fame. In women's football, Cheryl was a pioneer. She was the first female to be awarded the Alex Tobin Medal, the highest honour in Australian football. As well as making her mark on the ground with a ball, she also helped make the field more level for women in sport, raising issues of the inequity in pay, conditions and recognition. More than show other women what was possible in football, Cheryl also demonstrated to the world that fair play did not just apply in sport; it needed to be addressed in everyday life.

Cheryl learnt she was equal to the boys, and the boys learnt she was equal to them, and better, from about the age of seven. Growing up in Lambton, she played in teams with boys at school, and with a local club side. As Cheryl recalled when I spoke with her in 2017, on the field, she had to keep up.[27] But she wanted to be out there because she was good enough, and not to be given a break because she was female.

More than be good enough, Cheryl had demonstrated by her late teens that she was among the best. She was selected to be in the Matildas. Her journey as an extraordinary player, and as a pioneer, had begun. She helped bring change to the game, and to people's perspective of female players. As Cheryl told me, achieving equality was more important in her eyes than what she had done and achieved.

Around the time Cheryl Salisbury was first kicking a ball with the boys, Newcastle entered the National Soccer League. Newcastle KB United was formed in 1977 and joined the national competition the following year. For home games at the International Sports Centre, the team would attract thousands, including a supporters' group known as The Rowdies. Before a national rugby league team arrived, soccer filled the stadium. Helping draw the crowds were international players, including a cameo for Newcastle by Manchester United legend Bobby Charlton, and Hunter-nurtured greats, such as Craig Johnston.

Growing up at Lake Macquarie and playing on grounds throughout the Hunter, Craig knew he was following a tradition imprinted in the dirt by generations of British migrants who worked in the valley's mines and in Newcastle at the steelworks and dockyard. He admired them for being 'a hardy and tough old bunch'. Craig would need similar traits where he was headed: the cauldron of professional football in Britain.

In the mid-1970s, as a teenager, Craig carried his dream of being a professional soccer player to the other side of the world. The Hunter boy proved to be hardy and tough and tenacious, refusing to surrender his dream. He played for Middlesbrough Football Club then Liverpool FC in front of huge crowds. While he was based in England, Craig returned home for a couple of stints with KB United. He was stunned to see a full stadium in Newcastle.

'It was amazing', Craig says. 'I'd never seen anything like it in Australia.'

Craig would head back to Britain and create an iconic moment for Liverpool, helping take his side to victory against Everton by scoring a goal in the 1986 FA Cup final. Yet all the time he was overseas, Craig felt the pull of home. These days, Craig Johnston lives in the Newcastle area, where an extraordinary career was born.

'The Knights didn't exist then, so it was a soccer town.'

However, the roar of soccer crowds at the stadium was not enough to sustain KB United. It was no more by the mid-1980s. A succession of soccer teams came along, leading to the formation of the Newcastle United Jets Football Club. The Jets continue to pull crowds to the stadium, but nothing like the numbers for the Knights.

These days, McDonald Jones Stadium is synonymous with rugby league. A sign near the entrance to the stadium reads, 'You're on Knights Turf'. As if you need to be told. That sign could be erected anywhere in Newcastle, or anywhere in the valley.

On game days for the Knights, thousands travel from far and wide, swaddled in the team's colours, to the stadium. And they turn up, no matter the weather. In Newcastle, 'rain, hail or shine' is not so much a cliché but the creed for Knights fans. To the visitor, a Knights fan is a figure of admiration and wonderment. During the broadcast of the 2023 home-game final against the Canberra Raiders, playing great turned television commentator Brad Fittler observed the dramatic change in mood, and volume, of the 30 000-strong crowd when their team was in a tough patch, saying it suddenly went from being like a rock concert to like being in a library. Yet when things get really tough, a Newcastle crowd invariably raises its voice to lift the team – and the grandstands' roofs. As one, fans express not just their support for the Knights players but their deep sense of place by hollering three distinct syllables.

NEW-KAR-SUL!

Such is the roof-raising, shape-shifting power of the Knights that this stadium was rebuilt and reconfigured, making it better for rugby league and its fans. It went from oval to rectangular, with tens of millions of dollars poured into the stadium over the years. In effect, the Knights were given their own fortress to preside over.

When the Newcastle Knights joined the NSW Rugby League competition in 1988, it was, in a sense, history repeating. Newcastle had been in the competition when rugby league was introduced to Australia in 1908. Yet the Newcastle side, the Rebels, were gone the following year, in part because the team tired of the travel to and from Sydney. The players' focus shifted from participating in that competition to building up the game in the Hunter. The game that was born, in part, as a breakaway from rugby union to offer better conditions and support to the players found a natural home in Newcastle and the valley. Clubs and playing grounds emerged in the city's suburbs and villages, and throughout the Hunter, drawing crowds and creating champions. Young men became household names, including Clive Churchill and John Sattler. The Newcastle competition was a world unto itself, so much so that when the NSW Rugby League came knocking about 1980 to entice a local team to join its competition, there was relatively little interest. A few years later, momentum was building for a local team to join the bigger competition, and in 1987 Newcastle was invited to join. The team's name played into that of the city. Newcastle had its Knights. For decades, the city's official colours had been cinnamon and emerald. Even 'Newcastle's Own', the 35th Battalion of the AIF, had worn patches in those colours. But the Knights unveiled a new look. Their colours were to be red and blue. Change was coming to the sporting ground, and to the city. And part of that change was coming up the highway from Sydney.

In 1987, Tony Butterfield was a young man from Sydney's western suburbs who played for the Penrith Panthers. Late one night at Sydney's Central Station, Tony ran into a former coach of his, David Waite, who was returning from Newcastle. David told Tony he was helping build a new team there. Tony knew little about Newcastle, other than fleeting glimpses through the family's car window on the drive north. He particularly remembered the vast Sandgate cemetery on the edge of town – not exactly the most promising image to take away from a place.

The young forward had played a few games in Newcastle as well, but that was about the extent of his dealings with the town. Yet when he heard about the Knights, Tony Butterfield wanted to be in the team. He would tie his future to Newcastle.

Tony and two other Sydney recruits, Glenn Miller and Troy Clarke, rented an apartment at Bar Beach. In their footy shorts, the trio headed for the surf across the road and declared, 'How good is this!?' That night, they went into town, had a drink at a Hunter Street hotel, where a live band was playing and the place was packed. Tony thought to himself, 'These are all great people'.

While Newcastle made a good impression on Tony, he recalls that the arrival of outsiders, and the disruption to the local competition, was met with resistance. He recalls sometimes getting 'serious looks across the bar' from Newcastle rugby league players when he was out.

'It struck me that a lot of people had a chip on their shoulder about Sydney', Tony says. 'I thought, "You guys are crazy, you don't know what you've got here!"

'Maybe I'm wrong in saying it, not being a local, but just from the language, people were always having a crack at Sydney, as if Sydney was controlling them. And I think over a long period of time they felt they were downtrodden.'

The team's inaugural coach, Allan McMahon, encouraged the players to 'win these people over. If anybody wants a photo, wants to have a chat, welcome them in'.

While working on the team and their acceptance, these Knights were very much foundation players. Some of them, including Tony, helped lay the turf at the stadium.

By the time the Knights ran onto the field they had helped prepare for their first game on Sunday 28 February 1988, in the *Herald* Challenge Cup, against the much-favoured Manly-Warringah, they had attracted a crowd. About 21 400 turned up. Before the kick-off, Tony recalls, the players headed straight for the sidelines, facing the spectators and applauding them. The spectators 'went off'. Then the Knights demonstrated to the crowd what they were made of. The Knights beat the so-called 'silvertails' from Sydney's northern beaches, 24 to 12.

'But it was the manner in which we beat them', Tony explains.

'It was the Newcastle of old. It was hard work, it was, "Put the overalls on, let's get out there and pay the price". They were very simple [playing] instructions, which were very Newcastle in themselves. "Work, and work for your mate". That's what Newcastle was built on.'

Work, and work for your mate, and for your town. The team kept working and building through tumultuous times for both the game, and for the town. Posterity could not have devised a more dramatic script. In 1997, the year Newcastle was both commemorating the bicentenary of the arrival of the British in its harbour and commiserating the imminent closure of the steelworks, the Knights were on the cusp of giving the city and the valley its greatest triumph. They had made it through to the grand final, playing the club they had defeated in that first Challenge Cup game in 1988, Manly-Warringah.

To Tony Butterfield, who had been there from the start and was known as 'Butts' by most Novocastrians, this game marked the end of 10 long years when, for a lot of that time, 'nobody gave you a hope'.

For the fans, this moment gave them so much hope. In his memoir, Malcolm Reilly, who coached the Newcastle Knights in 1997, published a couple of poems composed by supporters and sent to the team. In their words and thoughts, the supporters revealed that the team being in the grand final meant more than the prospect of winning a competition; it was about restoring a region's self-esteem in a year when Newcastle had learnt it would not be Steel City for much longer.

Tony distinctly remembers those expectations of a city and a region, and they did provide inspiration, but they were not the main motivation for him.

'We could talk about all the great things after, but if you start getting lost in inspiration and all this sort of stuff, you perhaps don't focus on the things you need to do.'

As the team headed south for the grand final on 28 September 1997, at Sydney Football Stadium, Knights fans lined the route out of town to cheer the players on their journey.

The journey led to a historic moment for Australian rugby league, and for Newcastle.

The Knights defied expectations, pulled off the near-impossible and wrote the fairy tale, to use the description that television commentator

Paul Vautin applied to the 1997 grand final. In the final moments, with the score locked up and the players exhausted, the Knights' halfback Andrew Johns dashed along the sideline and threw a pass inside to Darren Albert. The young winger scored a try. Newcastle Knights had won the ARL grand final, 22 to 16.

As Darren Albert revealed in an interview with Channel Nine on the field straight after the game, the players had a call that lifted them in the last 10 minutes when they were running on empty: 'Newcastle'. Or NEW-KAR-SUL.

In Newcastle and throughout the valley, the result brought delirium and pandemonium by the trophy-full. The party lasted for days. The team's captain, Paul 'The Chief' Harragon, later described it as being like a New Year's Eve party, times a thousand, and he recalled an old veteran telling him he had not seen people celebrate like this since the end of the Second World War.[28] At a 'welcome home' function outside City Hall, the team showed off the trophy to the estimated 100 000 who had gathered, before Knights players joined The Screaming Jets on stage at a concert across the road in Civic Park.

Tony Butterfield reckons the win provided not just a reason for Newcastle to party, but prompted a change of self-perception.

'For me, what did Newcastle get out of it? They (the Knights) got respect. And Newcastle gained that respect.

'That's probably when I formed my strongest sense of, "The mob have found their self-respect". Not that they didn't have self-respect. Newcastle is a very proud town and has been through all sorts of things. The level of honesty and camaraderie that you find in a place like Newcastle I think is unique in Australia. This just took it to another level.'

What also went to another level was the community's passion for, and the intensity of the public gaze on, the Knights, especially the player who threw the winning pass in the grand final and would become the lynch pin of the team, Andrew Johns. In his memoir, Andrew wrote how the parochialism and loyalty of those in Newcastle was unmatched in Australia. He also noted that part of the city's culture was that people didn't dump on each other, and he acknowledged that trait helped him be protected from off-field incidents becoming public. 'Joey', as he is known, had been Newcastle's best chance of winning a premiership, of giving the town something to hold up. And when that was achieved, he was our best hope of the Knights doing it again. Which they did, in 2001. Well before the NRL named him an Immortal of rugby league, Andrew was already viewed that way, and treated as such, in Newcastle.

However, Andrew also wrote about the pressures of living a fishbowl existence in a one-team, rugby league–mad town. Andrew, who revealed he has a bipolar condition, was uncomfortable with being a living exhibit, constantly on display, in Newcastle.[29]

Tony Butterfield didn't feel that same level of scrutiny. What he felt was an intense loyalty in Newcastle towards its team, and, as a result, 'they made me that way, the town'. Tony retired from the Knights as a player after the 2000 season, but not from the game. He was pivotal in establishing the Rugby League Players' Association (RLPA), which he headed. All the while, he was studying business at the University of Newcastle. Tony jokes that he would apply in RLPA meetings, negotiating on behalf of the players, what he had learnt the night before in a lecture. The RLPA was registered as a trade union, a first for an Australian sporting body. Tony noticed how when people stopped to talk with him around Newcastle, it was not so much about the footy but issues of workers' rights. So even in retirement he was still very much at home in Newcastle.

In 2011, the Newcastle Knights were bought by a company of the Hunter mining magnate, Nathan Tinkler. The Knights' board had endorsed the offer, and club members also voted overwhelmingly for a takeover by the Tinkler Sports Group. Tinkler had pitched that the Knights were a community asset, and that he was investing in the team for the community. Tinkler, who had been named by BRW magazine as Australia's richest person aged under 40 in 2008, was spending up big in the community around that time. His name seemed to be everywhere, in business and sport. Since Tinkler had bought the Newcastle Jets a year earlier, and the injection of funds had bolstered the soccer team, there was great hope the same would happen to the cash-strapped Knights.

Tony felt that it wasn't just the Knights that were changing dramatically, so was the city. Newcastle's determination to resist the top end of town was being tested. He could see the growing interest of developers and the state government in Newcastle, and not all of that pleased him. For instance, he was disappointed so much land near the harbour was ending up in private hands.

'What happened with the Newcastle Knights reflected that [change]. That new breed of entrepreneur and player was coming into town.'

A team's and town's hopes in what Tinkler would bring wilted in the coming years. In 2012, Tinkler had handed back the Jets' franchise, and, with his empire shrinking, doubts were mounting about what the future held for the Knights. During the 2014 season, Tinkler and the Knights parted ways. While the NRL had taken interim ownership of the club, before the locally-based organisation The Wests Group took over the Knights, people still saw the team as theirs and continued to turn up to home games in droves.

And so it has been ever since. Through three successive seasons of coming last to fighting their way into the finals, the Knights have held onto the love and belief of a town. For the town to do any less would be tantamount to it rejecting a crucial part of itself.

In a game against the New Zealand Warriors in 2024, a Nine television commentator observed that the Knights had secured a hard, gritty, tenacious win and added that it was just like the city.[30] The Knights continue to personify how many outsiders see Newcastle and perhaps how many Novocastrians would like to be seen.

Tony believes the Knights and rugby league will continue to be entwined around the character of Newcastle.

'It's a game that requires intelligence in some positions, it requires ingenuity, it requires a lot of courage, a lot of perserverance, and a lot of hard work. And that's very much the Newcastle ethos.'

By virtue of what he has done for the team and the town, everyone considers Tony a Novocastrian. Even if he says more than once as we talk, 'I'm not a local'. But he is not a Sydneysider. Not any more. The young bloke who couldn't see the sense of Novocastrians having a chip on their shoulder when he arrived in 1987 now sees some value in that part of the Newcastle character. Especially as more Sydneysiders arrive.

'I think we need to work at still being that independent, strong-minded community, where we're not told what to do or how to think by Sydney.

'Maybe keep the chip on the shoulder. I think a small chip on any shoulder is a healthy, good disposition to have. It just keeps you on your toes, it maintains a little independence, perhaps integrity. I'd love to see us continue like that.'[31]

On the edge of the old villages, waiting to be consumed by the dreams of home builders and subsumed into suburbs, has been the bush.

It was in the bush fringing their home that the Leyland brothers found the track to their future.

Mal was 'five and a bit' and his brother Mike a few years older when their family emigrated from Britain to Australia in 1950. The Leyland family ended up in Newcastle, as the boys' father had a friend already living in the area.

At his first day at school, Mal confronted resistance. He was bashed up for being a 'Pommy'.

'After that, he was all right', Mal recalls of his schoolyard adversary. 'He was a mate then.'

The family lived at Waratah, then at Wallsend, or 'World's End'. Wherever the Leylands lived, a large rug hung on the wall. They had bought it in one of the ports on the voyage from Britain. The rug was woven with images of camels and pyramids and the Sphinx; it was a talisman of the wonders of travel and a reminder that there was something out there beyond 'World's End'.

Yet the boys also explored the world closer to home. In Wallsend, they loved to venture out of the order of the streets through a quarry and into the bush. The opportunity to wander into the natural environment broadened when the Leylands moved to a block of land in a new housing estate taking shape in the suburb of Hillsborough.

'That is where we learnt to love the Australian bush', says Mal. 'We learnt what lizards were like and what snakes were like. We weren't fearful. We ended up with a shingleback lizard as a pet for a while.'

Tracking along with their interest in the bush was a love of cameras and filming. This was spurred in 1956, when Mike won a cartoon drawing competition, with the prize being a trip to the Olympic Games in Melbourne. But for the teenager, that wasn't the only prize. His father had promised to buy him a movie camera if he won the competition, so he could film what he saw in Melbourne.

'The very first film he ever shot was of us going on a picnic around Newcastle. It was shot around Lake Macquarie', says Mal.

The boys also helped their father show latest-release movies in an old hall at the lake, which Mal says, 'was a good introduction to film presentation and to what audiences liked'. What really opened the world of moving pictures to the Leyland brothers was when their father installed a 50-foot (about 15.2 metres) antenna on the roof to pick up reception from Sydney. After all, Newcastle didn't have a television station yet. The brothers particularly enjoyed documentaries involving travel and wildlife.

'We were inspired by the work of David Attenborough and Armand Denis, and I think we figured we'd like to do that in Australia, because what we'd seen in Australia was very limited.

'We felt Australia had a lot to offer and we wanted to film it.'

The brothers developed their skills in Newcastle. After NBN Channel 3 began transmission in 1962, Mike was employed as a television cameraman, and Mal secured a job as a photographer at the *Newcastle Sun* newspaper.

'The early days of Channel 3 were experimental, and I had a great deal of freedom as a photographer. I think all of that made us better at what we were doing', reflects Mal.

Covering local news stories, however, was never going to constrain the Leylands. From the early 1960s, Mike and Mal began travelling into the interior to film documentaries, with the first being *Down the Darling*, in 1963. The brothers edited at home but later bought a house in Hamilton, which became their production headquarters. Then, as they grew, the Leylands bought a former armoured car building in Broadmeadow, using the strong room to store their film archives and equipment. So even as they became household names, the Leyland brothers kept their base in Newcastle.

Initially, the brothers reached an audience by tapping into what they had learnt as teenagers, arranging screenings of their documentaries in halls and suburban cinemas. Television caught up with the Leylands, and the brothers filled the gap that they realised was missing when they were kids. They put Australian landscapes and wildlife on our screens.

As a result, Mike and Mal Leyland became the eyes to the heart and soul of Australia. They transported us out of the suburbs and into the bush. Along the journey, they became stars, especially from 1976, with their television series, *Ask the Leyland Brothers*. The premise of the show was brilliantly simple. The brothers would visit and film places suggested by viewers. They took out an ad in *TV Week* magazine, inviting people to write to a post box in Newcastle with their suggestions. Mal Leyland remembers the first time they opened the post box.

'Nothing was in there, except a bit of paper, a note asking us to come into the post office. They had five bags of mail, thousands of letters.'

Ask the Leyland Brothers attracted huge audiences, as Mike and Mal made home movies for a nation. It was the brothers, and often their families, who were on the screen, but there was room for all of us on those journeys. In the way the Leylands told a story, we saw ourselves in them. But we also knew they were stars: 'brothers' was accorded a capital letter. They were the Leyland Brothers. What helped lodge the TV series in the mind – and on the lips – of many Australians was the theme music. It was also a product of Newcastle, written and performed for the Leyland Brothers by the Provost Brothers. Bruce and Barry Provost had moved to Newcastle from Grafton in 1958 and were regulars on television music shows, not just on Channel 3 but nationally as well, with *Six O'Clock Rock* and *Bandstand*. The Provost Brothers could have taken on the world. Another band of siblings, the Bee Gees, had invited the brothers to tour with them in the United States but Bruce and Barry declined. In Newcastle, you could be 20 feet from stardom and be unaware of it. And so it was with Barry Provost. When I was a boy, little did I know that the dignified and gentle man living a few doors up the street, the father of a mate of mine, could have made it big in America but instead chose to remain in Newcastle and raise his family in Merewether Heights. Even if I did know, Mr Provost wouldn't have made a big deal about it. And every week, it was his singing voice, and his brother's, hollering out from television sets in lounge rooms around the nation, inviting us to travel all over the countryside with the Leyland Brothers, but Barry Provost never made a big deal about that either. Which is just how Newcastle likes its stars.

Having taken Australians out into their country via the camera, the Leyland Brothers decided to bring a little of the outback to the fringe of the continent. They built Leyland Brothers World about an hour's drive north of Newcastle. The main feature was a scale replica of Uluru. After it opened in 1990, Leyland Brothers World brought in not just tourists but big debts. The venture collapsed, and the brothers went their separate ways publicly. Mike died in 2009. Mal has continued to film his travels, particularly with his family, and for many years has lived in Queensland. But he returns to Newcastle and loves heading to the beach, the scene of so many of his early photographic assignments for the *Newcastle Sun*.

'I would go to the beaches to find and photograph a page-three girl.'

Yet one part of his past that Mal Leyland cannot retrace are the places where he and his brother fell in love with nature and learnt to drive on rough tracks as preparation for their bigger adventures. As Mal says, with a touch of lament in his voice, 'The bush is now all suburbs'.

IN a few places, the bush – or at least, that sense of escape and invigoration that the natural environment gives you – has been reclaimed.

On the fringe of the city at Shortland is a tract of land that was, until the mid-1980s, a rugby club and playing fields. It is now the site of the Hunter Wetlands Centre. These 45 hectares of wetlands have been restored largely by community volunteers, planting more than 377 000 trees. In restoring the land to what it once was, natural life has also returned. The wetlands are a home for more than 200 bird species, some flying from half a world away to nest here. It is also a terrific space in which humans can while away a few hours, going for a paddle on the waters coursing through here or walking around the shores, observing a flourishing ecosystem. And that is part of the joy of this place. More than transform the landscape, the centre has shifted people's attitude to wetlands. Not so long ago, places like the Shortland site were considered swamps that bred nothing but mosquitoes, and the best option for them was to fill them in and build on them, turn them into playing fields, or dump garbage into them. Just before the formation of the wetlands group to save and restore this land, there were plans to fill in this area and develop a dump and a major highway. What could have been so easily lost is now considered internationally significant under the Ramsar Convention on Wetlands. Yet Novocastrians don't need a convention to ratify what they know. This place enriches their home, and their lives.

Virtually in the backyards of many Newcastle residents is another project of transformation and rejuvenation. The Fernleigh Track is a major recreational hub and visitor attraction that links Newcastle to Lake Macquarie, and the area's present to the past.

The track began life as a rail line, cut through the bush in the late 19th century to freight coal to Newcastle's port from the mines that had sprung up along the coast. With the collieries came little villages, so the line provided a means of transport for the miners and their families. It came to be known as the Belmont Line, as trains trundled to and from that Lake Macquarie community and Adamstown. Ironically, these two cornerstones of industrial Newcastle – the railway and mines – that pushed so much change through the area also preserved land that would be central to the reincarnation of the line as the Fernleigh Track. As local rail historian Ed Tonks has explained, land along the corridor could not be developed while the rail line and the collieries were operating.[32]

Yet in the 20th century, collieries along the line began to close, and mining villages were turned into suburbs, easily accessed by road. The rail line was less and less needed for transporting coal or people. By 1971, regular passenger services to Belmont ceased. Twenty years later, the final coal train left Lambton Colliery at Redhead, destined for Newcastle and history.

The Belmont Line was no more, and the scar of another time was slowly covered in growth and forgotten about. After all, the disused line was better forgotten about, otherwise it was just another uncomfortable reminder of how the city was changing – and decaying. But not everyone forgot about that 15-kilometre corridor between Adamstown and

Belmont. Even before the line closed, Newcastle Cycleways Movement looked ahead and proposed when the trains stopped using it, the track would be ideal for bikes and feet.

In 1994, around the time the Newcastle and Lake Macquarie councils bought the corridor, community members drew up a plan for the old rail line. The plan's authors proposed calling it the Fernleigh Track. The name 'Fernleigh' may have had echoes of the past, as that was the name of a colliery and a section of the rail line, but the plan was all about a very different future. The report was titled, *The Fernleigh Track: A living corridor*, and it envisaged a trail connecting communities, encouraging recreational activities, and helping preserve the area's environment and heritage.

'The Fernleigh Track offers an outstanding opportunity within suburbia to create a living corridor for the interaction of people, vegetation and wildlife within a bushland atmosphere', the report's authors wrote.[33]

More studies were done, but eventually words and plans, hopes and dreams led to funding and construction. Between 2003 and 2011, over five stages, the Fernleigh Track came into being between Adamstown and Belmont. In 2024, a 3.5-kilometre extension south from Belmont to Blacksmiths, known as the Fernleigh Awabakal Shared Track, was officially opened.

The Fernleigh Track transports walkers and joggers, cyclists and wheelchair users through a diversity of coastal environments, past the remains of collieries and railway stations, and deep into Awabakal culture. The track performs a wonderful sleight of hand on its users, allowing them to feel as though they are deep in the bush while they are often in the heart of suburbia. Sometimes houses' back fences are but metres away, yet the air is filled with birdsong and rustling tree canopies and a sense of escape. Newcastle is near yet so blissfully far. As a result, the Fernleigh Track is a magical place. Little wonder it is so popular, with more than 1000 people using the track on any given day.

As Sam Reich, from Newcastle Cycleways Movement, says of the track, 'It has become an iconic feature of the region, and a destination in its own right for many visitors, including bicycle tourists from around the world'.

Yet more than provide an escape for the city's residents and visitors, the Fernleigh Track is taking Newcastle somewhere.

'The success of the track has accompanied the concurrent extraordinary development of Newcastle as a modern city and region', asserts Sam Reich. 'It has spurred a significant increase in infrastructure development for cycling and walking, which, in turn, has helped transform the city streetscape, enhancing amenity, reducing traffic congestion and improving the environment.'

Perhaps the most famous parcel of bushland to be saved in Newcastle is Blackbutt Reserve. The 182 hectares of bushland tumble down the hills from New Lambton Heights and nudge into the suburbs. Consequently, Blackbutt makes those suburbs more valuable, and more liveable. Blackbutt is hemmed by major arterial roads, yet those roads, and all that traffic they carry, don't constrain the nature reserve; rather, when you're driving on one of those roads, the reserve provides respite through the windscreen. In the reserve are walking tracks and areas that allow visitors to get close to animals, including koalas, emus and kangaroos. Blackbutt is where generations of Novocastrians have been introduced to native wildlife. Blackbutt has hosted everything from family barbecues to 'bush' weddings in the 'burbs.

Since the 1930s, the reserve had been created from the skerricks and satchels of bushland saved from the foundered plans of subdivisions and returned soldiers' farmlets. More land was secured from a mining company, and it was gradually restored and rejuvenated. However, the gnawing demands of a growing city wanting to get places ever more quickly threatened and hacked at the reserve. There was a long, and ultimately successful, fight to stop a motorway slicing through a corner of the reserve. As one opponent wrote to the newspaper, if the roads department had tried something like this in Sydney, heads would have rolled.[34] Still, the widening of other roads claimed some of the bushland, while through the years, plans for housing and even mines had to be fended off. Until the 1970s, the Borehole Colliery operated in the area, and after it closed, the land was rehabilitated.

From all those bits and pieces of bush saved, secured, retrieved and reborn, Blackbutt has become bigger than the parts. The whole is so much a part of the soul of Newcastle. In there, we can see the wood for the trees. For, as life scurries around it, about it and through it, Blackbutt is the calming influence in a city that can, at times, trip over itself. Just as the beach does, Blackbutt reminds us to catch our breath. To breathe.

FOR many in Newcastle's suburbs, their window to the world was located in a white edifice squatting in a valley below The Obelisk. In that big white box were the offices and studios of the NBN Channel 3 television station. These days, little more than the news bulletin is produced locally, but in the early days of TV in Newcastle, all manner of programs were created in the big white box. Channel 3 was the city's mirror. We would see on the screen local presenters and performers. Perhaps more than any other organisation in Newcastle, what came out of that big white box in the valley shaped the world view of many Novocastrians. It still does. Even in the face of ever-growing choices on the screen, Newcastle and Hunter Valley people are a loyal lot and support NBN. Yet the location of the television station itself has changed. The big white box has been demolished, making way for a residential development, while NBN, or Nine NBN, as it is known these days, has moved into a building by the harbour.

Living just near where the white box used to be is a couple who brings the world into the homes of Novocastrians. Matt vanderWall and Brett Lynch are stars of Nine's program, *Travel Guides*.

Matt and Brett are not the only Newcastle residents on the show. The four members of the Fren family have also become audience favourites because of their ebullient personalities, and they often use Newcastle as their reference point for other places, far and wide. And usually those other places pale in comparison to Newcastle, according to the Frens.

As a result of the show's popularity, the Frens need no first names, and Matt and Brett need no surnames. Everyone knows them.

As a kid, Brett knew Newcastle, as he grew up in Maitland. Matt grew up on the NSW far north coast but visited relatives at Cessnock during holidays. Matt's first impression of Newcastle was one of ruins and exclusion zones, as he visited the city soon after the 1989 earthquake.

Matt and Brett met at Port Stephens, an hour's drive north of Newcastle, in 2002 and have been together ever since. They made Newcastle their home in 2003 and have lived in the city since then – when they are not travelling, that is.

When they moved to Newcastle, Matt and Brett 'were a bit worried' whether they would be accepted as a same-sex couple. Both were aware there was a gay 'enclave'. As a young man in the early 1990s, Brett would go to Pipers nightclub in Newcastle West, before it shut and, as he explains, the building 'was turned into a church!'.

Yet they quickly realised they didn't have to live in an 'enclave', and that the broader community was accepting and welcoming. Actually most people didn't give it a thought. Never mind the city's reputation as a masculine, working-class city; Matt believes because it has a university and has a comparatively high number of arts and cultural workers, along with progressive politicians, 'Newcastle evolved quicker than other places'.

For Matt and Brett, their belief they were in the right place would be tested by the results of Australia's same-sex marriage plebiscite in 2017. They had already married in New Zealand, having given up on their own country ever officially recognising their union. So they viewed the results of the plebiscite with much anticipation, especially the votes of their fellow Newcastle residents.

In the Newcastle electorate, 74.8 per cent voted 'yes' to same-sex marriage. That was the fifth highest result in NSW, and it was above the state average of 57.8 per cent and the national average of 61.6 per cent. Newcastle's council celebrated the local result, having already established a rainbow walk in Islington Park. The then-Lord Mayor, Nuatali Nelmes, said the result reflected the city's true heart.[35] For Matt and Brett, the result was one of relief.

'That kind of reaffirmed our decision to live here, because it would have been terrible to be a couple in a community where the vote was against you rather than for you, and who you are', says Brett.

Being a long-time couple, Matt and Brett know what each other are thinking. They riff off each other's thoughts, finish each other's sentences, and laugh at shared memories and experiences. They have accrued a lot of memories and experiences. So they laugh a lot.

They are a fun couple. And what you see on *Travel Guides* is what you get away from the camera. Which makes them fantastic on TV because they are not playing characters – they are who they are. Again, that makes them very much like the city they call home. No pretence.

Brett, who is a teacher, and Matt, who has worked in tourism and marketing, particularly for local government, had done a lot of travel together before they applied for *Travel Guides* in 2019. When they auditioned in Sydney, they had just disembarked from a Pacific cruise, so, as Matt says, 'we were very authentic with our luggage and in our holiday clothes'.

Matt and Brett were selected to join *Travel Guides*, but their first episode didn't air until 2021. For more than a year, they would head away for filming then return to Newcastle without telling a soul what they were up to.

'We slotted straight back into our normal life', says Matt. 'It wasn't until [the series] actually hit the TV that it hit us that Newcastle people like to see Newcastle people doing well.'

From that moment, their quiet lives were behind them. The unblinking gaze of the public eye was on them. They were now 'Matt and Brett'. Yet in Newcastle, the reaction was, from the outset, positive.

'No tall poppy syndrome', says Brett.

'It's like they're proud that we're representing Newcastle.'

Fame has not changed the way Matt and Brett live. They still go for their walks along the harbour foreshore, they dine at the local cafés and restaurants, and when they are approached by fans of the show, the interaction is respectful. Newcastle is their refuge.

'I think we're quite lucky that the footballers have been kind of trailblazers as well, they're quite accessible', says Brett. 'You can see the Knights players around town, and they get to go to a restaurant and have breakfast and no-one annoys them.

'I mean, we see [Silverchair's] Daniel Johns and we don't approach him, and other people don't as well', says Matt.

'You know I went to school with Gavin Morris!' enthuses Brett, seemingly oblivious to the idea that he is probably as recognisable as the NBN newsreader.

Which is one of the reasons why he and Matt are embraced in Newcastle. Brett is unaffected by his fame, let alone by any notions of grandeur.

During the 2024 series of *Travel Guides*, there was no hiding away in the hometown for Matt and Brett, and for the Frens. One of the episodes was titled 'Newcastle',[36] and it explored not just the city but other attractions around the Hunter. The episode began by outlining the stereotypes of Newcastle as a tough industrial city but then flipped the narrative by suggesting the place could be a diamond in the rough. The out-of-town guides cited the stereotypes as well, talking of coal and ships and surfers. The three young blokes in the series, Kev, Dorian and Teng from Melbourne, mentioned Newcastle would have been one of their last options for a holiday. However, the Frens waved the flag from the start, declaring Newcastle was the best place in the world not just to live but to holiday. By the end of the episode, the guides had experienced a gallery of photogenic settings and great adventures, preconceptions and stereotypes were tossed out, and all the guides scored the place highly. Young friends Karly and Bri reflected the changing attitude towards Newcastle, saying it seemed like a good place to spend time in rather than just pass through. They awarded it a maximum five stars as a travel destination. Naturally, so did the loudly, proudly biased Frens, as did Matt and Brett.

What the other travel guides saw, and what television viewers saw of Newcastle in that episode, is what Matt and Brett believe about their home. Newcastle is not just a good place. Newcastle is in a good place.

'Newcastle has been a city in transition for twenty-five to thirty years now', Matt muses, 'and it's like everyone is kind of along on that same journey. So the tall poppy stuff tends to exist where there is stagnation. Whereas I don't feel like Newcastle has had any stagnation for at least the [more than] twenty years that we have lived here.'

As Matt would know from his training and work experience, Newcastle is considered by many in marketing to be the 'Goldilocks city'. It is just the right size for companies to test goods and services. Products have flown or fallen based on the feedback of consumers in Newcastle. But marketing Newcastle itself, especially shutting the gap in perceptions between those who live here and outsiders, has been challenging, as Matt also knows. After all, that was his job for a time.

'Spending several years trying to move the visitor brand of Newcastle away from a dirty industrial city to something else was very difficult because the people here didn't see Steel City as a negative thing.

'And it's not a negative thing, but we say "Steel City" and we go, "This city was built on that manufacturing", whereas in Sydney if you say, "Newcastle, Steel City" they go, "Oh yeah, dirty industry." And it's like, "Yes, that was part of it, but that's not what made Newcastle what it is".

'It's like every bit of the past accumulates to make the present, and everything that's happening now will accumulate to make what I think is going to be a really bright future for Newcastle.'

And that's why Matt and Brett are staying put. They may get to explore the world on *Travel Guides*, but, as Matt and Brett told their large television viewing audience about Newcastle, there's no place like home.

CHAPTER SEVEN

CITY OF NOW WHAT?

As I write this, I keep glancing at a print on the wall. The image is a view from Nobbys looking towards Newcastle during a storm. The work was created about 1886 for publication in the *Picturesque Atlas of Australasia*. It is a scene of busyness, with the port dotted with ships, and a steamer is heading in from the churned-up sea, seeking the calmer waters of the harbour. The steamer is not quite out of trouble, as waves curl and crash over Macquarie Pier into the channel. In the foreground, a man on Nobbys is dashing for shelter, while the flags and signals flap, and smoke from the stacks of factories around town is blown by the southerly buster.

Almost 140 years on, that image seems to hold metaphors for Newcastle. Many believe change is blowing in, along with people, not just from the south but from all directions. The Visit Newcastle website refers to the city as 'one of Australia's best-kept secrets'.[1] However, the secret is out. By 2041, the city's population is expected to top the 200 000 mark, with an estimated 19 450 new dwellings needed by that time.[2] As a result, Newcastle continues to grow up and out.

It is all a far cry from Newcastle's origin as the destination of punishment, just one stop from the gallows. As the character pronouncing a sentence in the convict novel *Ralph Rashleigh* hollers, 'A most dreadful scoundrel, an atrocious villain. Send him to Newcastle'.[3]

People are no longer sent to Newcastle but choose to move here. And it would be safe to assume very few are dreadful scoundrels or atrocious villains. Successful businesspeople, brilliant creatives, young people starting out, families, retired couples; they're all coming here. And whereas many of the original European residents were considered stained by their time in Newcastle, now people want to be identified as Novocastrians. What's more, Novocastrians accept the recent arrivals adopting that identity. Again, it all seems so different from even a generation ago. In *Aftershock*, the novel Peter Corris set in post-earthquake Newcastle and wrote just a couple of years after the disaster, the private investigator Cliff Hardy is heading up the highway from Sydney and thinking about his destination. Newcastle, he ruminates, is 'a tough town where Sydneysiders can be thought of as invaders from another planet'.[4] Not so much these days. There is little distinction now between the invaders and the natives. No matter where you're from, if you love the place and wish to call it home, then that's as good as a birthright. You're a Novocastrian.

Among the myriad contributions and changes to Newcastle the new residents bring, one seems to be to the very lexicon of the place. We're even changing how we refer to our own town. Newcastle is increasingly called Newy. An advertising sign in the city poses the question of whether it is Newie or Newy. The sign declares that only a local would know.[5] As a local, I would argue the sign is asking the wrong question. What I would ask is since when was Newcastle Newie or Newy? I concede that somehow Newy seems in keeping with the still-casual character of the city. However, I prefer Newcastle. Perhaps, as a Novocastrian, I'm still loath to accept some changes to the place I call home by any name.

Change is a selling point for the city. Those driving into town will see a welcome sign that reads, 'Newcastle. See Change'. On one level, the catchphrase acknowledges what the city has become for many. Newcastle is a destination for those seeking a sea change. On another level, the phrase is a challenge and proclamation. Newcastle is no longer what you thought it was. Newcastle can be anything you imagine it to be. It is right there before your eyes.

Then again, you can't always see change, especially when it is the product of the imagination. In those instances, change comes from within. And so it has been for Shawn Sherlock. The life of Shawn Sherlock, in many ways, charts the recent life of the city he was born in.

Shawn is the owner of, and creative force behind, Foghorn Brewery. Or, to use the title he has given himself, he is Foghorn's Chief Brewing Officer. The craft brewery is seen as part of the transformation and rejuvenation of inner-city Newcastle. An old warehouse in King Street has been converted into a place where transformation is played out every day, as beer goes 'from grain to glass all under one roof', as Foghorn describes itself.[6] Under the time-seasoned trusses, the space is spiced with the smell of grains and a strong scent of optimism. This is the cologne Newcastle would like to put on before heading out, confident and ready to impress the rest of the world. This is the smell of the future in this town. Yet when Shawn and his then-business partner wandered into this warehouse in 2014, searching for somewhere to house their dream of brewing and serving beer in the heart of Newcastle, it held a vastly different atmosphere. For many years, this place had helped realise the dreams of the once-stereotypical Novocastrian, Normie and his mates from 'The Newcastle Song'. It had been a car dealership. By the time Shawn saw it, the warehouse was empty and ducoed in dust. As with so many buildings around town, time had moved on for this warehouse. But to Shawn, the intersection of time and position was perfect. He had found a home for an 1800-litre brewery, with the tanks right beside the bar, as he helped bring the warehouse back to life.

'When we opened in 2015, the fit-out was like nothing people had seen in town', Shawn explains in his baritone as rich as stout and brimming with passion.

The fit-out garnered industry awards for its innovation, but for those who walked through its doors, there was a sense of familiarity, of respect for what had come before, of where it was, as it retained an industrial look. This was a working space, not a fancy place.

'You know you walk into some places in Sydney and everyone is looking down their nose at you before you even sit down. This place is the antithesis of that.'

While the brewery was innovative, Shawn says, 'we did it in a way that brought people with us, and I think that's a Newcastle thing.

'Certainly the Newcastle that I grew up in, nobody looked down on anybody.'

Where Shawn grew up, he could literally look down on Newcastle. Near his home in Waratah West was a high point, Braye Park. From there, Shawn could scan the suburbs to the harbour and the city and around to the steelworks. He could see Kooragang, where his surveyor father was working on projects that would load ever greater volumes of coal onto ships.

'What I saw at the time was that it was my world and an industrial city. Whereas a lot of people grow up thinking of the place as a big country town or whatever, I wasn't one of those.'

Shawn could see the city's future from that hill. But not his future. He never imagined himself working in the steelworks or the other industries huffing and puffing along the estuary. Instead, he could look in another direction from Braye Park at his future. Off to the north-west, young Shawn could see the University of Newcastle. Although it was hard to make out the details of the campus; the halls of learning were heavily camouflaged by trees. Perhaps that said something about Newcastle then. You didn't want to stand out as being too smart in this town. Nonetheless, it was there at the university that Shawn would begin building a career as an academic and historian. However, in pursuing that path, he didn't turn his back on what this city was. Shawn's area of research was labour history and the Labor Party, especially the impact of the Hawke and Keating governments' policies. He began lecturing in 1999, the year BHP steelworks was closing. The irony was not lost on Shawn. He was teaching history as it happened. But history was also teaching Shawn about his hometown.

'I was living in a town that I was still really proud of, and I was reading and hearing all the death notices for Newcastle. But what I saw, just dealing with people on the ground, it didn't really correlate to what I was reading, and what history was telling me.

'People had lived through so many difficulties, just the closure of the steelworks wasn't going to be the thing that killed Newcastle. I just had a belief in that.'

The city had a future. The past told him that. What that future would look like, and how Newcastle would adapt, Shawn wasn't sure. But it would. Just as his city grappled with those unknowns, so did Shawn. With cutbacks and restructuring at Australian universities, Shawn began looking at a career beyond the campus and eventually followed his love of brewing. From 2006 to 2014, he worked at Murray's Craft Brewing Company on the NSW mid-north coast and at Port Stephens.

In 2012, he was awarded Australian Brewer of the Year. Shawn had crafted a new career and life direction. But it wasn't enough.

'The thing that appealed to me so much was the concept of being part of the revitalisation of Newcastle. It was really getting into full swing.'

The idea of a brew house in the heart of Newcastle took shape. Beer had been good to the entrepreneurial in Newcastle in the past. Just up the hill from the warehouse where Shawn and his business partner founded Foghorn is Woodlands, one of Newcastle's grand historic homes. The mansion was built in the 1870s for a local brewer, Joseph Wood. Yet with Foghorn, Shawn wasn't seeking his own fortune but helping encourage a change of fortune for his hometown.

'So many great things come from the town but the outside world, until relatively recently, has really only seen the negatives about the place.'

By more than its position, the brewery is proudly Newcastle. The name 'Foghorn' refers to the moaning of the ships bouncing off the water and through the inner city. Many of the beers also celebrate their source, with names such as 'Newy Pale Ale' and 'King Street Pale'.

'I love being an active agent of change in Newcastle', he says. 'And I love ... that locals actively are being part of the change, rather than it just being someone else from Sydney with money coming in.'

Without a hint of irony, Shawn describes himself as 'a glass half-full person', before declaring, 'I wouldn't be investing in the town and investing in everything that I am, if I wasn't positive about the future'.

'The old Newcastle couldn't sustain this business. It couldn't sustain the new restaurants around the place. So we're products of the new Newcastle, and all the positives that come with that, and I think there are more positives than negatives. I think the trick is to hang onto the strengths of what makes us the town that we are, while embracing the change. And I realise how glib that sounds, and how much like an advertising campaign for something, but it's the truth, and it's all we can do. And I see it happening all around.'

DESPITE what the 'welcome' sign leading into town says, Novocastrians don't always see change. Sometimes we choose not to see it or acknowledge it. We just keep driving, undertaking the journey, even if we're not sure of the destination. For many years, a mine's poppet head occupied land at a busy intersection in Newcastle West. This was not a former colliery site; rather, the tower of iron, which had been moved to here as an exhibit for the nearby musuem, was effectively filling a vacant block. The old poppet head was like an industrial sculpture, reminding us where we had come from and where we were at, as we drove past, heading somewhere. Only that mining artefact seemed to be telling us that the city was going nowhere, by taking up ground for no particular purpose. When inner Newcastle finally got moving again, the poppet head was shifted and an office block was constructed.

With the poppet head gone, many saw this as a sign for where Newcastle was heading. Or, at least, what the city was heading away from: mining.

In 1889, when the *Illustrated Sydney News* published a profile of Newcastle, the writer noted that 'so long as the age of steam lasts, Newcastle will be in the front of the colony's reputation', and that, for Newcastle, 'coal has been the beginning and end of its story'.[7] The age of steam is hanging around; Hunter coal continues to be burnt to generate electricity. But the end of an age is approaching, and many in Newcastle and the Hunter are preparing for a new chapter in their own lives.

In 2024, 135 years after that *Illustrated Sydney News* article, the University of Newcastle's Institute for Regional Futures released a report titled *Hunter Horizons: Navigating the future of work and workplaces in our region*. The report called the Hunter and Central Coast a region in transition, as it adjusted 'from the carbon intensive mining and energy industries that characterised its heavy industrial past to a more diverse and innovative knowledge and services-led economy'.[8] The report shows the biggest employment growth had occurred in health care and social assistance. In February 2024, more than 100 000 people worked in those sectors in the region. One of the other big employment areas has been construction, according to the report, with about 52 000 working in the sector. That would come as no surprise to Novocastrians, as they have watched buildings rising in the CBD and beyond. A point of pride to many is to count the cranes studding the cityscape.

Never mind looking up at the buildings, many Novocastrians are looking ahead. According to the *Hunter Horizons* report, the majority of residents in the region are willing to retrain and reskill, to change, as their home economy shifts. For the survey respondents in the Lower Hunter, including Newcastle, 70 per cent indicated they were willing to retrain.[9] Going by the *Hunter Horizons* report, coal has been shrinking as a jobs generator in the region. In February 2024, mining accounted for 3 per cent of employment in the Hunter.[10] However, coal remains, and will continue to be, a substantial part of Newcastle's story, according to the mining union's Robin Williams.

'I think we're still proportionately a coal city, there's still a lot of attachment to the coal industry. I appreciate there might not be mines directly in and around Newcastle, but we still have a fairly strong link to coal, and there are still a lot of people who live in and around those local communities, Newcastle and Lake Macquarie, who work in the coal industry or work in associated industries or service industries. So I think we're still fairly strong in that area.'

Robin acknowledges coal won't be part of the Newcastle and Hunter story forever, with a number of power stations and coal mines in the region scheduled to close.

'But I think we need to use the opportunity to make sure the Hunter Valley still remains relevant, with respect to renewables, building things, manufacturing. There's no reason why a lot of the infrastructure currently being utilised on mines and holdings couldn't be used for other things.'

A transition to being a clean energy hub won't happen quickly. For some time yet, Newcastle will remain a coal city, Robin says. It has to.

'You take the coal industry away tomorrow, we've got a lot of people who don't have jobs, and a lot of those people do live in Newcastle and surrounding suburbs', he argues.

'Unless there are some new technologies that the rest of the world wants and are generated here in the valley, I can't see any other way that the area will be less prosperous than it's been in the past.

'I think without some replacement industries, it could be not a good story for Newcastle and up the valley.'

As tourism grows in importance, Robin hopes that mining is not written out of the Newcastle story.

'I'd like to think people come to the area and do a bit of a tour not only in relation to wines but in relation to the history of coal mining.

'People in the future, in generations to come who don't really know about coal, that it was this stuff we dug up a long time ago, burnt it and we made power, people might struggle with that concept. But it might be an opportunity for people to go, "Oh, we might have a look at this and understand what happened in the past".'

What also happened in the past in Newcastle was steel making on a massive scale. Only Leigh Shears, the secretary of Hunter Workers, doesn't see it that way. When asked what sort of city he believes Newcastle is now, the union leader replies, 'I still very much believe we're the Steel City. We just don't have the steelworks. But we're still very much a working-class, manufacturing, trades town. I think that's still very solid'.

Hunter Workers covers the Newcastle Local Government Area, along with four other LGAs, in the Lower Hunter. Under its umbrella are 26 unions, with about 64 000 members. However, the name of the organisation reflects an acknowledgment that the region is changing. A few years ago, it changed to Hunter Workers from the Newcastle Trades Hall Council. Leigh says that reflects the change in the workforce, as some of the biggest membership growth has occurred in the health and community services sectors.

'We're broadly represented by women; it's not just blokes and manual labour.'

Newcastle's first Trades Hall, built in the 1890s, was in Hunter Street, with an ornate Italianate façade sculpted from stone. These days, Hunter Workers and a number of unions are in a building shrouded by trees in King Street. Emblazoned on the building's skin is a mural that reads 'Union Town'. Leigh reckons the mural is more than colourful; it is a statement of fact for Newcastle.

'It really depicts who we are', he asserts, saying union membership in the areas has remained steady.

'Whenever I think about Newcastle and the Hunter, I think "hashtag union town".'

'Our roots are really well established, and we're very much a working-class society.'

Leigh acknowledges the city is changing. Yet he rankles when people refer to the 'gentrification' of Newcastle. He feels it is a denial of what this city was, and is.

'They really don't like the Steel City representation, and [they argue] that Newcastle is something else. I think we're a fairly solid union town.'

Whether Newcastle is still a steel city and manufacturing hub is an argument frequently moulded and extruded for political purposes. Delivering a speech in Newcastle in early 2024, the Labor Prime Minister Anthony Albanese rattled off examples of locally produced steel bolstering national landmarks, including the mast from which the Australian flag flies above Parliament House in Canberra. While acknowledging the steelworks had gone, Albanese believed the city had the workforce, the resources and experience to continue manufacturing and developing technology, including in the area of renewable and clean energy, and it had a diversifying and innovative local economy. The PM also described the region as 'a hub of new skills, new technologies, new energy and new ideas'.[11]

As that transition takes hold in the Hunter, Leigh Shears forecasts Newcastle will remain a steel city and a union town.

'We won't be pouring steel out of vats', the union boss says, but Newcastle and the valley 'will be a massive manufacturing hub for renewable energy'.

'The Hunter will be a solid base for renewable energy, manufacturing and construction.'

WHILE its inhabitants regard their home as unique, Newcastle has frequently been compared with other places.

Throughout the 19th century and into the 20th, the comparisons often involved places in Britain, as though that made the promise of Newcastle less hollow. Some believed the beaches could make Newcastle a resort town like Brighton. JHM Abbott, the author of the 1943 book, *The Newcastle Packets and the Hunter Valley*, wrote that the city's industrial character meant it was 'surely destined one day to be the Birmingham of the Commonwealth'.[12] Perhaps Abbott was correct in comparing Newcastle and Birmingham, but in ways he couldn't foresee. The British industrial city was tossed into the economic doldrums in the second half of the 20th century, particularly after the 1980s, when a large number of businesses collapsed. While it still has industries, Birmingham has pushed to reinvent itself and is often promoted as a 'lifestyle' city.

Despite the comparisons, or perhaps in no small part because of them, through the years, Novocastrians worked at proving they and their home were incomparable. Now, many Novocastrians are less bothered by comparisons to other places than by the thought the city could become a satellite of Sydney or, worse, an extension of Sydney. That niggling thought has grown stronger with the renewed talk of constructing a high-speed rail network between Sydney and Newcastle, a topic that has come and gone for decades. If Newcastle were to become a part of Sydney, there is the question of character, and of who we are. The mere suggestion that Novocastrians could be seen as Sydneysiders or, worse, become Sydneysiders is beyond the pale.

'I will punch you in the mouth if you say Newcastle is a part of Sydney', declares Marcus Westbury, the Novocastrian who did so much to renew the city and help restore its residents' belief in what they have. 'The only people who hate people from Sydney more than [those from] Melbourne are people from Newcastle.

'Newcastle was beautifully ignored, and I fear I may be part of the reason Newcastle is not ignored any more.'

Now that Newcastle is not ignored, Marcus says the city has to work at keeping its own sense of who it is.

'I fear Sydney is swallowing Newcastle's identity. I think it's really important to evolve and keep our distinct identity.'

Dein Perry, who moulded Newcastle's industrial character into a cultural phenomenon, recalls when he moved to Sydney many years ago, he was struck by the difference in attitude. In Sydney, many sought to go with the flow in order to do well, whereas to Novocastrians, the definition of success was to chart your own course – especially if that meant going against the flow. But the Tap Dogs founder wonders whether that element of being a Novocastrian has been diluted for many who call Newcastle 'home'.

'They want to be with the trend, where I don't think we ever really wanted to be with the trend. They didn't want to be told how to live.'

With his frequent visits to his hometown, for business and to see family, Dein can chart what has changed in Newcastle since he left. One striking difference is right there on his lips.

'Back in the day there was no way you could get a latte', Dein says, while sipping at a barista's fine work.

To reflect on where the city may be headed, I turn to water. After all, that is what many in Newcastle do when they want some thinking space.

I return to where it all began for Newcastle, to the place where Lieutenant Shortland and his crew rounded the tooth-like island biting on the sky, as they ventured into the mouth of the river that the naval officer predicted would be a great acquisition to the young settlement. I follow the lines of art and the trails of those who have gone before me and stroll into the scene of that 19th-century *Picturesque Atlas of Australasia* print depicting the view from Nobbys. Only the day I head to Nobbys–Whibayganba, it is very different from the image depicted. There are no storms – at least not externally. It is a sublime late afternoon, with just enough of a breeze to soften the dregs of the day's heat.

Where I walk I'm flanked by water. To my right is the sea tousling the sand along Nobbys Beach. The waves squeeze the last of the energy out of a low that had loitered off the coast a few days earlier. You can just about see forever from Nobbys Beach on a day like this. To my left is the last reach of the Hunter River before it surrenders to the sea. Unlike the sea, the river wears a patina of brown, a legacy of the low. It is amazing how two bodies of water, so close to each other and both shaping this community, can have entirely different characters. That is, until they coalesce just beyond the breakwaters. The British writer Bernard Levin once noted that the power and prosperity of cities were writ in water. In his paean to cities, Levin observed that while rivers that cities were built on were usually slow, the people in these large centres seemed to defy the calm wisdom of the waterways by living at a breakneck pace.[13] Yet I think Newcastle has learnt to be calm from the river that flows by, and through, it. The river is a lulling, reassuring presence – most of the time. And when the Hunter does flood, carrying the flotsam and jetsam of lives disrupted or even taken upstream and washed to Newcastle, the river teaches us resilience. More than we are willing to acknowledge, we are shaped by the Hunter River. And Newcastle is a river city.

Between the river and the sea, I tread on the toil of convicts who built the original Macquarie Pier out to Nobbys, turning the island into an appendage of the mainland, and the port of Newcastle into somewhere less treacherous. I think of those poor blighters, cast out by Britain yet lashed to an empire's ambitions and imprisoned by water. Novocastrians tend to measure that renowned chip on our shoulder by distance, determining the prime source of our resentment, or resilience, lies 60 nautical miles to the south of here, in Sydney. Yet the chip can be measured by time. It began burrowing into the Novocastrian soul in 1804. As soon as those first exiled prisoners straggled ashore, Newcastle was destined to be a city of grievances.

The strata of grievances and deprivation, of unfairness and injustice seamed through Newcastle's character lie much deeper than the convict experience. Listen to the earth and you may hear the kangaroo entombed in Whibayganba bang his tail. The kangaroo reminds us this is not just an earthquake-prone area, but that the ground shifted dramatically for the First Nations residents around Yohaaba and Mulubina as soon as the Europeans arrived. To Gamilaroi and Weilwun woman and Newcastle cultural and educational leader Cherie Johnson, the ground continues to shift.

Cherie points out the establishment of the penal settlement had a brutal impact on the Aboriginal people, on their culture, and on the very land itself. The land has still not been regenerated.

'I would say the spirit of this place needs to be laid to rest, needs to settle. Peace needs to be made', she says. 'The only way you make peace with the past is to acknowledge it.'

By acknowledging that past, Cherie says, Newcastle will better understand itself.

'If you deny your past, if you deny your history, then who are you? Why would you do that? Why would we say Newcastle history started with the BHP? Why create a narrative that we are no more than coal miners?'

Cherie is devoted to helping bring about better understanding, and to finding a way forward. As well as being an artist and educator, Cherie is the founder and managing director of Speaking in Colour, an organisation that revolves around connecting people, particularly in educating businesses and teachers about Aboriginal culture.

'I think there is more of a desire to be connected', Cherie says of non-Aboriginal people in Newcastle.

Cherie has seen that desire through events such as NAIDOC Week and Ngarrama, which is held each 25 January in the city as an opportunity for people to come together, to reflect and learn about Aboriginal culture and history. But Cherie also sees it on a personal level, when older people approach her to learn more about Aboriginal culture, because their children and grandchildren have studied it at school, and they want to have that knowledge as well.

However, while there is a growing desire to connect, Cherie believes many still don't understand and realise the importance of that connection.

'If people did realise, then we wouldn't have had the outcome we had with the [Voice] referendum', she says.

In the 2023 Voice to Parliament referendum, the nation rejected the proposal to alter the Constitution to recognise the First Peoples of Australia by establishing an Aboriginal and Torres Strait Islander Voice. Nationally, the vote was 39.9 per cent for 'yes', and 60.1 per cent 'no'. In the Newcastle electorate, the majority voted 'yes'. But the margin was narrow, 53.5 per cent to 46.5 per cent.[14]

John Maynard says that result indicates Newcastle still has a way to go in its attitude towards, and embrace of, Aboriginal people. And we should make that journey, he points out, because Aboriginal culture and identity is all around us here.

'This region contains the greatest Aboriginal historical and cultural treasures in south-east Australia', John argues. 'We're very fortunate to call upon that material, and this is what we can tap into.'

Newcastle can be more than a tourism city, John emphasises. It can be an Aboriginal cultural tourism city, celebrating Australia's greatest and richest treasure.

'Aboriginal culture offers a roadway to attract people into this region. Unquestionably.'

Cherie Johnson points out if Newcastle embraces Aboriginal culture more tightly and deeply, the city will not just attract more people from the outside. It will help the city to grow from within.

'We haven't quite worked out who we are, and we're grabbing at different things. It's time for us to mature. By "mature", I mean we need to embrace all of our history and make informed decisions.

'Our past makes us who we are.'

Yet acknowledging our past does not have to limit who we can be, as Cherie makes clear. When I ask her what sort of city she thinks Newcastle is, the people connector with the welcoming smile replies without hesitating.

'Whatever we want it to be.'

On the afternoon I'm walking at Nobbys–Whibayganba, the banging and slapping of the kangaroo's tail would be muffled by the soft thud of jogging shoes, the gentle grind of bike chains, and the chatter of walkers along Macquarie Pier. A couple of young blokes with surfboards tucked under their arms run ahead, destined for the waves shoving into the wedge of sea between Nobbys and the southern breakwater. Occasionally, after big storms, board riders can surf in the harbour, as the swell pushes past the breakwaters. But it isn't that kind of topsy-turvy day. Rather, it is stunningly photogenic.

In these moments, Newcastle looks like a tourism city, a city of recreation, and a city connected with its beautiful environment. That seems to fit in with how the City of Newcastle sees the future.

In what it calls its community strategic plan, titled *Newcastle 2040*, the council forecasts that by then, 'Newcastle will be a liveable, sustainable, inclusive global city'.[15] Which is a bigger mouthful, and more complex to explain as an identity, than, say, Steel City.

The plan points out some of the challenges for Newcastle becoming the city envisioned. Among the challenges listed is moderate population growth, which would surprise those who believe Newcastle is being inundated with people. The report also talks about the local brain drain, particularly with younger residents leaving. That challenge is also explored in *Hunter Horizons*, the research paper by the University of Newcastle's Institute for Regional Futures. The institute found that about a third of the Lower Hunter workers surveyed were either very likely or somewhat likely to move to a metro area for a job opportunity.[16]

In defining and bolstering its future, and in an effort to keep its young and attract others to the area, Newcastle has promoted itself as a smart city. It has become a base for a string of firms and agencies, including the Commonwealth Scientific and Industrial Research Organisation (CSIRO) and the United Nations, which located a training centre at the university. And in tertiary education, the words 'smart' and 'city' have literally shifted closer to each other. The university has expanded, moving out from under the canopy of trees on the fringe of the city, and stamped its presence in the CBD. While it has retained its campus at Callaghan, the university also occupies reshaped and reimagined architectural landmarks in the city, such as NESCA House. The uni has also built a couple of structures in the CBD, including a bold statement that rises above, and looms over, Hunter Street, known as NUspace. Replacing any notion of an ivory tower with a modernist structure, NUspace brings the shock of the new, and hordes of students, to Hunter Street. The building anchors itself to the city via its large windows, which are filled with expansive views of inner Newcastle and the harbour. The university has not just moved into town; it has helped shift the demographics of Newcastle. In all, about 38 000 students are enrolled at the university. About 7400 of those are international students.[17] The sum of all those people and those who have graduated, with all their knowledge and ideas, has helped push Newcastle closer to its goal of being a smart city.

When I ask Distinguished Laureate Professor Roger Smith whether Newcastle is a smart city, he replies, 'I don't think we are'.

'I think we've got potential, but at this stage, it's potential not yet realised.'

Roger would know. He's not just one of the smartest people in Newcastle but he's used that extraordinary brain of his to make the community better. Actually, he has made the world better.

Roger is a renowned endocrinologist and medical researcher. In 1990, he was instrumental in establishing what would become the Hunter Medical Research Institute (HMRI), which has made many globally significant developments and is a cornerstone of Newcastle's 'Smart City' potential. So through his work, Roger Smith has changed and saved lives.

He also has some thoughts about what could improve the life of Newcastle, now and into the future.

'When I came to Newcastle in 1981, it was extremely parochial', says Roger, who was born in England. 'Almost everybody in Newcastle had been born in Newcastle, and their vision didn't extend very far down the Pacific Highway. And the general attitude was "We seem to be impoverished relatives of Sydney", and nothing happened in Newcastle. It happened in Sydney, and elsewhere.

'That's not true any more. We're part of a global community, and we're less parochial than we used to be. But now I'm more parochial, and I think of Newcastle as the best place on the planet!'

To Roger, Newcastle's future is very much as a city of the globe, a city of ideas, sharing its knowledge. He mentions HMRI as an area where 'we can become smarter in improving the health of our region but also the health of the planet'.

'That, to me, is what we should be doing, learning locally and applying globally.'

But in looking forward to this city of ideas and knowledge, Roger also sees Newcastle's past as being part of that. The industrial city he arrived at has literally shaped where he works and creates. He cites HMRI again as an example.

'You could think about a research institute as an elitist ivory tower, but that would not suit Newcastle. That would sit uneasily.'

The architecture of HMRI is reminiscent of a factory, he explains.

The facility would not look out of place beside some of the other industries that have been around Newcastle through the years.

'Think about it as a knowledge factory', Roger explains. 'It produces knowledge, it's useful, it's an utilitarian place. That suits our industrial background.'

In 2024, City of Newcastle recognised what Roger Smith has done for his adopted home, and for the world. He was named a Freeman of the City. He is the first scientist to receive the honour.

'I think it's exciting they chose to make a scientist a Freeman', Roger says. 'And it does mirror the changes occurring in Newcastle. It is an understanding our future will be knowledge based.'

Back to Roger's views on Newcastle's unrealised potential. For Newcastle to be the city it could be, Roger looks to the community's leaders thinking and acting both locally and globally. As an example, he proposes that on former industrial sites and at the coal-fired power stations in the region, alternative energy technologies and businesses can be developed. As well as encouraging new industries, the region can continue with those it has already established, such as mining, but by using 'green' approaches.

With all of that in mind, I ask Roger to finish this sentence: Newcastle, the City of ... ?

'Unbelievably privileged people, in the large part', he replies. 'But with privilege comes responsibility, so we have to make ourselves the best we can be. We have to make an equitable city. While most are privileged, that doesn't extend to everyone, so we have to help them.

'I've lived such a fortunate life. I'm certainly privileged to live in Newcastle.'

Sister Diana Santleben, the Dominican nun who has done so much to help many find their way in Newcastle, agrees with Roger as to what Newcastle can, and should, be.

'We can be the Smart City, we can be the alternative energy capital of Australia', the refugee and asylum seeker advocate says. 'But hopefully we can be a kind city too. Smart and kind.'

I WALK beyond Nobbys-Whibayganba, past what is seen as Newcastle's eastern limit. The breakwater, extended in the early years of the 20th century, leads towards the sea. The goal in the late 1800s had been to build the breakwater to a reef known as Big Ben.[18] Back then, it seemed just about every distinguishing mark, whether on land or water, was somehow referred back to the Mother Country, rather than acknowledging that these places already had names and held significance for many thousands of years. Now, watching the waves nudge into the eastern face of the breakwater, I think not of the British landmark but of time ticking away. I glance again at the waves. Time and tide, both ceaselessly sculpting this city, forever changing all of us here.

For what seemed like an eternity, time stood still in Newcastle's heart in 2024. Newcastle's own version of Big Ben, the City Hall clock, was not working, while the heritage timepiece received an overhaul. In a city where time seems to be ripping by, and the hourly chimes emanating from the tower echo with both assurance and a reminder that life goes on, the clock's still hands and deathly silence were disquieting. Once, as I looked up at one of the faces of the frozen clock, I thought about how much had changed in the life of this city, and in my life. The thoughts were tightly bound. My thoughts whooshed back about half a century, when there were horses on the streets of The Junction. Just behind the local primary school was a paddock and shed that brought the bush, and the hay- and manure-scented thrill of adventure, to suburban kids. For this was the base of Tracey's, an outfit that hired out horses and ponies by the hour, by the day, even by the week. You paid your money, you hopped on a horse and you rode it on a circuit through the streets into the city, or to the beach, or to pretty much anywhere you wanted. Where the horses wanted to go was a different matter. By the accounts of those who rode them, the nags were reluctant and irascible until the reins were pulled for home. Then they'd break into a canter, clip-clopping at a frightening pace along the bitumen, back to their owner, Wal Tracey. It was a different time. It is a different place. Or is it? As I stood looking at time unmoved at City Hall, a couple of kids raced by on an electric bike. I shook my head in admonishment. Then I thought of Tracey's.

Strolling along the breakwater, I pass monuments to those whose time had come. For this breakwater has become a memorial walk. On the rocks and blocks buttressing the breakwater are plaques etched with love and memories, verses and dates, honouring the departed. It seems like a good place to be memorialised, beside the sea and the harbour, as time washes over the plaques. Except in big seas, that is, when monstrous waves explode over the breakwater, burying the rocks in froth and spume, all the while scaring the hell out of the living and performing an act of aspersion for the dead. So this breakwater marks an ending. And perhaps a beginning. After all, this is where the sea starts.

Endings and beginnings. This city has contemplated those, often simultaneously, throughout its history, be it due to an earthquake, as buildings toppled and decisions were made what to do with a vacant site, or through major industrial upheavals. The AA Company's spruiking of its garden suburb concept for the Hamilton area a century or so ago declared Newcastle would always be an industrial centre. It couldn't imagine us being anything else. For generations, Newcastle people couldn't imagine anything else either. Then again, many companies have done the imagining for us through the years. None more so than BHP. And we know where that led. To an ending, and to a beginning. As John Howard said during his visit soon after the steelworks' closure had been announced, this region has a capacity to regenerate. What the then-prime minister called a capacity to regenerate, we who live here see as part of being a Novocastrian.

I cannot help but wonder what this city could have been if BHP had not built its steelworks by the river. If we weren't Steel City, what would have we been? Some people lament we're no longer Steel City. Yet were we Steel City for too long? In its relationship with the city, The BHP often seemed like the dominant partner. When that relationship ended, it felt devastating to the city. It felt like the end. But perhaps it was also a good thing. We could be whoever we wanted to be, now that we were no longer Steel City. The problem has been we don't know who we want to be. We remain uncertain as to who we are. It would seem we have been, for too long, the City of Now What?

Perhaps I should take another sip from the glass half-full of labour/Labor historian turned brewer Shawn Sherlock. Even in those days of worry and uncertainty in 1999, when the steelworks closed, he held on to hope for his hometown.

'I just always had optimism, and I still do about the place', says Shawn. 'It has probably worked out better than I anticipated. I could sit here and try and sound wise, but I don't think anyone could have anticipated exactly how the way it has turned out to this point. But I think the optimism was well placed.'

It is not as though all industry left town. As I look over to my left, beyond Stockton to the north, there is a blur of industries that scumble the sky by day and whose lights sparkle like a fairground attraction by night. Near the stacks and factories, Stockton Bridge sketches a curve in the sky. More than vaulting the Hunter River's North Arm, the bridge looks like an engineered rainbow. On one side is the city's main industrial area at Kooragang, the pot of gold that Newcastle, and the nation, has relied on for many years. In a literal sense, Stockton Bridge takes traffic to the community it is named after and funnels people to Port Stephens. But if we look at that bridge as a metaphorical rainbow for Newcastle, leading from its industrial traditions to somewhere else, then we are yet to see where it lands.

I HAVE reached the end.

The security and certainty of the breakwater surrender to the sea. On one of the blocks at the head of the breakwater is a plaque dedicated to Captain Donald McRae, RN. He lived from 1896 to 1963. As the plaque notes, he was Beach Master for the evacuation of Gallipoli in 1915, Newcastle Harbour Master from 1944 to 1952, and a master mariner. Out here, I can feel like I'm on the edge of the world, but Captain McRae's plaque is a reminder the world doesn't end at Newcastle.

I turn away from the sea and look back towards the city, about 2 kilometres away. From out here, I can't see the City Hall clock. But distance is not the only obstruction. There are so many taller buildings creeping towards the waterfront, a few even obscuring the clock tower. It looks like a growing wall, the sum of all those buildings, as if blocking Newcastle in, or keeping the rest of the world out. You may not be able to see the face of time from out here, but all those buildings mark the fact that time is passing. Newcastle is changing. And the city is not just changing at ground level – or in the space above. Just as it was with the earthquake that brought so much change to the surface, the most profound shifts are happening much deeper. For those who have helped determine what the face of Newcastle is, or what it could be, the fear is that the city could be losing some of what makes it what it is. In the eyes of architect Brian Suters, for instance, we don't have to reach for the sky. We already have something wonderful.

'We have created a good city, a liveable city', he tells me. 'Sydney's not really liveable unless you're in the very high echelon. Newcastle's a town with a balance of wealth and working people.'

'Can we keep that?' I ask.

Brian frowns and scrunches his lips before replying.

'I'd like to think we can.'

A liveable city. It is one of the aspirations in the City of Newcastle's 2040 plan, and it is a term that has been used time and again by those who I have spoken with about what we are, what we could be, and how we could be seen by the rest of the world.

'It's really simple for me', asserts tourism and marketing man turned *Travel Guides* TV star Matt vanderWall. 'I want Newcastle to be recognised as one of the world's most liveable cities, because I think it already is.'

When asked what sort of city we could become, Matt uses that word again. Liveable.

'I think that we just want to be the liveable city. Because a great place to live is a great place to visit, and if it's a great place to live and a great place to visit, it's a great place to invest. And then the city will keep growing and keep getting better from that.'

As to what his husband and fellow *Travel Guides* star, Brett Lynch, sees Newcastle becoming, he replies, 'One great big Spiegeltent!'

'I just feel like it's going to be a collection of old and new, and I just feel like it's going to be more welcoming and more accepting, because I do see it as constantly evolving.

'I think people will grow up and get comfortable with where they live and not feel like they need to be judged by other people.'

With a twinkle in his eyes and a chuckle, Brett adds, 'It's time to start judging other people instead!'

Ever since it was founded, Newcastle has been judged and labelled. It has been Sydney's Siberia, a hell hole. It has been Coalopolis. Steel City. Rock City. A surf city. A smart city aspiring to be an even smarter city. Increasingly, a tourism city. While the first Europeans may have violently disagreed, it has always been a liveable place. The many generations of First Nations custodians of the land have demonstrated and celebrated that. And now, to more and more people, it is Liveable City.

How others have judged and labelled us is often how we have seen ourselves. However, Newcastle doesn't have to be any one of those things. We have been all of them. And we are much more than all of those things. A community is the sum of its parts. It is the product of many lives and times. That is what Newcastle is. Just as all humans are. Just as we Novocastrians are.

The possibilities for us, and the prospects of what our city will grow into, are both daunting and exciting. We don't have to be like Normie, believing you should never let a chance go by. Some chances are best let go or not even grasped in the first place. But where we are at this point, there are so many opportunities to make Newcastle the city we imagine it can be. And because of all that Newcastle has been, and all that it has had, what it is and will continue to be is the City of Us. We are Newcastle.

ACKNOWLEDGEMENTS

Following Ernest Hemingway's advice that authors should write about what they know, I figured Newcastle was an obvious subject for me. After all, I would be writing about the place where I was born and spent most of the first 20-odd years of my life, and to where I have returned. I would be writing about home. Little did I know ...

Newcastle has been a journey of knowledge for me. My journey has been marked by the generosity of many guides. My thanks to each and every person who spoke with me, or wrote to me, for the book. I also thank the many people who have spoken with me during my career as a journalist and broadcaster, including my time at the *Newcastle Herald* and more recently at 1233 ABC Newcastle. The sum of your knowledge and perspectives of Newcastle has not only enriched my journey, it has helped make this book what it is.

For pointing me in the right direction, thank you: Sue Ryan, Coordinator of Local Studies at Newcastle Region Library; Julie Baird, Director of Museum, Archives and Learning, City of Newcastle; Peter Toedter; Vikas Bangia, Newcastle Harbour Master, Port Authority of NSW; Professor Roberta Ryan; Jasmine Sullivan; Honarary Associate Professor Howard Bridgman; Paul Bevan; Emeritus Professor Tim Roberts, Patron of Hunter Region Botanic Gardens; Alek Schulha; Greg Bryce; Christopher Saunders; Ed Tonks; Newcastle Art Gallery Foundation Chair Suzie Galwey; Cathy Tate; Lisa Allan, *Newcastle Herald* editor; Rod Thompson, *Newcastle Weekly* editor; Tim Ryan, Merewether Surfboard Club; Warren Smith; Therese Spruhan, a wonderful writer; the members of the Gerund Dining Club, a deep reservoir of Newcastle-related knowledge; Lucas Coleman, Executive Manager Corporate Affairs, Port of Newcastle; Carmen Leyland; Margaret Connolly; Dermod and Morgan Kavanagh; Art Ryan; and military historian David Dial. Emeritus Professor John Maynard, I deeply appreciate all the advice you have given me, and the knowledge that you have shared with me.

My thanks to all those who helped me with gaining permission to quote from others' works. And my thanks to those poets, authors and musicians for creating the work that has said so much about this city and its people.

Thank you to Katherine McLean, Director of Hunter Writers' Centre, for facilitating a day's residency at Nobbys Head-Whibayganba as part of the Lighthouse Arts program.

My gratitude and thanks to David Hampton, Head of Exhibitions and Cultural Collections at Newcastle Museum, and to Brooke Murphy for reading the manuscript and for your invaluable advice and suggestions. Thank you to sports journalist extraordinaire Robert Dillon for reading the footy section, and for your guidance, strengthening that part of the manuscript. My thanks to Shawn Sherlock for reading sections of the manuscript and sharing your knowledge of Newcastle. Thank you to Brydie Piaf for your artistry with a camera, and for your courage in taking on the task of photographing my portrait. And thank you to historian and author Ian Hoskins for advising me at the start of the project.

My thanks and appreciation, Bob Hudson, for your generous words about this book, and for your brilliant creativity, including with *that* song.

Thank you to Elspeth Menzies, Executive Publisher at NewSouth Publishing, for taking on the book and encouraging me to keep journeying. My thanks as well to Joumana Awad, NewSouth's project editor for *Newcastle*, for guiding the book towards publication, to Alex Ross for the cover design, and to Josephine Pajor-Markus for the internal design.

My thanks and huge appreciation, Jocelyn Hungerford, for your insightful and judicious editing, making this a better book, and for your patience and camaraderie. Thank you to proofreader Edward Caruso for your fine eye.

Thank you to my colleagues at 1233 ABC Newcastle, particularly, Lucia Hill, Bridget Murphy and my friend, producer and sounding board, Cara O'Brien.

My thanks to all the librarians and booksellers who helped guide a Newcastle boy through the world of words, and thank you for still spreading the word – and words, including mine.

My love and thanks to my father, Dafydd, for sharing your memories of Newcastle and gently steering my own memories back on track when they needed it. And my undying love and gratitude for my late mother, Jean, whose own memories, and my memories of her, have helped shape this book.

Boundless love and hugs for my two sons, Tom and William, for your support and making time for me, even while you are on your own creative journeys. My thanks and appreciation to Jo for all you've done for me.

To my partner Jane, for your patience and gentle coaxing, for lending me your ear and – when needed – your shoulder, for reading what I wrote, for your advice, and for sharing your thoughts and your life with me, there are not enough words …

If I have inadvertently forgotten to thank anyone, and for any mistakes I have made in *Newcastle* (and, for that matter, in Newcastle), forgive me.

Finally, to everyone who has been a part of my life in Newcastle, who has helped me learn and grow, who has been patient with me as I have learnt and grown, and who has enriched my understanding of what it means to be a Novocastrian, thank you. I hope you see yourself in this book.

SELECT BIBLIOGRAPHY

BOOKS

Abbott, JHM. *The Newcastle Packets and the Hunter Valley*. The Currawong Publishing Company. Sydney. 1943.
Apter, Jeff. *The Book of Daniel*. Allen & Unwin. Sydney. 2018.
Armstrong, John (editor). *Shaping the Hunter*. Newcastle Division of the Institution of Engineers, Australia. 1983.
Avalon, Phil. *From Steel City to Hollywood*. New Holland. Sydney. 2015.
Barnard, Marjorie. *Macquarie's World*. Angus and Robertson. Sydney. 1971 (reprint).
Barney, Norm (with Terry Callan). *Bert Lovett's Between the River and the Sea*. Saucy Jack Publications. Newcastle. 1989.
Bevan, Scott. *Bill: The life of William Dobell*. Simon & Schuster Australia. Sydney. 2014.
Bevan, Scott. *Return to the Hunter*. No Shush Press. Toronto. 2023.
Bingle, John. *Past and Present Records of Newcastle, New South Wales*. Bayley, Son, and Harwood. Newcastle. 1873.
Blackley, Roger. *The Art of Alfred Sharpe*. Auckland City Art Gallery in association with David Bateman Ltd. Auckland. 1992.
Bladen, FM (ed.). *Historical Records of NSW: Vol. IV. Hunter and King: 1800, 1801, 1802*. Charles Potter, Sydney, 1896.
Boyd, Dan. *The Gravy Train Doesn't Stop Here Anymore*. Self-published. November 2000.
Brown, Kevin and Jurisich, Mark. *The Nobbys Collection*. Self-published. Newcastle. 1993.
Callen, Terry. *Bar Dangerous*. Newcastle Region Maritime Museum and Runciman Press. Newcastle. 1986.
Carruthers, Steven L. *Japanese Submarine Raiders 1942*. Casper Publications. Narrabeen. 2006.
Chegwidden, Cath. *Mighty Mayfield Then and Now: Book I: The Early Years*. Newey Printing Company and Cath Chegwidden. 2022.
Claridge, William R. *The Pommy Town Years: Memories of Mayfield and other tales of the twenties*. William Michael Press in conjunction with the University of Newcastle. 2000.
Clark, CMH. *A History of Australia*, Vols. II and V. Melbourne University Press. 1975 (reprint) and 1981.
Clouten, Keith H. *Reid's Mistake*. Lake Macquarie Shire Council. 1967.
Conrick, Chris. *The Northern District Surf Lifesaver*. SLSA, Newcastle Branch. Merewether. 1989.
Corris, Peter. *Aftershock*. Bantam Books. Sydney. 1991.

Cusack, Dymphna. *Southern Steel*. Constable. London. 1953.
de Mierre, HC. *Clipper Ships to Ocean Greyhounds*. Harold Starke Ltd. London. 1971.
Dick, Howard; Stevenson, Iain; Carolin, Mike; Pemberton, Barry; Rex, Lindsay; Cox, Rex, and; Priest, Russell. *ANL: A fleet history of Australian National Line, 1957–1999*. Nautical Association of Australia. Victoria. 2020.
Dillon, Robert. *Hard Yards: The story of the Newcastle Knights*. Newcastle Herald. 2018.
Dunn, Mark. *The Convict Valley*. Allen and Unwin. Sydney. 2020.
Ellis, Elizabeth. *Rare & Curious: The secret history of Governor Macquarie's Collector's Chest*. The Miegunyah Press, Melbourne, and State Library of New South Wales. 2010.
Falkus, Hugh. *Master of Cape Horn*. Victor Gollancz Ltd. London. 1982.
Farrelly, Alan and Morrison, Ron. *Newcastle*. Rigby Limited. Adelaide. 1968.
Fleming, Steven. *Velotopia: The production of cyclespace in our minds and our cities*. nai010 publishers. Rotterdam. 2017.
Gunson, Niel (editor). *Australian Reminiscences & Papers of L.E. Threlkeld: Volumes I & II*. Australian Aboriginal Studies No. 40. Ethnohistory series No. 2. Australian Institute of Aboriginal Studies. Canberra. 1974.
Giles, Zeny. *Caught in the Light: A celebration of Newcastle*. Catchfire Press. Newcastle. 2002.
Gillies, Ben and Joannou, Chris, with Alley Pascoe. *Love & Pain*. Hachette. Sydney. 2023.
Gray, Sheilah. *Newcastle in the Great Depression*. Newcastle History Monographs No. 11. Newcastle Region Public Library. Newcastle. 1984.
Halligan, Marion. *Lovers' Knots*. Minerva. Port Melbourne. 1993.
Harragon, Paul, with Brett Keeble. *One Perfect Day*. Pan Macmillan Australia. Sydney. 1999.
Hugill, Stan. *Sailortown*. Routledge & Kegan Paul Ltd. London. 1967.
Hunter, Cynthia (editor). *Riverchange*. Newcastle Region Public Library, 1998.
Jenkins, David. *Battle Surface! Japan's submarine war against Australia, 1942–44*. Random House Australia. Milsons Point. 1992.
Johns, Andrew, with Neil Cadigan. *The Two of Me*. HarperCollins Publishers. Sydney. 2007.
Jones, Captain William HS. *The Cape Horn Breed*. Ibex. Albert Park, Victoria. 1999 (reprint).
Keating, Julie. *Merewether & The Junction: Nineteenth century industrial towns*. Self-published. 2016.
Keating, Julie and Wetherall, Lachlan. *Adamstown & Broadmeadow ... the early days of settlement*. Self-published. 2020.
Klepac, Lou. *Shay Docking Drawings*. The Beagle Press. Forestville. 1990.
Levin, Bernard. *Enthusiasms*. Sceptre. London. 1987.
Lingard, Eric (editor). *Newcastle 150 Years*. Oswald L Ziegler for The Publicity Sub-Committee of the Greater Newcastle 150th Anniversary Celebrations Committee. 1947.
Loney, Jack. *Australian Shipwrecks: Volume 2: 1851 to 1871*. Reed. Sydney. 1980.
Mack, John. *The Sea: A cultural history*. Reaktion Books. London. 2011.
MacLean, Mark. *A Year Down the Drain: Walking in Styx Creek, January to December*. The Hunter Press. Hamilton. 2011.
Macquarie, Lachlan. *Journals of his Tours in New South Wales and Van Diemen's Land, 1810–1822*. First edition published by the Trustees of the Public Library of NSW. 1956. Facsimile reprint published by Library of Australian History. North Sydney. 1979.

Maitland, Barry and Stafford, David. *Architecture Newcastle: A guide*. RAIA (Newcastle Division). Newcastle. 1997.

Marsden, Susan. *Newcastle: A brief history*. Newcastle City Council. 2004.

Maynard, John (editor). *Awabakal Word Finder and Dreaming Stories Companion*. Keeaira Press. Southport, Queensland. 2004.

Maynard, John. *Fight for Liberty and Freedom*. Aboriginal Studies Press. Canberra. 2024.

McManus, Phil; O'Neill, Phillip; and Loughran, Robert (editors). *Journeys: The making of the Hunter Region*. Allen & Unwin. St Leonards. 2000.

Melville, Rosemary. *A Harbour from a Creek: A history of the Port of Newcastle*. Newcastle Port Corporation. 2014.

Morrison, Ron and Elizabeth. *Newcastle: Heart of the Hunter*. Exisle Publishing. Wollombi. 2007.

Mortlock, JF. *Experiences of a Convict*. Part Four. Originally published in London, Brickhill and Bateman, 1865. Sydney University Press edition edited by GA Wilkes and AG Mitchell and published in 1966.

Murray, Joan. *The Vision Splendid*. Newcastle Christ Church Cathedral. 1991.

Murray, Les. *New Selected Poems*. Duffy & Snellgrove. Sydney. 1999.

The Newcastle Nautical Almanac, Directory and Guide to the Port of Newcastle for the Year 1881. R.C. Knaggs and Co. Newcastle. 1881.

North, Marilla (editor). *Singing Back the River: A miscellany of selected writings by and for Vera Deacon*. Yarnspinners Press Collective. Leura. 2019.

O'Donoghue, John. *Essington Lewis: I Am Work*. Currency Press. Paddington. 1987.

Olson, William. *Down the Breakie*. Allen & Unwin. Sydney. 1988.

Piaf, Brydie. *The Sunrise Swimmers of Merewether Ocean Baths*. Self-published. 2018.

Pierce, Peter (editor). *The Oxford Literary Guide to Australia*. Oxford University Press. Australia. Melbourne. 1993.

Pointon, Rick. *Hey Rock 'n' Roll*. Newey Printing Company and Rick Pointon. Newcastle. 2020.

Prunster, Ursula. *Shay Docking: The landscape as metaphor*. A.H. & A.W. Reed Pty Ltd. Frenchs Forest. 1983.

Reilly, Malcolm, with Ian Heads. *Reilly: A life in rugby league*. Ironbark. Sydney. 1998.

Sheather, Gaye. *Rock This City: Live music in Newcastle, 1970s–1980s*. Hunter Press. Hamilton. 2016.

Silver, Lynette Ramsay. *The Battle of Vinegar Hill: Australia's Irish Rebellion*. The Watermark Press. Sydney. 2002.

Smith CE. *Dr James Mitchell*. Newcastle History Monographs No. 1. Newcastle Public Library. 1966.

Stannard, Bruce. *Ben Lexcen: The man, the keel and the cup*. Faber and Faber. London. 1984.

Threlkeld, LE. *An Australian Grammar, Comprehending the Principles and Natural Rules of the Language, as Spoken by the Aborigines, in the Vicinity of Hunter's River, Lake Macquarie, &c. New South Wales*. Stephens and Stokes, 'Herald Office', Sydney. 1834.

Threlkeld, LE. (Re-arranged, condensed, and edited, with an appendix by John Fraser). *An Australian Language as Spoken by the Awabakal, the People of Awaba or Lake Macquarie (Near Newcastle, New South Wales), being an account of their language, traditions, and customs*. Charles Potter, Government Printer. Sydney. 1892.

Tonks, Ed. *Beneath Tidal Water: The story of Newcastle's harbour collieries*. Headframe Publishing. Charlestown. 1985.

Tucker, James. *Ralph Rashleigh*. Pacific Books. 1962.

Turner, JW. *James and Alexander Brown, 1843–1877.* Newcastle History Monographs No. 4. Newcastle Public Library. Newcastle. 1968.

Turner, JW (ed.). *Newcastle as a Convict Settlement: The evidence before J.T. Bigge in 1819–1821.* Newcastle History Monographs, No. 7. Newcastle Public Library. Newcastle. 1973.

Turner, JW. *Manufacturing in Newcastle, 1801–1900.* Newcastle Public Library. 1980.

Turner, JW. *When Newcastle was Sydney's Siberia.* Hunter History Publications. Stockton. 1980.

Turner, JW. *Coal Mining in Newcastle, 1801–1900.* Newcastle History Monographs No. 9. Newcastle Region Public Library. 1982.

Von Bertouch, Anne. *What Was It? Before it was a gallery.* Hunniford's Lane Press. Newcastle. 1989.

Wafer, Jim; Southgate, Erica; and Coan, Lyndall. *Out in the Valley: Hunter gay and lesbian histories.* Newcastle History Monograph No. 15. Newcastle Region Library. 2000.

Walsh, Paul F (ed.). *Novocastrian Tales.* Elephant Press. New Lambton. 1997.

Watson, Don (introduction). *The Wayward Tourist: Mark Twain's adventures in Australia.* Melbourne University Press. Melbourne. 2006.

Westbury, Marcus. *Creating Cities.* Niche Press. Melbourne. 2015.

Windross, John; and Ralston, JP. *Historical Records of Newcastle, 1797–1897.* Federal Printing and Bookbinding Works. Newcastle. 1897. Facsimile reprint by Library of Australian History. North Sydney. 1978.

REPORTS, JOURNAL ARTICLES AND BROCHURES

Archaeological and Heritage Management Solutions Pty Ltd. *Section 87/90 Aboriginal Heritage Impact Permit #1098622. Excavation Report for SBA Architects Pty Ltd.* May 2011.

Broken Hill Proprietary Company Limited – Australia. *The B.H.P. Review: Jubilee Number.* June 1935.

Brown, Russell; Spencer, Brenda and Williamsz, Patricia. 'The Fernleigh Track: A living corridor. An Action and Management Plan for the Adamstown-Belmont Railway Line.' September 1994. Report prepared as an assignment for an Associate Diploma of Applied Science (Landscape). Report in Lake Macquarie City Council's Local Studies collection.

City of Newcastle and Bluecoast Consulting Engineers. *Stockton Bight Sand Movement Study.* 2020.

City of Newcastle. *Newcastle 2040: Community Strategic Plan.* 2022.

City of Newcastle. *Newcastle 500 Community Consultation Strategy.* Updated February 2023.

City of Newcastle. *Newcastle Destination Management Plan, 2021–2025.*

City of Newcastle. *Newcastle Local Housing Strategy.* 2021 (updated).

Ernst & Young. *Newcastle Urban Transformation and Transport Program Benefits Realisation Summary Report.* Hunter and Central Coast Development Corporation. 20 August 2021.

Institute for Regional Futures, The University of Newcastle, in collaboration with NGM Group. *Hunter Horizons: Navigating the future of work and workplaces in our region.* The University of Newcastle. June 2024.

Institute for Regional Futures, The University of Newcastle. *The Hunter Matters: Regional insights.* November 2023.

Merewether National Surfing Reserve Committee. *Merewether National Surfing Reserve*. March 2009.
NSW Legislative Assembly. *Report of the Royal Commission Appointed to Inquire into and Report upon the Safety and Health of Workers in Coal Mines*. 1939.
The Planning and Regulatory Group, Newcastle City Council. Newcastle Archaeological Management Strategy, 2015.
NSW Government. *Newcastle Coastal Geotrail*. 2020.
Port of Newcastle. *2024 Trade Report*. 2025.
Regional Australia Institute. *Big Movers 2023*. August 2023.
Rising Tide. *2023 People's Blockade' Participants' Handbook*.
Roberts, David Andrew and Eklund, Erik. 'Australian Convict Sites and the Heritage of Adaptation: The Case of Newcastle's Coal River Heritage Precinct' in *Australian Historical Studies*, 43:3, 2012.
Suters, Brian (curator). *Menkens Centenary Exhibition*. Newcastle Region Art Gallery, 19 October–19 November 1978.
Talbot, Norman. *The Seafolding of Harri Jones*. Nimrod Pamphlets No. 2. Printed in Maitland. 1965.

SONGS

Bryce, Greg. 'Rock 'n' Roll Town.' Copyright, Greg Bryce. 2016.
Cook, Allan. 'The Star and the Slaughter.' Rondor. 1980.
Hudson, Bob. 'The Newcastle Song.' Leeds Music. 1973.
Sleeman and Hennessy. 'Our Town.' Newcastle Permanent Building Society. 1978. Sleeman and Hennessy Pty Ltd. Lyrics by Garry Sleeman.

FILM

Perry, Dein (director and executive producer). *Bootmen*. Bootmen Productions Pty Limited. 2000.

WEBSITES

Anglican Newcastle <newcastleanglican.org.au>
Australian Broadcasting Corporation <abc.net.au>
Australian Dictionary of Biography <adb.anu.edu.au>
Australian Maritime Safety Authority <amsa.gov.au>
Australian War Memorial <awm.gov.au>
City of Newcastle <newcastle.nsw.gov.au>
Coal and Community <coalandcommunity.com>
Frank the Poet <frankthepoet.blogspot.com>
Geoscience Australia <ga.gov.au>
Greg and Sylvia Ray's Photo Time Tunnel <phototimetunnel.com>
Hunter Living Histories <hunterlivinghistories.com>
ID Community <profile.id.com.au>
Lost Newcastle Facebook page
Mews Publishing (Chris Helme's website) <chrishelme-brighouse.org.uk>
Newcastle United Jets Football Club <newcastlejetsfc.com.au>
Newcastle Industrial Heritage Association <niha.org.au>
New South Wales Electronic Regional Archives <nswera.net.au>

Our Newcastle <ournewcastle.info>
Parliament of New South Wales <parliament.nsw.gov.au>
Prime Minister of Australia <pm.gov.au>
Port of Newcastle <portofnewcastle.com.au>
Research Data Australia <researchdata.edu.au>
Sailfest <sailfest.com.au>
Trove <trove.nla.gov.au>
University of Newcastle <newcastle.edu.au>
Visit Newcastle <visitnewcastle.com.au>
Yahoo Serious <yahooserious.com>

AUTHOR INTERVIEWS AND CORRESPONDENCE
Amponsah, Mary. 26 March 2025.
Anderson, Dave. 21 August 2024.
Anderson, Philippa. 2 September 2024.
Avalon, Phil. 9 October 2024.
Badger, Margaret. 26 February 2024.
Bangia, Vikas. 13 February 2024.
Banney, David. 3 February 2024.
Baremgayabo, Farida. 26 March 2025.
Biggins, Jonathan. 10 February 2024.
Body, Justin. 5 July 2024.
Bowyer, Katherine. 6 February 2024.
Boyd, Ron. 7 December 2023.
Brooks, Aubrey. 5 June 2024.
Bryce, Greg. 19 March 2025.
Butcher, Glenn. 7 February 2024.
Butterfield, Tony. 20 November 2024.
Carter, Frank. 18 January 2024.
Cooper, William T. 13 January 2007 and 9 April 2013.
Cuppaidge, Virginia. 29 April 2024.
D'Accione, Pina. 21 July 2025.
Della Grotta, Antonio and Della Grotta, Leo. 8 November 2024.
Dodd, Garry. 8 January 2024.
Everingham, Christine. 8 August 2024.
Fielding, Saretta. 17 February 2025.
Fleming, Steven. 13 May 2024.
Freedman, Tim. 20 and 22 November 2024.
Hudson, Bob. 26 May 2022; 23 January 2023 and 2 February 2023 (emails).
Inglis, Reg. 11 January 2024.
Joannou, Chris. September 2021.
Johnson, Bill. 20 May 2024.
Johnson, Cherie. 17 February 2025.
Johnston, Craig. 25 May 2025.
Jones, Greg. 27 March 2024.
Jones, Tom. 12 January 2024.
Le Messurier, John. 18 April 2024.
Leyland, Mal. 29 January 2024.
Lynch, Brett. 23 May 2024.

Maynard, John. 21 November 2023.
McKean, Murray. 3 July 2024.
McLean, Katherine. 11 December 2023.
Melville, Rosemary. 12–13 December 2023.
Mitzevich, Nick. 19 December 2023.
Moore, Billy. 12 April 2024.
Moylan, Stan. 17 May 2025.
Newman, Dianne. 13 September 2024.
Noble, Stuart. 13 February 2024.
Paczynski, Halina. 10 January 2024.
Peschar, John. 11 January 2024.
Perry, Dein. 17 February 2023.
Piaf, Brydie. 3 October 2024.
Pointon, Rick. 10 February 2024.
Reich, Sam. 22 February 2024.
Santleben, Diana. 29 August 2024.
Sarwar, Muhammad Zaid. 26 November, 2023.
Schofield, Zack. 7 December 2023.
Shears, Leigh. 19 December 2024.
Sheather, Gaye. 6 February 2024.
Sherlock, Shawn. 10 October 2024.
Slater, Neil. 9 August 2024.
Smith, Roger. 21 January 2025.
Suters, Brian. 30 January and 13 February 2023.
Tate, John. 18 September and 30 September 2024.
Tinson, Mark. 12 February 2024.
vanderWall, Matt. 23 May 2024.
Walmsley, Grant. 10 February 2024.
Watson, Steve and Watson, Sylvia. 4 October 2024.
Westbury, Marcus. 2 February 2024.
Williams, Robin. 29 May 2024.
Wynter, Sarah. 4 April 2025 (email).

NOTES

INTRODUCTION
1. Figures from 'Newcastle Destination Management Plan, 2021–2025'. City of Newcastle, p. 2.
2. *Big Movers 2023*. Regional Australia Institute. August 2023, p. 22.
3. Quoted in Abbott, JHM. *The Newcastle Packets and the Hunter Valley*. The Currawong Publishing Company. Sydney. 1943, p. 20.
4. Quoted from *Historical Records of New South Wales, Volume 5*, p. 367 and p. 362 in Di Gravio, Gionni. 'The many names of Newcastle – Mulubinba', Hunter Living Histories website at <hunterlivinghistories.com>. 30 August 2013.
5. The song, 'Our Town', was written by Sleeman and Hennessy in 1978. Released on a promotional record, with another Sleeman and Hennessy song, 'We Made It (On Our Own)', on the A-side. Newcastle Permanent Building Society.
6. From the Visit Newcastle website at <visitnewcastle.com.au>.
7. 'The Newcastle Song.' Words and music by Bob Hudson. Leeds Music. 1974.

CHAPTER ONE: HARBOUR CITY
1. Figures from '2024 Trade Report'. Port of Newcastle. March 2025, and the catchphrase is from Port of Newcastle's website, <portofnewcastle.com.au>.
2. The excerpt from the journal (*A Journal of the proceedings of His Majesty's Bark Endeavour on a voyage round the world, By Lieutenant James Cook, Commander, commencing the 25th of May 1768–23rd of October 1770* – in the State Library of NSW collection) appears on the Hunter Living Histories website, <hunterlivinghistories.com>.
3. The plaque, mounted in 1926, is affixed to the former Longworth Institute building in Scott Street, Newcastle East.
4. Letter from J Shortland, Jun. to J Shortland, Sen., 10 September 1798, reproduced at Hunter Living Histories website, <hunterlivinghistories.com>.
5. Letter from Lieutenant William S Coke to his sisters, Newcastle, 2 August 1827. Copied from the Brookhill Hall Collection, Derby Central Library. Copy held as 'Letters from William S Coke, 1824–1828' in the Newcastle Libraries' Local History Library.
6. Dunn, Mark. *The Convict Valley*. Allen and Unwin. Sydney. 2020, p. 30.
7. Tucker, James. *Ralph Rashleigh*. Pacific Books. 1962, p. 226.

8   Tucker, James. *Ralph Rashleigh*, p. 232.
9   Quoted in the 'Newcastle Coastal Geotrail' information brochure. State of NSW through Regional NSW. 2020.
10 A copy of the sketch can be seen at the State Library of New South Wales website, <transcripts.sl.nsw.gov.au/page/extract-letter-lieut-john-shortland-hms-reliance-his-father-10-September-1798-series-2338-no-2>.
11 Windross, John & Ralston, JP. *Historical Records of Newcastle, 1797–1897*. Federal Printing and Bookbinding Works. Newcastle. 1897. Facsimile reprint by Library of Australian History. North Sydney. 1978, p. 6.
12 Whiteley's comment and a reproduction of his painting, 'Nobby's Head and the Entrance to Newcastle', are on pages 46–47 of *The Nobbys Collection*, collated and published by Kevin Brown and Mark Jurisich in 1993.
13 The story is recounted in *Awabakal Word Finder and Dreaming Stories Companion*, edited and compiled by John Maynard. Keeaira Press. Southport. 2004, p. 49.
14 The map is reproduced in 'Barrallier's Surveys of the Hunter Region (1801–1802)' on the Hunter Living Histories website, <hunterlivinghistories.com>.
15 Quoted in Bladen, FM (ed.). *Historical Records of NSW. Vol. IV. Hunter and King. 1800, 1801, 1802*. Charles Potter, Sydney. 1896, pp. 413–414. Translation from French to English by Kenneth Dutton.
16 Information from Loney, Jack. *Australian Shipwrecks. Volume 2: 1851 to 1871*. Reed. Sydney. 1980, pp. 178–179.
17 Journal entry for Monday, 3 August 1818, in Macquarie, Lachlan. *Journals of his tours in New South Wales and Van Diemen's Land, 1810–1822*. First edition published by the Trustees of the Public Library of NSW. 1956. Facsimile reprint published by Library of Australian History. North Sydney. 1979, p. 135.
18 Journal entry for Tuesday, 4 August 1818, in Macquarie, Lachlan. *Journals of his tours in New South Wales and Van Diemen's Land, 1810–1822*, p. 136.
19 Quoted in Melville, Rosemary. *A Harbour from a Creek: A history of the Port of Newcastle*. Newcastle Port Corporation. 2014, p. 43.
20 *The Newcastle Nautical Almanac, Directory and Guide to the Port of Newcastle for the Year 1881*. R.C. Knaggs and Co. Newcastle. 1881, p. 73.
21 I spoke with Calvin for the 'Harbour Lives' series I wrote for the *Newcastle Herald* in 2022. Calvin was quoted in Part 8 – 'The point of punts and "pirates"', published 3 September 2022.
22 'Stockton Bight sand movement study.' City of Newcastle and Bluecoast Consulting Engineers. 2020, p. 85.
23 Information provided to the author in an emailed statement by Glen Hayward, Port of Newcastle's Executive Manager of Marine and Operations, 20 July 2022.
24 Carruthers, Steven L. *Japanese Submarine Raiders 1942*. Casper Publications. Sydney. 2006, p. 199.
25 'Newcastle's iconic, phallic-shaped Queens Wharf Tower set for demolition, 30 years after it was erected.' Robert Virtue, Jenny Marchant and Craig Hamilton. ABC Newcastle. 29 November 2017. abc.net.au.
26 Hugill, Stan. *Sailortown*. Routledge & Kegan Paul Ltd. London. 1967, p. 289.
27 I spoke with ferry worker Steve Hoggart for a series I wrote, titled 'Harbour Lives', for the *Newcastle Herald*. Part of my interview with Steve appeared in 'The point of punts and "pirates"', published on 3 September 2022, p. 24.
28 Quoted from Behrman, Cynthia Fansler. 'Victorian myths of the sea', in Mack, John. *The Sea: A cultural history*. Reaktion Books. London. 2011, p. 144.

29　Jones, Captain William HS. *The Cape Horn Breed*. Ibex. Melbourne. 1999 (reprint), p. 202.
30　de Mierre, HC. *Clipper Ships to Ocean Greyhounds*. Harold Starke Ltd. London. 1971, p. 89.
31　Falkus, Hugh. *Master of Cape Horn*. Victor Gollancz Ltd. London. 1982, pp. 123–124.
32　Barney, Norm (with Terry Callan). *Bert Lovett's Between the River and the Sea*. Saucy Jack Publications. Newcastle. 1989, p. 37.
33　Hugill, Stan. *Sailortown*, p. 288.
34　Hugill, Stan. *Sailortown*, p. 289.
35　Both Hugill, on page 280 of *Sailortown*, and Jones, on p. 192 of *The Cape Horn Breed*, referred to the *Sydney Morning Herald* article.
36　'AGY-5380. Honeysuckle Development Corporation (1992–2008)/Hunter Development Corporation (2008-2018).' NSW State Archives Collection.
37　Inscription in the stone, seen by the author at Wickham in April 2023.
38　Gordon McDonnell, from the Henry Lawson Society of NSW, discussed that in an interview for a story I wrote about the building, 'Push to turn words into action to protect historic School of Arts building and its poetic past', published in the *Newcastle Herald* on 10 September 2020.
39　*Sydney Morning Herald*, 20 August 1866, quoted in Turner, JW. *Manufacturing in Newcastle, 1801–1900*. Newcastle Public Library. 1980, p. 41.
40　*The State Dockyard: Its wartime establishment and production: January, 1942–December, 1945*. T.H. Tennant, Government Printer. Sydney. 1946, p. 10.
41　Dick, Howard; Stevenson, Iain; Carolin, Mike; Pemberton, Barry; Rex, Lindsay; Cox, Rex; and Priest, Russell. *ANL: A Fleet History of Australian National Line, 1957–1999*. Nautical Association of Australia. Melbourne. 2020, p. 195.
42　Quoted in Melville Rosemary. *A Harbour from a Creek*, p. 19.
43　Figures from Port of Newcastle's '2024 Trade Report', p. 5.
44　'2023 People's Blockade Participants' Handbook.' Rising Tide, p. 6.
45　Craig Carmody, interview with the author for *Return to the Hunter*, 6 December 2022.
46　Evidence of William Eckford, pilot, 21 January 1820. Quoted in Turner, JW (ed.). *Newcastle as a Convict Settlement: The evidence before J.T. Bigge in 1819–1821*. Newcastle History Monographs, No. 7. Newcastle Public Library. Newcastle. 1973, p. 112.
47　Interview with the author. Parts of that interview with Margaret Olley were used in a story I wrote, 'Affair of the heart', which was published in the 'Weekender' section of the *Newcastle Herald*, 5 November 2005, pp. 6–7.
48　Halligan, Marion. *Lovers' Knots*. Minerva. Melbourne. 1993, p. 7.
49　Keneally, Tom. *The People's Train*. Vintage. Sydney. 2009, p. 237.
50　Cusack, Dymphna. *Southern Steel*. Constable. London. 1953, p. 3.
51　Cusack, Dymphna. *Southern Steel*, p. 21.

CHAPTER TWO: THE CITY'S HEART

1　Letter reproduced in 'Toothache Cure at Root of Exhibit', *Newcastle Herald*, 12 May 2007.

2   Quote from *Following the Equator* in Watson, Don (introduction). *The Wayward Tourist: Mark Twain's adventures in Australia*. Melbourne University Press. 2006, p. 65.
3   See Turner, JW. *When Newcastle Was Sydney's Siberia*. Hunter History Publications. Stockton. 1980.
4   Silver, Lynette Ramsay. *The Battle of Vinegar Hill: Australia's Irish Rebellion*. The Watermark Press. Sydney. 2002, p. 9.
5   Information from Lynette Ramsay Silver's book, *The Battle of Vinegar Hill*, p. 183.
6   Dunn, Mark. *The Convict Valley*, p. 44.
7   Barnard, Marjorie. *Macquarie's World*. Angus and Robertson. Sydney. 1971 (reprint), p. 67.
8   'Instructions for Administration of Settlement', quoted in Turner, JW (ed.). *Newcastle as a Convict Settlement: The evidence before J.T. Bigge in 1819–1821*, p. 179.
9   Barnard, Marjorie. *Macquarie's World*, p. 102.
10 Tucker, James. *Ralph Rashleigh*, p. 218.
11 Tucker, James. *Ralph Rashleigh*, p. 221.
12 Evidence of William Evans, Assistant Colonial Surgeon at Newcastle, 18 January 1820. Quoted in Turner, JW (ed.). *Newcastle as a Convict Settlement: The evidence before J.T. Bigge in 1819–1821*, p. 112.
13 Evidence of Morris Landers, gaoler at Newcastle, 20 January 1820. In Turner, JW (ed.). *Newcastle as a Convict Settlement: The evidence before J.T. Bigge in 1819–1821*, p. 135.
14 Bingle, John. *Past and Present Records of New South Wales*. Bayley, Son, and Harwood. Newcastle. 1873, p. 7.
15 Macquarie, Lachlan. *Journals of His Tours in New South Wales and Van Diemen's Land, 1810–1822*, p. 135.
16 Evidence of James Clohesy, Stone Mason, January 1820. Quoted in Turner, JW (ed.). *Newcastle as a Convict Settlement: The evidence before J.T. Bigge in 1819–1821*, p. 162.
17 Interview with the author for 'Garden Rambles', broadcast on ABC Newcastle, 12 October 2024.
18 Documentary details from Yahoo Serious' website at <yahooserious.com>.
19 Kavanagh, Paul. 'Upon the Architect Frederick Menkens'. Reprinted in the catalogue for 'Menkens Centenary Exhibition'. An exhibition arranged by Brian Suters. Newcastle Region Art Gallery, 19 October–19 November 1978.
20 Suters, Brian. Introduction in the catalogue for 'Menkens Centenary Exhibition'.
21 Brian John Suters AM died on 17 April 2025. He was honoured with a memorial service at Newcastle City Hall on 9 May 2025. For the section about him, I have kept the writing in the present tense.
22 Cusack, Dymphna. *Southern Steel*. Constable. London. 1953, p. 16.
23 '30 Years On – Commemorating the 1989 Newcastle Earthquake' at Geoscience Australia website, <ga.gov.au/news/30-years-on-commemorating-the-1989-newcastle-earthquake>.
24 Corris, Peter. *Aftershock*. Bantam Books. Sydney, 1991, p. 45.
25 'Australian Convict Sites and the Heritage of Adaptation: The Case of Newcastle's Coal River Heritage Precinct', David Andrew Roberts and Erik Eklund. *Australian Historical Studies*, 43:3, 2012, p. 379.
26 'Newcastle Steelworks Closure.' Legislative Assembly Hansard, 7 May 1997. Parliament of NSW website, <parliament.nsw.gov.au>.

27 Westbury, Marcus. *Creating Cities*. Niche Press. Melbourne. 2015, pp. 52–53.
28 Westbury, Marcus. *Creating Cities*, p. 153.
29 'City of Newcastle: Dwelling type.' City of Newcastle website, <Profile.id.com.au/Newcastle/dwellings>.
30 'Newcastle Urban Transformation and Transport Program' Benefits Realisation Summary Report' (prepared by Ernst & Young). Hunter and Central Coast Development Corporation. 20 August 2021, p. 3.
31 Friends of National Trust Newcastle/Hunter Valley Facebook page, <facebook.com/FriendsOfNationalTrustNewcastleHunter>.
32 West End Newcastle Dairy Farmers Towers website, <westendnewcastle.com.au/dairy-farmers-towers>.
33 Diary entry for Monday, 9 May 1825, reproduced in Gunson, Niel (editor). *Australian Reminiscences & Papers of L.E. Threlkeld. Volume I*. Australian Aboriginal Studies No. 40. Ethnohistory series No. 2. Australian Institute of Aboriginal Studies. Canberra. 1974, p. 88.
34 Clark, CMH. *A History of Australia*, Vol. II. Melbourne University Press. 1975 (reprint), p. 151.
35 Letter to G Burder and WA Hankey, 27 March 1826, reproduced in Gunson, Niel (editor). *Australian Reminiscences & Papers of L.E. Threlkeld. Volume II*. Australian Aboriginal Studies No. 40. Ethnohistory series No. 2. Australian Institute of Aboriginal Studies. Canberra. 1974, p. 202.
36 Quoted in Gunson, Niel (editor). *Australian Reminiscences & Papers of L.E. Threlkeld. Volume I*, p. 45.
37 London Missionary Society report, December 1825. Reproduced in Gunson, Niel (editor). *Australian Reminiscences & Papers of L.E. Threlkeld. Volume II*, p. 194.
38 Letter to G Burder and WA Hankey, 23 April 1825, in Gunson, Niel (editor). *Australian Reminiscences & Papers of L.E. Threlkeld. Volume II*, p. 181.
39 Information from the catalogue for 'Richard Browne: A focus exhibition'. Newcastle Art Gallery. 30 June – 12 August 2012.
40 Threlkeld, LE. *An Australian Grammar, Comprehending the Principles and Natural Rules of the Language, as Spoken by the Aborigines, in the Vicinity of Hunter's River, Lake Macquarie, &c. New South Wales*. Stephens and Stokes, 'Herald Office', Sydney. 1834, p. 82.
41 Quoted in Gunson, Niel (editor). *Australian Reminiscences & Papers of L.E. Threlkeld*, p. 6.
42 Threlkeld, LE. *A Key to the Structure of the Aboriginal Language* … Kemp and Fairfax. Sydney. 1850, reprinted as part of *An Australian Language as Spoken by the Awabakal, the People of Awaba or Lake Macquarie (Near Newcastle, New South Wales), being an account of their language, traditions, and customs* by LE Threlkeld, re-arranged, condensed, and edited, with an appendix by John Fraser. Charles Potter, Government Printer. Sydney. 1892, p. 88.
43 Threlkeld, LE. *The Gospel by St Luke Translated into the Language of the Awabakal*. Charles Potter, Government Printer. Sydney. 1891, reprinted as part of *An Australian Language as Spoken by the Awabakal …*, p. 126.
44 Threlkeld, LE. *A Key to the Structure of the Aboriginal Language*, p. 120.
45 Journal entry for Thursday, 6 August 1818, in Macquarie, Lachlan. *Journals of His Tours in New South Wales and Van Diemen's Land, 1810–1822*, p. 137.
46 Dunn, Mark. *The Convict Valley*, pp. 54–55.
47 Dunn, Mark. *The Convict Valley*, p. 54.

48 Letter from Lieutenant William S Coke to his father, Newcastle, 10 August (finished 25 August) 1827. Copied from the Brookhill Hall Collection, Derby Central Library. Copy held in the Newcastle Libraries' Local History Library.
49 Kelly, Matthew. '6500-year-old heritage junked.' *Newcastle Herald*, 21 May 2011, p. 7.
50 'Section 87/90 Aboriginal Heritage Impact Permit #1098622. Excavation Report for SBA Architects Pty Ltd.' Archaeological and Heritage Management Solutions Pty Ltd. May 2011, p. 102.
51 Kelly, Matthew. '6500-year-old heritage junked.' *Newcastle Herald*, 21 May 2011, p. 7.
52 I wrote about the Deep Time project in a feature story titled 'Virtual Digging', published in the 'Weekender' section of the *Newcastle Herald*, 18 November 2017, pp. 4–6.
53 'Section 87/90 Aboriginal Heritage Impact Permit #1098622. Excavation Report for SBA Architects Pty Ltd.' Archaeological and Heritage Management Solutions Pty Ltd. May 2011, p. 13.
54 The report being referred to was Suters Architects, 'Newcastle Archaeological Management Plan', vol. 1 (unpublished report), Newcastle, 1997, was quoted in Roberts, David Andrew and Eklund, Eric. 'Australian Convict Sites and the Heritage of Adaptation: The Case of Newcastle's Coal River Heritage Precinct', p. 369.
55 Lyrics from 'The Newcastle Song'. Music and lyrics by Bob Hudson. Leeds Music. 1973. Bob Hudson kindly gave permission for me to quote lyrics from 'The Newcastle Song'.
56 Email from Bob Hudson to author. 23 January 2023. Leeds Music, 1973.
57 Newcastle writer Zeny Giles wrote about the café in an essay, 'Angelo Bourtzos and the Newcastle Niagara', published in her book, *Caught in the Light: A celebration of Newcastle*. Catchfire Press. Newcastle. 2002, pp. 39–44.
58 Figure quoted in 'Four million trips later: Light rail marks five-year milestone', Sage Swinton, *Newcastle Herald*, 17 February 2024, p. 26.
59 Claridge, William R. *The Pommy Town Years: Memories of Mayfield and other tales of the twenties*. William Michael Press in conjunction with the University of Newcastle. 2000, p. 86.
60 My story, 'Cycling design expert Steven Fleming wants cars gone from Hunter Street', was published on the *Newcastle Herald* website at <newcastleherald.com.au> on 3 August 2019.
61 Fleming, Steven. *Velotopia: The production of cyclespace in our minds and our cities*. nai010 publishers. Rotterdam. 2017, p. 182.

CHAPTER THREE: PUB ROCK CITY

1 My thanks to local hotel historian Ed Tonks for doing the Hunter Street pub count.
2 The letter, dated 26 June 1978, is reprinted in Pointon, Rick. *Hey Rock 'n' Roll*. Newey Printing Company and Rick Pointon. Newcastle. 2020, p. 227.
3 This story is recounted by Rick Pointon in his book, *Hey Rock 'n' Roll*, pp. 50–57.
4 Sheather, Gaye. *Rock This City. Live music in Newcastle, 1970s–1980s*. Hunter Press. Hamilton. 2016, p. 184.
5 For more about this time read 'Uncle Doreen's family drag album', by Jim Wafer

in *Out in the Valley*, edited by Jim Wafer, Erica Southgate and Lyndall Coen. Newcastle History Monograph No. 15. Newcastle Region Library. 2000.
6   Email from Bob Hudson to the author, 26 May 2022.
7   Sheather, Gaye. *Rock This City. Live music in Newcastle, 1970s–1980s*, p. 36.
8   Lyrics from 'The Star and the Slaughter'. Written by A Cook. Rondor. 1980.
9   See 'Uncle Doreen's family drag album', p. 98.
10 I spoke with John O'Donoghue for a story I wrote titled 'Dramatic end', published in *Weekender, Newcastle Herald*, 22 July 2017, p. 11.
11 Ellis, Elizabeth. *Rare & Curious: The secret history of Governor Macquarie's collector's chest*. The Miegunyah Press, Melbourne, and State Library of New South Wales. 2010, p. 141.
12 'Painter sees beauty in Newcastle', *Newcastle Morning Herald*, 30 March 1945.
13 I interviewed David Thomas on 16 August 2013 for my book, *Bill: The life of William Dobell*. Simon & Schuster Australia. Sydney. 2014.
14 I interviewed John Olsen on 27 September 2016, as research for an essay I was writing for Newcastle Art Gallery for its exhibition, *John Olsen: The city's son*, 5 November 2016 – 19 February 2017. My thanks to the gallery's director, Lauretta Morton, for the essay commission.
15 Von Bertouch, Anne. *What Was It? Before it was a gallery*. Hunniford's Lane Press. Newcastle. 1989, p. 2.
16 Von Bertouch, Anne. *What Was It? Before it was a gallery*, p. 25.
17 'Newcastle emerges as the new street art capital.' 30 September 2022. On City of Newcastle website, <newcastle.nsw.gov.au>.
18 Information from The Lock-Up website, <thelockup.org.au>.
19 Gleeson, James. 'The World of Art' in the *Sun-Herald*, 20 October 1963, p. 67.
20 'Art and Culture' at City of Newcastle website, <newcastle.nsw.gov.au/explore/art-and-culture>.

CHAPTER FOUR: CITY OF COAL AND STEEL
1   'Instructions for Administration of Settlement', 24 December 1818, quoted in Turner, JW. *Newcastle as a Convict Settlement: The evidence before J.T. Bigge in 1819–1821*, p. 177.
2   Quoted in Hunter Living Histories, University of Newcastle website, 'Proposed Development on the Convict Lumber Yard', 14 July 2009, <hunterlivinghistories.com/2009/07/14/proposed-development-on-the-convict-lumber-yard>.
3   My interview with Kel Richards was used in a story I wrote, 'Talking like a convict', published in the *Newcastle Herald*, 8 May 2021, p. 15.
4   Roberts, David Andrew and Eklund, Eric. 'Australian Convict Sites and the Heritage of Adaptation: The Case of Newcastle's Coal River Heritage Precinct', in *Australian Historical Studies*, 43:3, 2012, p. 369.
5   Suters Architects, 'Newcastle Archaeological Management Plan', vol. 1 (unpublished report), Newcastle, 1997.
6   Planning and Regulatory Group, Newcastle City Council. 'Newcastle Archaeological Management Strategy, 2015.' 2015, p. 15.
7   Threlkeld, LE. *An Australian Grammar*, p. 82.
8   Turner, JW (ed.). *Newcastle as a Convict Settlement: The evidence before J.T. Bigge in 1819–1821*, pp. 138–141.
9   Figures from a table in Turner, JW. *Coal Mining in Newcastle, 1801–1900*.

Newcastle History Monographs No. 9. Newcastle Region Public Library. 1982, p. 17.
10 Evidence of William Evans, Assistant Colonial Surgeon at Newcastle, 18 January 1820, in Turner, JW (ed.). *Newcastle as a Convict Settlement: The evidence before J.T. Bigge in 1819–1821*, p. 104.
11 Bingle, John. *Past and Present Records of Newcastle, New South Wales*. Bayley, Son, and Harwood. Newcastle. 1873, p.12.
12 Quoted in Farrelly, Alan & Morrison, Ron. *Newcastle*. Rigby Limited. Adelaide. 1968, p. 28.
13 The poem, 'For the Company Underground' (1839), is reproduced in full at <https://frankthepoet.blogspot.com/2011/01/for-company-underground.html>. This is a research project by Mark Gregory, titled 'Frank the Poet – Francis McNamara – 1811–1861.
14 Quoted in Clouten, Keith H. *Reid's Mistake*, Lake Macquarie Shire Council. 1968, p. 95.
15 Turner, JW. *James and Alexander Brown, 1843–1877*. Newcastle History Monographs No. 4. Newcastle Public Library. 1968, p. 15.
16 Quoted in Turner, JW. *Coal Mining in Newcastle, 1801–1900*, p. 56.
17 Turner, JW. James and Alexander Brown, 1843–1877, p. 17.
18 Turner, JW. James and Alexander Brown, 1843–1877, p. 49.
19 'Newcastle, N.S.W.: The Port of the North.' *Illustrated Sydney News*. 27 June 1889, p. 12.
20 'Newcastle, N.S.W.: The Port of the North.' *Illustrated Sydney News*. 27 June 1889, p. 12.
21 Shoebridge, JW. 'Winning the Coal', in Armstrong, John (ed.). *Shaping the Hunter*. Newcastle Division of the Institution of Engineers, Australia. 1983, p. 45.
22 Marsden, Susan. *Newcastle: A brief history*. Newcastle City Council. 2004, p. 15.
23 Figures taken from the table 'Output of Coal for Northern District' in Windross, John and Ralston, JP. *Historical Records of Newcastle, 1797–1897*, pp. 60–61.
24 Much of this information comes from the chapter, '"Perseverance will command success": Engineering manufacture', by Dheera Phong-anant and Ian Stewart in Armstrong, John. *Shaping the Hunter*. My thanks to the authors.
25 'John Brown' by JW Turner in Australian Dictionary of Biography at <adb.anu.edu.au/biography/brown-john-5388>.
26 'Death of John Brown.' *Central Queensland Herald*, 13 March 1930. Retrieved from Trove at <nla.gov.au/nla.news-article7026756>, courtesy of the Coal and Community website at <coalandcommunity.com>.
27 'Late Mr Brown: Funeral service.' *Sydney Morning Herald*, 8 March 1930. Retrieved from Trove at <trove.nla.gov.au/newspaper/article/28045538>.
28 'Late Coal Baron'. *Recorder*. 10 March 1930. Retrieved from Trove at <trove.nla.gov.au/newspaper/article/95861103>.
29 Murray, Les. 'The Smell of Coal Smoke', in *New Selected Poems*. Duffy & Snellgrove. Sydney. 1998, pp. 70–71.
30 Quoted in Tonks, Ed. *Beneath Tidal Water: The story of Newcastle's harbour collieries*. Headframe Publishing. Charlestown. 1985, pp. 4–5.
31 For more information, see the Cato Street Conspiracy website at <catostreetconspiracy.org.uk>.
32 Turner, JW. *Coal Mining in Newcastle, 1801–1900*, p. 41.

33 Quoted in Windross, John and Ralston JP. *Historical Records of Newcastle, 1797–1897*, p. 49.
34 Quoted from *Daily Telegraph*, 27 September 1884 in the James Fletcher entry in the Australian Dictionary of Biography at <adb.anu.edu.au/biography/fletcher-james-3538>.
35 Turner, JW. *Coal Mining in Newcastle, 1801–1900*, p. 119.
36 The banner can be seen in a 1904 photograph in the Snowball collection in the Newcastle Public Library, reproduced in Hunter, Cynthia (editor). *Riverchange*. Newcastle Region Public Library, 1998, p. 103.
37 *Newcastle Morning Herald*, 20 September 1888, quoted in Keating, Julie and Wetherall, Lachlan. *Adamstown & Broadmeadow: The early days of settlement*. Self-published. 2020, p. 5.
38 Lingard, Eric (ed.). *Newcastle 150 Years*. Oswald L Ziegler for The Publicity Sub-Committee of the Greater Newcastle 150th Anniversary Celebrations Committee. 1947, pp. 4–5.
39 Lingard, Eric (editor). *Newcastle 150 Years*, p. 11.
40 Farrelly, Alan. *Newcastle*, p. 101.
41 Farrelly, Alan. *Newcastle*, p. 102.
42 My thanks to Emeritus Professor Tim Roberts, Patron of the Hunter Region Botanic Gardens, for providing that quote from the *Newcastle Morning Herald*, 9 June 1881.
43 Quoted in 'The B.H.P. Review. Jubilee Number'. Broken Hill Proprietary Company Limited – Australia. June 1935, p. 24.
44 Clark, CMH. *A History of Australia*, Vol. V. Melbourne University Press. 1981, pp. 415–416.
45 Thanks to Alek Schulha, from Hunter Multicultural Communities Inc, for giving me a copy of the 'Welcome to Australia! Welcome to Newcastle!' booklet. The information about finding a job at BHP is on page 2 of the undated document.
46 Maynard, John (ed). *Awabakal Word Finder & Dreaming Stories Companion*, p. 44.
47 The figures are based on documents provided by Aubrey Brooks. Thanks, Aub.
48 Gray, Sheilah. *Newcastle in the Great Depression*. Newcastle History Monographs No. 11. Newcastle Region Public Library. 1984, p. 12.
49 Quote from the foreword written by Essington Lewis for 'The B.H.P. Review', p. 3.
50 Quoted in Jenkins, David. *Battle Surface! Japan's submarine war against Australia, 1942–44*. Random House Australia. Milsons Point. 1992, p. 251.
51 Farrelly, Alan. *Newcastle*, p. 104.
52 Farrelly, Alan. *Newcastle*, p. 107.
53 'Newcastle steelworks closure.' Legislative Assembly Hansard on Parliament of New South Wales website, <parliament.nsw.gov.au>. 7 May 1997.
54 That comment was reported in Ian Kirkwood's report, 'Announcement a boardroom betrayal: Carr', published in the *Newcastle Herald*, 30 April 1997, p. 6.
55 'Newcastle steelworks closure'. Legislative Assembly Hansard on Parliament of New South Wales website, <parliament.nsw.gov.au>. 7 May 1997.
56 'Newcastle Steelworks Closure'. Legislative Assembly Hansard on Parliament of New South Wales website, <parliament.nsw.gov.au>. 7 May 1997.
57 Senator John Tierney, quoted in Hansard on Parliament of Australia website, <parlinfo.aph.gov.au>. 2 September 1977, p. 6231.

58 O'Neill, Phillip and Green, Roy. 'Global economy, local jobs', in McManus, Phil; O'Neill, Phillip and Loughran, Robert (eds). *Journeys: The making of the Hunter Region*. Allen & Unwin. St Leonards. 2000, p. 109.
59 Speech to Paterson Liberal Party function, Newcastle on the Department of the Prime Minister and Cabinet website, <pmtranscripts.pmc.gov.au>. 16 July 1997.
60 From 'The Gravy Train Doesn't Stop Here Anymore', in Boyd, Dan. *The Gravy Train Doesn't Stop Here Anymore*. Self-published. November 2000.
61 'The Last Day Tomorrow ... What Then': My Thoughts. Aubrey Brooks. 'Muster Point – BHP Newcastle, 1913–1999' Facebook site. Reproduced with Aubrey Brooks' permission.
62 'With history on its side, city can recover.' Paradice, WEJ, opinion piece published in the *Newcastle Herald*, 30 April 1997, p. 3.
63 'Death blow for "steel city" as Molycop workers clock out forever.' Madeline Link. Published in the *Newcastle Herald*, 9 February 2024.
64 I spoke with Jan Senbergs for my book, *The Hunter* (ABC Books, 2012), which was reprinted in my book, *Return to the Hunter*, No Shush Press, 2023.
65 Much of the information about this tour comes Chris Helme's excellent piece, 'The Newcastle Steelworks Brass Band from Australia and its 1924 visit to the UK', published on his website, <chrishelme-brighouse.org.uk>. 23 September, 2017.
66 Cusack, Dymphna. *Southern Steel*, p. 4.
67 O'Donoghue, John. *Essington Lewis: I Am Work*. Currency Press. Paddington. 1987, p. 93.
68 O'Donoghue, John. *Essington Lewis: I Am Work*, p. 10.
69 'Doing nothing "not an option": Treasurer concedes region deserves more' by Michael Parris, in the *Newcastle Herald*, 18 June 2024.
70 Our Newcastle website, <ournewcastle.info/policies>.

CHAPTER FIVE: SURF CITY

1 Quoted in Mack, John. *The Sea: A cultural history*, p. 165.
2 Threlkeld, LE. *An Australian Grammar*, p. 93.
3 Threlkeld, LE. *An Australian Grammar*, p. 89.
4 Reproduced in Turner, JW (ed.). *Newcastle as a Convict Settlement: The evidence before J.T. Bigge in 1819–1821*, p. 186.
5 Mortlock, JF. *Experiences of a Convict*. Part Four. Originally published in London, Brickhill and Bateman, 1865. Sydney University Press edition edited by GA Wilkes and AG Mitchell and published in 1966, p. 162.
6 A letter to the editor headlined, 'Newcastle', published in the *Sydney Gazette and New South Wales Advertiser*, 29 October 1829, p. 2. Retrieved from Trove at <trove.nla.gov.au/newspaper/article/2193720>.
7 Information from 'Newcastle Coastal Geotrail' pamphlet.
8 Conrick, Chris. *The Northern District Surf Lifesaver*. SLSA, Newcastle Branch. Merewether. 1989, p. 65.
9 Maynard, John (ed.). *Awabakal Word Finder and Dreaming Stories Companion*, p. 53.
10 Threlkeld, LE. *An Australian Grammar*, p. 84.
11 Gunson, Niel (ed.). *Australian Reminiscences & Papers of L.E. Threlkeld, Volume I*, p. 65.

12 The information about Mitchell comes from Smith CE. *Dr James Mitchell.* Newcastle History Monographs No. 1. Newcastle Public Library. 1966.
13 Halligan, Marion. *Lovers' Knots.* Minerva. Port Melbourne. 1993, p. 56.
14 The plaque is reproduced on the back cover of 'Merewether National Surfing Reserve', published by the Merewether National Surfing Reserve Committee. March 2009.
15 'A Letter from Newcastle.' Written by WR and published in the *Sydney Gazette,* 15 August 1818, p. 4. Retrieved from Trove at <trove.nla.gov.au/newspaper/article/2178141>.
16 For more on this, read Keating, Julie. *Merewether & The Junction.* Self-published. 2016, pp. 10–11.
17 A letter to the editor headlined, 'Newcastle', published in the *Sydney Gazette and New South Wales Advertiser,* 29 October 1829, p. 2.
18 Reay, Audley. *Memories of the Hunter and Newcastle in the Eighties.* Self-published. Undated, p. 6. In the Newcastle Local History Library collection.
19 This line of Jones' poetry is reproduced in Pierce, Peter (editor). *The Oxford Literary Guide to Australia.* Oxford University Press Australia. Melbourne. 1993, p. 82.
20 Talbot, Norman. *The Seafolding of Harri Jones.* Nimrod Pamphlets No. 2. Printed in Maitland. 1965.
21 Reay, Audley. *Memories of the Hunter and Newcastle in the Eighties,* p. 8.
22 Reay, Audley. *Memories of the Hunter and Newcastle in the Eighties,* p. 7.
23 'New Year's Day'. *Newcastle Morning Herald and Miners' Advocate,* 2 January 1913, p. 5.
24 Details about Ben Lexcen's early life from Stannard, Bruce. *Ben Lexcen: The Man, The Keel and The Cup.* Faber and Faber. London. 1984, pp. 17–24.
25 Martin, James. 'Memorandoms', believed to have been written in London about 1792. Reproduced in Walsh, Paul F (ed). *Novocastrian Tales.* Elephant Press. New Lambton. 1997, p. 10.
26 'Glenrock Lagoon: Old favourite still visited.' *Newcastle Morning Herald,* 11 October 1933. From Newcastle Local History Library files.
27 John Bingle used that term to describe the walk in his *Past and Present Records of Newcastle, New South Wales.* Bayley, Son, and Harwood. Newcastle. 1873, pp. 11–12.
28 Some of these details are from the Hunter Living Histories website: <hunterlivinghistories.com/2012/08/31/origins-of-king-edward-park>.
29 Some biographical information, and a reproduction of the painting, can be found in Blackley, Roger. *The Art of Alfred Sharpe.* Auckland City Art Gallery in association with David Bateman Ltd. Auckland. 1992.
30 'An art gallery for Newcastle', *Newcastle Morning Herald,* 13 September 1892, p. 6.
31 'The Hill Reserve', *Newcastle Morning Herald,* 27 August 1890.
32 Sharp, Alfred. 'A Day in Burwood Glen', published in the *Newcastle Morning Herald,* 2 January 1889, p. 2.
33 Information from the Newcastle Car Club website at <mgcarclub.com.au/kep>.
34 'Park the protests, let city soak up spotlight.' *Newcastle Herald,* 23 November 2017.

CHAPTER SIX: CITY OF VILLAGES

1. Quoted by James, Bob. 'Changing the Record', in *Riverchange*, Cynthia Hunter (ed.), Newcastle Region Public Library. 1998, p. 89.
2. 'Opening of a Rotunda in Lambton Park', *Sydney Morning Herald*, 1 December 1890, p. 5. Accessed via Trove at <trove.nla.gov.au/newspaper/article/13792422>.
3. Information from Australian War Memorial website, <awm.gov.au/collection/U51475>.
4. Information from the Clarence Smith Jeffries entry in the Australian Dictionary of Biography at <adb.anu.edu.au>.
5. 'Early Mining.' *Newcastle Morning Herald and Miners' Advocate*. 18 November 1929, p. 9. Accessed via Trove at <trove.nla.gov.au>.
6. For more on the formation of the Minmi Rangers, read John Maynard's essay, 'What "1884" means to football in Northern NSW' at the Newcastle Jets website at <newcastlejetsfc.com.au>.
7. Lyrics reproduced with permission from Subsidence Advisory NSW. You can see Maurie Mole singing his subsidence song at the NSW Government website at: <www.nsw.gov.au/subsidence-advisory/subsidence-emergencies>.
8. I spoke with Pina D'Accione while researching a story I wrote, 'An Italian village helps build a city', published in the *Newcastle Herald*, 20 November 2021, pp. 4–7.
9. For more information on Mayfield, read Chegwidden, Cath. *Mighty Mayfield Then and Now: Book I: The early years*. Newey Printing Company and Cath Chegwidden. 2022. The advertisement, from the *Newcastle Directory and Almanac*, 1887, is reproduced on p. 220.
10. These details from Claridge, William R. *The Pommy Town Years*, pp. 34, 72 and 76.
11. Figures accessed at the City of Newcastle website, <profile.id.com.au/Newcastle/overseas-arrivals>.
12. Information on the camps derived from Gray, Sheilah. *Newcastle in the Great Depression*, p. 18.
13. Vera Deacon wrote about her experiences during the Great Depression in 'Making Do and Lasting Out', which was originally published in *Depression Down Under*, edited and published by Len Fox, Potts Point, 1977, and reproduced in *Singing Back the River*. Conceived and edited by Marilla North. Yarnspinners Press Collective. Leura. 2019.
14. 'Fierce riot at Newcastle', *Canberra Times*, 15 June 1932, p. 1, via Trove at <trove.nla.gov.au/newspaper/article/2285602>.
15. I am indebted for much of the information about the Tighes Hill riot to Sheilah Gray's *Newcastle in the Great Depression*, pp. 37–46.
16. Gray, Sheilah. *Newcastle in The Great Depression*, p. 78.
17. Maynard, John, *Fight for Liberty and Freedom*. Aboriginal Studies Press. Canberra. 2024 (revised and updated), pp. 133–135. For the council's reconciliation commitment, John quotes from the council's *Walking Together*, no. 7, March 1994, p. 14.
18. I interviewed William T Cooper for my book, *Bill: The life of William Dobell*, on 13 January 2007 and 9 April 2013.
19. *Portrait Painter to the Birds*. Australian Broadcasting Corporation, in association with BBC TV. 1992.
20. MacLean, Mark. *A Year Down the Drain. Walking in Styx Creek, January to

December. The Hunter Press. Hamilton. 2011. Mark writes about what he imagines and hopes for in a number of places in his book, but this reference is from p. 122.

21 Lingard, Eric (editor). *Newcastle: 150 Years*, p. 23.
22 Adriaan Johannes 'John' Peschar died on 6 December 2024. He was aged 96. For the section about him, I have kept the writing in the present tense.
23 Interview with the author on ABC Newcastle, Saturday, 22 June 2024.
24 I interviewed Chris Joannou for an essay, which was never published, at The Edwards in September 2017.
25 Chris recounts these times in his life in the memoir he co-wrote with Ben Gillies (and Alley Pascoe), *Love & Pain*, Hachette. Sydney. 2023.
26 Information from Keating, Julie and Wetherall, Lachlan. *Adamstown & Broadmeadow ... the early days of settlement*. Published by Julie Keating. Newcastle. 2020, pp. 62–63.
27 I spoke with Cheryl for a profile published in the *Newcastle Herald* on 16 September 2017, and at <newcastleherald.com.au> as 'Cheryl Salisbury kicks goals in life'.
28 Harragon, Paul, with Brett Keeble. *One Perfect Day*. Pan Macmillan Australia. Sydney. 1999, p. 211.
29 Johns, Andrew, with Neil Cadigan. *The Two of Me*. HarperCollins Publishers. Sydney. 2007. Andrew writes about life in Newcastle in chapter 17, 'King of the castle'.
30 Heard on Fox Sports coverage of the Newcastle Knights and New Zealand Warriors match, 5 May 2024.
31 Much of the information about the history of the Newcastle Knights comes from Robert Dillon's *Hard Yards: The story of the Newcastle Knights* (*Newcastle Herald* 2018), and from talking with Robert. My thanks to Robert for sharing his knowledge.
32 I spoke with Ed Tonks as research for a series I wrote about the Fernleigh Track, published in the *Newcastle Herald*, 29 January – 5 February 2022.
33 Brown, Russell; Spencer, Brenda and Williamsz, Patricia. 'The Fernleigh Track: A living corridor. An Action and Management Plan for the Adamstown-Belmont Railway Line.' September 1994. Report prepared as an assignment for an Associate Diploma of Applied Science (Landscape). Report in Lake Macquarie City Council's Local Studies collection, p. 4.
34 'Blackbutt Reserve: "Would this happen in Sydney?", J Mood, New Lambton, published in the *Newcastle Sun*, 7 September 1966. From Newcastle Local History collection, Q719.3/BLA.
35 'Council welcomes marriage equality vote.' City of Newcastle. 14 November 2017, City of Newcastle website, <Newcastle.nsw.gov.au>.
36 *Travel Guides*, Season 7, Episode 8, 'Newcastle'. Broadcast on the Nine network on 14 July 2024.

CHAPTER SEVEN: CITY OF NOW WHAT?

1 Visit Newcastle website at <visitnewcastle.com.au>.
2 Estimations from 'Newcastle Local Housing Strategy'. City of Newcastle. 2021 (updated), p. 3.
3 Tucker, James. *Ralph Rashleigh*, p. 83.

4   Corris, Peter. *Aftershock*, p. 35.
5   The advertisement is on the 'Paul McCartney mural' wall near the intersection of Hunter Street and Stewart Avenue in Newcastle West.
6   Foghorn Brewery website at <foghornbrewery.com.au>.
7   'Newcastle, N.S.W.: The Port of the North. *Illustrated Sydney News*. 27 June 1889, p. 12.
8   *Hunter Horizons: Navigating the future of work and workplaces in our region*. Institute for Regional Futures, The University of Newcastle, in collaboration with NGM Group. The University of Newcastle. June 2024, p. 14.
9   *Hunter Horizons*, p. 27.
10 *Hunter Horizons*, p. 13.
11 Anthony Albanese spoke at the Hunter Nexus Dinner, 16 February 2024. A copy of his speech can be found at the Prime Minister of Australia website at <pm.gov.au/media/hunter-nexus-dinner>.
12 Abbott, JHM. *The Newcastle Packets and the Hunter Valley*, p.35.
13 Levin, Bernard. *Enthusiasms*. Sceptre. London. 1987, pp. 90–92.
14 'Voice Referendum live results and updates', ABC News website at <abc.net.au/news/elections/referendum/2023/results>, 2 November 2023.
15 *Newcastle 2040*. Community Strategic Plan. City of Newcastle. 2022, p. 9.
16 *Hunter Horizons*. pp. 24–25.
17 Figure obtained from 'AskUoN', University of Newcastle website at <askuon.newcastle.edu.au>.
18 Big Ben is referred to in an *Illustrated Sydney News* article, 'The Nobby Rock, Newcastle', 25 November, 1871, p. 189. Reproduced at the Hunter Living Histories website, <hunterlivinghistories.com>.

www.ingramcontent.com/pod-product-compliance
Lightning Source LLC
Chambersburg PA
CBHW021342300426
44114CB00012B/1039